Troubling Truth and Reconciliation in Canadian Education

Edited by
SANDRA D. STYRES AND ARLO KEMPF

Troubling Truth and Reconciliation in Canadian Education

Critical Perspectives

UNIVERSITY *of* **ALBERTA** PRESS

Published by
University of Alberta Press
1-16 Rutherford Library South
11204 89 Avenue NW
Edmonton, Alberta, Canada T6G 2J4
Amiskwacîwâskahican | Treaty 6 |
Métis Territory
uap.ualberta.ca | uapress@ualberta.ca

Copyright © 2022
University of Alberta Press

Library and Archives Canada Cataloguing in Publication
Title: Troubling truth and reconciliation in Canadian education : critical perspectives / edited by Sandra D. Styres and Arlo Kempf.
Names: Styres, Sandra D., 1961– editor. | Kempf, Arlo, editor.
Description: Includes bibliographical references.
Identifiers: Canadiana (print) 20210371889 | Canadiana (ebook) 20210372273 | ISBN 9781772126006 (softcover) | ISBN 9781772126181 (EPUB) | ISBN 9781772126198 (PDF)
Subjects: LCSH: Critical pedagogy—Canada. | LCSH: Transformative learning—Canada. | LCSH: Culturally relevant pedagogy—Canada. | LCSH: Culturally sustaining pedagogy—Canada. | LCSH: Indigenous peoples—Education—Canada. | LCSH: Indigenous peoples—History—Study and teaching—Canada. | LCSH: Reconciliation—Study and teaching—Canada. | LCSH: Canada—Race relations—Study and teaching. | LCSH: Canada—Ethnic relations—Study and teaching.
Classification: LCC LC196.5.C2 T76 2022 | DDC 370.11/5—dc23

First edition, first printing, 2022.
First printed and bound in Canada by Houghton Boston Printers, Saskatoon, Saskatchewan.
Copyediting and proofreading by Kay Rollans.

All rights reserved. No part of this publication may be reproduced, stored in a retrieval system, or transmitted in any form or by any means (electronic, mechanical, photocopying, recording, or otherwise) without prior written consent. Contact University of Alberta Press for further details.

University of Alberta Press supports copyright. Copyright fuels creativity, encourages diverse voices, promotes free speech, and creates a vibrant culture. Thank you for buying an authorized edition of this book and for complying with the copyright laws by not reproducing, scanning, or distributing any part of it in any form without permission. You are supporting writers and allowing University of Alberta Press to continue to publish books for every reader.

University of Alberta Press gratefully acknowledges the support received for its publishing program from the Government of Canada, the Canada Council for the Arts, and the Government of Alberta through the Alberta Media Fund.

This book has been published with the help of a grant from the Canadian Federation for the Humanities and Social Sciences, through the Awards to Scholarly Publications Program, using funds provided by the Social Sciences and Humanities Research Council of Canada.

Contents

vii **Foreword**
JAN HARE

xiii **Acknowledgements**

xv **A Troubling Place to Start**
Reconciliation in Collapse
ARLO KEMPF, SANDRA D. STYRES, LIZA BRECHBILL
AND LUCY EL-SHERIF

I
Theoretical Perspectives on (Ir)reconciliation
Polishing the Silver Covenant Chain

3 **1 | Discovering Truth in the Post-TRC Era**
Morality and Spirituality Discourses in the Reconciliatory
Journeys of Schools
FRANK DEER

15 **2 | Indigenous Resiliency, Renewal, and Resurgence in
Decolonizing Canadian Higher Education**
MICHELLE PIDGEON

39 **3 | Uncomfortable Realities: Reconciliation in Higher Education**
DAWN ZINGA

65 **4 | Contested Knowledges: Indigeneity, Resistance, and
Black Theorizing in Academia**
GEORGE J. SEFA DEI (NANA ADUSEI SEFA TWENEBOAH)

81 **5 | Some of Us Are More Canadian Than Others**
Pedagogies of Citizenship and Learning Racialized Settlerhood
LUCY EL-SHERIF AND MARK SINKE

103   **6 | The Performativity of Reconciliation**
Illusory Justice and the Site C Dam
RACHEL YACAAʔAŁ GEORGE

121   **7 | Beyond Curricula**
Colonial Pedagogies in Public Schooling
TOBY ROLLO

II
Reconceptualizing Reconciliation in Education
Teaching and Learning in Right Relation

141   **8 | Reconciliation and Relational Ethics in Education**
SANDRA D. STYRES AND ARLO KEMPF

161   **9 | Exploring Tensions in Taking Up the Call for Reconciliation in Teacher Education**
LYNNE WILTSE

183   **10 | Troubling Trespass**
Moving Settler Teachers Toward Decolonization
DANIELA BASCUÑÁN, MARK SINKE, SHAWNA M. CARROLL, AND JEAN-PAUL RESTOULE

201   **11 | Talking It Through, Talking Through It**
A Dialogue on Indigenizing Education
CELIA HAIG-BROWN AND RUTH GREEN

223   **12 | Recalling the Spirit and Intent of Indigenous Literatures**
JENNIFER BRANT

247   **13 | Teaching Indigenous Studies in a Time of Reconciliation**
An Anticolonial Approach Toward Postcolonial Awareness
DAVID NEWHOUSE AND ROBIN QUANTICK

281   **14 | Contemporary Colonialism and Reconciliation in Higher Education**
A Decolonial Response Through Relationality
JEANNIE KERR AND AMY PARENT

295   **Contributors**

Foreword

SINCE THE 2015 RELEASE OF THE Truth and Reconciliation Commission of Canada's (TRC) final report and the accompanying policy directives in its calls to action,[1] reconciliation has fast become a vehicle for attention, expression, and action. Even as tensions around the possibilities of better relations between Indigenous and settler societies surfaced amid the work of the TRC, I believed that if reconciliation held the moment, it held promise. As an Indigenous scholar, educator, and administrator, I could see the ways reconciliation as a discourse was being transposed into faculties of education and K to 12 schooling across Canada. Reconciliation as a framework for education has inspired formalized responses in postsecondary education institutions that include strategic plans, task-force recommendations, symposia, symbolic representations on campus, Indigenous advisories or boards, Indigenous community engagement initiatives, and professional development for staff and faculty. Faculties of education have introduced required coursework in Indigenous education or integrated Indigenous curriculum across their programming, hired Indigenous faculty, created reconciliation councils, and hosted reconciliation events. I continue to observe the strong and focused way the concept of reconciliation takes hold in educational spaces, especially when it facilitates decolonization and, more recently, Indigenization.

As part of this reconciliation movement, I developed a massive open online course (MOOC) called Reconciliation Through Indigenous Education: a free online professional learning opportunity for educators that has been taken by over 60,000 participants worldwide. In line with the TRC's calls to address the consequences of colonial schooling, I wanted educators to deepen their knowledge of Canada's colonial history and how an assimilationist education has produced different outcomes for Indigenous learners in comparison to their non-Indigenous counterparts. I wanted them to interrogate their own personal and professional positionings to understand how they are implicated in colonial systems of education and to recognize the contributions of Indigenous knowledges to teaching and learning. I wanted them to see how their relationship to land and place is another entanglement in settler colonialism, and to develop strategies for respectful engagement with Indigenous families and communities. I hoped that the MOOC would contribute to the much-needed transformation in K-to-12 and postsecondary education.

However, like so many other scholars and educators, I have become impatient towards reconciliation. While I appreciate that reconciliation has raised awareness about settler-colonial histories and even prompted educators to engage more deeply in reconciliation practices and pedagogies, it simply has not done enough to dismantle the colonial and normative structures in our education systems. In recent work, I questioned whether reconciliation offered hope or was just hype.[2] I reflected on whether education is a deeply transformative site for reconciliation, recognizing how debated and diversely understood the latter concept is for teacher candidates and teacher educators. As an Indigenous scholar teaching Indigenous and settler learners and giving oversight to Indigenous programs, I take issue with the accelerated trend towards reconciliation in education that continues to emphasize Indigenous-settler relations while deemphasizing the ways postsecondary institutions can be more responsive and accountable to the aspirations and needs of Indigenous learners and communities.[3] My responsibility as Associate Dean of Indigenous Education at the University of British Columbia is to mobilize Indigenous education priorities across a large faculty of education with a goal towards empowering Indigenous learners and communities in their own journeys towards resurgence and educational sovereignty. Yet I see the challenges to such important ambitions when reconciliation is enacted through settler understandings and intentions.

The editors of this book express their own exasperation with reconciliation as a motivation for this edited collection, pointing to the growing anti-Indigenous racism, illegal incursions on Indigenous lands and rights, and heightened inequities within Indigenous and racialized communities as a result of COVID-19. These instances of racial and Indigenous injustice, sanctioned by state mechanisms and practices of settler colonialism, give the editors pause to ask the difficult questions about "whether reconciliation is dead, whether it ever existed, and indeed whether it is a worthy idea (if not an impossibility)."[4] Though the editors recognize the limitations of reconciliation, they simultaneously acknowledge the possibilities that reconciliation holds for social and educational transformation. So, what we can appreciate most about this book is that it engages with the idea of *troubling* the concept of reconciliation within educational spaces rather than dismissing reconciliation altogether. As a result, the editors are strategic and productive in what they bring together for the readers in the book's structure, content, and perspectives.

In pushing the boundaries of reconciliation as both a hopeful and productive framework for educational change, this book brings to the fore the opportunities and limitations of reconciliation through a rights-based discourse that upholds self-determination, self-governance, and sovereignty. If we are to dismantle oppressive mechanisms of postsecondary institutions and create a framework for reconciliation that is accountable to Indigenous communities, then we need to look to the TRC's forty-third call to action, which calls upon "federal, provincial, territorial, and municipal governments to fully adopt and implement the *United Nations Declaration on the Rights of Indigenous Peoples* [UNDRIP]."[5] This would create a new relational and political dynamic between postsecondary institutions and Indigenous communities through responsibilities to advance human rights standards set out in UNDRIP. If higher education defended Indigenous rights to education, language, and culture, then Indigenous priorities of self-determination and sovereignty expressed in control over their lands, resources, and knowledges could also be upheld.[6]

The Government of Canada has adopted legislation to implement UNDRIP through Bill C-15, which calls on laws to be consistent with the United Nations' declaration. Bill C-15 requires the government to prepare a plan of action to address injustices, combat prejudice, and eliminate all forms of violence and discrimination, including systemic discrimination against Indigenous peoples. Further, all relations with Indigenous peoples must be based on the recognition of self-determination. In the province of British Columbia, where UNDRIP has been in legislation since 2019, the challenge for Indigenous people has not been recognition of Indigenous rights, but commitments by government to apply and uphold these rights. It is striking that chapters in the first half of this edited collection link this rights-based discourse to postsecondary education activities and processes by highlighting the significance of treaty and sovereign rights in creating equitable and socially just institutional environments for Indigenous learners, faculty, and communities. While self-determination and sovereignty are the basis on which the editors, and a good number of the authors, contextualize their conversations, it is apparent that postsecondary institutions must be knowledgeable and willing to accept the unique legal and political status of Indigenous people and Nations if they are to be held accountable to Indigenous aspirations. The authors signal strategies and approaches to assist higher education in this work.

Another significant feature of *Troubling Truth and Reconciliation* is that it takes readers beyond the common critiques of reconciliation, which tend to focus on peaceful co-existence, the history of residential schooling, or the disconnection of reconciliation from decolonization. Instead, each chapter moves the reader forward through writings that interrogate reconciliation, drawing on the authors' diverse roles, responsibilities, and research. Through complicating reconciliation, the authors in this book attend to Indigenous concerns of reclamation, resurgence, decolonization, Indigenization, restitution, and solidarity. By orienting us towards what matters to Indigenous people, the authors create a space for Indigenous-settler engagement with reconciliation that is grounded in responsibility and relationality to Indigenous people. This is exemplified in the writings of contributing authors, including leading Black anticolonial scholar George J. Sefa Dei, higher education scholar and Simon Fraser University Associate Dean of Indigenous Education Michelle Pidgeon, ally scholar Celia Haig-Brown, Indigenous activist-turned-scholar Ruth Green, and Canada Research Chair in Indigenous Education Frank Deer, to name just a few of the contributors to this valuable text.

If we are to destabilize our understandings of reconciliation in educational contexts as this edited collection propels us to do, then we need models, strategies, and approaches that help actors of postsecondary institutions to effectively breach the limits of reconciliation in educational practices, policies, and ideologies. The authors of this book generate possibilities for readers through their experiences, perspectives, and research. We seek inspiration from the challenges they face in their practices with preservice teachers, graduate students, and colleagues, as well as in K to 12 school settings, to help us understand our collective responsibilities towards creating socially just education on Indigenous lands. Though the authors gesture towards reconciliation in their educational approaches (as, for instance, authors Amy Parent and Jeannie Kerr demonstrate in Chapter 14), the frameworks that underpin the collective work of this text are decolonial and Indigenizing—frameworks that are necessary to address the uneven power relations that operate in mainstream education institutions.

At the heart of the TRC's final report are the stories of residential school survivors. Their stories are testaments to the resiliency of Indigenous people. They speak the truth of colonial violence mediated through schooling. We cannot heal our spirits, we cannot reconcile our past, nor can postsecondary education be accountable to Indigenous learners and communities without this truth. And yet reconciliation continues to proceed ahead of the truth. We must always create spaces for survivors to share their experiences of residential schooling. Their narratives are our legacy, giving us courage, strength, and hope to tell new stories needed to reimagine educational alternatives for Indigenous learners and communities and to transcend the limits of reconciliation as a framework for educational change.

Troubling Truth and Reconciliation is a collection of these kinds of stories, told through the arguments, perspectives, experiences, and research of the editors and authors. It seeks something more than the current status quo of helping non-Indigenous folks engage with reconciliation.

Dr. Jan Hare
Professor and Canada Research Chair (Tier 1) in Indigenous Pedagogy
University of British Columbia

NOTES

1. Truth and Reconciliation Commission of Canada, *Final Report*; *Truth and Reconciliation Commission of Canada: Calls to Action* (hereafter cited as TRC calls).
2. Hare, "Reconciliation in Teacher Education."
3. McCarty and Lee, "Critical Culturally Sustaining."
4. Kempf et al., "A Troubling Place to Start," this volume.
5. TRC calls, no. 43.
6. Bellier and Préaud, "Emerging Issues."

BIBLIOGRAPHY

Bellier, Irène, and Martin Préaud. "Emerging Issues in Indigenous Rights: Transformative Effects of the Recognition of Indigenous Peoples." *The International Journal of Human Rights* 16, no. 3 (2012): 474–88.

Hare, Jan. "Reconciliation in Teacher Education: Hope or Hype?" In *Reconceptualizing Teacher Education: A Canadian Contribution to a Global Challenge*, edited by Anne M. Phelan, William F. Pinar, Nicholas Ng-A-Fook, and Ruth Kane, 19–38. Ottawa: University of Ottawa Press, 2020.

McCarty, Teresa L., and Tiffany S. Lee. "Critical Culturally Sustaining/Revitalizing Pedagogy and Indigenous Education Sovereignty." *Harvard Education Review* 84, no. 1 (2014): 101–23.

Truth and Reconciliation Commission of Canada. *The Final Report of the Truth and Reconciliation Commission of Canada*. 6 vols. Montreal: McGill-Queen's University

———. *Truth and Reconciliation Commission of Canada: Calls to Action*. Winnipeg: National Centre for Truth and Reconciliation, 2015. https://ehprnh2mwo3.exactdn.com/wp-content/uploads/2021/01/Calls_to_Action_English2.pdf.

Acknowledgements

WE FIRST ACKNOWLEDGE THE traditional territory upon which we as editors have worked to coordinate this collection at the University of Toronto. We draw upon the work of the Deepening Knowledge Project at the Ontario Institute for Studies in Education to note that this land has a long and tangled (hi)story that carries the storied footprints of the Wendat, Haudenosaunee, and Anishinaabek nations. Tkaronto (Toronto) has a treaty with the Mississaugas of the Credit River First Nation and is part of the Dish With One Spoon, an agreement to share the land between the Anishinaabek and the Haudenosaunee Nations. We also offer an acknowledgement to each of the places upon which the contributing authors have worked on their own chapters. This book represents the complexities of place and placefulness.

In following an ethics of relationality and moving toward reconciliation, we seek to polish the Silver Covenant Chain and, in doing so, to restore the relationship between the Onkwehonwe (Original) and settler peoples of this land— a relationship based in honour and deep respect. Land acknowledegments have and continue to be sites of resistance and sociopolitical contestation. As such, this land acknowledgement serves as a starting point for readers that needs to be taken beyond recitation. It requires deeper exploration and self-reflection. We challenge all readers, but particularly non-Indigenous readers, to consider how you will take up your responsibilities in the places you inhabit.

We also wish to thank the contributors to this edited collection. You are the book, and we are honoured to work with all of you. Thanks to Mat Buntin at the University of Alberta Press for his long-standing support of this work. Our deep gratitude, as well, to the reviewers who generously offered their time and guidance.

Finally, thank you to Liza Brechbill and Lucy El-Sherif, contributing authors and graduate students who supported various aspects of this work. We also want to extend a thank you to Rosalinda Furlan, another graduate student who worked diligently to help us put the manuscript together.

ARLO KEMPF,
SANDRA D. STYRES,
LIZA BRECHBILL,
AND LUCY EL-SHERIF

A Troubling Place to Start

Reconciliation in Collapse

WE WOULD LIKE TO BEGIN OUR journey by acknowledging the complex histories of those whose traditional lands we are on and the ways those storied landscapes have informed the various writings that have contributed to this book. While as authors we may be geographically, culturally, and linguistically disparate in terms of where we are located, we all wrote and thought on the ancestral lands of Indigenous Peoples across what we now call Canada. These lands exist first and foremost in storied relationship to Indigenous Peoples who have existed and who continue to exist on them since time immemorial—that is, time before we can imagine time. As we consider the project undertaken here—this collaboration— we recognize the importance of relationship. To be in good relationship with one another requires several interconnected factors, including but not limited to a sincere acknowledgement of whose traditional lands we are all on; an understanding that big systemic structures, such as educational institutions that have been erected on lands and spaces that exist in relationship to Indigenous Peoples, continue to guide the contemporary practices of Canadian colonialism and genocide; an understanding of the historical and contemporary realities of Indigenous-settler relationships; and a mindful, purposeful, and respectful restoration of land and treaty rights.

This edited volume comes at a critical time in Canada's relationship with Indigenous Peoples and Nations. Reconciliation, resurgence, and the politics of education have become critical conversations worldwide, highlighting the importance of addressing Indigenous rights and equity, particularly in education. Following Tuck and Yang, we note the distinction between Indigenous rights and mainstream human rights discourse(s).[1] As we began working on this volume, we were mourning the unnecessary death of Colten Boushie, a young Cree Red Pheasant First Nation man, and the subsequent acquittal of his killer Gerald Stanley, a White Canadian farmer, by an all-White jury. As time passed, our attention shifted to the illegal incursions onto Wet'suwet'en lands by the Canadian Government. As Indigenous and non-Indigenous allies across Canada conducted coordinated protests in solidarity with Wet'suwet'en land defenders, some declared that reconciliation was dead (the latter prompting Tanya Talaga to argue that reconciliation is not, in fact, dead, but "never truly existed"[2]), and calls emerged to shut down Canada. Protestors delayed trains to Toronto, Montréal, Winnipeg, Prince George, and elsewhere. In sharp contrast was the palpable bigotry of many angry settlers who resented, in equal parts it seems, both the assertion of Indigenous sovereignty and the inconvenience of closed railways and delayed shipments of goods. The idea that Indigenous people might get in the way of, or negate in even the smallest way, the project that is the Canadian state was once again proven violently unthinkable in the popular discourse of Canadian settler coloniality.

As we were completing this book, we were working in isolation, hoping for the best as the world grappled with the COVID-19 global pandemic. We watched what it looked like for Canada to *really* shut down. We watched as the government laid out a plan for middle-class and wealthy people to survive the sickness and slow the spread, telling us to take sick days, use separate bathrooms, and stock up on essentials—we watched as the plan failed to address the needs of low-income folks, much less those of Indigenous communities with limited access to healthcare, overcrowded and substandard housing, and, in a great many cases, a lack of clean water. We watched a discourse of responsible citizenship emerge in which being "good" meant taking extreme measures—far beyond the level of inconvenience—and engaging in a total restructuring of daily life. We watched this knowing that such measures were a matter of life and death. We also noted, however, that such a shutdown of Canada was unimaginable and unforgivable in the hearts and minds of many settler Canadians only weeks earlier during the rail blockades—yet sovereignty is also a matter of life and death for many Indigenous Peoples. With armed police taking aim at peaceful protestors and with life-sustaining lands and waters at risk of destruction, this is not a simply theoretical proclamation but a clear and present danger to life. As we recast and lean into what being a good citizen means in light of social distancing, the ethics of self-isolation, and other COVID-19 requirements, we note the inability of most Canadians to even conceptualize being Canadian in relation to sovereign Indigenous Peoples and lands. We note, sadly, that we are a long way from the day in which common understandings of what it means to be a "good" Canadian (and ergo a good citizen, a good neighbour, a good parent, a good person) might include fulfilling our responsibility to relationships with Indigenous Peoples and Nations. Indeed, as the incursion into Wet'suwet'en lands illustrates, we are a long way from living up to the 2015 Truth and Reconciliation Commission's (TRC) ninety-second call to action, which pushes Canada to: "commit to meaningful consultation [by] building respectful relationships, and obtaining the free, prior, and informed consent of Indigenous peoples before proceeding with economic development projects."[3]

The TRC's final report also identified education as a critical site for Indigenous resurgence and reconciliation, characterizing Canada's actions as cultural genocide.[4] The 2019 National Inquiry into Missing and Murdered Indigenous Women and Girls (MMIWG) went a step further by identifying Canada's actions as simply genocide. The MMIWG Inquiry report, *Reclaiming Power and Place*, explains that the term *genocide*

> was first used by the Polish-Jewish legal scholar Raphael Lemkin at a conference in Madrid in 1933...In Lemkin's construction of the idea, genocide would have two phases that could contribute to establishing the political domination of the oppressor group. The first included the destruction of the "national pattern of the group," and the second phase included what he called the "imposition of the national pattern of the oppressor," which could be imposed on the population that remained in the territory, or on the territory itself within the context of colonization of the land by a new group.[5]

The TRC argued that residential schooling was part and parcel of Canada's cultural genocide. Although survivors of the residential school system have been telling stories about the deaths of children at these schools for decades, the Canadian government and many of its citizens have openly resisted the notion of genocide within the nation's borders. This resistance became much more difficult in 2021 with the discoveries of mass and unmarked graves at several former residential schools in British Columbia, Saskatchewan, and Manitoba, which shed new light on the truth of survivors' stories. Using the language of the MMIWG Inquiry, we argue here that education (K to 12 and postsecondary) is a central terrain for the "imposition of the national pattern of the oppressor," which has served and frequently does serve to destroy the "national patterns" of Indigenous peoples.[6] Sheila Cote-Meek, Leanne Simpson, Lee Maracle, and many others have, for some time now, asked very hard questions about settler colonialism and schooling, and have called for a variety of approaches to educational justice.[7] Echoing the calls of a variety of Indigenous activists and scholars, and unlike the TRC's declaration of cultural genocide, the MMIWG Inquiry's explicit naming of genocide as a contemporary Canadian issue demands that we recognize a truly problematic question of concurrency: How do we take up reconciliation in the midst of genocide? Following the MMIWG Inquiry report, Canadian Prime Minister Justin Trudeau publicly accepted the findings and identification of contemporary Canadian genocide. This acknowledgement from the heart of governmental Canadian settler space suggests a mainstreaming of the notion of cultural genocide, and to a lesser degree of the notion of genocide. Reconciliation in education is a complex and challenging endeavour that necessitates first identifying the effects of settler colonialism on educational practices, and then finding ways to decolonize those practices. It is also fraught to consider (or conceive of) these undertakings in the context of ongoing colonialism—like trying to dry off while you are still in the shower with the water running. The MMIWG Inquiry report states that decolonizing approaches seek to untangle colonialism and "re-establish Indigenous Nationhood."[8] It further states that key to decolonizing approaches is the recognition of Indigenous peoples' "inherent rights"[9]—that is, their rights of self-determination, self-governance, and sovereignty. We are committed to this, and this volume supports these ideas. We acknowledge that we are situated within an impossible task of synthesizing reconciliation and genocide. We offer this complex and messy notion of situatedness in order to contextualize the works undertaken here, highlighting the live tensions and challenges of reconciliation rather than suggesting that syntheses are, or even can be, forthcoming.

This volume seeks to offer a series of contributions to this complex moment and landscape, which we hope will deepen and extend the current literature and thinking regarding colonization and decolonization in Canadian education. The authors who have generously shared their insights and experiences in these pages are mostly Indigenous. Settler scholars, both racialized as White and racialized as non-White, have also contributed. For the most part, the authors in this collection are people who can, one way or another, be called teachers. The complexity of contributors' social locations and experiences within and across the works in this volume makes speaking with one voice all but impossible in terms of a simple statement about what this book does or intends. However, for those of us who worked to assemble this collection, the work was, from the outset, guided by a refusal to accept and leave uncontested mainstream reconciliation discourses.

We understand the idea of *troubling* reconciliation to be inclusive of both the limitations and the possibilities of walking in right relations. With the police killing of Chantel Moore and the death of Regis Korchinski-Paquet at police hands, we note the persistent failure of Canadian governmental agents to stop killing Indigenous people. With ongoing police violence aimed at Indigenous protestors within contemporary racial justice movements, we note Canada's refusal to stop annexing and occupying Indigenous lands. These, and the instances cited above, offer powerful evidence of the limitations of reconciliation. Indeed, these state practices of settler colonialism lead us (and many others) to wonder whether reconciliation is dead, whether it ever existed, and indeed whether it is a worthy idea (if not an impossibility). The meaning of reconciliation is, however, highly varied. Some of these meanings are positive, and we recognize that many see reconciliation as a site of possibility. So, while we explicitly orient this volume as coming out of and moving toward a highly critical reading of reconciliation, we recognize our role as that of troubling reconciliation: problematizing it, not dismissing it.

We watch as many school boards and universities fumble awkwardly through land acknowledgements. Universities often assert commitments to "Indigenize the academy" (a phrase potentially emblematic of Tuck and Yang's notion of "settler moves to innocence," in which such commitments are rhetorical rather than structural in nature)[10] and develop grammars of colonial benevolence while simultaneously holding firm on practices of colonial reproduction. This professional context intersects and interlocks with personal positions of advantage and disadvantage. We recognize our own complicity in the colonial work of the university and the concurrent responsibility to engage in anticolonial work from our respective locations and positionalities. This is to say that we are aware of the contradictions and concomitant challenges of working in and for spaces that are sites of coloniality as critical scholars and people. We acknowledge that we are enmeshed as actors in some of the very processes identified in these pages. Nonetheless, guided by hope and humility, this collection undertakes the work of anticolonial change in education. We are pleased to be able to bring together a variety of thinkers and perspectives focused on the concerns raised above. We believe the contributing authors to this book offer significant diversity of thought, approach, and sociopolitical location, each with their own focal points and theoretical engagements.

Overview of the Book

This volume is framed in two parts. Part I focuses on theoretical approaches to reconciliation, and Part II addresses the more practical issues of reconciliation in education.

Part I, entitled "Theoretical Perspectives on (Ir)reconciliation: Polishing the Silver Covenant Chain," focuses on theoretical perspectives that trouble mainstream discourses of reconciliation. We borrow the phrase *polishing the Silver Covenant Chain* from the Haudenosaunee practice of intentionally working to renew and maintain trade and treaty relationships.[11] The "trouble" with reconciliation is that current conversations related to the mainstream reconciliation discourse (e.g., the hollow work of Indigenization often taken up by universities alongside the maintenance of settler-colonial practices as mentioned above) remain mired in colonial discourses and representations. The chapters in this section explore the complexities of legislation, identity, and recognition; Indigenous-settler relationships, resurgence, and nation building; the politics of curricula and programming; and systemic undertakings concerning resurgence and colonial restitution in education.

Frank Deer opens Part I with a discussion about the role of spirituality in processes of reconciliation and the value of Indigenous knowledge in education. Drawing connections between spirituality and morality, Deer asserts that Indigenous spirituality cannot be reduced to a codified set of rules or intellectual structures. Deer explores the tension between spirituality and morality in reconciliation by troubling the relationship between truth, knowledge, and morality.

Michelle Pidgeon moves the conversation forward in her chapter by examining the challenges of Indigenizing the academy in Canadian higher education institutions. Pidgeon identifies these processes as sites where Indigeneity thrives alongside resistances. She concludes her chapter by looking forward, beyond the reconciliation project, to a transformation of system and society that empowers Indigenous peoples' aspirations of education.

In the third chapter, Dawn Zinga explores the uncomfortable realities inherent to practicing reconciliation in higher education contexts. She delves into these tensions using the concept of ethical space within the institutional structures themselves. Zinga challenges us to consider the ways that power, privilege, and cognitive imperialism impact administrative organizations and research structures, as well as student and faculty relationships and experiences. Zinga is critical of reconciliation discourses that simply provide the opportunity for institutions to make token advancements while continuing to perpetuate harm and ongoing colonial violences. Zinga specifically calls upon upper administration and faculty to critically examine their roles and responsibilities as treaty people on stolen land.

George J. Sefa Dei focuses his discussions in Part I on the ways Black and Indigenous scholars have sought to theorize their own experiences by raising key issues of Indigeneity and resistance in academia. Dei highlights the need to investigate how both colonialist and anticolonialist philosophies and practices have been developed to advance scholarship and politics. Anticolonial work offers important insight into the politics of reconciliation discourse. Dei argues that Black, Indigenous, and racialized scholars' knowledge production must challenge relations of power at the epistemological level while always centring their liberatory and social change goals. He argues for the need to be deeply critical of institutional and intellectual systems of power that perform mental gymnastics to perpetuate hypocritical intellectual work that does not challenge social constructs or engage with lived realities—in particular, work that nostalgically hearkens back to an artificially constructed "glorious past." This chapter contributes to important new scholarship on Black and Indigenous solidarity and decolonization, highlighting concomitant theoretical alignments and challenges.

The next chapter, by Lucy El-Sherif and Mark Sinke, troubles the relationship between race and settler subjectivity. El-Sherif and Sinke assert that White supremacy is inscribed in racial hierarchy: a phenomenon that acts to erase the complex and contested relationships that people of colour, particularly Muslim Canadians, have to space, place, and belonging within Canadian borders. The authors challenge all settler Canadians to ask themselves: How do I learn a hierarchy of belonging to a place premised on Indigenous removal, erasure, and genocide? El-Sherif and Sinke argue that relational encounters offer opportunities to expose how one is or is not claimed by the national polity and settler subjectivities. They challenge readers to consider the impact of race on the national imagination's understanding of what it means to be Canadian.

Rachel yacaaʔaɬ George, in her chapter, highlights how reconciliation is used to mask Indigenous destruction through colonial wastelanding, and argues that we need to distinguish very clearly between reconciliation and justice. Reconciliation for residential school injustices is, as she describes it, a current Canadian national "obsession"—one that is being used as an alibi against working towards issues of sovereignty and land and water rights. In other words, Canadian politicians trumpet reconciliation even as they pursue colonial land grabs and Indigenous destruction, unimpeded by the spirit of reconciliation they proclaim. George illustrates the ways reconciliation is appropriated by settler colonialism and shows that decolonization and environmental justice must be viewed as inseparable.

In the final chapter of Part I, Toby Rollo argues that the education of Indigenous children and youth must be returned to Indigenous communities in order to fulfill the goals that reconciliation requires and demands. Rollo offers a historical account of colonial education in Canada, and of the ways that it has been adapted over time to serve goals of assimilation. Rollo argues that the decolonization of education requires more than Indigenization. They call for a rejection and dismantling of the colonial order, providing an effective bridge into Part II.

Part II, "Reconceptualizing Reconciliation in Education: Teaching and Learning in Right Relation," moves the conversation forward by focusing on the ways we can use decolonizing approaches to critically interrogate reconciliation and reframe the ways we think about and do education. This section considers the ways in which teaching can be an act of critical reconciliation in K to 12 classrooms and higher-learning contexts.

Sandra D. Styres and Arlo Kempf, the editors of this volume, open Part II by raising the question of whether or not reconciliation between settler states and Indigenous Peoples is ontologically conceivable in North America. After self-locating with regard to this writing, the authors offer a discussion about prevalent national settler-colonial discourses around land and power in the United States and Canada, and provide a brief statistical analysis of race-based inequity facing Indigenous Peoples in Canada. Like George in Part I, they state that while Canada shines a spotlight on the "reconciliation project," violent colonial encounters continue unabated. Styres and Kempf argue that the relationships between Indigenous Peoples and Canada cannot be fixed simply though apology; recognition, restitution, and critical social action that honours Indigenous treaty and sovereignty rights are needed. The authors propose a view of relational ethics for working in right relation in education, with a specific focus on the teacher education context.

In the next chapter, Lynne Wiltse focuses on a three-year collaborative research project with Indigenous and non-Indigenous participants that explored the complexities, hesitancies, and demands placed on students, teachers, and teacher candidates in Canadian education in a time of reconciliation. She highlights the importance of disrupting damaging colonial narratives that have been used to perpetuate harm. She then addresses the concept of storying, which can be used to heal and to educate. Wiltse finishes the chapter with a short discussion on the importance of pedagogies of discomfort in teacher education and the need to recognize the plurality of challenges facing those who are dedicated to decolonial processes in education. She calls on all settlers to take responsibility for reconciliation and find ways to reckon with, disrupt, and unsettle their relationships, identities, and investments with the historical and contemporary impacts of settler colonialism in Canada.

Daniela Bascuñán, Mark Sinke, Shawna Carroll, and Jean-Paul Restoule focus their chapter on the research findings from a study that examined the strategies teacher candidates use to engage in meaningful teaching about Indigenous perspectives and treaty relationships in their teaching practices. The study had the larger goals of supporting Indigenous students in the classroom, contributing to making antiracist citizens, and supporting Indigenous communities more broadly. Participants were asked to examine the multiple ways they incorporate Indigenous knowledges into their teaching practices, their successes, and the barriers they face. Despite the national conversations related to the colonial project, the authors found that participants still did not understand or engage with notions of reconciliation. The authors identify the pitfalls of educational methods of inclusion and invite readers to engage in critical reflection while resisting pedagogical initiatives rooted in colonial discourse and hegemony.

The next chapter, from Celia Haig-Brown and Ruth Green, brings together a senior non-Indigenous academic and a junior Indigenous activist-turned-academic in a dialogue about the complexities of Indigenizing postsecondary education. The authors assert that Indigenization is not to be taken as a new or popular trend, but rather as a paradigmatic shift in education. As a troubling of reconciliation, the authors caution that the rush to reconcile has led to performative and token gestures rather than the deep and meaningful action called for by the TRC.

Jennifer Brant then compels the reader to consider the role of Indigenous literature in the implementation of the TRC's calls to action by attending to the spirit and intent of Indigenous literatures. By contextualizing the TRC through her approach to Indigenous Maternal Pedagogies, Brant discusses the possibilities and challenges of using Indigenous literatures, and the importance of drawing on reconciliatory pedagogies and worldviews that embrace learners holistically and create learning environments that speak to the hearts and minds of students. Brant asserts that the learning environment created through her use of Indigenous Maternal Pedagogies offers a space where students can be their whole selves and learn from positions of strength. She asks educators to use Indigenous literature to engage with complex questions around reconciliation. She is, moreover, adamant that it is vital that the work of dismantling colonial narratives take place in non-Indigenous spaces before Indigenous literatures are used to simply counteract those narratives. Brant tells us that educators can do this dismantling work by drawing on topics such as treaty, policy, and Indigenous sovereignty to set the foundations and contextualize conversations, hearts, and minds to be inspired by Indigenous literature and testimony.

In the next chapter, David Newhouse and Robin Quantick reflect upon the experience of piloting a redesigned introductory Indigenous studies course at Trent University in the fall 2017 and winter 2018 semesters in preparation for the introduction of an Indigenous content requirement in the fall 2018 semester. The authors argue that, over the last half century, the teaching mission of Indigenous studies has remained consistent in its anticolonial approach. The chapter records student reactions to the pilot course and critically explores the politics, challenges, and opportunities that result from teaching students who take such courses only to meet a program requirement. This chapter documents the course's teaching environment, anticolonial framing, and role in creating postcolonial consciousness. Importantly, it offers lessons for instructors embarking on a similar journey, and is instructive in the context of similar courses and course requirements in universities across Canada.

Finally, situating relationality as fundamental to reconciliation work in higher education, Amy Parent and Jeannie Kerr consider the potential of collaborative pedagogies in navigating the current context of ongoing colonial violence in Canada, offering a powerful exploration of the notion of working and being in right relation. They assert the utility and potential of embodying their respective subjectivities in the contexts of Indigenous-settler relations and positionalities to grapple with the impacts of settler denial and student resistance to coursework on colonial history generally, and on the Indian residential school system in particular. The authors do not propose collaborative pedagogy as an answer for decolonizing education. Rather, they use it to contextualize their teaching practices as gestures towards reconciliation by challenging the colonial relations that continue to permeate higher education in Canada.

The works collected in this volume are by no means intellectually unified, and the authors included here offer divergent, competing, and sometimes contrasting views, terminology, and arguments. For example, Lynne Wiltse' discussion of research and teacher education is decidedly distinct from that of Daniela Bascuñán, Mark Sinke, Shawna Carroll, and Jean-Paul Restoule. As well, it is important to note that because of these diversities, each of the contributing authors have chosen to take up the issue of capitalization of certain terms (e.g, Indigenous, Settler, Elder) in their chapters in various ways. We celebrate the complex, diverse, and contested nature of the voices included in this volume. They make up, we hope, a rich intellectual tapestry that offers a diversity of approaches to troubling reconciliation. In this sense, the authors here are a group of trouble *makers*. Woven throughout, we find a consistent rejection of mainstream understandings of reconciliation discourses, a breach of dominant conversations about Indigeneity in Canadian education, and a commitment to moving forward, critically, in right relations.

As you read this volume and engage with the various chapters, we challenge you to consider how you will take up your responsibilities for being on these lands, whether they be treatied lands or unceded and untreatied territories. As all settler Canadians (including newcomers, regardless of their stories of arrival) have benefitted from these treaty relationships, we ask you to consider how you reconcile this advantage with the brutality of past and present genocidal practices against Indigenous Peoples. Decolonization and decolonial processes are multifaceted and complex. We hope this work offers a series of entry points for deeper understandings. We contend that settler-colonialism, in both its historical and contemporary forms, is inherently violent, serving to reinforce settler moves to innocence and claims to futurities.[12] We ask you to think about what reconciliation means to you personally, what your reconciliatory responsibilities are, and how to reconcile your own place within a violent colonial history—a history that is still very much present. We are grateful to all the contributing authors who have, each in their own ways, critically troubled the challenging and provocative truths about reconciliation.

NOTES

1. Tuck and Yang, "Decolonization Is Not a Metaphor."
2. Talaga, "Reconciliation Isn't Dead," para. 18.
3. *Truth and Reconciliation Commission of Canada: Calls to Action*, no. 92.i.
4. Truth and Reconciliation Commission of Canada, *Final Report*, 1:3–4.
5. National Inquiry into Missing and Murdered Indigenous Women and Girls, *Reclaiming Power and Place*, 1a:50. Hereafter cited as MMIWG Inquiry report.
6. MMIWG Inquiry report, 1a:50.
7. See Simpson, "Land as Pedagogy"; Maracle, *My Conversations with Canadians*; Cote-Meek, *Colonized Classrooms*.
8. MMIWG Inquiry report, 1b:170.
9. MMIWG Inquiry report, 1b:171.
10. Tuck and Yang, "Decolonization Is Not a Metaphor," 9.
11. See Venables, "Polishing the Silver Covenant Chain."
12. Tuck and Yang, "Reconciliation Is Not a Metaphor."

BIBLIOGRAPHY

Cote-Meek, Sheila. *Colonized Classrooms: Racism, Trauma and Resistance in Post-Secondary Education.* Toronto: Fernwood, 2014.

Maracle, Lee. *My Conversations with Canadians.* Toronto: Book*hug Press, 2017.

National Inquiry into Missing and Murdered Indigenous Women and Girls. *Reclaiming Power and Place: The Final Report of the National Inquiry into Missing and Murdered Indigenous Women and Girls.* 2 vols. Ottawa: MMIWG Inquiry, 2019. https://www.mmiwg-ffada.ca/final-report/.

Simpson, Leanne Betasamosake. "Land as Pedagogy: Nishnaabeg Intelligence and Rebellious Transformation." *Decolonization: Indigeneity, Education & Society* 3, no. 3 (2014): 1–25.

Talaga, Tanya. "Reconciliation Isn't Dead. It Never Truly Existed." *Globe and Mail,* February 29, 2020. https://www.theglobeandmail.com/opinion/article-reconciliation-isnt-dead-it-never-truly-existed/.

Truth and Reconciliation Commission of Canada. *The Final Report of the Truth and Reconciliation Commission of Canada.* 6 vols. Montreal: McGill-Queen's University Press, 2015.

———. *Truth and Reconciliation Commission of Canada: Calls to Action.* Winnipeg: National Centre for Truth and Reconciliation, 2015. https://ehprnh2mwo3.exactdn.com/wp-content/uploads/2021/01/Calls_to_Action_English2.pdf.

Tuck, Eve, and K. Wayne Yang. "Decolonization Is Not a Metaphor." *Decolonization: Indigeneity, Education & Society* 1, no. 1 (September 2012): 1–40.

Venables, Robert. "Polishing the Silver Covenant Chain: A Brief History of Some of the Symbols and Metaphors in Haudenosaunee Treaty Negotiations." *History of Relations With our Brothers 1613 to Today*, Onondaga Nation website, last updated March 10, 2011. https://www.onondaganation.org/history/2010/polishing-the-silver-covenant-chain-a-brief-history-of-some-of-the-symbols-and-metaphors-in-haudenosaunee-treaty-negotiations/.

I

Theoretical Perspectives on (Ir)reconciliation

Polishing the Silver Covenant Chain

1

FRANK DEER

Discovering Truth
in the Post-TRC Era

Morality and
Spirituality Discourses
in the Reconciliatory
Journeys of Schools

CURRENTLY, DISCOURSES ON
reconciliation in primary and secondary schools in Canada are developing in
response to the 2015 Truth and Reconciliation Commission of Canada's (TRC)
final report, as well as its ninety-four calls to action. While it may be useful to
invoke the TRC final report and its calls to action to inform these discourses, these
reconciliatory points of inquiry are, necessarily, generic insofar as they are intended
to reflect the needs of all indigenous peoples from across Canada. What has emerged
from the activities of the TRC is not just incisive discussion regarding how we may
correct the harms of the past as they were manifest in Indian residential schools,
but a developing imperative to come to understand the rich diversity of indigenous
peoples in Canada in an ethos of reconciliation.

In order to engage in adequate explorations of the unique experiences of
indigenous peoples, for which specific manifestations of indigenous knowledge,
heritage, consciousness, and tradition are relevant, deliberate ways in which we
approach their meaning and application are necessary. Although frequently explored
topics such as treaties may represent learning opportunities for which resources and
cogent paradigms are readily available, learning about perspectives in other areas

such as morality and spirituality in indigenous contexts may not be as accessible and the role of educators in articulating these areas may not be readily understood by students or the general public.

This chapter will explore how reconciliation may incorporate varied views of spirituality and morality, and how such views affect the goals of TRC-based reconciliation. It will investigate how philosophical underpinnings of belief and truth may incorporate indigenous knowledge and traditions. Central to the intent of this chapter, however, is the need to address how reconciliation may be approached in a manner that departs from the frequent, singular focus upon just the TRC's calls to action. In its final report, the TRC conceptualizes reconciliation as an appeal for respectful conversation, improved relationships, and mutual understanding across nations. In an attempt to lay out what is epistemically necessary for these conversations and relationships to be possible, this chapter looks at Western perspectives on morality and reconciliation to which indigenous contexts— topics of developing interest in primary and secondary education in Canada—are relevant. It explores these as one entry point into understanding an essential part of indigenous knowledge, heritage, consciousness, and tradition. The chapter will conclude with a discussion of the implications of these perspectives for teaching and learning, ultimately arguing that reconciliation in educational contexts relies on more than just learning indigenous content. It relies on developing a capacity for moral decision-making.

An Introduction to Reconciliation in Education

Reconciliation—herein defined as the movement of improving relationships between indigenous and non-indigenous peoples while maintaining an understanding of how past events have adversely affected these relationships—may be regarded as a particularly Canadian discussion in response to the truths of the residential school genocide. In spite of this apparent focused regard for how primary and secondary education was handled by government and religious authorities for much of the nineteenth and twentieth centuries, reconciliation in the post-TRC era has extended beyond schooling issues to many dimensions of Canadian society.[1] Topics such as health and wellness, language and culture, and labour-market participation are captured in the calls to action. These calls have broadened the discussion of how relationships between indigenous peoples and Canadians may be improved.[2]

Conversations regarding reconciliation in Canada are still developing. The vast majority of the calls to action that emerged from the TRC were directed toward federal and provincial/territorial levels of government. Further institutions such as postsecondary schools, religious groups, and other public offices are cited; however, the TRC's focus on the two principal levels of government reflects the sort of responsibility it imagined to be most appropriate within the body politic. As the report underlines, "it will take sustained political will at all levels of government and concerted material resources" in order to realize progress.[3] The federal government's responsibilities in this regard may be understood in the contexts of both its past role in the establishment and administration of residential schools and its current duties within treaty and constitutional relationships. Provincial areas of responsibility include, among other things, the responsibility to deliver and administer key social welfare services such as those of health and public education. As a consequence, these two levels of government have been noticeably engaged in discussions on reconciliation (with varying degrees of involvement and authenticity) in numerous events, initiatives, and other activities that are, ostensibly, in the public interest.[4]

While most of the TRC calls to action direct reconciliatory imperatives toward these two levels of government (with some positive responses having come from those corners), many nongovernmental institutions and community representatives have demonstrated interest in and commitment to the general goal of reconciliation. Public institutions such as universities and community organizations such as churches have been taking part in conversations and initiatives that minister to the goals of reconciliation—conversations and initiatives that are intended to improve relations with indigenous peoples while also coming to terms with difficult histories. The general conversation on reconciliation in Canada has extended beyond the interface indigenous peoples have had with government and has become inclusive of many for whom the calls to action were not nominally directed.[5]

The general discussion of reconciliation has, perhaps understandably, extended to those involved in primary and secondary schooling.[6] Indigenous histories, experiences, and perspectives have become increasingly essential when engaging in the creation of educational programming in schools. Many who are affiliated with primary and secondary education have committed themselves to exploring indigenous content, histories, and social issues. In many settings, the educational programming for children and youth includes important dimensions of First Nations, Métis, and Inuit languages, literacies, mathematics, and other areas of indigenous knowledge, heritage, consciousness, and tradition. School administrators and teacher leaders who have a role in developing and encouraging teachers to account for the emergent value associated with this relatively new area of indigenous education are becoming more responsive. This responsiveness is associated with the notions that indigenous content should be shared and celebrated, and that it should inform the development of a balanced perspective on indigenous experience in Canada.[7]

The reconciliation movement in public education, as well as the more dated movement toward integration of indigenous perspectives, has not developed without critical reception.[8] Much of the criticism toward these developments has been manifest in general public discourses as well as institutional resistance.[9] Despite this pushback, many governmental and educational authorities have pressed forward with this new chapter in Canadian history—one in which indigenous perspectives are employed in appropriate ways. Thus, many education leaders in Canada have assumed the responsibility of facilitating the development of appropriate learning opportunities that will support a sustainable and educationally fecund journey toward reconciliation. Many school principals, superintendents, and administrators who occupy positions of power have ventured into this area in a manner that is inclusive of divergent indigenous perspectives. This inclusive approach has allowed many indigenous elders and community members to provide leadership and knowledge that is essential to this process.

Exploring Reconciliation

Curricular and noncurricular initiatives, activities, and policies that would need to be developed and delivered in order to support a journey toward reconciliation have become central to school and district initiatives. Currently, primary and secondary schools rely on a small number of topical points of inquiry to facilitate discussions of indigenous experience in Canada.[10] Of these topics, two are most frequently featured, and are central to the efforts of the many schools that have committed to engaging in reconciliation: treaties and culture. This is no surprise, as treaties and culture are important elements of the TRC's calls to action, which guide many of these reconciliatory efforts—but these are not the only important points of departure. Another area of inquiry that must be included in curricula is morality.

TREATIES

Treaties are accords between indigenous peoples/nations and government agents, both past and present, that establish international relationships, land transfers, and government responsibilities. They have become an important conceptual lens through which the indigenous experience may be understood, especially when it is situated within a legal/constitutional context.[11] Treaties are often cited as a source upon which those interested in reconciliation may frame the existing relationships between indigenous and non-indigenous peoples. Learning about treaties between Canadian (as well as pre-Canadian) governments and indigenous peoples may be useful when discussing possibilities for educational initiatives. The educational value of treaties in Canada has led provincial authorities, postsecondary faculty, and others to develop programming and supporting resources for teachers and students to explore this topic.[12] Beyond legal and constitutional dimensions, treaties provide opportunities for historical and social learning for students and may serve as a useful point of inquiry for primary and secondary learners.

The broad focus on treaties as a bona fide dimension of school programming has contributed to the development of, directly and indirectly, a "lens" for understanding the indigenous experience in Canada. Since treaties have important and perhaps inseparable connection to the indigenous nations with which they are associated, this lens is valuable. Non-indigenous Canadians may be understood as those whose ancestral roots are from another country or part of the world. (This understanding may provide a way of understanding non-indigenous people through the histories and politics out of which those people have come.) Indigenous peoples, on the other hand, are repeatedly viewed and perhaps understood through their respective treaty/constitutional realities. In the era of reconciliation and for decades before, teachers and students have frequently taught and learned about First Nations, Métis, and Inuit cultures and peoples in terms of their particular treaty, which may offer inferential information about what region of Canada they are from as well as their respective language(s). Such treaty-based observations and discussions can condition the manner in which students understand indigenous peoples, but may offer useful starting points in the journey toward reconciliation.

Treaty and constitutional dimensions of First Nations, Métis, and Inuit peoples may also be a useful way of facilitating reconciliatory discussions by offering points of inquiry into the indigenous experience in Canada. Treaty issues risk, however, being limiting insofar as they may be seen as focusing upon legislative dimensions at the expense of topics that are more germane to other social realities.

CULTURE

Another issue that has emerged as a source for interfacing with indigeneity in primary and secondary schools in Canada is that of culture—specifically, spirituality. Although public schools often do not explicitly use the framing of spirituality, many public school staff have begun exploring spiritual perspectives of indigenous knowledge and consciousness. Similar to treaties and constitutional consideration, the topic of spirituality may be useful as an initial frame through which to acquire knowledge on indigenous histories, experiences, and cultures. The inclusion of spiritual frames that reflect belief systems and worldviews of indigenous peoples has become more ubiquitous as schools strive to be involved with reconciliation journeys and to engage in what is often referred to as "indigenization." This has been marked by the emergence of, for instance, high school pow wows, the inclusion of indigenous elders in school programming, and the development of curricula that incorporate activities such as sweat lodge ceremonies.[13]

There is no single rationale for why spirituality has become an important dimension of indigenous education; indeed, there is little empirical research of a pan-Canadian nature on this topic. However, the published work that is available points to the value of knowledge for indigenous community activities, and thus of the solicited participation by indigenous families and community members who can create guiding narratives and principles for schools and teachers to follow when considering such things as indignous ceremonies.[14] Schools continue to be particularly welcoming of community contributions from indigenous elders. It is through discourse with indigenous communities and elders that the topic of spirituality and morality emerge.[15]

MORALITY

The inclusion of morality in school programming reflects philosophical perspectives that may be essential to understanding indigenous worldviews. Vine Deloria Jr. notes the importance of religious and spiritual realities, making a conceptual bridge between these topics and that of morality:

> The real interest in the old Indians was not to discover the abstract structure of physical reality but rather to find the proper road along which, for the duration of a person's life, individuals were supposed to walk. This colorful image of the road suggests that the universe is a moral universe. That is to say, there is a proper way to live in the universe. There is a content to every action, behavior, and belief...There is direction to the universe...Nothing has incidental meaning and there are no coincidences.[16]

Deloria's stance on issues of morality highlights an area of tension between concepts of morality held by indigenous peoples and those held by non-indigenous peoples (many of whom are informed by monotheistic orientations). Deloria comments on this tension, noting that the role of indigenous people in the United States has been to "change the American conception of a society from that of a complex of laws designed to protect property to one in which liberty is not a matter of laws, coercive power, or a shadow of government but is characterized by manners of a moral sense of right and wrong."[17]

There is a discernable difference between the sources of morality for those with traditional indigenous orientations compared to the sources of those for whom morality is informed by traditions such as Christianity. Indigenous religion and spirituality, and the moral frames to which they may be affiliated, are frequently not delineated in a manner that leads to a set of reduced and generalizable rules similar to those in the Christian and Hebrew bibles. Rather, they may be best regarded as a process of discerning morality. As Gregory Cajete has written, "the traditional First Nations' metaphysical belief system did not adhere to an overall, organized description. It was a way of life, not carefully catalogued delineation of major and minor doctrines, subdoctrines, and corollary beliefs. Theology, to the Aboriginal, was a process rather than an intellectual structure."[18]

◁ ▷

Given that this process of discerning morality is clearly experiential in nature and not governed by codified, categorical rules, the educational opportunities ought to be designed to take advantage of available indigenous sources of knowledge and pedagogies.

A logical extension from this discussion of morality and how it may be situated in contemporary discourses on reconciliation, including how it is reflected in the work of the TRC, is best achieved by using religious, spiritual, and other cultural dimensions of the indigenous experience as a means of achieving initial understanding and eventual establishment of empathy in non-indigenous teachers and learners.[19] To this end, such indigenous perspectives are becoming more frequently reflected in many facets of Canadian public school curricula and beyond. A better understanding and development of morality may be supported in curricular and noncurricular initiatives through authentic experiential processes in which students have the opportunity to act and do. The opportunity for educators here is to view student agency as the primary apparatus for managing and developing conceptions of morality.

This view may be controversial for those whose understandings of morality are codified, religiously justified, and brokered by people they view as authorities. Central to this possible tension is how different indigenous and non-indigenous actors situate truth in the conversation of morality.

On Knowledge, Belief, and Truth

Currently, teachers and schools are exploring indigenous manifestations of morality. For example, many teachers have included an indigenous teaching about truth in their classroom. This teaching is believed to be a traditional aspect of a moral framework espoused by, among others, Anishinaabe peoples in Canada. It is also one element of the seven teachings (an indigenous framework). As Cyndy Baskin, Bela McPherson, and Carol Strike explain, in this context, the truth teaching is customarily described as the deliberate exercise of "coming to know, and trying to understand...[that] truth also encompasses the overarching picture as we try to understand both the past and the present."[20] Many school districts that have made a commitment to exploring indigenous perspectives in their respective educational programming are using the seven teachings in some manner, especially in primary schools.

The seven teachings, as understood by Baskin, McPherson, and Strike, are as follows:

1. **Respect:** Showing honour to someone or something, considering the wellbeing of everything, and treating everything with deference or courtesy
2. **Wisdom:** The practice of balance in all things
3. **Love:** Treating people with special care and kindness
4. **Honesty:** Being sincere, open, and trustworthy
5. **Humility:** Placing the needs of others first, and avoiding criticizing others

6. **Courage:** Showing personal bravery in the face of fear and doing what needs to be done even when it is difficult or frightening

7. **Truth:** Coming to know and trying to understand the previous six teachings and focusing on the overarching picture as we try to understand both the past and the present[21]

In this understanding, the indigenous teaching of truth bears some similarity to classical Western philosophical views on truth, belief formation, and justification. However, any exploration of truth (whether in indigenous or non-indigenous contexts) benefits from a conceptualization of what knowledge is and how this concept is situated in the work of establishing truth.

Knowledge, in a general Platonic sense, may simply be regarded as that which is established when a true belief is justified.[22] I will call this the Platonic tripartite definition. This definition of knowledge has been criticized for, among other reasons, its problematic presumption of how justification may be achieved and its focus on empirical forms of justification.[23] Edmund Gettier crystallized the potential issues with this traditional view of knowledge. His work became known as the "Gettier Problems": a series of hypothetical situations that demonstrate that belief and its justification may be affected by situational circumstances.[24] Coupled with caveats such as those of the Gettier Problems and with amendments such as the conclusive reasons condition,[25] knowledge, in the classical Platonic tripartite definition, has two main referent types around which it is built: empirical referents and those that may be understood through reason.[26]

This brief overview of how knowledge may be conceptualized is necessary in order to situate ourselves in the journey toward understanding the moral landscape of humanity. This is because knowledge is one of the desired products of our life journey. Moreover, the way in which we understand truth has a bearing on how we obtain this goal. The Platonic tripartite approach to truth (as well as frameworks that employ an "extra condition" to accommodate problems with justification, such as the conclusive reason condition mentioned above) can offer us a sense of the role that truth plays in obtaining knowledge.

Truth was described by Thomas Aquinas as the correlation of thought and object (i.e., our belief in something is a true belief if it corresponds with reality). A more robust definition of truth comes from Kant's categories of the understanding, which allow for coherence with our own subjective perspectives. As Chris Rohmann once wrote, "Our subjective perceptions may not accurately capture reality...[This] is addressed by the coherence theory, according to which something can be said to be true if it is consistent with the other elements in a coherent conceptual system."[27]

Rohmann's synthesis of coherence theory emphasizes a further element to this journey toward knowledge: belief. In establishing knowledge, a person's belief that something is true is essential. As Paul Kleinman once intimated while describing the tripartite theory of knowledge, "a person can't know something to be true without first believing that it is true."[28] A fundamental description of what knowledge is may be captured in the phrase "knowledge is established when a belief is true and justified."[29]

Earlier, it was suggested that this classic, Platonic description of truth bears important similarities with the indigenous views on truth as explored in the seven teachings framework. This correspondence may be reflected in several ways. One crucial point of correspondence—the focus of this discussion—is the process of knowledge generation and acquisition and, more specifically, the manner in which human agency is a driving force for such processes. As is frequently the case for classical theories of truth and how it may be established, the source of belief and judgment of what is true lies with the human agents engaged in these processes. The indigenous teaching of truth implies a similar process (as do the other six teachings). It is within the scope of our collective and individual journeys toward moral truth to discover, discuss, and even negotiate that which is true. Discovering what I believe to be true is my responsibility. Although the justification of a truth may go beyond my individual responsibility (many truth claims require more than my intuition and may require external verification or support to adequately establish justification), Plato's condition of belief must emerge from our own consciousness.

There are two principles associated with the seven teachings framework that may lead us to a caveat with regard to truth as an element of these teachings. The first is the condition of process and the associated role of human agency in the journey toward knowledge. The second involves the form that the seven teachings take. These teachings are repeatedly presented as discernable concepts. However, this may unjustly essentialize individual concepts. Such essentializations are not the point. Rather, "the manner in which the constituent elements of the seven teachings are conceptualized is not necessarily fixed and therefore not necessarily consistent from context to context, although the general spirit of the teachings is retained."[30] So the caveat is this: the seven individual teachings ought not to be regarded as delineated and independent of one another but rather as a wholistic set of moral guidelines that require balance in their observation and use.[31] This observation opens the door toward one philosophical tradition among many—that of *intuitionism*.

Intuition and the Search for Moral Truth

Gregory Cajete asserted that the religious worldviews of indigenous peoples in North America are not reduced to specific, unalterable doctrines to which we must adhere.[32] Rather, these worldviews are better regarded as a way of life. The variability of these perspectives has an essential quality that should not be overlooked: that of pliability in a particular national and/or cultural context. The pliability in the indigenous teaching of truth may be understood in terms of how one must reconcile truth in particular situations and cultural contexts. *Intuition*—the capacity to believe something in an a priori manner—provides philosophical grounding that complements Cajete's position.

William Ross developed a position on intuitionism that proposed the existence of prima facie duties that humans carry out to varying degrees.[33] Ross's position states that human beings possess moral intuition, that this intuition necessitates intuitive moral duties, and that these duties are not absolute. For Ross, human consciousness is the source from which morality emerges; there is no need to invoke external sources as religious doctrine to justify morality. The appearance of Ross's intuitive duties as a delineated framework may be understood thus: "Given that it is this intuition-based morality that informs ethical decisions and actions, it may be no surprise that conceptualizing ethics in a sort of framework, just as we see with the seven teachings, occurs."[34] Ross emphasizes that one must weigh intuitive duties in the contexts in which they are relevant. For example, if one intuitive duty is in conflict with another, the duty that is seen to be more important will be acted upon— possibly at the expense of others.[35]

As Canadian public schools respond to the post-TRC reconciliation movement, teachers and school administrators appear to have palpably initiated or renewed their embrace of spiritual content such as the seven teachings. There have been many observations about the opportunities schools have to follow this course, but it is the before-mentioned topic of human agency that merits examination at a time when the development of initiatives requires consideration of resources. Sources that are employed by teachers have become an important consideration in the development of curriculum that explores indigenous spiritual content. Although teachers may frequently rely upon sources such as established curriculum and text-based resources for the purposes of general program development, many schools are utilizing indigenous peoples and other less-conventional resources to support curriculum development related to reconciliation. The development of curriculum ought to focus on supporting the learning of indigenous cultural content, but not *just* on this. It should also focus on the development of students' capacity for moral decision-making. In order to engage in such development in an appropriate way, indigenous elders, community members, and traditional narratives associated with indigenous spiritual and religious beliefs are examples of resources that have been used for program development. Although such unconventional sources of knowledge may provide insight into the content and nature of indigenous spiritual perceptions of truth and morality, it is on the intuitive agency of human beings that moral decision-making relies.

NOTES

1. Frideres, *First Nations*.
2. *Truth and Reconciliation Commission of Canada: Calls to Action*.
3. Truth and Reconciliation Commission of Canada, *Final Report*, 6:4.
4. Chandler-Olcott and Hinchman, "Reconciliation."
5. See Korteweg and Russell, "Decolonizing + Indigenizing."
6. Newbery, "Canoe Pedagogy."
7. Deer, "Institutional and Community Capacity."
8. Montero and Dénommé-Welch, "Reconciliation through Education."
9. Grande, "Refusing the University."
10. Deer, "Moral Landscape."
11. Stonechild, *The Knowledge Seeker*; Lawrence, *"Real" Indians*.
12. Deer, "Institutional and Community Capacity."
13. Hamm, "Walking with Place."
14. Montero and Dénommé-Welch, "Reconciliation through Education."
15. Ellerby, *Working with Indigenous Elders*.
16. Deloria, *Spirit and Reason*, 46.
17. Deloria, *Spirit and Reason*, 73.
18. Cajete, *Look to the Mountain*, 12.
19. Aitken and Radford, "Learning to Teach."
20. Baskin, McPherson, and Strike, "Using the Seven Sacred Teachings," 194.
21. Baskin, McPherson, and Strike, "Using the Seven Sacred Teachings," 182–196.
22. Kleinman, *Philosophy 101*.
23. Hospers, *Introduction to Philosophical Analysis*.
24. Gettier, "Is Justified True Belief Knowledge." One Gettier problem, the cow in the field, shows that truth claims may be based on perceived good evidence that turns out to be nonexistent. For further exploration of epistemological issues, see Ichikawa and Steup, "Analysis of Knowledge."
25. The conclusive reasons condition is an account of knowledge and a response to the counterexamples of Gettier. In this account, a proposition's truth is understood according to the reasons for understanding that truth.
26. Sidgwick, *Methods of Ethics*.
27. Rohmann, *A World of Ideas*, 411.
28. Kleinman, *Philosophy 101*, 42.
29. Ichikawa and Steup, "Analysis of Knowledge."
30. Deer, "Moral Landscape," 3.
31. Stonechild, *The Knowledge Seeker*.
32. Cajete, *Look to the Mountain*.
33. Ross, *The Right and the Good*. Ross conceptualized a set of seven intuitive duties: promise keeping, fidelity, gratitude for favours, beneficence, justice, self-improvement, and nonmaleficence.
34. Deer, "Moral Landscape," 5.
35. Pojman and Fieser, *Ethics*.

BIBLIOGRAPHY

Aitken, Avril, and Linda Radford. "Learning to Teach for Reconciliation in Canada: Potential, Resistance and Stumbling Forward." *Teaching and Teacher Education* 75 (2018): 40–48.

Baskin, Cyndy, Bela McPherson, and Carol Strike. "Using the Seven Sacred Teachings to Improve Services for Aboriginal Mothers Experiencing Drug and Alcohol Misuse Problems and Involvement with Child Welfare." In *Well-Being in the Urban Aboriginal Community: Fostering*

Biimaadiziwin, a National Research Conference on Urban Aboriginal Peoples, edited by David Newhouse, Kevin FitzMaurice, Tricia McGuire-Adams, and Daniel Jetté, 179–200. Toronto: Thompson Educational Publishing, 2012.

Cajete, Gregory. *Look to the Mountain: An Ecology of Indigenous Education.* Durango: Kivaki Press, 1994.

Chandler-Olcott, Kelly, and Kathleen Hinchman. "Reconciliation." *Journal of Adolescent and Adult Literacy* 62, no. 2 (2018): 133–35.

Deer, Frank. "The Institutional and Community Capacity for Aboriginal Education: A Case Study." *In Education* 19, no. 3 (2014): 3–16.

———. "Moral Landscape of Indigenous Knowledge in Learning, Initial Thoughts for Primary and Secondary Education." In *Encyclopedia of Educational Philosophy and Theory* (living digital reference), edited by Michael Peters. Singapore: Springer, 2018. https://doi. org/10.1007/978-981-287-532-7_641-1.

Deloria, Vine, Jr. *Spirit and Reason.* Golden: Fulcrum Publishing, 1999.

Ellerby, Jonathan. *Working with Indigenous Elders.* Winnipeg: Aboriginal Issues Press, 2006.

Frideres, James. *First Nations in the Twenty-First Century.* Don Mills: Oxford University Press, 2011.

Gettier, Edmund. "Is Justified True Belief Knowledge?" *Analysis* 23, no. 6 (1963): 121–23.

Grande, Sandy. "Refusing the University." In *Dissident Knowledge in Higher Education,* edited by Marc Spooner and James McNinch, 168–89. Regina: University of Regina Press, 2018.

Hamm, Catherine. "Walking with Place: Storying Reconciliation Pedagogies in Early Childhood Education." *Journal of Childhood Studies* 40, no. 2 (2015): 56–66.

Hospers, John. *An Introduction to Philosophical Analysis.* 3rd ed. Englewood Cliffs: Prentice Hall, 1988.

Ichikawa, Jonathan Jenkins, and Matthias Steup. "The Analysis of Knowledge." In *Stanford Encyclopedia of Philosophy* (living digital reference), edited by Edward N. Zalta. Stanford: The Metaphysics Research Lab. Last modified March 7, 2017. https://plato.stanford.edu/entries/ knowledge-analysis/.

Kleinman, Paul. *Philosophy 101: A Crash Course in the Principles of Knowledge, Reality and Values.* Avon: Adams Media, 2013.

Korteweg, Lisa, and Russell, C. "Decolonizing + Indigenizing = Moving Environmental Education Toward Reconciliation." *Canadian Journal of Environmental Education* 17 (2012): 5–14.

Lawrence, Bonita. *"Real" Indians and Others: Mixed-Blood Urban Native Peoples and Indigenous Nationhood.* Vancouver: UBC Press, 2004.

Montero, Kristiina, and Spy Dénommé-Welch. "Reconciliation through Education: A Review of *Achieving Indigenous Student Success: A Guide for Secondary Classrooms." Journal of Adolescent and Adult Literacy* 62, no. 2 (2018): 241–43.

Newbery, Liz. "Canoe Pedagogy and Colonial History: Exploring Contested Spaces of Outdoor Environmental Education." *Canadian Journal of Environmental Education,* 17 (2012): 30–45.

Pojman, Louis, and James Fieser. *Ethics: Discovering Right and Wrong.* 8th ed. Boston: Cengage Learning, 2017.

Rohmann, Chris. *A World of Ideas: A Dictionary of Important Theories, Concepts, Beliefs, and Thinkers.* New York: Ballantine Books, 1999.

Ross, William David. *The Right and the Good.* Oxford: Oxford University Press, 1930.

Sidgwick, Henry. *The Methods of Ethics.* 7th ed. Indianapolis: Hackett Publishing Company, 1981.

Stonechild, Blair. *The Knowledge Seeker: Embracing Indigenous Spirituality.* Regina: University of Regina Press, 2016.

Truth and Reconciliation Commission of Canada. *The Final Report of the Truth and Reconciliation Commission of Canada.* 6 vols. Montréal: McGill-Queen's University Press, 2015.

———. *Truth and Reconciliation Commission of Canada: Calls to Action.* Winnipeg: National Centre for Truth and Reconciliation, 2015. https://ehprnh2mwo3.exactdn.com/wp-content/uploads/2021/01/ Calls_to_Action_English2.pdf.

2

MICHELLE PIDGEON

Indigenous Resiliency, Renewal, and Resurgence in Decolonizing Canadian Higher Education

A question was asked of me when I was a doctoral student: Why are Indigenous peoples even trying to be here if it's such a bad place for them? "Here," in this instance, was the university. The question came as a form of resistance to the critique I had of the institution's systemic biases towards Indigenous ways of knowing and being. This question has stayed with me ever since. I've had to ponder long and hard about it. It constantly affronts me on an almost daily basis, whether I'm at a meeting with "Indigeneity" on the agenda or in the classroom working with undergraduates on why Indigenous education matters—whether I'm having to react to the latest policy or program change that excludes Indigenous students or just being present on campus. Being present, being seen, is a constant reminder that Indigenous peoples are here, persisting, resisting, and thriving!

The story that opens this chapter is my story. I share it to engage us in relationship with the calls to action of the Truth and Reconciliation Commission of Canada (TRC), in which all Canadians are asked to take up the work of truth and reconciliation.[1]

This includes those working within the educational system who must reconcile their role in the colonial project of assimilation and genocide against Indigenous peoples. This chapter centres Indigenous people's views of Canadian higher education—from this lens, from this place, and from this time. In troubling reconciliation as it is currently being taken up across the Canadian higher education system, the work of decolonization must take hold with the aim of empowering Indigenous peoples. In looking to the past, we can better understand our future and continue the work and visioning required to fully understand what a decolonized and transformed Canadian education system will be.

I raise my hands in deep respect to those Indigenous scholars who started this work in Canadian higher education long before I entered the academy: Verna Kirkness, Jo-ann Archibald, Marie Battiste, Blair Stonechild, David Newhouse, Michael Marker, and so many others. Their intentional acts of troubling the academy, pushing for decolonization and Indigenous ways of knowing over the last fifty years means that now the next generation is ready to continue their work and advance Indigeneity as it has been envisioned by our ancestors. I pause, too, to raise my hands and heart to all of our Indigenous academic knowledge holders who have gone before us.

It is with a well-honed awareness of the already-existing bias that Indigenous peoples enter into the Canadian higher education system. Indigenous peoples see higher education as a tool of decolonization,[2] and consequently they persist through determination and intentional acts of resiliency (e.g., succeeding with Indigenous integrity intact), renewal (e.g., Indigenous voice and vision for Indigenous student success), and resurgence (e.g., cultural practices and language revitalization).

As an Indigenous academic, there is deep responsibility in the words that I write; there are intentional actions of troubling commonly held beliefs, biases, and assumptions that Canadians have about Indigenous peoples, particularly students. I have to be reflective of what Leigh Patel calls the "pauses" that are needed in the writing process: "the sort of rupture[s] and change[s] to being and learning that may be appropriate to counter the built up habits of colonialism."[3]

Within these pauses, writing can become an intentional act of decolonization. Still, we must remain mindful that writing continues to be a tool of colonization, and the pressure within the academy to publish or perish looms over many of us in the academy—students, faculty, postdoctoral fellows, and sessional instructors. Still, we challenge the academy from within: each of us with distinct measures of "success" against Western forms of accountability. Writing as a decolonizing praxis takes on a broader sense of responsibility for the words written, the intention set out in the writing, and the audiences for the work. Writing, therefore, becomes a tool to educate, empower, and assert Indigenous voices and perspectives within (and outside) the academy. It becomes a way of laying claim to Indigenous knowledges and ways of being that are relevant and need to be shared collectively. Indigenous writing processes honour the principle of reciprocity and responsibility as Indigenous scholars work with Indigenous communities' self-determination and empowerment.

I paused, as Patel encourages, when reading Martin Nakata's work on Indigenous higher education in Australia, and his critique of the simplicity of positioning Indigenous self-determination in the absence of critically "engag[ing] in the complexity of contemporary space in which we as Indigenous peoples find ourselves today."[4] He argues:

> In practice, both the equity and social inclusion agenda and decolonizing knowledge framework are utilized in support of the goals of Indigenous self-determination. These frameworks assist in the normalization of the logic and sense of political and cultural self-determination as the goals and grounds for Indigenous higher education practice. As a consequence of this normalization, we think less about the underlying assumptions of these or how we take them for granted as our frames of reference. They sit in our practice and reasoning as if that has been the way things have always been.[5]

Patel intentionally used anticolonial frameworks within her own decolonizing project to ensure "a pause from the overuse of decolonization, with the intention of better leveraging both terms."[6] Eve Tuck and K. Wayne Yang remind us that in taking up the work of decolonizing, we are not simply thinking of decolonization as a metaphor. As they argue, "When metaphor invades decolonization, it kills the very possibility of decolonization; it re-centers whiteness, it resettles theory, it extends innocence to the settler, it entertains a settler future. Decolonize (a verb) and decolonization (a noun) cannot be easily grafted onto pre-existing discourses/ frameworks, even if they are critical, even if they are anti-racist, even if they are justice frameworks."[7]

I fully recognize the academic debates within these theoretical frames by Indigenous and non-Indigenous scholars. My intent is not to dismiss them, but to fully embrace them in the recognition that settler colonialism, through land, has immediate and long-lasting consequences. In fact, colonial practices are not "something of the past" nor are they something Indigenous peoples just need to get over. In higher education, Marie Battiste calls on us to understand that the role of place (i.e., the lands and waters) and the influence of time (i.e., the way in which the past, present, and future directly influences Indigenous contemporary realities) are critically important as we move Indigeneity forward within the academy. Tuck and Yang urge us to consider the incommensurability of higher education and decolonization that is centred in and "accountable to Indigenous sovereignty and futurity";[8] decolonizing education without clear articulation of the practices and policies that address land and the ongoing impacts of colonization may not actually move the Indigenization of the academy forward in ways that empower Indigenous peoples. Indigenization—the centring of Indigenous ways of knowing and being within the relationship of lands and waters, the animate and the inanimate—cannot happen without meaningful decolonizing efforts. Consequently, we must be critical of calls for reconciliation that only focus on how settler Canadians better understand the intergenerational impacts of residential schools and continue to dismiss the colonial, systemic causes of the inequities between Indigenous people and settlers in this country. The TRC, in its final report and calls to action, was clear in the need for *truth* and reconciliation. Within this process, all Canadians must understand the truth of colonization in this country, as it was enacted by residential schools and other assimilationist policies. True reconciliation will be present when structures, policies, processes, and people themselves have done the work of decolonization, and when Indigenization is woven into the Canadian fabric rather than a "tokenized checklist" approach to inclusion.[9] We act intentionally when we push against and trouble the nuanced subversive coloniality existing within our higher education system. In part, this is done by calling out the interconnections and overlaps between Indigenization, decolonization, and reconciliation. More importantly, it is done by critically reflecting (and acting) on how each approach (or multiple approaches) may intentionally contribute to the futurity and resurgence of Indigenous ways of knowing, being, and self-determination.

There is value in listening to a niggling in the recesses of one's heart that is telling you a pause is needed. In our training as Indigenous scholars, we are reading about and immersed in discussions of decolonization, anticolonial analysis, and centring our ways of knowing and being—and we need to pause, as Patel reminds us to do, to ensure that we are not taking for granted frames of reference that have been colonized. Vanessa de Oliveria Andreotti and colleagues speak of a continuum of decolonization approaches within higher education from the view that "everything is awesome" and no decolonization practices are required to "beyond-reform," which sees decolonization occurring through the dismantling of systemic violence through subversive educational use of spaces, resources, hacking, and hospicing.[10] There is also recognition by these scholars that there is no promise or guarantee of systemic change nor is there any assurance that Indigenous knowledges will not be co-opted by the very institution we are aiming to change. Therefore, Nakata and others call for a clear interrogation of the assumptions that inform our work from practices to policies and suggest that it is necessary to take on a subversive stance in using the academy for Indigenous means.[11] This means leveraging the resources of the academy to advance Indigenous resurgence through the university practices of teaching, research, and service—for example, seeking research funds that empower community-led research projects where the resources and capacity-building are within the community rather than retained within the institution only. Mentoring Indigenous students and future scholars is a key part of enacting Indigenous resurgence. Central to this mentorship is taking on research that matters to the mentees' communities, that is informed from their cultural frameworks, and that builds capacity at the community level. Some aspects of systemic change require consideration of the role of allyship with others who are working from antiracist, diversity, inclusion, social justice, and/or other equity-seeking frameworks to intentionally address settler roles and responsibilities. This work is not the responsibility of Indigenous peoples in the academy and it may be that in some cases these various groups have competing interests. In some ways, having various equity-seeking groups competing for resources is an ongoing colonial practice of dividing and conquering. The key is to decipher ongoing, systemic acts of resistance to necessary changes from moments when we can actually come together to unite in our shared responsibilities to make those changes. We must work together, too, to understand our shared responsibilities. Above all, we must not be lulled into the complacency of believing that this work belongs to other people or another time.

Postsecondary institutions, especially universities, are recognized as places of "cognitive imperialism: a form of mind control, manipulation, and propaganda that serves elites in the nation."[12] In this chapter, I focus on Euro-Western postsecondary institutions. As Canadian citizens and treaty peoples, Indigenous people have legal right and title to education in these institutions.[13] Most First Nations, Métis, and Inuit students do in fact attend these institutions, and these institutions are then called on to support Indigenous students' journeys where they take them, and to ensure that Indigenous students' postsecondary experiences honour who they are as Indigenous people.[14] Furthermore, without Indigenous engagement with the educational system, the system will only further perpetuate colonial practices through marginalization and continued attempts to erase Indigenous peoples. Remembering that, as Linda Tuhiwai Smith has said, these systems are created by humans, and therefore are inherently flawed, and therefore can be changed, the hope is that with Indigenous engagement and presence, the postsecondary system will transform.[15] In essence, this vision of change troubles the colonial legacy of education and acknowledges that colonization has not "gone away"; it is part of Canadian society, and it is reflected in the colonial governance structures (e.g., government, education, health) that directly impact the day-to-day experiences of Indigenous peoples in Canada (e.g., systemic racism). Contemporary colonization can be as subversive as it is covert, and we can no longer afford to ignore it.

Collective Responsibility and Sharing in Higher Education

> Of all the teachings we receive, this one is most important: Nothing belongs to you of what there is, of what you take, you must share.
> —Chief Dan George, *My Heart Soars*

As the teaching from Chief Dan George reminds us, we have an inherent responsibility to share what we have learned—this is my responsibility as an Indigenous higher education scholar. Indigenous peoples have always had an education system that was inclusive of the lifespan and higher learning.[16] In this regard, the Canadian higher education system is relatively young, with the first two universities being established in 1663 (Universitié Laval, Québec) and 1785 (University of New Brunswick).[17] These universities and others were essentially established by financial contributions from church organizations in partnership with provincial governments. The churches therefore were implicit in the colonization project within the Canadian education system that extends beyond their role in residential school history.

What is often omitted in the telling of the story of the establishment of the Canadian postsecondary system was that, in fact, these campuses were built on unceded Indigenous territories.[18] Contemporarily, the Canadian higher education system consists of over sixty-eight universities and fifty-one colleges operating as public institutions, with some provincial jurisdictions also allowing for private universities, colleges, and institutes.[19] Higher education in Canada is governed at the provincial level, with federal support through federal transfer agreements. Provincial and territorial governments are the overseers, regulators, and legislators of the institutes, colleges, and universities within their jurisdiction.[20]

These institutions—as part of the colonial project—were established with an inherent belief about whose knowledge counts and who belongs within the ivory tower. The Indian Act, first established in 1867, dictates the federal colonial project with regard to education. As Blair Stonechild notes, the federal government is responsible according to the act, for providing K to 12 schooling for First Nations, but sees itself as only socially, not legally, responsible for providing higher education.[21] Consequently, exposing the truth of the colonial and violent history of Canadian higher education is critically important in moving Indigenization efforts forward in these institutional spaces that were never intended to be inclusive of Indigenous peoples.

The 200-year history of Canadian higher education also connects to the history of residential schools (the first established in 1831, the last closed in 1996), as these institutions trained those educators, social workers, and other professionals to perpetuate violence against Indigenous families. All this was done under the guise of the assimilationist policies (i.e., the Indian Act 1876) that Sir John A McDonald intentionally set out to "take the Indian out of the child," and notably the establishment of residential schools in Canada.[22] Further, prior to the 1960s, any First Nations person who went to university was enfranchised—that is, they involuntarily lost their status. This meant that the federal government no longer formally recognized them as First Nations, and they lost all financial support and all other treaty rights provided through the Indian Act.[23] Such intentional assimilation and other intentional policies marginalized Aboriginal peoples' full participation as citizens of Turtle Island, or what we now call North America.

Within these reflections, a core question emerges: How has Indigeneity been used to reclaim and decolonize the academy in a manner that empowers Indigenous peoples? Indigeneity in this sense means going beyond bringing art and cultural representations into the hallways; it must also go beyond simply including Indigenous content in the curriculum. Indigeneity is grounded in Indigenous ways of knowing and being—relationality to land, to one's cultural frameworks and languages. It is the empowerment of Indigenous sovereignty across academic structures and policies (e.g., governance, ethics boards, and tenure and promotion) and it is a resistance to and disruption of ongoing colonial practices in these spaces. Looking back to think forward, I have organized my thoughts in the rest of this chapter around three interconnected sections: (1) Responsibility of Self-Determination, Resiliency and Policies; (2) Renewal through Relevant Programs; and (3) Resurgence of Praxis. I conclude with a deep imagining of what a decolonized system would look like. Tuck and Yang's calls for decolonization to empower a decolonial praxis are upon Canadian higher education.[24] Decolonial praxis, in the words of Levi Gahman and Gabrielle Legault, is a set of "dynamic processes, reflexive methods, and interdependent practices of unsettling the structural apparatuses, systemic mechanisms, and everyday (yet power-laden) routines that reassert colonial social relations."[25] In thinking about what Indigenous and non-Indigenous peoples can do as agents within the higher education system to ultimately transform the system in relation to reconciliation, decolonization, and Indigenization, several responses and responsibilities come to mind. The TRC's calls to action, the United Nations Declaration of the Rights of Indigenous Peoples (UNDRIP), and the reports from the National Inquiry into Missing and Murdered Indigenous Women and Girls (MMIWG), for instance, all include proposed actions that have direct implications for postsecondary education. The work we are called to do requires changes in how and why we do things—from our pedagogical approaches, to our ways of enacting self-governance within a bicameral governance structure, to our research and service endeavours. More importantly, none of this work can be done without sustained responsible relationships with Indigenous peoples and communities. To decolonize the institution—to go beyond token acts, and to truly engage in reconciliation and Indigenization—colleges and universities must take up the principle "nothing about us without us" in their relationships with diverse Indigenous communities (e.g., Indigenous faculty, staff, Elders, and students within their campuses), and specifically the holders of the territories upon which the institutions reside. In this relationship, an ethics of relationality must be enacted. This ethics would transform the work of a university, leveraging it to advance Indigenous communities—whether urban, rural, or remote—to further their goals of Indigenous economic sustainability, education, and employment opportunities, and improve the cultural, physical, mental, and emotional wellness for their people. Praxis calls upon all of us to act, to change, and to empower. In order to respond to that call, we must understand what we are aiming for.

Responsibility of Self-Determination

In a policy paper written for the Assembly of First Nations, Dr. John Borrows asserts that Indigenous peoples are self-determining when "Indigenous law and governance…operate in its own sphere of authority." He further specifies:

> Areas of Legislative Jurisdiction should be pursued in relation to:
>
> (1) Control of Federal Service Delivery through Self-Determination Recognition Legislation.
> (2) Protection of Culture and Communities through National Legislation related to:
>   a. Indigenous Child Welfare
>   b. Indigenous Languages
>   c. Religious Freedoms
>   d. Cultural Heritage
>   e. Dispute Resolutions and Tribal Courts
> (3) Indigenous Economic Development and Resource Protection through Legislation related to:
>   a. Gaming
>   b. Business Development and Support
>   c. Oil, Gas, Minerals
>   d. Forests, Air, Agriculture and Water[26]

Under international treaty law, Canada is obligated to respect the First Nations' right of self-determination. In *Indian Control of Indian Education*, the National Indian Brotherhood envisioned self-determination as Indigenous control and ownership over an Indigenous education system. [27] This education system would be informed by Indigenous customs, practices, and ways of knowing. These knowledge systems would directly inform pedagogical practices, curriculum, and programs by and for Indigenous peoples across the lifespan (e.g., early childhood, K to 12, postsecondary, adult, and community-based education).

Indigenous self-determination in higher education becomes how Indigenous peoples choose to bring themselves into the academy: what knowledge(s) or gifts they share,[28] and how they articulate their goals and objectives of being in these spaces. Self-determination is enacted through the multiple ways that the system is transformed from policies to practices for Indigeneity to thrive both within and outside the academy. I agree with Robin D.G. Kelley's cautions, made in the context of African American university student protests and the inequitable treatment of African Americans by police in the United States: "The fully racialized social and epistemological architecture upon which the modern university is built cannot be radically transformed by 'simply' adding darker faces, safer spaces, better training, and a curriculum that acknowledges historical and contemporary oppressions."[29] Similarly, Indigenization of the academy is not going to simply happen with the cluster hires of Indigenous scholars or the creation of institution-wide strategic plans. These actions alone will neither change the system nor allow for self-determination. Arguing for better linkages between university systems and Indigenous educational needs, Nakata advocates for a middle ground—something others might call "walking in two worlds"—rather than the "us-versus-them" perspective: "In higher education we need to prioritize a fuller and different Indigenous engagement with the world of ideas. We must see our work as an ongoing effort to think about the challenges in the difficult middle ground rather than foreclose on the possibilities that reside there by a fetish for solidifying the boundaries between Indigenous and non-Indigenous worlds."[30] To elaborate using the example of cluster hires, welcoming Indigenous academics as a cohort is an attempt to value the collective relationality. However, such hiring practices do nothing to challenge the system's valuing of individual success and competition (e.g., sole-author publications, primary investigators on research grants) more than collective and collaborative work (e.g., co-authored papers, co-teaching). Self-determination could be supported if tenure and promotion policies and processes were decolonized. This would involve including Indigenous academics (either from within the institution or from outside if lack of representation exists within the institution) in tenure and promotion policy renewal.

When a scholar is assessed for promotion or tenure, much weight is placed on research and publication. What this looks like in Indigenous contexts may differ from what has typically been expected. Including Indigenous members, either from within our outside of the institution, on review panels assessing Indigenous academics for promotion or tenure would integrate Indigenous values and perspectives into these processes, enacting decolonized policies. To further decolonize this process, at minimum, all members of these committees would undergo professional development to understand the diversity and complexity of Indigenous research and scholarship. An Indigenous scholar's career trajectory would be understood based on relationality—with regard to the communities to whom they are responsible and the context of their discipline (e.g., how decolonized the discipline itself is). In this regard, Indigenous community representatives with whom the researcher has been working could speak to the nature of research relationships and their impact. The members of the tenure and promotion committees must also have an understanding that certain modes of Indigenous research, and of subsequent knowledge mobilization, may take longer to mobilize within the academy. For example, for Indigenous scholars who are doing community-based work, their first responsibility is giving back to the community through the development of curriculum materials before peer-reviewed articles. Scholars may encounter publication-barriers due to the nature of their knowledge mobilization (e.g., time to publication, racism, lack of publication venues that would accept Indigenous-focused scholarship). Committees with this type of training, and with Indigenous representatives, would then be empowered to recognize and support Indigenous self-determination as it is reflected in their Indigenous colleagues' academic CVs.

Such decolonized policies and processes of recruitment, hiring, tenure, and promotion must come with systemic changes to support networks and challenge assumptions that are being made—for instance, that in being hired together as a group, they will inherently get along, understand how to support each other, and navigate their disciplines and the academy successfully. However, this alone changes neither the system nor the structures by which these academics would be reviewed for tenure and promotion, as illustrated above. Unless the system provides that policy directive as well as intentional supports in the system itself, Indigenous cluster hires will continue to be set up to fail in a system that is essentially saying to them, "You only belong if you conform to colonial standards of what it means to be an academic."

Even in thinking through what it means to be Indigenous in the academy, I am reminded of the immense cost—emotionally, spiritually, physically, and intellectually—on Indigenous faculty, students, and staff—particularly those standing up to, speaking out and reminding others about, watching for, reading and writing about, reacting and responding to, and pushing against colonization, racism, and so on. This cost is high for the too-few Indigenous staff in Aboriginal student services, that lone Indigenous faculty member in a department, and that single Indigenous student in the classroom to take on alone. Expecting these individuals to speak for and represent everything Indigenous is simply untenable and unsustainable. In addition to the reason for their being at the institution (e.g., as an educator, researcher, learner, supporter), Indigenous peoples in the academy are now also called upon to be educators for all, advocates for all things Indigenous, and mentors to the next generations. In the spirit of the TRC's calls to action, it is now time for all of us in these systems to be stepping up, speaking out, and, more importantly, changing practices to support Indigenous ways of knowing and being (i.e., Indigeneity) within the academy. As a preliminary guide in this journey of transformation, the next section considers how Indigenous resiliency is enacted through policy.

Resiliency and Policies

In 1972, the National Indian Brotherhood (now the Assembly of First Nations) released a two-volume report entitled *Indian Control of Indian Education*. It articulated a vision of Indigenous education across the lifespan, inclusive of policies, programs, and practices, outlining how the Canadian education system could support Indigenous education. This visionary document has influenced current practices, programs, and policies around Indigenous education across the country.[31] For example, the *Accord on Indigenous Education* from the Association of Canadian Deans of Education takes up the work of *Indian Control of Indian Education* by ensuring that all K to 12 teachers are educated to work with Indigenous students.[32] British

Columbia's Aboriginal Education Enhancement Agreements enact the values of the Indigenous Brotherhood document by having local First Nations and Métis communities/organizations direct how Aboriginal education occurs within their school districts.[33] Within higher education, we see the intentional development of policies and Indigenous strategic plans aimed at supporting Indigenous student success. This may look like setting targets for Aboriginal admissions into the first year of university or the creation of specific programming to support Indigenous student transition into university. Other institutions have set institutional priorities in response to the TRC's calls to action. After a consultation process, Simon Fraser University's Aboriginal Reconciliation Council put forward its commitments to reconciliation in the 2017 report *Walk this Path with Us* and established a CAD9 million fund to follow through on them. Putting these policies to practice remains the ongoing challenge for most institutions as they struggle with the resource allocations, both financial and human, that are required to make the institutional changes called for by Indigenous peoples and their allies.[34]

Understanding that Indigenous peoples are self-governing and that all those First Nations who have treaties with the Canadian government should be considered treaty peoples fundamentally changes the relationship Indigenous peoples have with the federal, provincial, and Indigenous government relationship.[35] Indigenous "membership" in their local nations' band registry is bound by policy. First Nations peoples' ability to attend postsecondary is a complicated interaction between federal Aboriginal postsecondary funding policies, provincial Aboriginal postsecondary policy, and band/nation policies (related to funding for postsecondary education). In *The New Buffalo*, Blair Stonechild provides a detailed history of the relationship between policy and education for Indigenous peoples:

> The spirit of the treaties is such that First Nations were to receive something of significant value, and, in the case of the Numbered Treaties, this was largely represented by the demand for education that would enable future generations to share in the bounty of Canada. This access to opportunity extends to post-secondary education and implies that First Nations individuals should have unlimited access to any training for which they qualify. In addition, Aboriginal people should have the right to establish and control post-secondary institutions as a means of ensuring culturally appropriate and effective programs.[36]

The decolonizing of institutions through Indigeneity, as argued earlier, goes beyond simply adding more curriculum or more programs. While such initiatives help, deeper transformation is required by policy actors in our institutions so they fully understand the treaty relationship of First Nations peoples to postsecondary education and the institutional responsibility required to address these obligations. I often reflect on the fact that if these policies are not acted upon in ways that positively impact Indigenous students' experiences, whether in the classroom or at the front counter of a student affairs department, then collectively we are failing them. For example, in some of my undergraduate classes I ask, "How does policy affect you as a student?" It surprises me when non-Indigenous students say, "It doesn't really." Indigenous students, on the other hand, tend to speak about the broader policies, like the Indian Act; even so, they may not see how postsecondary institutional policies directly impact them. Through the research they do for their assignments, self-reflection writing, and facilitated dialogue within class, both settler and Indigenous students come to see the interconnected web of policies at an institutional level that touches on almost every aspect of their student experience.

Policy matters. Period. Policy has been a tool of colonization. So, the question now is: Can policy become a tool of decolonization? And if so, how? While there are currently policies in place in many institutions across the country, there is still a clear need for more policy work to be inclusive of Indigeneity across all aspects of postsecondary education. Currently, there are specific admissions, financial aid, and housing policies for Aboriginal students. There may also be program-level policies about designated registration seats or proportional representation for Aboriginal students, which are aimed at increasing Aboriginal student enrolments within particular fields of study.[37] However, very few policies exist for the cultural responsibilities that draw some Indigenous students away from their studies to attend winter ceremonies or tend to their family's cultural responsibilities when a death occurs in their communities. In other instances, the practice of cultural ceremony is limited in scope and/or removed in some institutions due to the "challenges" of working with the various campus units (e.g., fire department and campus security to coordinate sweats on campus) and complaints about, for instance, the smell of smudge being too similar to cannabis and/or people being allergic to the smoke.

Policies that allow for interinstitutional mobility are important for Indigenous students. One such policy, the British Columbia Transfer Guide,[38] equips students with the means to attend multiple institutions over the course of their postsecondary career and, ideally, not "lose" credits or time. For financial, family, and housing needs, and sometimes even educational ones, Indigenous students stop and start out of institutions to make the system work for them. This is another example of resiliency; Indigenous student persistence rates challenge the common institutional standard of four years to complete an undergraduate degree. Whether intentional or not, Indigenous students are pushing against these expectations by journeying through multiple institutions to gain experiences, credentials, and a relevant education.[39]

Decolonizing governance structures of postsecondary institutions that are inclusive and respectful of Indigenous governance practices is another example of Indigenization—for example, the creation of specific seats for Indigenous representation in the Senate and/or Board of Governors and the creation of Elders Advisory Councils and/or positions such as Indigenous Advisor to the President for senior executives. Even at the faculty levels, there are increasing Associate Dean positions with specific mandates related to Indigenous education. There have also been shifts in research funding opportunities for Indigenous faculty, lecturers, and graduate students, and research ethics boards have been doing work around decolonizing ethics procedures following the Tri-Council's policy statement about improving research relationships with Indigenous communities.[40] Other institutions have been intentional in taking up the work of Indigenization through their employment equity frameworks.[41] Elsewhere, I have written about the dangers of tokenism with regard to Indigenization efforts.[42] I believe this is what Nakata is also urging Indigenous scholars to be mindful of—ensuring that the practices and protocols that we might bring into an institution are overseen and directed by Indigenous peoples or at minimum, with Indigenous peoples. The next section speaks specifically to the power and influence relevant programs have in Indigenous renewal and self-determination.

Renewal Through Relevant Programs

Kirkness and Barnhardt called for institutions to develop more culturally relevant programs and services for Indigenous students.[43] Learning, however, cannot be relevant if the learning environment is intolerant of Indigenous peoples. The calls for renewal and resurgence of Indigenous culture and ways of knowing through Indigenization of academic programs does bring to light a tension that is worth exploring further in this section. The tension is this: creating specific Indigenous programs within institutional spaces that have not done the work of decolonization—or, even worse, that fail to see the institution as an ongoing actor in colonization—raises questions about the sustainability of such programs without broader institutional reform.[44]

For Indigenization of higher education to be actualized, it is key for the institutions to be relevant to Indigenous people. This work has been happening in Canadian higher education for decades. First Nations studies and Native teacher education, fields that have been emerging in academia since the 1970s, were the first Indigenous-specific fields of academic study in Canada. Today, institutions are hosting courses and programs in Indigenous medicine, law, forestry, business, social work, and other disciplines. Science, technology, engineering, and mathematics fields are also aiming to be more inclusive of and relevant to Indigenous peoples.

Indigenous-centric institutions such as the First Nations University (est. 1978), Blue Quills College (est. 1931), Nicola Valley Institute of Technology (est. 1983), Saskatchewan Indian Institute of Technologies (est. 1976), and the First Nations Technical Institute (est. 1985) were founded on Indigenous ways of knowing and being. These institutions are direct examples of Indigenous resurgence. Indigenous institutions offer a recentring of ways of knowing and being, of cultural protocol, and of institutional processes. The Indigenous Adult and Higher Learning Association (IAHLA) represents over forty-two institutes and colleges in British

Columbia alone, and "strives to support Aboriginal adult and post-secondary institutes through research, professional development, and networking opportunities."[45] Similarly, the Indigenous Institutes Consortium (IIC), established in 1994, represents nine Indigenous-controlled postsecondary and training institutes located within Ontario with a mandate and purpose similar to the IAHLA. Since 2001, the National Association of Indigenous Institutes of Higher Learning (NAIIHL, of which IAHLA and IIC are members) has been promoting and enhancing Indigenous languages and cultures.[46] These examples are provided to show how the resiliency of Indigenous commitment to relevant education has influenced the landscape of Canadian higher education.

I've heard non-Indigenous senior leadership, when asked how the institution should be supporting Indigenous student success, express that "every space should be a safe place for our Indigenous students." This senior leader was explicitly stating that, regardless of the program, class, or campus office an Indigenous student was in, they were in a safe space, an inclusive space, a respectful space for them to bring their Indigenous selves into the institution fully and completely. However, there are fallacies and tensions in speaking about "safe spaces" when Indigenous peoples and others who are marginalized (because of their gender, race, ability, etc.) continue to experience racism and discrimination on a daily basis, and when institutions seem unable to address these issues, whether they happen in the classroom, residence hall, or any other part of campus.

Safe spaces connect directly to relevant programs. The lateral violence and systemic racism that Indigenous students experience cannot be ignored; learning cannot be relevant if the learning environment is intolerant to Indigenous peoples themselves. Simply making curriculum more "inclusive" of Indigenous content will do little to create campus (and societal) cultures of inclusion and respect for diversities. Inclusion isn't enough; it alone will not disrupt the colonial system. What is needed are deep shifts across the system to dismantle systemic colonialism so that Canadian postsecondary institutions are not only sites of decolonization and reconciliation but are key agents in changing society as a whole—so that Indigeneity thrives. Yet resistance to this system transformation is ongoing. The question that needs to be asked is: "How will Canadian higher education institutions respond to creating this cultural shift of inclusion and respect on their campuses?"

One response from universities to the TRC's calls to action has been to mandate a required first-year Indigenous content course in Canada for all undergraduate students as part of their undergraduate degree requirements. There has been mixed reaction to this mandated approach. In some instances, the mandated course creates an unsafe learning environment, with Indigenous students having to deal with ill-prepared, non-Indigenous instructors who lack the relevant content knowledge and/or have little to no professional experience working with Indigenous peoples, and with outright violence from non-Indigenous classmates who resent being "forced" to learn. Indigenous instructors of these courses may also face problems in the forms of discrimination and racist taunts. It is further worth noting that these instructors tend to be contingent faculty (e.g., sessionals or limited-term lecturers), Indigenous graduate students, or untenured faculty whose course evaluations are used to renew contracts as part of tenure and promotion materials. Negative course evaluations have a direct impact on the future employment opportunities of Indigenous instructors, faculty, and graduate students.[47]

Indigenous postsecondary institutions and Indigenous programs and services within Euro-Western institutions must negotiate with institutional governance structures and provincial ministries regarding their governance, curriculum, programs, and services. Indigenous programs, services, and even institutions co-exist in a colonial system that constantly (both subtly and overtly) challenges their ways of being and undermines credibility due to societal and systemic racism that deems anything labelled "Indigenous" to be of lesser quality. These inherent biases are systemic and perpetuated by the people within these institutions who, today, still see Indigenous peoples as being less than other Canadians. In their attempts to decolonize the institution, in their pursuit of a transformed space free of biases and prejudices, in their commitments to reconciliation and Indigenization, Indigenous and non-Indigenous administrators, scholars, activists, and community members will have to constantly address issues of structural racism and patriarchy.[48] This leads to a discussion of the resurgence of praxis.

Resurgence of Praxis

Indigenous peoples have always known education. Teaching, learning, embedding lessons in language, hands-on learning, witnessing work, and honouring inter-generational learning have always been part of Indigenous praxis. Everyone is a learner and a teacher at the same time. These Indigenous ways of being are the exact practices that the Western education system has sought to erase. Sandy Grande suggests that what is needed is a reframing of the discourses surrounding univer-sities, particularly "within settler societies, [where] the university functions as an apparatus of colonization: one that refracts the 'eliminative' practices, modes of governance, and forms of knowledge production" of Indigenous peoples.[49] By drawing on Indigenous scholars who write from their locations in Canadian higher education (e.g., Archibald, Donald, Kirkness, Battiste, Stonechild, Styres, Tuck, Andreotti, Restoule, and others), we can work to decolonize postsecondary institu-tions from within, intentionally enacting Indigeneity in teaching, scholarship, and relationships, and challenging colonial policies and practices that aim to assimilate, alter, or silence Indigenous voices and perspectives. Leigh Patel reminds us to take up the work of decolonization within the institution, noting this structure is only "countered by attending to the ways that we come into relation through coloniality."[50] Within higher education research, student services, administration, and academic programs across this country, we see the increased development of co-op and other experiential learning opportunities, more integration of place-based and ecological knowledge, more connection to "real-world" experiences, and calls for including Elders and Knowledge Holders within our institutions.

A resurgence of practices calls to the fore Indigenous ways of knowing and understanding as acts of Indigenization and pushes efforts of anticolonial and decolonial education by *doing* the work, *being* the work, and *living* as Indigenous scholars. It includes the direct and sometimes subversive acts that Indigenous peoples use to bring who they are into the academy. This may be the incorporation of Indigenous languages within a syllabus or classroom; it may be the act of bringing the university to Indigenous communities through resources, staff, and opportunities that are directed and guided by Indigenous community members. It is about wholistically, physically, emotionally, culturally, and intellectually bringing who one is as an Indigenous person into the academy. An Indigenous person does not see their role or roles in postsecondary as separate but rather as interconnected parts of their whole person (i.e., educator, researcher, community member, advocate, cultural practitioner, parent, sibling, cousin).

Being intentionally mindful of what, and with whom, we share is a decision each person has to make in their own teachings (e.g., what to keep private and what to share publicly).[51] Therefore, in intentionally bringing who we are as Indigenous people—our lived beings—into these academic spaces, we are asserting Indigenization. We push decolonizing praxis through the ways we do our work within the academy. While I hear Nakata's skepticism about self-determination in education, I remain optimistic that through our presence of being who we are—our whole selves, in ethical relationships with those around us (e.g., colleagues, students in classrooms, the communities we serve)—Indigenous scholars will continue to influence transformation for ourselves, our peoples, those in relationship with us, and ultimately the system itself.

A clear example of this is Indigenous scholars who integrate their cultural knowledges into their research process unapologetically, asserting that how they do research is informed by who they are. Another is Indigenous scholars who, engaging in community-based language revitalization, see the inherent value of time spent in community, with community, and being there for community. These Indigenous concepts of time and relationality push against the Western academic expectations of research for publishing and individual career advancement.

In advocating for more of this intentional presence in the academy, I am also aware of the costs I mentioned earlier. I'm not asserting that all will be fine. I know it won't. Indigenous students, faculty, staff, and administrators will still encounter subtle (and sometimes not so subtle) forms of racism, ignorance, and negative resistance to our presence and practices. However, in being present and enacting change through our navigation of the academy with cultural integrity—like the other Indigenous scholars who came before us—we become the next change makers who will expand the multiple pathways and opportunities for the next seven generations to thrive. In turn, settler colleagues, particularly those who see themselves as allies to decolonization and Indigenization, can be part of the system-wide change by taking up their collective responsibilities of reconciliation.

Responsibilities of Reconciliation

In a time of reconciliation, it seems that the memory of ongoing Indigenous resistance to colonization has been forgotten and the calls for system-wide decolonization and transformation remain unheard, ignored, or, worse, tokenized within the higher education system.[52] There is consciousness raising (the land acknowledgements occurring at various campus events across Canadian postsecondary institutions are one example of this). These acknowledgements symbolize that there is some understanding of relationship to place; there is a teaching in the acknowledgement of the peoples on whose land we live. Yet the stories that underpin colonization (e.g., land seizure, displacement) are the stories of the higher education system, which many do not know or choose to ignore. So, among the teachings of land acknowledgements, there is a responsibility to tell the true histories of the lands upon which our campuses are built.

I was a doctoral student attending a conference when I heard the untold truth of how the establishment of higher education directly resulted in Indigenous dislocation, disruption, and erasure from Indigenous lands. Sandy Grande was telling the story in relationship to the establishment of the United States' Ivy League institutions. As Grande noted, these institutions would not have been built had federal and state governments at the time not given them land titles to unceded Native American territories. These land titles were seen as acts of colonial reciprocity; institutions built in this way then had the mandate, or perhaps just the good intention, to have Native Americans attend them.[53] In this situation, institutions of higher education across the United States are "an arm of the settler state—a site where the logics of elimination, capital accumulation, and dispossession are reconstituted."[54] Grande's reflections spoke of true cost of the dislocation, the forced removal, and the dismal reciprocity (e.g., limited or no financial compensation) that followed the dispossession of Indigenous peoples from their traditional territories, not honouring treaties and related agreements. We know this history of dispossession and relocation in Canada, too. Like in the United States, unceded Indigenous lands were given for the establishment of universities and colleges with a similar extension of "tolerance" of Indigenous people being admitted to these higher education institutions under the guise of moral and social obligation. This continues in Canada today.[55]

Indigenization in practice directly calls on all involved in higher education to examine their place within the academy and their responsibilities to support Indigenous peoples. This is a direct challenge to reconciliation as it is currently enacted across postsecondary campuses. It means shifting power and privilege. It is uncomfortable at times to be unsettled, which Paulette Regan calls for in *Unsettling the Settler Within*.[56] It is now, with the nation's attention on issues of reconciliation, that these shifts and unsettlings must occur. Some of what is already happening across postsecondary classrooms today, such as more relevant curriculum and pedagogical practices for Indigenous learners, is the direct result of decades of advocacy. Other examples include decolonizing teaching practices, workshops, and the multitude of resources (e.g., massive open online courses, podcasts, websites) that are intentionally focusing on supporting the unsettling and relearning necessary for reconciliation. The decades of advocacy, starting with community participatory action movements, are also behind the paradigm shift towards Indigenous inclusivity and decolonized research methodologies.[57] It is in the spaces of decolonization and reconciliation, in these reflections of policies, programs, and practices, that one can pose the question: How can we imagine the futurity of a decolonized and Indigenized postsecondary institution?

Imagining a Decolonized Higher Education System

Pause...Close your eyes...Take a deep breath...
You are outside. You can feel the fresh spring grass underneath you.
You hear the rustling of the leaves and the sounds of birds above...
You also hear a drum, like a heartbeat, gently present around you.
You have a sense of calm and balance upon smelling the aroma of
sweetgrass and sage lingering in the air.
Open your eyes.
You are in a circle.
An Elder has just opened with a cultural prayer.
You are part of the journey.
You are here to do the work.
You belong.
You are part of the circle.

The vignette above is drawn from the collection of experiences I've had, both in research contexts and in being a guest on another's territory. I have been part of various groups taking up the work that needs to be done, and have been invited by others to witness their own process. These diverse perspectives and roles within a process of enacting change provide multiple pathways to enter and engage in the work ahead. It is this simple yet powerful process of enacting Indigenous protocol and practices, of setting expectations, and of responsibilities that we are all now collectively embarking upon in Canada. Reflecting back on the discussion of policy, program, and practices, a truly decolonized institution would place Indigeneity at its centre; how the academy governs, discusses, and enacts being would be inclusive of Indigenous ways of knowing and being. Indigenous students would feel part of the circle; they would be welcomed, and they would be empowered; they would be fully Indigenous. They would experience how the policies, programs, and practices intended to support their success were authentically and respectfully inclusive of the diversity of the nations upon which the institution was built. They would be renewed by attending classes and events around campus. Their families would feel safe in sending them to the institution and welcome them home once they completed their journey. Elders and Knowledge Holders would provide guidance, not just as an afterthought, but as a clear and central part of every decision-making forum. Visitors to the campus would know that they were on Indigenous lands in a decolonized institution by more than just the signage and artwork. These visitors would have a deeper understanding of the stories of these Indigenous lands that connect historical and contemporary Indigenous presence and resiliency. This understanding would expand to that of knowing that the geographic colonial boundaries of what is today Canada and the United States are, in fact, all Indigenous lands: Turtle Island, where Indigenous territories expanded more north to south than east to west. Reframing this understanding of place and time to be inclusive of Indigenous understandings would be a true act of decolonization and reconciliation.

Decolonization involves intentional actions—actions upon actions that have ripple effects of change across our institutions and, ultimately, Canadian society. In reading this chapter, I ask you, the reader: How are you going to enact changes in your practices? In your relationships? In your presence within an institution? How are you going to take up your responsibilities towards reconciliation, decolonization, and Indigenization? In working together, it is possible; inaction is not an option. It is now your turn.

NOTES

1. *Truth and Reconciliation Commission of Canada: Calls to Action.* See also Truth and Reconciliation Commission of Canada, *Honouring the Truth* (hereafter cited as TRC executive summary).
2. Battiste, *Decolonizing Education.*
3. Patel, "Countering Coloniality," 358.
4. Nakata, "Rights and Blights," 289.
5. Nakata, "Rights and Blights," 292.
6. Patel, "Countering Coloniality," 360.
7. Tuck and Yang, "Decolonization Is Not a Metaphor," 3.
8. Tuck and Yang, "Decolonization Is Not a Metaphor," 35.
9. Pidgeon, "More Than a Checklist," 78.
10. Andreotti et al., "Mapping Interpretations," 26, 29, 31.

11. Nakata, "Rights and Blights." See also Andreotti, "Conflicting Epistemic Demands"; Ahenakew et al., "Beyond Epistemic Provincialism"; Shahjahan, "From 'No' to 'Yes'"; Kelley, "Black Study, Black Struggle"; Grande, "Refusing the University"; Battiste, Bell, and Findlay, "Decolonizing Education."

12. Battiste, Bell, and Findlay, "Decolonizing Education," 83.

13. Battiste, *Decolonizing Education*.

14. Pidgeon, "More Than a Checklist"; Pidgeon, "Pushing against the Margins."

15. Smith, "SSHRC Research Panel."

16. See, e.g., Battiste and Barman, *First Nations Education*; Royal Commission on Aboriginal Peoples, *Report*, vol. 3; Styres, *Pathways for Remembering*; Stonechild, *The New Buffalo*.

17. Jones, "Introduction to Higher Education."

18. See https://native-land.ca to learn on whose territory your campus resides.

19. "Responsibility for Education," Council of Ministers of Education, Canada, accessed June 28, 2021, https://www.cmec.ca/299/Education-in-Canada-An-Overview/index.html.

20. Jones, "Introduction to Higher Education."

21. Indian Act, R.S.C. 1985, c. I-5, s. 114-117. See also Stonechild, *The New Buffalo*.

22. TRC executive summary.

23. TRC executive summary; Royal Commission on Indigenous Peoples, *Report*; Stonechild, *The New Buffalo*.

24. Tuck and Yang, "Decolonization Is Not a Metaphor."

25. Gahman and Legault, "Disrupting the Settler Colonial University," 6.

26. Borrows, *Policy Paper*, 1.

27. National Indian Brotherhood, *Indian Control*.

28. Kuokkanen, *Reshaping the University*.

29. Kelley, "Black Study, Black Struggle," para. 11.

30. Nakata, "Rights and Blights," 302.

31. Pidgeon, Archibald, and Muñoz, "Editorial: *Indian Control*."

32. Archibald et al., *Accord on Indigenous Education*.

33. Kitchenham et al., *Aboriginal Education Enhancement*.

34. Pidgeon, "More Than a Checklist."

35. Battiste, *Decolonizing Education*.

36. Stonechild, *The New Buffalo*, 137.

37. Shotton, Lowe, and Waterman, *Beyond the Asterisk*; Pidgeon, "Pushing against the Margins"; Pidgeon, "Moving beyond Good Intentions."

38. For more information on the British Columbia Transfer Guide, see http://www.bctransferguide.ca/.

39. Archibald et al., *Aboriginal Transitions*.

40. CIHR, NSERC, and SSHRC, "Research Involving the First Nations."

41. Canadian Association of University Teachers, "Indigenizing the Academy."

42. Pidgeon, "More Than a Checklist."

43. Kirkness and Barnhardt, "First Nations and Higher Education."

44. See Pidgeon, "Moving beyond Good Intentions"; Pigeon, "More Than a Checklist."

45. "About Us," Indigenous Adult and Higher Learning Association, accessed June 29, 2021, http://iahla.ca/about/.

46. As of July 7, 2021, the website for the NAIIHL (http://naiihl.org/) was inactive. According to the Office of the Commissioner of Lobbying of Canada, the NAIIHL registration status is inactive. See the Lobby Canada entry on the NAIIHL (https://lobbycanada.gc.ca/app/secure/ocl/lrs/do/vwRg?cno=315365&regId=) for more details.

47. Canadian Association of University Teachers, "Recognition of Increased Workload."

48. Kelley, "Black Study, Black Struggle."
49. Grande, "Refusing the University," 48.
50. Patel, "Countering Coloniality," 360.
51. See, e.g., Debassige, "Building on Conceptual Interpretations."
52. Pidgeon, "More Than a Checklist."
53. Grande, "Refusing the University."
54. Grande, "Refusing the University," 1.
55. Gahman and Legault, "Disrupting the Settler Colonial," 6; See also Royal Commission on Aboriginal Peoples, *Report.*
56. Regan, *Unsettling the Settler.*
57. Pidgeon, "Moving between Theory."

BIBLIOGRAPHY

Ahenakew, Cash, Vanessa de Oliveira Andreotti, Garrick Cooper, and Hemi Hireme. "Beyond Epistemic Provincialism: De-Provincializing Indigenous Resistance." *AlterNative: An International Journal of Indigenous Peoples* 10, no. 3 (2014): 216–31. https://doi.org/10.1177/117718011401000302.

Andreotti, Vanessa de Oliveira. "Conflicting Epistemic Demands in Poststructuralist and Postcolonial Engagements with Questions of Complicity in Systemic Harm." *Educational Studies* 50, no. 4 (2016): 378–97. https://doi.org/10.1080/00131946.2014.924940.

Andreotti, Vanessa de Oliveria, Sharon Stein, Cash Ahenakew, and Dallas Hunt. "Mapping Interpretations of Decolonization in the Context of Higher Education." *Decolonization: Indigeneity, Education & Society* 4, no. 1 (2015): 21–40. https://decolonization.org/index.php/des/article/view/22168/18470.

Archibald, Jo-ann, John Lundy, Cecilia Reynolds, and Lorna Williams. *Accord on Indigenous Education.* Delta: Association of Canadian Deans of Education, 2010. https://csse-scee.ca/acde/wp-content/uploads/sites/7/2017/08/Accord-on-Indigenous-Education.pdf.

Archibald, Jo-ann, Michelle Pidgeon, and Colleen Hawkey. *Aboriginal Transitions: Undergraduate to Graduate Studies: Phase I Final Report.* Victoria: Ministry of Advanced Education, British Columbia, 2009.

Battiste, Marie. *Decolonizing Education: Nourishing the Learning Spirit.* Saskatoon: Purich, 2013.

Battiste, Marie, and Jean Barman, eds. *First Nations Education in Canada: The Circle Unfolds.* Vancouver: UBC Press, 1995.

Battiste, Marie, Lynne Bell, and L.M. Findlay. "Decolonizing Education in Canadian Universities: An Interdisciplinary, International, Indigenous Research Project." *Canadian Journal of Native Education* 26, no. 2 (2002): 82–95.

Borrows, John. *Policy Paper: Implementing Indigenous Self-Determination through Legislation in Canada.* Ottawa: Assembly of First Nations, 2017. https://www.afn.ca/wp-content/uploads/2018/09/2017-04-20-Implementing-Indigenous-self-determination-through-policy-legislation.pdf.

Canadian Association of University Teachers. "Indigenizing the Academy." CAUT Policy Statement, approved November 2016. https://www.caut.ca/about-us/caut-policy/lists/caut-policy-statements/indigenizing-the-academy.

———. "Recognition of Increased Workload of Academic Staff Members in Equity-Seeking Groups in a Minority Context." CAUT Policy Statement, approved November 2015. https://www.caut.ca/about-us/caut-policy/lists/caut-policy-statements/recognition-of-increased-workload-of-academic-staff-members-in-equity-seeking-groups-in-a-minority-context.

CIHR [Canadian Institutes of Health Research], NSERC [Natural Sciences and Engineering Research Council of Canada], and SSHRC [Social Sciences and Humanities Research Council]. "Research Involving the First Nations, Inuit, and Métis Peoples of Canada." In *Tri-Council Policy Statement: Ethical Conduct for Research Involving Humans*, 107–32. Ottawa: Secretariat on Responsible Conduct of Research, 2015. https://ethics.gc.ca/eng/policy-politique_tcps2-eptc2_2018.html.

Debassige, Brent. "Building on Conceptual Interpretations of Aboriginal Literacy in Anishinaabe Research: A Turtle Shaker Model." *Canadian Journal of Education* 36, no. 2 (2013): 4–33. https://journals.sfu.ca/cje/index.php/cje-rce/article/view/1273.

Gahman, Levi, and Gabrielle Legault. "Disrupting the Settler Colonial University: Decolonial Praxis and Place-Based Education in the Okanagan Valley (British Columbia)." *Capitalism Nature Socialism* 30, no. 1 (2017): 1–20. https://doi.org/10.1080/10455752.2017.1368680.

Grande, Sandy. "Refusing the University." In *Toward What Justice? Describing Diverse Dreams of Justice in Education*, edited by Eve Tuck and K. Wayne Yang, 47–65. London: Routledge, 2018.

Jones, Glen A. "Introduction to Higher Education in Canada." In *Higher Education Across Nations,* 2 vols., edited by M. Joshi and Saee Paivandi, 1:1–38. Delhi: B.R. Publishing, 2014.

Kelley, Robin D.G. "Black Study, Black Struggle." *Boston Review*, March 1, 2016. http://bostonreview.net/forum/robin-d-g-kelley-black-study-black-struggle.

Kirkness, Verna J., and Ray Barnhardt. "First Nations and Higher Education: The Four R's—Respect, Relevance, Reciprocity, Responsibility." *Journal of American Indian Education* 30, no. 3 (1991): 1–15. http://www.jstor.org/stable/24397980.

Kitchenham, Andrew, Tina Ngaroimata Fraser, Michelle Pidgeon, and Karen Ragoonaden. *Aboriginal Education Enhancement Agreements: Complicated Conversations as Pathways to Success.* Victoria: British Columbia Ministry of Education, 2016. https://www.bced.gov.bc.ca/abed/research/AEEA-Final_Report_June_2016.pdf.

Kuokkanen, Rauna. *Reshaping the University: Responsibility, Indigenous Epistemes and the Logic of the Gift.* Vancouver: UBC Press, 2007.

Nakata, Martin. "The Rights and Blights of the Politics in Indigenous Higher Education." *Anthropological Forum* 23, no. 3 (2013): 289–303. https://doi.org/10.1080/00664677.2013.803457.

National Indian Brotherhood. *Indian Control of Indian Education.* Ottawa: Assembly of First Nations, 1972.

Patel, Leigh. "Countering Coloniality in Educational Research: From Ownership to Answerability." *Educational Studies* 50, no. 4 (2014): 357–77. https://doi.org/10.1080/00131946.2014.924942.

Pidgeon, Michelle. "More Than a Checklist: Meaningful Indigenous Inclusion in Higher Education." *Social Inclusion* 4, no. 1 (2016): 77–91. https://doi.org/10.17645/si.v4i1.436.

———. "Moving between Theory and Practice within an Indigenous Research Paradigm." *Qualitative Research* 19, no. 4 (August 2019): 418–36. https://doi.org/10.1177/1468794118781380.

———. "Moving beyond Good Intentions: Indigenizing Higher Education in British Columbia Universities through Institutional Responsibility and Accountability." *Journal of American Indian Education* 53, no. 2 (2014): 7–28.

———. "Pushing against the Margins: Indigenous Theorizing of 'Success' and Retention in Higher Education." *Journal of College Student Retention: Research, Theory & Practice* 10, no. 3 (2008): 339–60. https://doi.org/10.2190/CS.10.3.e.

Pidgeon, Michelle, Jo-ann Archibald, and Marissa Muñoz. "Editorial: *Indian Control of Indian Education*—40 Years Later." *Canadian Journal of Indian Education* 36, no. 1 (2013): 1–4.

Regan, Paulette. *Unsettling the Settler Within: Indian Residential Schools, Truth Telling, and Reconciliation in Canada.* Vancouver: UBC Press, 2010.

Royal Commission on Aboriginal Peoples. *Report of the Royal Commission on Aboriginal Peoples.* 5 vols. Ottawa: Indian and Northern Affairs Canada, 1996.

Shahjahan, Riyad A. "From 'No' to 'Yes': Postcolonial Perspectives on Resistance to Neoliberal Higher Education." *Discourse: Studies in the Cultural Politics of Education* 35, no. 2 (2014): 219–32. https://doi.org/10.1080/01596306.2012.745732.

Shotton, Heather, Shelly C. Lowe, and Stephanie J. Waterman, eds. *Beyond the Asterisk: Understanding Native Students in Higher Education.* Sterling: Stylus, 2013.

Simon Fraser University Aboriginal Reconciliation Council. *Walk This Path With Us: Report of the SFU Aboriginal Reconciliation Council.* Vancouver: SFU, 2017.

Smith, Linda Tuhiwai. "SSHRC Research Panel." Unlisted panel discussion at the Annual Conference of the Canadian Society for the Study of Education, Regina, SK, May 2018.

Stonechild, Blair. *The New Buffalo: The Struggle for Aboriginal Post-Secondary Education in Canada.* Winnipeg: University of Manitoba Press, 2006.

Styres, Sandra D. *Pathways for Remembering and Recognizing Indigenous Thought in Education : Philosophies of Iethi'nihsténha Ohwentsia'kékha (Land).* Toronto: University of Toronto Press, 2017.

Truth and Reconciliation Commission of Canada. *Honouring the Truth, Reconciling for the Future: Summary of the Final Report of the Truth and Reconciliation Commission of Canada.* Winnipeg: National Centre for Truth and Reconciliation, 2015. http://www.trc.ca/assets/pdf/Executive_Summary_English_Web.pdf.

———. *Truth and Reconciliation Commission of Canada: Calls to Action.* Winnipeg: National Centre for Truth and Reconciliation, 2015. https://ehprnh2mwo3.exactdn.com/wp-content/uploads/2021/01/Calls_to_Action_English2.pdf.

Tuck, Eve, and K. Wayne Yang. "Decolonization Is Not a Metaphor." *Decolonization: Indigeneity, Education & Society* 1, no. 1 (2012): 1–40.

3

DAWN ZINGA

Uncomfortable Realities

Reconciliation in Higher Education

I AM TROUBLING RECONCILIATION by focusing on uncomfortable realities associated with reconciliation within higher education. More specifically, I will be exploring how the broader institutional context complicates reconciliation and how upper administration and faculty within universities have choices to make about whether reconciliation will be engaged in meaningful ways or simply paid lip service. I will explore the differences between lip service and meaningful engagement, paying particular attention to examples of both in higher educational contexts. Considering the importance of engaging in challenging conversations around upholding the status quo, I explore understandings of political contexts and what it means to engage in reconciliation through the narratives we have been told, the narratives we tell ourselves, and the narratives that universities want to be told about their institutions and their engagement in reconciliation. This exploration draws upon ethical space to consider the roles that contested terms such as *allyship* and *intellectual freedom* play in both meaningfully engaging with and impeding reconciliation. Issues of power and privilege are drawn into this conversation as I explore how the motivations behind the invocation of allyship and intellectual freedom must be examined alongside their practical application in higher education contexts.

Higher education contexts set the backdrop for our journey through the uncomfortable realities associated with reconciliation within Canadian universities. By exploring difficult truths and uncomfortable realities, I examine the tensions and challenges that universities face in their attempts to address the Truth and Reconciliation Commission of Canada's (TRC) calls to action.[1] A TRC video about reconciliation identifies the act of national reconciliation as a long process that involves Indigenous and non-Indigenous peoples collectively establishing how to go forward in respectful relations.[2] It says reconciliation is about changing how we educate children and young people, acknowledging what we have been taught and what we have learned, deconstructing that teaching and learning, and examining it in conjunction with what treaty history and the testimony from residential school survivors offer as teachings. Educational institutions are seen by the TRC as both the primary vehicles in achieving reconciliation and as among the institutions most responsible for causing and perpetuating the harm that needs to be reconciled as we move into respectful relations. There are choices that need to be made in terms of how non-Indigenous Canadians[3] will acknowledge treaty responsibilities—including living in respectful relationship with Indigenous peoples—and move forward toward reconciliation. Relations of power and privilege, as well as our complicity and roles in the networks created by these relations, have to be examined and reconfigured if we are to engage meaningfully in reconciliation.

Higher Education Contexts

The educational experiences of everyone within Canadian educational systems are fundamentally entwined within relations of power and privilege. According to Foucault, individuals are at once both vehicles and recipients of power relations.[4] Essentially, every individual in the university is implicated in relations of power; they can be controlled and oppressed by that power and they can act to reinforce and reassert networks of power. Awareness of our own roles in supporting, reinforcing, reasserting, disrupting, troubling, and challenging the networks of power that exist are crucial to understanding the uncomfortable reality that universities are deeply implicated in colonialism, continue to support Eurocentrism, and actively engage in what Marie Battiste has termed "cognitive imperialism."[5]

Battiste argues that within Canadian education contexts, Indigenous knowledges have been omitted or so poorly represented as to be largely absent. Education in these Canadian contexts has been based on a Eurocentric foundation of knowledge that devalues other ways of knowing. Furthermore, this context creates an environment of cognitive imperialism and racism for Indigenous students. Battiste likens cognitive imperialism to a "whitewashing" of the mind that privileges and centres Western or mainstream peoples while diminishing and dehumanizing Indigenous peoples as uncivilized and less than others.[6] Battiste does not limit this experience to residential schools, stating that it continues in provincially and federal funded schools at all levels of education from elementary through to postsecondary. While she recognizes that there are new initiatives and commitments at all levels to improve education within Canada for Indigenous students, she sees such initiatives as being rendered ineffective by the resistance and barriers created by the layers of cognitive imperialism within Canadian systems of education. Within university contexts, Eurocentric traditions around knowledge production and acceptance have created layers of cognitive imperialism that serve to control and influence the norms and traditions within the university about what is legitimate and important, and what is therefore supported and resourced. It is embedded in all the decisions that are made and how everything is evaluated. It continues to marginalize and alienate Indigenous students, Indigenous faculty, their knowledges, and their peoples. According to Battiste, cognitive imperialism serves to render Eurocentric superiority invisible, providing an illusion of Canadian education as being "neutral and universal," thus positioning anyone who has trouble fitting in as the problem and deflecting attention from the systemic inequities within the system of education and its structures.[7]

This permeation of Eurocentric superiority and the perception of education as neutral and universal can be disrupted easily if one knows where to look. Eve Tuck and Sandy Grande each offer windows into Indigenous faculty experiences that disrupt the view of universities as providing neutral and universal education and outline the invasive and entrenched Eurocentric superiority throughout policies and procedures.[8] The employment precarity experienced by Indigenous faculty and sessional instructors as well as concerns around hiring practices and workload point to an educational context that is neither neutral nor universal. Howard Ramos and Peter Li examined 2016 Canadian census data to determine the proportional representation of visible minority individuals within faculty positions and found that 16% of faculty positions were held by visible minority professors. When comparing their proportion in the general population with their proportional representation within faculty positions, Ramos and Li discovered that individuals who were identified as Aboriginal in the census were the most underrepresented racialized group in university professor positions (0.08%).[9] The precarious employment situations and challenges described by Tuck and Grande trouble understandings of university contexts and help examine why Indigenous faculty members represent less than 1% of all faculty positions. This strongly suggests that many people do not experience Canadian education as neutral or universal at any of its levels.

Eurocentric superiority is also front and centre in the experiences of Indigenous faculty members who are seeking tenure and promotion. The marginalization and alienation of Indigenous faculty referred to by Marie Battiste has also been clearly documented by others.[10] For all faculty members, obtaining tenure and promotion secures a sense of employment permanence. Prior to those attainments, faculty members exist within a state of precarious employment. This sense of precarity is more striking and intense for Indigenous faculty, as it is reinforced by the lack of appropriate representation at all organizational levels. They also experience marginalization, tokenism, and reduced opportunities (e.g., mentorship, networking, and funding). Indigenous faculty members also expressed a lack of confidence that collective agreements (where they exist) and/or university administration adequately consider their best interests.[11]

Examining higher education contexts and the associated readiness to engage in the work of reconciliation repeatedly reveals that systemic and structural racism continue to be roadblocks that routinely go unaddressed. Carl E. James and Selom Chapman-Nyaho interviewed minoritized faculty members who reported that hiring process experiences and discussions around equity and diversity were very challenging. More specifically, participants indicated that the discomfort of mainstream faculty with equity and diversity issues was masked by discussions that included terms such as "institutional fit" or "most excellent candidate" or "fit into the culture of the faculty," and that, in some instances, blatant discrimination was expressed, including references to an applicant's accent and questions of whether the students would take an applicant of a particular background seriously.[12] Sara Ahmed focused on the need to unsettle institutional tendencies of masking potential discrimination in hiring practices by appealing to "best fit" or specific qualifications by challenging such conversations.[13] Ahmed voiced this position over a decade ago, yet minoritized individuals are still reporting experiences of discrimination in the hiring process and the workplace. This underscores the importance of addressing such issues.

According to one of the Indigenous participants in James and Chapman-Nyaho's study, even after Indigenous faculty are hired, it is not smooth sailing. These faculty members are often burdened by the expectations associated with being an "Indigenous hire." Participants in the study reported feeling that the assumptions that went along with the image of being Indigenous were layered on top of the expectations that most junior faculty experience in attempting to fill the position into which they were hired. This was supported by research conducted by my colleague Sandra D. Styres and myself. Like James and Chapman-Nyaho, we found that Indigenous faculty members reported experiencing discrimination in hiring practices, feeling that their work was precarious and often unsupported, and feeling the burden of representing some image of Indigeneity predetermined by the university and colleagues while also remaining true to their own sense of identity and the expectations of their community.[14]

Participants in both studies reported a lack of mentorship in navigating university structures and processes towards promotion and tenure as well as costs associated with playing, or not playing, the game of academic tokenism. Indigenous faculty members spoke about how playing the game meant meeting certain expectations and not stepping outside of them by pushing too much. Essentially, they described the need to assimilate into the faculty body while still representing their Indigeneity within the academy in an "acceptable" way. Those who didn't play the game—who instead stepped outside expectations to challenge university procedures and pushed to address issues relevant to Indigenous and other minoritized individuals—reported being shut down, shut out of opportunities, and at times warned that they were hurting their chances to advance within the university. Participants in both studies also reported other unrecognized burdens that they faced, such as being one of only a few individuals who Indigenous students could approach to discuss issues that they were facing within the university or the overwhelming demand for them to supervise Indigenous students and serve on their committees. While they found this work rewarding, they also found that the university did not recognize the extra work associated with there being very few Indigenous faculty for much higher numbers of Indigenous students.

James and Chapman-Nyaho also wrote about the ways that higher administration can give the perception of supporting and advancing Indigenous faculty members while in practice actually sabotaging those individuals. This is not new; the federal government has a long-standing practice of putting First Nations communities in positions where they are set up to fail and then blaming the community for the failure. In higher education contexts, James and Chapman-Nyaho have identified these types of approaches as examples of Palmer's glass cliff phenomenon.[15] The glass cliff phenomenon is the tendency for equality efforts to create new forms of inequality. These new forms are used to explain away discrimination by saying that it is not discrimination, but some other justified belief or action, or by justifying the basis of the discrimination. James and Chapman-Nyaho apply the glass cliff phenomenon specifically to Indigenous faculty and other faculty who are appointed to leadership positions in difficult times or under circumstances in which the likelihood of failure is highest. Examples of this can be seen when Indigenous faculty members are put into precarious leadership positions—as in the case of Angelique EagleWoman, who resigned from her position as Dean of Lakehead University's law school—and in cases where junior, pretenure Indigenous faculty are asked to fulfill leadership positions when they should instead be supported in establishing a solid research program and a strong dossier for promotion and tenure.

In the case of Angelique EagleWoman, Lakehead University appeared to be directly addressing the TRC's calls to action by hiring the first female Indigenous law school dean in 2016. However, a case can be made for the application of the glass cliff phenomenon. By the spring of 2018, Dean EagleWoman announced her resignation, citing systemic racism and discrimination. In various interviews following the announcement of her resignation, EagleWoman stated that she had hope that Lakehead could accomplish its goals in time but that she could no longer continue the work given the levels of racism and discrimination she faced.[16] While I am not privy to the particulars of the situation at Lakehead, an examination of the publicly available information suggests that the situation can be explained by the difference between surface responses to the TRC that do not address Eurocentric superiority and its influence within all aspects of higher education, and deep, carefully thought-through responses to the TRC that involve an examination of cognitive imperialism and Eurocentric superiority. Knowing university contexts, it is fair to say that the decisions to hire a female Indigenous dean and to embed Indigenous content throughout the law program were subject to lengthy discussions and consultation. Comments made by Dr. Dennis McPherson, an Indigenous faculty member at the law school, and members of the school's Aboriginal Advisory Committee support claims of entrenched racism and the application of the glass cliff phenomenon.[17] Thus, I would argue EagleWoman's resignation offers evidence that the systemic and structural racism and discrimination within the university was not addressed, and the university was unprepared to confront and work through the uncomfortable realities associated with engaging in reconciliation.

While it is not possible to think through every potential issue that could arise, university administrators owe it to their students and to all who work within the university to consider the issues that are likely to arise and to have a plan for addressing those issues. In the case of the TRC and reconciliation, universities are struggling to understand what reconciliation means both philosophically and practically. On a surface level, there seems to be an appreciation of the types of experts who may need to be hired and of the fact that Indigenous content needs to be represented. There is, however, no clear evidence of a nuanced understanding of how to return to respectful relations. As an individual who has the benefit of being born into a white, Euro-Canadian, blue-collar family, I recognize that I have a responsibility to uphold my treaty obligations around respectful relations, to call into question what is meant by these discussions, to encourage others to unpack what is happening, and to have challenging and frank discussions about what is being brought into the hiring process. Furthermore, my obligations and those of my mainstream colleagues go beyond the hiring processes to other aspects of the cultures of the places where we live and work. My understanding of reconciliation and respectful relations does not come from my education within Canadian educational contexts but from my resistance to that education and from the tutelage offered by Indigenous colleagues and Elders with whom I am privileged to engage.

In a keynote address, Marie Battiste spoke about how everyone who has experienced Canadian education has been marinated in Eurocentrism and subjected to cognitive imperialism.[18] While significant volumes of research have been devoted to the implications of Canadian education from residential schools to current educational experiences for Indigenous students, there has been less uptake of what this means for everyone else educated in Canadian systems. At the most foundational level, I would argue that Canadian education systems have left non-Indigenous Canadians—particularly those who identify or can be identified as part of the majority or mainstream—ill-equipped to understand and engage with the challenges presented by reconciliation. It is not surprising that universities are struggling with the TRC and reconciliation as they are Eurocentric organizations whose very structures, policies, and cultures violate respectful relations with Indigenous peoples on a daily basis. They are staffed by individuals who have been drinking the Eurocentric

Kool-Aid since elementary school and now need to learn how to examine the difficult truths and uncomfortable realities embedded in their own education and belief systems, and in Canada's history, to move forward into respectful relations with Indigenous peoples.

This is just a quick snapshot of the higher education contexts in which reconciliation is being pursued and of the experiences of Indigenous faculty within those contexts. While these contexts vary in details and degree in the university campuses across Canada, every institution is complicit in the perpetuation of what we are trying to reconcile. EagleWoman's resignation was just the first of several resignations by Indigenous faculty who were hired in response to the TRC but faced systemic racism and discrimination that blocked institutional movement toward engaging in reconciliation and addressing the TRC's calls to action. Universities cannot meaningfully engage in reconciliation without examining and troubling the complicity of university structures and systems in perpetuating coloniality.

Ethical Space

Ethical space presents one way in which individuals can meaningfully engage in reconciliation. It offers an opportunity to examine and explore the difficult truths and uncomfortable realities embedded in individuals' experiences of education, their current belief systems, the ways in which those systems were formed, and Canada's history to move forward into respectful relations with Indigenous peoples. In previous work, I have engaged with the concept of ethical space and its practical implications in relation to reconciliation and working with Indigenous communities.[19] According to Willie Ermine, who draws upon Roger Poole, ethical space is the creation of a space in which ethical action and conversation can occur. For Poole, the possibility of ethical space is created when two individual sets of intentions confront each other. Ermine specifically applies this idea to the space created when Indigenous and Western knowledge systems collide or bump up against one another. Poole and Ermine agree that the space between the sets of intentions is full of possibilities as well as the interests, assumptions, and biases that individuals carry into the space with them. This space is not inherently ethical; often, the clash of worldviews results in misunderstanding or more negative outcomes such as marginalization or oppression, which may be expressed through actions. Residential schools are examples of such actions. However, Poole and Ermine contend that the space can become ethical if the parties entering it are willing to engage with each other and with the associated worldviews and intentions in a way that supports careful examinations of what each individual is bringing to the space, of uncomfortable realities, and of ways of moving forward positively.[20]

In interviews with Daniel Coleman, Ermine discusses ethical space as a neutral space to be engaged. He speaks about how he personally used it as a space where he could engage with Indigenous and Western worldviews.[21] He also speaks about how ethical space provides an opportunity to reassert control by challenging the assumptions embedded in institutions and systems that shape our lived realities and perpetuate the privileging of one worldview over another. Ermine challenges individuals to engage meaningfully in ethical space and to examine their own involvement in the perpetuation of unhealthy relationships between Indigenous peoples and settler Canadians. The goal of this challenge is to examine the status quo and create significant push back against the systems and institutions that continue to perpetuate and legitimate the status quo. Because Ermine recognizes that such work can be done theoretically without any practical change, he also challenges individuals to find practical ways to apply their engagement in ethical space.

Understanding treaties and treaty violations is another important step on the road toward reconciliation, and one that can be examined in ethical space. Battiste stresses the relevance of treaties and the necessity of educating Canadians about the history, contexts, and current importance of treaties in terms of their "constitutional significance in contemporary life."[22] She also calls attention to how "racism and Eurocentric superiority, and apathy" continue to be effective strategies that serve to mask the complicity of both the government and its citizens in the continued denial of treaty rights and obligations.[23] The narratives shared by Battiste find resonance with the work of other Indigenous scholars. Notably, Corey Snelgrove, Rita Kaur Dhamoon, and Jeff Corntassel share Battiste's focus on education as a way forward and argue for the importance of insurgent education within a decolonizing strategy.[24] They identify the importance of localizing Indigenous struggles so as to avoid "Free Tibet Syndrome," which refers to the settlers' preference to focus their decolonizing efforts on far-away places rather than looking in their backyard.[25] These researchers, along with JoLee Sasakamoose, Shauneen Pete, and, notably, Graham Smith, also stress the need to disrupt the politics of distraction by centring Indigenous struggles on and for land.[26] They argue that this can and should be implemented in formal and informal contexts such that the disruption compels accountability and action towards making amends and changes. They also identify the important role of discomfort in the process, arguing that disruption and discomfort are central in moving towards decolonization. I argue that ethical space is often triggered by a willingness to consider uncomfortable realities and to tolerate (and at times embrace) the discomfort within ethical space. In "My Tribe, My Heirs," Pamela Palmater agrees with the importance of treaties as nation-to-nation agreements about living in peace and friendship and being centred on land. She sees the importance of the spirit and intent of treaties and speaks about the narratives that offer context and outline the current impact of the treaty relationships. According to Palmater, "this isn't about feeling bad or guilty; it's about undoing as much of the harm done as possible."[27] One should embrace being a treaty person as a way of life. In Palmater, I see the lesson that one should engage in ethical space as a treaty person, trouble one's own understandings, push through the discomfort to honour treaty relationships and responsibilities, and consider how to move forward in respectful relation without getting mired in guilt.

Ermine states that there is a deceptive convenience for non-Indigenous people in being shielded by the systems and institutions that privilege them. He argues that such shelter serves to entangle non-Indigenous people in the system and co-opts them to replicate and reinforce negative interactions and oppression. Engagement in ethical space offers an alternative and an opportunity to engage meaningfully in reconciliation by confronting uncomfortable realities and considering how one can move forward. Essentially, it provides an opportunity to trouble our own understandings of these uncomfortable realities and work through them. Susan Hill writes about what reconciliation means in the context of Canada's relationship with the Grand River Haudenosaunee in three broad areas: land claims (reconciling financial debts to First Nations communities); education (language revitalization and community-controlled education); and environmental responsibility (shared values around environmental responsibility and ethics).[28] These are important ways to think about and engage in reconciliation, and ethical space offers an opportunity for meaningful engagement. In the area of education, I have argued that ethical space can be used effectively in teaching.[29] Below in this chapter, I expand on this idea to address reconciliation more directly within higher education contexts, as education has been identified within the TRC as one of the primary vehicles for reconciliation.

It can be difficult to understand how ethical space might be applied as a way of engaging in reconciliation within higher education contexts. Instead of theorizing about how it might be applied, I am going to draw upon the teachings generously shared with me by my Indigenous colleagues, Indigenous scholars, and Indigenous Elders. I am going to share narratives about places where ethical space had a role to play—times when uncomfortable realities emerged, and individuals were presented with a choice: engage in ethical space and critically examine those uncomfortable realties or shy away from them, turn away from ethical space, and embrace the status quo.

Uncomfortable Realities

Canadian education systems have a long-standing history of embracing the status quo and telling particular narratives about "Canada the good" while turning away from opportunities to tell different, more complex narratives and to engage in ethical space. The former narratives—those we are told and those we tell ourselves, each other, and the broader world—inform our own understandings about the ways in which we live in connection with and apart from one another. Ethical space allows us to examine those narratives, troubling the ways they have been shaped and the ways they shape how we see the world. Ethical space can be pivotal in opening eyes, ears, minds, and hearts to some uncomfortable realities that Indigenous scholars have been sharing for some time.

An entire book could be devoted to the sharing of these realities. In this limited space, I will share my understanding of what many have to say within the context of higher education. For instance, as already discussed, Battiste argues that cognitive imperialism and its presence within and shaping of Canadian education systems, including higher education, has reinforced a hierarchy of privilege and entitlement that serves to further marginalize Indigenous peoples while supporting the success of Canadians. In other words, she argues cognitive imperialism amounts to cognitive racism. Linda Tuhiwai Smith also speaks to cognitive racism through the lessons she has been offering throughout her long and prestigious career. One of Smith's more recent lessons calls our attention to the effect of normative ideologies—Battiste's cognitive imperialism—on the ways research impact is defined, measured, and evaluated.[30] Her focus within the area of defining and measuring research impact illuminates two different, but equally interesting, uncomfortable realities. The first is the identification of how normative ideologies within universities and granting agencies create the rules of play or engagement around what is valued, counted, and seen to be worthy of resource and grant dollar support. The second and larger area of focus is on the irony that while Indigenous research is primarily all about impact on communities and on working to address the impacts of hundreds of years of colonialism, this is not the type of impact that universities and granting agencies are looking to measure with their metrics. Social transformation of the type sought through Indigenous research is not likely to feature prominently, if it features at all, in an individual researcher's impact metrics. The metrics capture citations and numbers of publications but not community engagement or how an individual's work shifts people's worldviews or encourages deeper engagement in reconciliation.

One of the more poignant realties that Smith points out is the history of these normative ideologies within university and research contexts. Indigenous research is being measured and judged through lenses created by normative ideologies that have supported unethical research on Indigenous peoples (though, of course, it was sanctioned by ethics boards as "ethical" at the time)—research that identified Indigenous peoples as deficient and saw their knowledges as less advanced. While there have been changes—it is now generally understood that research about Indigenous peoples must be done in partnership with Indigenous peoples, and preferably led by Indigenous primary investigators—it is naïve to believe that the historical influences of normative ideologies do not continue to influence what universities and granting agencies see as worthy or how they measure impact. Ironically, while these changes to ethical processes and funding priorities are evidence of the impact of Indigenous research, they have not necessarily changed how individual Indigenous researchers are evaluated and supported. Smith identified how Indigenous researchers have formed research networks of support that are what she terms "a form of resistance to marginalization."[31]

Battiste agrees with Smith that normative ideologies have historically marginalized Indigenous research, and that any advances in how Indigenous research is valued and accepted is relatively recent and still troubled by cognitive imperialism and its effects. She also identifies that the current context of universities operating under the perception of "limited resources" requiring increased enrolments has led to a focus on increasing the number of Indigenous students enrolled in universities.[32] Unfortunately, she has found that this focus on increased enrolment has not led to a serious questioning of Eurocentrism and its influence on university structure and climate. Battiste problematized the term *indigenization*, arguing that it is another way to affirm the superiority of Eurocentrism and support assimilation.[33] Battiste and Smith both point to the absence of an effort to untangle the narratives associated with Eurocentrism, explore the past and present impacts of normative ideologies within the higher education context, and assert that cognitive imperialism / normative ideologies are alive and well. They identify the narratives that universities want to hear and tell about themselves, pointing to the fact that these narratives tend to perpetuate unexamined, normative ideologies that hinder reconciliation instead of highlighting universities' lack of engagement in changing these narratives.

Cognitive imperialism is indeed alive and well within higher education contexts; I see it regularly in the university. It is as if those within the universities are draught horses with blinders on, allowing them to look ahead and work towards their strategic plans without being able to see everything that is happening around them or what has happened behind them. The blinders have been placed on them through their experiences within education systems. Individuals either prefer the view that they have become accustomed to or have difficulty removing those blinders. This unwillingness to disengage from cognitive imperialism results from a lack of effort to untangle and examine the histories associated with Eurocentrism. It further results from an inability and/or unwillingness to see the past and current impacts of Eurocentrism and to consider what other narratives have to offer.

Jo-Ann Episkenew offers a personal reflection on her own experiences with Eurocentrism in higher education.[34] She speaks about how her university's language around making Indigenous students more comfortable came to grate on her nerves, but for a long time she could not pinpoint what it was that bothered her so profoundly. Episkenew deconstructed the language that was used in the university and came to understand that this language implied that Indigenous students are like guests who need to be made comfortable during their stay; this is what was bothering her. She was further disturbed by the embedded assumption that the Indigenous students were not as prepared or were lacking in some way so as to need special programming or resources to manage in the university. Episkenew writes about how she was given advice on how to grow or change to fit into the university context, but that following this advice would have changed her into someone she was not and did not want to be. University personnel saw this as a way to assist her in growing into her position and doing things properly. She saw it as a clear example of Eurocentrism: an assumption that there was an obvious, "correct" way to go about things to which the lessons she had learned from her community on establishing relationships did not conform.

Brock University, the institution in which I currently work, provides an excellent example of what Indigenous scholars are identifying and what I have been taught by my Indigenous colleagues to see and question. I can see how this university has become invested in particular narratives that are not conducive to engaging in reconciliation. Since 2010, there has been a resurgence at Brock that is tied to its namesake, Major General Sir Isaac Brock, and to the War of 1812. The Market, one of Brock's primary eating and gathering places, received a mural in 2010 entitled "Reverberation." The mural depicts elements of the War of 1812 and elements of Brock University's origins. That same year, the Royal Canadian Military Institute lent Brock portraits of Sir Isaac Brock and Chief Tecumseh, which were installed at a prominent and busy corner above the Market. In 2013, a statue of Sir Isaac Brock was commissioned; it was installed at the university in 2015. This is the same year that Brock University's official street address was changed to 1812 Sir Isaac Brock Way and that Shirley CheeChoo was installed as the university's Chancellor. An analysis of this time period reveals the uncomfortable reality that Brock University can be seen as pursuing some kind of indigenization while at the same time glorifying its connections to patriarchy and Eurocentrism. These two narratives seem to run parallel to each other, and are not being considered in terms of what they are collectively saying about the institution.

This certainly supports Battiste's argument that within universities, indigenization is just another method of assimilation and affirmation of Eurocentrism. Brock is actively trying to make the university more welcoming to Indigenous students and trying to increase Indigenous student enrolment while addressing the TRC's calls to action. The university has renewed Chancellor CheeChoo for two years and has created a new position, Vice Provost of Indigenous Engagement—all of which speaks to an investment in addressing the TRC's calls. Yet there is no conversation about how the actions taken by the university to strengthen its connections to the War of 1812 will impact Indigenous students. Similarly, while Indigenous Student Services has been given more space and better facilities, there is no engagement in conversation about its positioning near the portraits and mural.

In conversations with current Brock students in March of 2017, I learned that the majority of mainstream students do not notice the mural or portraits as much more than background. Indigenous students, on the other hand, see them vividly. As one Indigenous student said, "If I want to go to Aboriginal Student Services I have to either take a very careful and circuitous route or go past the mural. In the mural, I see my ancestors being trampled under the boots of soldiers. I don't go by the mural and I don't eat in the Market." It seems that Brock has been operating with blinders on—looking ahead towards a goal of addressing the TRC calls to action but failing to see what is happening around that goal or the history that has influenced and continues to influence the university's ties to Eurocentrism. However, there are promising signs that the blinders may be coming off. Since my conversations with students, the university has removed the mural, added a Vice Provost of Indigenous Engagement, and committed to hiring more Indigenous faculty.

Settlers Teaching Indigenous Content

Eurocentrism and ethical space can play interesting roles in the debate around who should be teaching courses with Indigenous content in higher education. This debate offers significant opportunities to engage in ethical space.

There are many different factors that come into play when making such a decision within higher education. Some of the most relevant factors include the following: the principle of "nothing about us without us," intellectual freedom, Indigenous faculty workload, and hiring practices. Currently, there are many non-Indigenous faculty and instructors teaching courses with varying levels of Indigenous content in Canadian universities. There is also a push within these universities to include more Indigenous content in a wide range of courses in response to the TRC. Eurocentrism frequently informs this debate with its inherent assumptions that Western mainstream approaches to teaching and learning, and instructors trained in these approaches, offer the "correct" way to deliver such material. As already discussed, Indigenous scholars such as Battiste and Smith have written about how pervasive Eurocentric attitudes have influenced research, teaching, and the overall perception of Indigenous peoples and communities. It is not surprising that these pervasive attitudes and modes of thought would also influence the delivery and instructor assignment for Indigenous content courses. Indigenous faculty, instructors, students, and communities have legitimate concerns that Indigenous content taught without their involvement can further replicate the Eurocentric views and cognitive imperialism that make it extremely difficult to move forward in reconciliation efforts. Such teaching often uses deficit models and perpetuates deficit thinking about Indigenous peoples. Ethical space offers an opportunity to engage in a meaningful examination of the relevant factors involved in decisions around who is assigned to teach Indigenous content courses.

Mount Saint Vincent University offers a practical example of the debate around the teaching of Indigenous content courses. A social media controversy was triggered in May 2018 when Mount Saint Vincent University assigned a non-Indigenous professor to teach a course about the residential school system. Academic freedom clashed with the principles of self-determination and participation that serve as the roots of "nothing about us without us." Multiple newspaper articles made it clear that the criticisms leveled at Mount Saint Vincent were not directed at the individual faculty member but at what was seen as a violation of Indigenous peoples' lived experiences in residential schools and the impact of those experiences. Rebecca Thomas, a Mi'kmaw community activist, was quoted saying, "There's no voice better than first voice."[35] The principle that courses and content about Indigenous peoples should be taught by Indigenous peoples—part of the principle of "nothing about us without us"—is rooted in the understanding that, historically, such practices have resulted in gross misrepresentations and laid the foundation of much of what needs to be reconciled. Patti Doyle-Bedwell, a Mi'kmaw faculty member at Dalhousie, has cited the importance of Indigenous faculty within universities: "Part of reconciliation is making space for Indigenous faculty members at universities and Indigenous knowledge perspectives."[36] In contrast, in a letter to the provost of Mount Saint Vincent, Mark Mercer, then the president of the Society for Academic Freedom and Scholarship, wrote: "The race or ethnicity of the professor is not an academic ground, and, thus, should not be a consideration."[37] Mount Saint Vincent faculty member Sherri Pictou is a Mi'kmaw woman who supported a settler colleague teaching the residential school course. During the controversy, Pictou was quoted as stating that she had "full confidence" in her colleague and that such work "cannot fall just on the backs and labour of other Indigenous academics."[38]

This debate offers significant opportunities to engage in ethical space and examine the deep issues that have to be explored when universities make decisions around the teaching of Indigenous content. The principle of "nothing about us without us" pushes up against institutional concerns such as academic freedom and departmental governance that include the assessment of instructor suitability, course offerings, and instructor assignment. There is a fundamental importance associated with having an Indigenous scholar teach from a lived-experience approach, outlining the complex levels of discrimination within residential school experiences and the legacy associated across generations with those experiences. Rebecca Thomas wrote an opinion piece for the *Washington Post* that spoke eloquently to many of these issues and to the heavy burdens placed on Indigenous faculty and instructors.[39] This raises the question of how those burdens can be shared so that the work of decolonizing is not solely the work of Indigenous scholars, while also respecting the importance of first voice. In the case of Mount Saint Vincent, members of the university did seem to engage in ethical space to some degree in determining how they would respond to the very public criticism of their decision. They demonstrated a willingness to engage in the tough questions that emerged out of their decision by holding a consultative session with Indigenous and non-Indigenous faculty. The outcome of that consultation was to uphold the assignment of the non-Indigenous faculty member and to support the assignment by indicating that the faculty member's background and approach to teaching was consistent with a commitment to engaging in reconciliation as a partnership.

It is important to point out that what happened at Mount Saint Vincent is not an isolated incident in terms of non-Indigenous faculty or instructors teaching courses with significant levels of Indigenous content. It is unusual in terms of the media attention that it triggered. Such assignments are relatively common within higher education and, given the pervasiveness of cognitive imperialism, they do not usually raise red flags or garner much attention. The social media controversy around the situation at Mount Saint Vincent may trouble and push back against that complacency.

Complacency and lack of attention do not mean that everyone in the university sees non-Indigenous faculty and instructors teaching Indigenous content as appropriate. Frances Henry and Audrey Kobayashi conducted interviews with racialized and Indigenous faculty members in Canadian universities. Some Indigenous interviewees expressed concerns about and identified tensions associated with non-Indigenous faculty teaching Indigenous content both in terms of appropriateness and in terms of what might be included or edited out of these courses.[40] Many interviewees also mentioned the heavy workload and high expectations placed on Indigenous faculty. Sandra D. Styres and I similarly found that both Indigenous students and faculty members expressed significant concerns about the teaching of Indigenous content by non-Indigenous faculty or instructors and about the workload burden faced by Indigenous faculty members.[41] Additionally, we found a number of concerns expressed by non-Indigenous faculty around fears of appropriation and of making mistakes when teaching or referring to Indigenous content. Jean-Paul Restoule also addressed concerns among Canadian educators from elementary to higher education who expressed fears around appropriation and making mistakes in covering curriculum about Indigenous issues. These educators reported an overall lack of confidence in their abilities to cover such curriculum. Restoule challenged educators to see mistakes as opportunities for learning, arguing that instead of asking "Do I have the right to teach this material?" educators should ask "What is my responsibility?"[42]

There are times when teaching or co-teaching a course with Indigenous content is an appropriate way for a non-Indigenous educator to uphold their treaty responsibilities, for instance if there has been consultation with Indigenous advisory councils and/or Indigenous faculty and co-teaching or teaching is deemed necessary due to the burden that would otherwise be placed on Indigenous faculty or to ameliorate some of the backlash and bullying faced by Indigenous faculty when they teach Indigenous content. Consideration has to be given to whether or not stepping up in a given case is supportive of Indigenous colleagues or actually undermines arguments for the need to hire more Indigenous faculty. There are also times when choosing to teach an Indigenous course when there is an Indigenous faculty member or instructor available and willing to teach the course is an act of imposing dominant privilege and institutional power. Engaging in ethical space—that is, space in which assumptions, biases, privilege, and other ways of knowing are all meaningfully examined and participants seek a solution that respects treaty responsibilities and respectful relations—offers universities a way to move forward in reconciliation efforts.

Engaging in ethical space and examining these tough questions around treaty responsibilities, the principle of "nothing about us without us," intellectual freedom, university governance, faculty workload, and hiring practices can lead toward meaningful steps in reconciliation. There has to be a balancing of the various factors; falling back on status quo and past practice should not be an option if higher education institutions are committed to reconciliation. Restoule offers a place to start by asking people to question what their responsibilities are when choosing a course of action. Intellectual freedom does not absolve faculty members of responsibility. In my understanding, intellectual freedom is intended to protect faculty members from persecution and to provide them with the freedom to teach a variety of material of their choosing. It does not absolve a faculty member from the responsibility to defend or explain positions or information that they have chosen to introduce or exclude. Academic freedom does not protect faculty from human rights complaints associated with charter rights and freedoms. We all need to consider what our treaty responsibilities are and how those responsibilities should inform our choices within higher education.

Reconciliation, Relationships, and Responsibilities

As I move into talking about reconciliation, relationships, and responsibilities, I need to make it very clear that I am addressing non-Indigenous individuals. As a Euro-Canadian myself, I cannot speak to Indigenous sovereignty, self-determination, and participation, as it is neither my place nor my responsibility to do so; my voice is irrelevant and inappropriate in such conversations. It is my responsibility to speak to other non-Indigenous individuals about respectful relations and how we might engage in such relations and uphold treaty rights. Understanding respectful relations as captured in the treaties and our responsibilities as treaty people is a place to start in our journey toward reconciliation.[43] For many people, the first step is coming to understand that all Canadians are treaty people. Though not all land in Canada falls under treaty agreements, as a country, Canada traces its origins back to treaties and stolen, unceded lands. We need to be aware that our standard of living is a direct result of the land that was appropriated, and that Canada has a complex and often dark history of not upholding treaty rights and failing to be in good relationship with Indigenous peoples. We also need to be aware of what we have been taught through our systems of education and how Eurocentrism and cognitive imperialism have provided us with particular lenses through which we view Indigenous peoples, communities, and associated concerns.

Within higher education contexts, we need to be mindful not only of the history of Canada's failure to maintain respectful relations and uphold treaty rights but also of the legacy that continues to inform current-day realities faced by our Indigenous students and colleagues. We need to be aware that there are significant events outside academia that carry into our learning spaces. In 2018 alone, there were several court cases that shook Indigenous communities and called into question whether progress towards reconciliation had been made at all. In Saskatchewan on February 9, 2018, a white farmer was acquitted of first-degree murder and manslaughter for the shooting of Colten Bushie. This was quickly followed by the acquittal of a white man in the murder case of Tina Fontaine, a 15-year-old Indigenous woman. Just over four months later, on June 27, 2018, there was an Ontario case in which a non-Indigenous man was acquitted of the shooting death of an Indigenous man. These verdicts sent shockwaves through Indigenous communities that reverberated in university hallways and classrooms, where the challenges that Indigenous defendants and victims face in obtaining justice in the Canadian justice system—a system that damages the relationships that we are trying to reconcile by continuing to impose its colonial views—are routinely studied and discussed. More recently, we have witnessed the discovery of unmarked graves at the sites of residential schools in British Columbia and Saskatchewan as well as the tragic death of Joyce Echaquan in a Québec hospital.

Consider a lawn-care metaphor: If you continue to mow your lawn and use that mowing to address the weeds, then your lawn will continue to have weeds. If instead you go and remove the weed by the root, you will eventually eliminate the weeds. Similarly, if we continue to see our responsibility as simply engaging in conversation about what is happening without examining the root of the issue— and if we fail to engage in ethical space to examine and trouble our biases and ways of knowing to see how they contribute to the root causes—then we will continue to gloss over the issues and fail in attempts at reconciliation.

In a conference panel, Jacqueline Ottman discussed universities' attempts at reconciliation and spoke about the long history of Canadian education systems silencing Indigenous voices and ways of knowing while continuing to perpetuate hidden curriculum and codes that entrench unconscious bias in individuals. It is this encouragement and support of unconscious bias that has not been eliminated from the Canadian justice system, other social and governmental institutions, and education systems. This must be addressed before respectful relations can occur. Ottman also stated that it was time for non-Indigenous people to embrace respectful relations and walk alongside their Indigenous colleagues. Jan Hare, in the same panel, challenged non-Indigenous colleagues to consider what role and responsibility they have in walking alongside Indigenous colleagues.[44]

What does it mean to walk alongside Indigenous colleagues? What role and responsibility do we hold as non-Indigenous colleagues? Many Indigenous scholars suggest that it means one needs to be self-aware, engage in decolonizing oneself, recognize how to support Indigenous colleagues and priorities, uphold treaty obligations, and know when to use your voice and position and when to be silent and step aside.[45] Many non-Indigenous scholars have struggled with these questions. One of the popular responses has been to become an "ally" or a "settler ally." It is not uncommon to hear people identify in this way during academic talks, at other events throughout conferences, and in various contexts within higher education settings. While the focus of this chapter is not on allyship—I do not have the space to fully address this concept and the associated scholarly work— it is important to briefly consider the idea and its implications for reconciliation as it is an uncomfortable reality that requires individuals to explore some difficult truths.

The term *ally* in contemporary Indigenous contexts has always made me uncomfortable. I have spent significant time trying to unpack why it disturbs me so profoundly. I know that I do not feel *ally* to be a term that an individual can choose on their own as it does not seem genuine to proclaim oneself to be someone else's ally. But this does not address the root of my discomfort with the term, as I am also uncomfortable when someone is named an ally by others. Upon much reflection, my trouble with the term is that it is both unnecessary and a way of absolving responsibility while imposing a relationship that may not be appropriate and may also not exist. It is a way in which an individual can achieve distance from uncomfortable realities to which they are historically connected. It strikes me that self-identifying as an ally can be equivalent to stating that, while your people may have contributed to and supported what has been and continues to be perpetrated against Indigenous peoples, you are neither connected to your people nor are you part of that system—you have defected to the other side and you are a "good person." I see ally-identification as unnecessary; it seems much more important to identify as a treaty person and to learn about respectful relations and your treaty obligations. There is no need to set yourself aside, but there is a need to examine yourself in all your complicity and to look to what you have not been taught: how to engage in respectful relations as a treaty person.

Consider some of what has been written about allies in the context of Indigenous and non-Indigenous relations. Nancy Peters has written about white allies and how they change their habits of mind to become open to other ways of knowing the world. She stresses that allies hold a responsibility to address racism and stand in support of Indigenous peoples while continuing to engage in critical reflection. Peters challenges non-Indigenous Canadians to leave their "white cultural bubbles" and engage in ethical space.[46] Len Findlay argues that no one can decolonize themselves on their own but only through dialogue and cooperation with others. According to Findlay, allyship "requires the explicit and recurrent disavowal of authority over the Other, and the willingness to help, when needed, under indigenous leadership, and most emphatically not as some paternalistic savior or corporate thief from away."[47] Peters also writes about the importance of working as an ally and of knowing who you are, and Isobel Findlay writes about how she recognized her own complicity, how she had internalized racism, and the importance of ethical alliances.[48] Kathy Snow wrote about becoming a "Settler Ally" in her graduate work. Though she offers no definition of the term, she does indicate that the role of a settler ally is to educate scholarly gatekeepers and to put Indigenous participants ahead of their own goals, ego, and institutional parametres. Snow argues for the importance of being accountable even when it is uncomfortable to contradict established processes. She also states that allies need to remain mindful of dynamics of power and privilege, negotiate their roles in research and in sharing narratives, build and sustain relationships, and be open to critical reflection personally and from others.[49] Ironically, I do not disagree with what these authors have argued—only with the need to introduce the label of *ally* or *settler ally*. I encourage non-Indigenous Canadians to trouble the term *ally* and to consider whether or not such a label is necessary or helpful in moving towards reconciliation.

Turning the focus back to reconciliation, I argue that what *is* necessary and helpful is the self-awareness that Indigenous scholars have suggested. It is also necessary and helpful to be willing to engage in ethical space to examine your own prejudices and biases, to learn to be in respectful relationship, and to uphold your responsibilities. Though not easy, this engagement in ethical space leads to awareness at different levels over time. For example, Len Findlay writes that, before he was aware of his complicity, he would have been resistant to having that complicity pointed out to him: "I believed in knowledge monopolies and racist hierarchies, although I, and my teachers and peers, would have been outraged if accused of either."[50] Essentially, while Findlay could at one point see complicity and racism in others, he was not open to seeing it in himself. Only later in his journey was he able become aware of his own role. Findlay stresses that universities are facing a similar challenge of entering into reconciliation as part of the solution (rather than part of the problem), but that doing so requires them to recognize their role in advancing colonialism and its objectives. Engaging in ethical space requires that one be open to past and present complicity. One must further be willing to move towards understanding that what they believe or have believed may need to be deconstructed and reconceptualized before they can move forward. In the postsecondary context, universities often employ equity-focused policies and services but rarely consider the influence of Eurocentrism on how these policies and services are designed and carried out. Enakshi Dua's and Nael Bhanji's examination of equity-related services in Canadian universities focused on the question of whether or not such policies and services were effective in addressing individual and systemic racism. They found that the existence of these policies and services met some legal obligations but were only successful in creating what they referred to as a "mask" that covered up discrimination and could recode incidents as nonincidents.[51] If policies and services do not offer opportunities for engaging in ethical space and considering one's complicity alongside one's responsibilities, then they are likely to continue to perpetuate the very things they are intended to address.

This pattern can also be seen outside policy and service in the everyday interactions within universities. For Henry and Kobayashi, the fundamental problem of everyday racism is that it is not seen by the perpetrators as racism. Even when the harm it causes *is* seen, the racist roots of that harm are often explained away by the absence of a conscious or overt intent to harm.[52] This puts Indigenous faculty in the position of experiencing racism on a daily basis but not having those microaggressions recognized. When it is pointed out to individuals that what they have said or done or failed to do is offensive and racist, they are often disbelieving, resistant, or hostile. These individuals are often committed to an image of themselves that is not racist, that is defined by being an open educator or, sometimes, being committed to social justice. Ironically, those committed to social justice are often most resistant to understanding that they could say or do something racist. Cecil Foster recognizes that those that we might expect to behave better or to know better based on their level of education and position to teach others often fail to do so.[53] Carl E. James has argued that such individuals often see themselves as immune to or exempt from racism. James goes on to discuss how mainstream faculty often evoke colour blindness to say that race does not enter their deliberations, and he questions how race can be so embedded in the experiences of visible minority faculty and yet so absent from those of white faculty.[54]

The common threads in the case of policies and services as well as in everyday interactions are those of missed opportunity and lack of awareness. Instead of recognizing an opportunity to have a critical conversation and open up a dialogue within ethical space, individuals resist, deny, or identify the issue as belonging to someone else. If mainstream faculty are to uphold their treaty obligations, a racist incident is an ideal time to consider what constitutes respectful relations and how to move forward positively from such an event. As faculty, we often challenge our students to consider how they know what they know, to be more self-aware, to be critical of what they are learning, to actively engage in critical reflection, to trouble concepts and ideas, and to consider how they are complicit in processes around them. Why do so many of us resist engaging in those same things when it comes to understanding how we can be in respectful relationship with Indigenous peoples, see ourselves as treaty people, and meet our responsibilities as we move towards reconciliation?

I have shared various narratives to demonstrate how complicated it is to move forward in reconciliation within higher education contexts, and yet, at a fundamental level, how simple it might be. The narratives that I have shared present the uncomfortable realities associated with why universities are struggling to address the TRC in any meaningful way. I have argued that ethical space provides us with an avenue to examine our own complicity and resistance while also providing a space to come to understand how we might come to be in respectful relations with Indigenous peoples and uphold our responsibilities as treaty people. When we think about reconciliation in terms of ethical space, it is simple. The barriers and resistance we, as non-Indigenous Canadians, insert into the process—barriers that we erect to protect ourselves from the narratives that were excluded from our education—only complicate reconciliation. Narratives and testimony from those who experienced the residential school system and narratives and testimony from those who continue to experience the legacy of Eurocentrism and cognitive imperialism trouble and disrupt non-Indigenous Canadian understandings of self and "Canada the good." Ethical space provides us with the opportunity to reconsider the narratives that we have been told and that we tell ourselves while also being open to other narratives that provide a different perspective. We can cling to the status quo, ignore the identification of contemporary Canadian genocide, and continue to perpetuate the damage— or we can look towards other teachings and ways of being in respectful relationship. Responses to COVID-19 have shown that Canadians are capable of making significant changes in a short period of time. However, engagement in reconciliation has not been a key part of these changes nor of contemporary Canadian life in general. Palmater calls for us to embrace being treaty people as a way of life.[55] The question that remains is: How will you answer?

NOTES

1. *Truth and Reconciliation Commission of Canada: Calls to Action.*
2. Truth and Reconciliation Commission of Canada, "What Is Reconciliation."
3. In this chapter, the term *Indigenous* refers to the original or first peoples of any land, including First Nations, Métis, and Inuit, unless otherwise specifically noted. The terms *non-Indigenous Canadians* and *non-Indigenous* refer to individuals residing in what is known as Canada who have a personal or ancestral history of immigration to Turtle Island.
4. Foucault, *Power/Knowledge.*
5. Battiste, "Reframing the Humanities," 3.
6. Battiste, "Reframing the Humanities," 3.
7. Battiste, "Reconciling Indigenous Knowledge," 4.
8. Tuck, "Biting the University"; Grande, "Refusing the University."
9. Ramos and Li, "Differences in Representation."
10. Battiste, "Mi'kmaw Symbolic Literacy." See also Dua and Bhanji, "Mechanisms to Address Inequities"; Grande, "Refusing the University"; Henry and Kobayashi, "Everyday World"; James and Chapman-Nyaho, "Would Never Be Hired"; L.T. Smith, *Decolonizing Methodologies*; L.T. Smith, "Art of the Impossible."
11. James and Chapman-Nyaho, "Would Never Be Hired"; Henry and Tator, "Interviews with Racialized Faculty"; Stewart, *The Visitor.*
12. James and Chapman-Nyaho, "Would Never Be Hired," 100–02.
13. Ahmed, "End Up Doing the Document."
14. Zinga and Styres, "Addressing the TRC."
15. Palmer, Nathan, "Walking Off the Glass Cliff: Race, Gender, and Leadership," *Sociology in Focus*, November 17, 2014, http://www.sociologyinfocus.com/2014/11/17/walking-off-the-glass-cliff-race-gender-leadership/ (web page discontinued).
16. Fiddler, "Professor, Aboriginal Committee"; Prokopchuk, "Indigenous Leaders Call"; Yang, "Celebrated Indigenous Law School Dean."
17. Fiddler, "Professor, Aboriginal Committee."

18. Battiste, "Ecological, Ethical, Inclusive."
19. See Styres et al., "Walking in Two Worlds"; Zinga, "Teaching as the Creation."
20. Ermine, "Ethical Space: Transforming"; Poole, *Towards Deep Subjectivity*.
21. Ermine, "Ethical Space in Action"; Ermine, "What Is Ethical Space?"
22. Battiste, "Narrating Mi'kmaw Treaties," 3.
23. Battiste, "Narrating Mi'kmaw Treaties," 6.
24. Snelgrove, Dhamoon, and Corntassel, "Unsettling Settler Colonialism."
25. Snelgrove, Dhamoon, and Corntassel, "Unsettling Settler Colonialism," 22.
26. Sasakamoose and Pete, "Towards Indigenizing University Policy"; G. Smith, "Indigenous Struggle."
27. Palmater, "My Tribe, My Heirs," 40.
28. Hill, *The Clay*.
29. Zinga, "Teaching as the Creation."
30. L.T. Smith, "Art of the Impossible." See also Battiste, "Reframing the Humanities," 1–17.
31. L.T. Smith, "The Art of the Impossible," 34.
32. Battiste, "Reconciling Indigenous Knowledge," 126.
33. Battiste, "Reconciling Indigenous Knowledge," 127.
34. Episkenew, "Indigenizing University Administration."
35. Rebecca Thomas, quoted in Canadian Press, "Mount Saint Vincent University," para. 10.
36. Patti Doyle-Bedwell, quoted in Bundale, "Professors Condemn University," para. 14.
37. Mark Mercer, quoted in Bundale, "Professors Condemn University," para. 6.
38. Sherri Pictou, quoted in Quon, "University Stands by Professor," paras. 9–10.
39. Thomas, "Canada Needs More Space."
40. Henry and Kobayashi, "The Everyday World."
41. Styres and Zinga, "Student Experiences"; Zinga and Styres, "Addressing the TRC."
42. Restoule, "Everything Is Alive," 35.
43. See Battiste, *Living Treaties*.
44. Hare and Ottman, "Indigenous Perspectives."
45. See Battiste, *Decolonizing Education*; Donald, "CAE/ACFE Panel on Reconciliation"; Hare and Ottman, "Indigenous Perspectives"; LaDuke, "Building a Multicultural Democracy"; L.T. Smith, "Art of the Impossible"; L.T. Smith, "Decolonizing and Strengthening Indigenous Research."
46. Peters, "Learning for Ethical Space," 271.
47. L. Findlay, "Smug Settler," 75.
48. Peters, "Learning Shame"; I. Findlay, "Weaving the Interdisciplinary Basket."
49. Snow, "Being a Settler Ally in Research."
50. L. Findlay, "Smug Settler," 69.
51. Dua and Bhanji, "Mechanisms to Address Inequities."
52. Henry and Kobayashi, "The Everyday World."
53. Foster, foreword to Stewart, *You Must Be a Basketball Player*.
54. James, "Why You Were Hired."
55. Palmater, "My Tribe, My Heirs."

BIBLIOGRAPHY

Ahmed, Sara. "You End Up Doing the Document Rather than Doing the Doing: Diversity, Race Equality and the Politics of Documentation." *Ethnic and Racial Studies* 30, no. 4, (June 2007): 590–609.

Battiste, Marie. *Decolonizing Education: Nourishing the Learning Spirit.* Saskatoon: Purich Publishing, 2013.

——. "Ecological, Ethical, Inclusive, Cognitively Just Citizenship in Canada." Keynote address to the Annual Conference of the Canadian Society for the Study of Education, Regina, SK, May 2018.

——, ed. *Living Treaties: Narrating Mi'kmaw Treaty Relations.* Sydney: Cape Breton University Press, 2016.

——. "Mi'kmaw Symbolic Literacy." In Battiste, *Visioning a Mi'kmaw Humanities*, 123–48.

——. "Narrating Mi'kmaw Treaties: Linking the Past to the Future." In Battiste, *Living Treaties*, 1–15.

——. "Reconciling Indigenous Knowledge in Education: Promises, Possibilities, and Imperatives." In Spooner and McNinch, *Dissident Knowledge in Higher Education*, 123–48.

——. "Reframing the Humanities: From Cognitive Assimilation to Cognitive Justice." In Battiste, *Visioning a Mi'kmaw Humanities*, 1–17.

——, ed. *Visioning a Mi'kmaw Humanities: Indigenizing the Academy.* Sydney: Cape Breton University Press, 2016.

Bundale, Brett. "Professors Condemn University for Handing of Residential-Schools Course Controversy." *National Post*, May 14, 2018. https://nationalpost.com/news/canada/university-condemned-for-handling-of-residential-schools-course-controversy.

Canadian Press. "Mount Saint Vincent University Under Fire over Residential Schools Course Taught by White Professor." *The Star: Halifax Edition*, May 11, 2018. https://www.thestar.com/halifax/2018/05/11/mount-saint-vincent-university-under-fire-over-residential-schools-course-taught-by-white-professor.html.

Donald, Dwayne. "CAE/ACFE Panel on Reconciliation." Panel presentation at the Annual Conference of the Canadian Society for the Study of Education, Regina, SK, May 2018.

Dua, Enakshi, and Nael Bhanji. "Mechanisms to Address Inequities in Canadian Universities: The Performativity of Ineffectiveness." In Henry et al., *The Equity Myth*, 206–38.

Episkenew, Jo-ann. "Indigenizing University Administration or Tâwaw cî? (Take 2)." In M. Smith, *Transforming the Academy*, 64–68.

Ermine, Willie. "Ethical Space in Action." Interview with Daniel Coleman. The Different Knowings Speaker's Series, McMaster University. Recorded October 1, 2010. YouTube video, 5:28. https://www.youtube.com/watch?v=ZUfXu3gfVJ8.

——. "Ethical Space: Transforming Relations." Paper presented at the National Gathering on Indigenous Knowledge, Rankin Inlet, NU, May–June 2005.

——. "What Is Ethical Space?" Interview with Daniel Coleman. The Different Knowings Speaker's Series. Recorded October 1, 2010. YouTube video, 7:18. https://www.youtube.com/watch?v=85PPdUE8Mbo.

Fiddler, Willow. "Professor, Aboriginal Committee Stand By Lakehead U Dean Who Quit amid Allegations of Racism." *APTN National News,* April 23, 2018. http://aptnnews.ca/2018/04/23/professor-aboriginal-stand-by-lakehead-u-dean-who-quit-amid-allegations-of-racism/.

Findlay, Isobel. "Weaving the Interdisciplinary Basket: Building Resilient and Knowledgeable Communities and Economies." In Battiste, *Visioning a Mi'kmaw Humanities*, 107–22.

Findlay, Len. "From Smug Settler to Ethical Ally: Humanizing the Humanist via Solidarity... Interrupted." In Battiste, *Visioning a Mi'kmaw Humanities*, 69–88.

Foster, Cecil. Foreword to *You Must Be a Basketball Player: Rethinking Integration in the University*, by Anthony Stewart, 3–6. Halifax: Fernwood Publishing, 2009.

Foucault, Michel. *Power/Knowledge: Selected Interviews & Other Writings 1972–1977*. Edited by Colin Gordon. Translated by Colin Gordon, Leo Marshall, and Kate Soper. New York: Pantheon Books, 1977.

Grande, Sandy. "Refusing the University." In Spooner and McNinch, *Dissident Knowledge in Higher Education*, 168–89.

Hare, Jan, and Jacqueline Ottman. "Indigenous Perspectives: Moving Forward in Higher Education." Panel presentation at the Annual Conference of the Canadian Society for the Study of Higher Education, Regina, SK, May 2018.

Henry, Frances, Enakshi Dua, Carl E. James, Audrey James, Audrey Kobayashi, Peter Li, Howard Ramos, and Malinda S. Smith, eds. *The Equity Myth: Racialization and Indigeneity at Canadian Universities*. Vancouver: UBC Press, 2017.

Henry, Frances, and Audrey Kobayashi. "The Everyday World of Racialized and Indigenous Faculty Members in Canadian Universities." In Henry et al., *The Equity Myth*, 115–54.

Henry, Frances, and Carol Tator. "Interviews with Racialized Faculty Members in Canadian Universities." *Canadian Ethnic Studies* 44, no. 2 (2012): 75–99.

Hill, Susan M. *The Clay We Are Made Of: Haudenosaunne Land Tenure on the Grand River*. Winnipeg: University of Manitoba Press, 2017.

James, Carl E. "'You Know Why You Were Hired, Don't You?' Expectations and Challenges in University Appointments." In Henry et al., *The Equity Myth*, 155–70.

James, Carl E., and Selom Chapman-Nyaho. "'Would Never Be Hired These Days': The Precarious Work Situation of Racialized and Indigenous Faculty Members." In Henry et al., *The Equity Myth*, 84–114.

LaDuke, Winona. "Building a Multicultural Democracy: Religion, Culture and Identity in America." Keynote address to the Annual Conference of the Environmental Studies Association of Canada, Regina, SK, May 2018.

Palmater, Pamela. "My Tribe, My Heirs and Their Heirs Forever: Living Mi'Kmaw Treaties." In Battiste, *Living Treaties*, 24–41.

Peters, Nancy. "Learning for Ethical Space: Capacity Building for White Allies of Aboriginal Peoples." In *Connected Understanding: Linkages between Theory and Practice in Adult Education. Proceedings of the 29th National Conference of the Canadian Association for the Study of Adult Education*, edited by Susan M. Brigham and Donovan Plumb, 268–73. Montréal: Canadian Association for the Study of Adult Education, 2010.

———. "Learning Shame: Colonial Narratives as a Tool for Decolonization." In Battiste, *Visioning a Mi'kmaw Humanities*, 149–68.

Poole, Roger. *Towards Deep Subjectivity*. New York: Harper & Row, 1972.

Prokopchuk, Matt. "Indigenous Leaders Call for 'Immediate Change' in Wake of Ontario Law School Dean's Resignation." *CBC*, April 24, 2018. https://www.cbc.ca/news/canada/thunder-bay/aboriginal-law-dean-no-support-1.4632680.

Quon, Alexander. "Halifax University Stands by Professor after Controversy over Course on Residential Schools." *Global News*, May 15, 2018. https://globalnews.ca/news/4210494/halifax-msvu-residential-schools-course/.

Ramos, Howard, and Peter Li. "Differences in Representation and Employment Income of Racialized University Professors in Canada." In Henry et al., *The Equity Myth*, 46–64.

Restoule, Jean-Paul. "Everything Is Alive and Everyone Is Related: Indigenous Knowing and Inclusive Education." In M. Smith, *Transforming the Academy*, 32–36.

Sasakamoose, JoLee, and Shauneen Pete. "Towards Indigenizing University Policy: kakwe-iyiniwasta kihci-kiskinwahamâtowikamikohk wiyasiwâcikanisa." *Education Matters* 3, no. 1 (2015): 1–11.

Smith, Graham. "Indigenous Struggle for the Transformation of Education and Schooling." Keynote address to the Alaskan Federation of Natives Convention, Anchorage, AK, October 2003.

Smith, Linda Tuhiwai. "The Art of the Impossible: Defining and Measuring Indigenous Research?" In Spooner and McNinch, *Dissident Knowledge in Higher Education*, 21–40.

———. "Decolonizing and Strengthening Indigenous Research." Panel at the Congress of the Humanities and Social Sciences, Regina, SK, May–June 2018.

———. *Decolonizing Methodologies: Research and Indigenous Peoples.* 2nd ed. New York: Zed Books, 2012.

Smith, Malinda S., ed. *Transforming the Academy: Essays on Indigenous Education, Knowledges and Relations.* Edmonton: University of Alberta, 2013.

Snelgrove, Corey, Rita Kaur Dhamoon, and Jeff Corntassel. "Unsettling Settler Colonialism: The Discourse and Politics of Settlers, and Solidarity with Indigenous Nations." *Decolonization: Indigeneity, Education & Society* 3, no. 2 (2014): 1–32.

Snow, Kathy. "What Does Being a Settler Ally in Research Mean? A Graduate Student's Experience Learning from and Working within Indigenous Research Paradigms." *International Journal of Qualitative Methods*, 17 (2018): 1–11.

Spooner, Marc, and James McNinch, eds. *Dissident Knowledge in Higher Education.* Regina: University of Regina Press, 2018.

Stewart, Anthony. *The Visitor: My Life in Canada.* Halifax: Fernwood Publishing, 2014.

Styres, Sandra D., and Dawn Zinga. "Student Experiences and Two Canadian Universities' Responses to Truth and Reconciliation Commission's Calls to Action." Paper presented at the Ireland International Conference on Education, Dublin, Ireland, April 2018.

Styres, Sandra D., Dawn Zinga, Sheila Bennett, and Michelle Bomberry. "Walking in Two Worlds: Engaging the Space Between Indigenous Community and Academia." *Canadian Journal of Education* 33, no. 3 (2010): 617–48.

Thomas, Rebecca. "Canada Needs More Space for Indigenous People in Academia." *Washington Post,* May 19, 2018. https://www.washingtonpost.com/news/global-opinions/wp/2018/05/19/canada-needs-more-space-for-indigenous-people-in-academia/?noredirect=on&utm_term=.3d930aa24859.

Truth and Reconciliation Commission of Canada. *Truth and Reconciliation Commission of Canada: Calls to Action.* Winnipeg: National Centre for Truth and Reconciliation, 2015. https://ehprnh2mwo3.exactdn.com/wp-content/uploads/2021/01/Calls_to_Action_English2.pdf.

———. "What Is Reconciliation?" Vimeo video, 2:55. https://vimeo.com/25389165.

Yang, Jennifer. "Celebrated Indigenous Law School Dean Resigns Claiming Systemic Racism." *Toronto Star*, April 11, 2018. https://www.thestar.com/news/canada/2018/04/11/celebrated-indigenous-law-school-dean-resigns-claiming-systemic-racism.html.

Zinga, Dawn. "Teaching as the Creation of Ethical Space: Indigenous Student Learning in the Academy/University." In *Indigenous Education: New Directions in Theory and Practice,* edited by Hulia Tomlins-Jahnke, Sandra D. Styres, Spencer Lilley, and Dawn Zinga, 277–309. Edmonton: University of Alberta Press, 2019.

Zinga, Dawn, and Sandra D. Styres. "Addressing the TRC in Higher Education: The Role of Faculty and Senior Administrators." Paper presented at the Ireland International Conference on Education, Dublin, Ireland, April 2018.

4

GEORGE J. SEFA DEI
(NANA ADUSEI
SEFA TWENEBOAH)

Contested Knowledges

Indigeneity, Resistance,
and Black Theorizing
in Academia

WRITING ON TURTLE ISLAND SOIL,
I acknowledge the traditional custodians of this Land[1] and pay homage and respect
to our ancestors and Elders, both living and dead.

There is an embodiment of knowledge that shapes one's intellectual
consciousness and the pursuit of politics. In this chapter, I take the concept of the
personal as intellectual to reflect upon and interrogate what I will call "the crisis
of legitimacy" of the Western academy. Using the same framework, I examine
the significances of the embodiment of the scholar, the body politics required for
survival as an academic and intellectual, and the power of language use in academia.
The knowings of the Black subject are always, in academia, held in suspicion until
they are "proven." This dynamic is revealed in the constant questioning of Black
bodies' legitimacy as knowers and theorists able to make sense of or comprehend our
own lived experiences. Throughout the chapter, the label *Black* can be extended in the
political sense to include the racialized, colonized, and Indigenous subject, resisting
from the fringes or margins of the academy. In other words, following British social
movements and racialized politics of earlier times, the word *Black* symbolizes all
oppressed groups or peoples of colour. In this liminal space, decolonization for the

Black subject becomes the radical things we do around Land, place, space, and names to ensure that education becomes a nurturing experience sustained in a healthy, spiritually centred space.

Perhaps, and much more importantly, the embodiment of knowledge for the Black/racialized/Indigenous subject is about the spaces we occupy and the knowledges that come with this spatialization. In contemporary times, when we have peoples and communities struggling with issues of mutual recognition, borders, security, water rights, control of spaces, problematics of settlements on stolen Lands, and yearnings for freedom of movement and freedom of return to homelands, we cannot take Land and sovereignty as mere intellectual exercises. These are struggles over life and death. We must acknowledge our relative privileges and what history has accorded unto us. It is oxymoronic to think that the colony's dominant cultural group has no privileges.

It is an honour to receive an invitation to contribute to this collection. My entry point into the discussion of troubling reconciliation is to complicate the stories we bring by way of narratives of colonization and decolonization from different vantage points, even when we talk about Indigeneity and what it means to be Indigenous. In the current moment, in which reconciliation has gained tremendous currency, I wonder what it is we are attempting to reconcile. What does such reconciliation mean when certain stories have not been on the table for discussion in the first place? The Land question is central to these discussions, and there are many voices, many answers, to the question of what Land means. For me, knowledge—that is, questions of what counts as knowledge and whose knowledge counts—becomes a starting point.

I am in search of a critical reading of (African) humanism that privileges ideas of connectivity, relationality, complementarity, reciprocity, sharing, and mutual interdependence as cherished moral values of human beings acting with a collective sense of purpose and meaning in life. While this chapter focuses on this type of critical reading, it is applicable to the broader concept of reconciliation in that anti-Black and anti-Indigenous ideologies are co-related. They serve the same White-supremacist and capitalist purposes, and must be dealt with in order to even begin to speak about authentic reconciliation. As I have stated elsewhere, Land is something we all have claims to somewhere, and we all are entitled to develop an association with and ties to Land.[2] Claiming a piece of Land is not just about claiming a physical location or a concrete material possession. It is about claiming a past, culture, history, rootedness, and heritage, as well as spiritual and psychic memories. The Land is the source of life. It is the water we drink and the air we breathe. We walk and root our existence on the Land. The Land makes us who we are. Land is given to us not as our permanent property but for our temporary use while we exist on this Earth. Temporary caretakers and custodians have no identity except in relation to this Land.[3] Land is also about knowledge. Indigenous communities teach us that the Land is everything. It encompasses the social, cultural, spiritual, physical, and metaphysical realms of existence.[4] For example, for many Indigenous people, evoking the Land brings to mind teachings about environment, social justice, equity, leadership, and the social good.[5] It is about place, space, spirit, and soul. Rivers, Seas, Oceans, Earth, and Sky show relations to Land beyond physical realities. Because Land is an embodiment of knowledge, we stand to learn a lot from it. Consequently, this text is about everything we do with and around the Land as place and space for knowing the physical, spiritual, and nonmaterial realms of existence. We should be able to speak about the ways certain bodies are denied their knowledges or even legitimate claims to know while on a given Land or space. This understanding of the importance of Land should resonate with the reader as they weave through my chapter.

Race and Knowledge Production

We must think about institutional structures and the validation of knowledge systems relationally and historically. For example, the effects of colonialism and White settler-colonial violence has been felt everywhere. However, colonialism and White colonial violence is also continually resisted. Resistance is about the intertwining contingencies of histories. Some key question arise: Are we (as educators, learners, and communities) always able to bring these connections to bear on our readings of human existence? Specifically, I am asking about the (im)possibility of sharing a common narrative around racial injustice in society. If it is not possible, how are we to account for this disjuncture and the continuing manifestations of social inequities? Is this impossibility because we come from different geographies, spaces, histories, and experiences, and embody different identities? That is, to what extent do gender, class, sexuality, religion, (dis)ability, citizenship, and other aspects of identity complicate the racial experience for us, and how does race complicate our experience of them? Could it be that many of us simply deny (racial) injustice, preferring to move heavens to pretend we don't see what is staring us in the face? While we must hang on to all these possibilities in the search of answers to our questions, I would like us to reflect more particularly on the question of the denial of race and racism as I have both a political and an intellectual investment in the discussion. Of course, the reader is welcome to bring their own, unique standpoints and entry points to this reading.

Because race is about rewards, entitlements, punishment, and oppression meted out to bodies differently, we should expect denial especially from those who benefit from their race. White arrogance, impunity, and racialized complacency assume that our world is changing for the better. For example, in the academy, White arrogance reveals itself in the dominant body's continued assertion of power to determine terms of legitimate intellectual debates, establish the rules of acceptable functioning in these spaces, and evaluate what is scholarly and worthy of political pursuits. Some Black, Indigenous, and racialized scholars fall for this crap. We distance ourselves from our own communities by not speaking about the salience of race and Indigeneity. In challenging claims of multiple Indigeneities, we buy into the merit badges of White academia, mimicking Eurocentric theories that hardly speak to the lived realities of Black, Indigenous, and racialized groups. We see power in the "White talk" of neoliberalism. We see a liberalized politics of intersectionality as a panacea to building communities for change. From where I sit as a Black/African racialized body, there is limited truth to this delusion especially since, as we all know, the more things seem to change the more they remain the same! Therefore, I call on us as educators, learners, researchers, policy workers, and community workers to intellectually and politically mobilize all efforts to challenge the easy normalization of race, racism, and systemic violence from our sites of difference (e.g., gender, sexuality, class, [dis]ability, religion, language, and culture). We must decry the watered-down understanding of intersectional politics and the diffused understanding of power—one that understands power to be equally distributed among groups. There is and will always be a colonial dominance to contend with. We can no longer afford to remain silent. As scholars, our academic spaces and our self- and collective absorptions do not insulate us from social criticisms and Black, Indigenous, and racialized rage. In the face of inaction, our intellectual rhetorics have long served to reveal our deep-seated hypocrisy.

Those who evoke powerful phrases such as "Black Lives Matter," "No Justice No Peace," and "No Justice on Stolen Lands" fight for a better society, a different world, and a new humanism that might emerge from an honest dialogue about and practices of resisting ongoing racialized, classed, and gendered colonizations and impositions. "Black is Human" is a new phrase for me. Anti-Blackness and anti-Indigeneity are among the most pressing social problems for academic scholarship to engage with as part of the project of decolonization. This fact requires a new antiracist, anticolonial framework to change the mantra of making our communities "great again" to one that renders visible how our communities have never been allowed to be great or to flourish in greatness. Our greatness has been prevented by the stories, histories, and violences of Eurocolonial racism, colonialism, and settler colonialism, and the gender, sexual, patriarchal and homophobic violence, inclusive of segregated work forces and ableism.

The law is important, although sometimes I feel we place too much faith in it and are met with disappointment. The relevance of a law is understood in relation to what the law says, where the law applies, and who constructs the legal. For laws to be effective, they must be deemed just by those they bind, and be acceptable to them. A law that seeks to protect the powerful cannot be deemed important to the poor and powerless even if it has ramifications on those same people. The law-and-order politics that characterize Euromodernity only work for some. Race-related and settler-colonial injustices and other forms of systemic violence continue to plague our society.

We often speak of how racism, colonialism, and oppression are not just theories. In fact, no amount of theory around, theorization about, or pursuit of law for social justice can adequately address the incessant problems of gender and sexual violence, ableism, class exploitation, the many forms of systemic injustice that confront the unwelcome migrant, police racial profiling of Black and Indigenous bodies, and the disproportionate incarceration of Black, African, and Indigenous youth. The law can address the question of power and power sharing if institutional responsibility and complicity are on the table for serious discussion. However, it also takes an ethics of caring, social responsibility, and personal implication for these violences to even become topics of open, public conversations, let alone critical dialogues and action.

Anti-Blackness and Indigeneity

Following many others, I understand anti-Blackness to be a sociohistorical and political dimension of Black existence that speaks to the everyday Black individual. It consists of the systemic hostilities and violences mapped onto the Black body and life in profound, concrete, and spiritual ways.[6] These violences are racialized, classed, gendered, and sexualized; they manifest in culture, politics, and knowledge. It is this expansive understanding that extends the meaning of anti-Blackness beyond anti-Black racism. This anti-Blackness speaks to the curious interface of body, skin, culture, and race that foments and cements a breathing culture and climate of anti-Blackness.[7] There is a global anti-Blackness that draws on the synergies of Blackness and Africanness in negative ways to ensure colonial projects and logics of White supremacy. Such anti-Blackness is endemic to the normal functioning of White capitalist society, placing Black and African peoples at the bottom of racial hierarchy and in the service of capitalist and Western hegemonic ideologies and practice. Anti-Black, anti-immigrant, and anti-Indigenous stances are co-relational in the ways they serve and sustain White supremacy and capitalist racial logics.

Anti-Blackness also extends beyond "thingification"[8] to a perceived lack of rational thought, the abnormality of the Black body, and the dis-normalness of Black behaviour (i.e., our perceived lack of morality and ethics). Thingification, in Aimé Césaire's usage, speaks to the White-supremacist objectification of the body and the denial of its subjectivity. The body is simply acted upon as a "thing" or "object," and rendered an unthinking self. The White-supremacist subject does not see Black and African peoples as human agents. The denial of African personhood and humanity downplays the saliences of anti-Black racism, how this form of racism is particularly virulent, and how it differs from other forms of racism and oppressions in practice and manifestation. It is significant to note that discounting the severity of issues for Black bodies and interpreting this reality as "oppression Olympics" is itself indicative of anti-Blackness.

It is crucial to understand intersectionality through a lens of multibodism: the fact that multiple bodies and subjectivities exist in relation to one another, each with their own relative complicities, privileges, and responsibilities.[9] It is, thus, troubling when intersectionality is anti-Black—that is, when it is posited in clever ways that deny race as a significant and unique entry point to oppression. I am specifically speaking here about the neoliberal and conservative counter-reaction that takes place when antiracist actors place race at the centre of these discussions. Here, these reactions read intellectual shifts as a privileging of race to the exclusion of other identities. I have often spoken of the relative saliencies of different oppressions with regard to race.[10] The negation of African and Black diasporic Indigeneity in the White settler-colonial context—something I discuss in the next sections—is another manifestation of anti-Blackness. This often leads to a further misreading of the nature and particular significance of Black resistance and politics. To be absolutely clear, I do not put forward a call for Black exceptionalism.

I have often wondered why it is that claims of Blackness are met with repeated calls for us to recognize the heterogeneity and multidimensionality of Blackness. Interestingly, we do not always hear these calls for heterogeneity in the context of Indigenous experiences. Similarly, I have come to realize that Black and African scholars who specialize in and/or focus on Black and African experiences risk being charged with having "narrow academic interests." Yet this charge is neither extended to Indigenous scholars who specialize in Indigenous studies, nor to White scholars who specialize in European studies.

Notwithstanding the fact that race cannot be ignored, any response to anti-Blackness must be about more than race radicalism. The anticolonial response to anti-Blackness must seek to destroy hegemonic Whiteness, its implications for the nation-building project, and its pursuit of the "idealized White racial subject."[11] Within the (Western) academy, the political masquerade of knowledge production must also be addressed. Specifically, anti-Blackness must be engaged with within the (Western) academy, within its prism of masquerading politics of knowledge production and validation in the (Western) academy. The violence of the (Western) academy reveals itself in the myriad manifestations of anti-Blackness and anti-Indigeneity (e.g., negation and devaluation of Black and Indigenous scholarship, absented presence of Blackness, and the prevailing codes of global anti-Blackness). We need to unpack who and what is currently included or excluded in conversations about what constitutes "theory" and "theorizing." In other words, we need to ask: What knowledges are left out? As Black, racialized, and Indigenous scholars, our counter-hegemonic critiques can be neither instructed nor validated by or through White Eurocentric prisms because our critiques resist these very prisms. That is, they resist forced compliance to the dominant paradigms that set the tone, norms, and standards for what counts as theory and theorizing.[12]

The problem of epistemic surveillance, upheld by the power of Eurocentricity, is a problem within the academy. We see this in the validation and hierarchies of particular bodies of knowledge, in the analytical skills and tools we develop, in ideas of "meritocracy" and "excellence," and in the ability of Whiteness to "regulate without regulating."[13] We see White imaginings and constructions of Blackness and

Indigeneity that deny Black and Indigenous subjectivity and agency, and that turn our bodies into property to be owned and, conveniently, excluded. We see it, too, in the dominance and control of colonial theorizing that reveal a deepening schism of multiple and different (e.g., colonial and anticolonial) realities and repeated struggles to contest knowledge. Resisting dominant intellectual discursive tropes comes at high spiritual, emotional, psychological, and physical costs for Black, Indigenous, and racialized bodies. The academy induces us to be, and rewards us for being, "colonial mimics,"[14] only then deeming us contributors to scholarship. We are told to present our counter, alternate, and subaltern theories in ways that are understandable to prevailing dominant scholarship if we are to gain broader appeal, whatever that is. Unfortunately, any resistance we mount against this situation places us in multiple binds with profound sociocultural, emotional, spiritual, and material costs. For example, our continuing resistance to becoming intellectual imposters[15] as a result of colonial mimicry and having to keep up appearances only furthers a form of structural epistemicide for us. That is, it is not just that colonial mimicry leads us to be intellectual imposters; it is that our struggle to remain true to our authentic selves, souls, and spirits as Black, African, Indigenous, and racialized scholars is intimately tied to colonial mimicry and intellectual imposter syndrome.

Black and African Indigeneities

Black and African Indigeneity is a complex subject. There was Africa (*Abibiman*) before the Land was colonially named "Africa." This is significant as it recognizes African and Black Indigenous peoples who cannot be dismissed or swept away. If nothing else, this recognition has merits for anticolonial politics.[16] It is a recognition that pays homage to the "ancestry of experience" of Black and African peoples as a powerful knowledge base from which to theorize about social life and political practice.[17] The recognition also serves to push for and validate Black theorizing as a knowledge within African Indigenous conceptions of the Universe (cosmology) as interdependent, interrelated, and interconnected; the nature of being and reality (ontology) as "fundamentally spirit and spiritual with material manifestations";[18] and the affirmation of values (axiology) as prioritizing interpersonal relations as well as collective, communal, and community gain. Such Black theorizing also works with other philosophical assumptions—for instance, the interface of body, mind, and soul interconnection, or *Suahunu*, the trialectic space.[19] Clearly, this knowledge is neither unique to nor a monopoly of African and Black peoples. It is a knowledge base shared by all global Indigenous peoples. This affirmation highlights the embeddedness of African ways of knowing as ideas that ground a different theorization of social reality.

We must also assert theories of Black and African Indigeneity from the different geographies of Blackness and Africanness, recognizing that White supremacy is global and exists in Africa, the Caribbean, South America, Asia,

Europe, Australia/Oceania, and North America. We must acknowledge, too, how global White supremacy within different communities perpetuates anti-Blackness, anti-Indigeneity, transphobia, homophobia, and other forms of oppression. In the academic context, we must also acknowledge that many dominant, racialized, Indigenous, and colonized bodies within education themselves perpetuate this oppression. It is imperative, therefore, that we combat White supremacy within multiple schooling and community spaces.

We must ask: When we speak about, learn about, hear about, and see different communities, which type of representation tends to be centred, imposed, and upheld as a singular, dominant narrative? Which types are most often erased? Erased representations include but are not limited to Black, African, Indigenous, and other racialized and colonized peoples with their own Indigenous histories. What does this mean within the realm of classrooms, schooling, and curriculum? How can taking an anticolonial approach to education work to unveil the nuances and complexities of our identities and see how schooling impacts various groupings within our communities both similarly and differently? For example, within Latinx community contexts, we must acknowledge the experiences and voices of Black/Afro-Latinxs, Indigenous peoples, and Black/Afro-Indigenous peoples in schooling and beyond to truly bring liberation for all Latinx peoples. This includes centring the shared histories and resistances of global Black and African continental and diasporic bodies, as well as global Indigenous peoples and global Black/Afro-Indigenous peoples outside of the context of Latin America and its diaspora.

The Politics of Black Theorizing

Can Black and African peoples think? This question is a humorous theoretical obfuscation whereby theory is presumed equivalent to European thinking.[20] It is not just that theory is not universal, but also, that theory itself is in need of interrogation. The fact is that theory has generally been considered a product of particular bodies. Early European ideological formations masqueraded under the guise of theory to animalize, devalue, and debase African humanity and human-ness.[21] Enlightenment philosophers such as Plato, Aristotle, Locke, Hume, Kant, Hegel and many others "fashioned the content and contours of modern White-supremacist thinking and conduct."[22] Black theorizing emerged to subvert and reject Euroconstructions and "Western modernist claims of neutrality, objectivity, rationality and universality" of science and what is knowledge.[23]

In highlighting Black theorizing, my focus is not on Black canons, but on how some of us have theorized as Black scholars—that is, our ways of sense and meaning making, knowledge production, interrogation, validation, dissemination, and use, and how we see ourselves as "knowing subjects."[24] Black theorizing has roots in Black radical intellectual traditions that speak to the sociology of knowledge. We know that, throughout human history, Black theorizing in the social sciences and humanities has revolved around contested conceptions of Negritude philosophy, pan-Africanism, Black Nationalism, Fanonian anticolonialism, postcolonial and diasporic literature theories, Afrocentrism, African-centred thought, intersectionality theory, critical race theory, critical antiracist theory, and BlackCrit, to mention a few. In examining these ideas, a long history of Black and African philosophical traditions of liberation emerges, which stresses the necessity of inculcating African learners with an African cultural foundation from which to view other global cultures.[25] As Theresa Perry and Lisa Delpit note, drawing from the Egyptian principles of *Maat*, the African conceptions of the "human" and "humanness" are about "righteousness, truth, honesty, propriety, harmony, order and reciprocity."[26] They are also about relations, connections, and complementarity.[27]

Today, there continues to be a growing need to investigate the nature of colonial and anticolonial philosophies and practices that have been developed to advance scholarship. For example, we must understand how the study of the "science of racism," which incorporates the logic of Western-educated scholars, has failed to fully engage with a more global consideration of Indigenous knowledge, science, and practice. It has, that is, failed to interface with multiple worldviews, world senses, and world sensations. The continuing struggle to shed from ourselves the enduring legacies of colonial and imperial thinking requires that we not conflate the "sociology of knowledge with epistemology," a genetic fallacy.[28]

Clearly, Black theorizing is not monolithic. I am specifically coming from the school of the dialectic of theory, practice, and politics to ask: What does it mean to theorize and think as a Black scholar? If "to know is to act," then how do we employ knowledge for the purpose of cultural criticism and social change?[29] The theories we develop and engage with are intellectual and strategic political choices. There is a particular politics and thinking process that has led some Black, Indigenous, and racialized scholars down the path of radicalism, coupling academic intellectualism with social responsibility. In effect, theory must be a weapon of change. Black scholarship and intellectuality must be relevant to Black communities.

The indomitable spirit of Black and African learners is evident in their survival in the hostile environment of the Western academy. Black life constitutes "a counter-white *episteme*, a mode of knowing and being that [is] deconstructive, reconstructive, and transformative of what it means to be Black."[30] The Black intellectual tradition has been a philosophy born of struggle and resistance; hence, as Black, Indigenous, and other racialized scholars, we must see our roles in the academy as activist scholars. We must work with "facticity and possibility" and an understanding that the pursuit of knowledge and scholarship should make a material difference in the lives of our communities.[31] A key question remains: How do we bring a "sense of social and deep personal existential accountability" to our work as Black scholars and move from "knowledge-getting" to "knowledge-doing"?[32]

Our theorization as scholars needs to focus on our collective empowerment, self-definition, and knowledge politics from the vantage of our personal agency as living and knowing subjects. The theoretically holistic prism of an Indigenous epistemology must counter Eurocentric epistemes and be informed by our lived experiences in relation to questions of trust, ethics of caring, empathy, and personal accountability with a knowledge that is inclusive of experiences, emotions, and feelings.

The urgency of understanding the complexity of Black and African experiences calls for groundbreaking subversive Black thinking and practice. We must engage knowledge to challenge Black exclusions—with the occasional exception of references to Fanon, and perhaps to Césaire—from decolonial theorizing.[33] This calls for outside-the-box questions: How do we, in our theorizing, begin to trouble our deeply held convictions, racialized assumptions, or even common-sense understandings that merely serve to maintain and sustain the current sociopolitical order? How have the theories, epistemological frameworks, and ideologies with which we have chosen to engage truly become weapons of change? And what speculative imaginaries from Black perspectives are called for as we counter-vision a different, new world? Black theorizing must interrupt certain powerful mythologies about ourselves—for instance, the idea that Black and African Peoples everywhere are all immigrants from somewhere, that we have no history, that we are not a colonized population, and that we have no Land.[34] Black theorizing must subvert our ongoing colonial enactments and investments. Black theorizing must allow us to speak with each other in ways that makes solidarity possible in the first place.

Critical Friends and a Beginning to a Conclusion

We need a genuine intellectual partnership to address the crisis of legitimacy in the academy. This partnership is only possible in the spirit of critical (i.e., intellectual) friends. Allyship is not enough. Allies are becoming increasingly suspect for their lack of action and commitment to change. The term *ally* is thus becoming increasingly discredited. So, I end with two more questions. First, how do we define and problematize allyship? Second, how does a critical friend differ from someone who engages in allyship?

Allies are simply those who see themselves in coalitions and shared struggles with a determination to work together. This is, however, a definition of a hopeful politics and not necessarily what allies actually do when in such coalitions. Why do I say this? From the position of the dominant body, allies presume that they have "arrived": they have been decolonized and are no longer oppressors. Allies do not centre their own complicities, implications, relative power, or histories of privilege, and they do not look at how these directly and subconsciously inform their own political practices. Allies are also not willing to seriously give up power and privilege so easily. They hang on to their privileges and largely see their part in the struggles as being to "help" someone else, but not themselves. They tend to morally distance themselves from the "bad ones," the oppressors. In the academy, scholarly allies could still insist on dominant theorizing as the hallmark of the true scholar, not realizing that the failure to recognize Black and Indigenous exclusions from theorizing and to challenge what is assumed to constitute theory in academia are themselves crises of intellectual legitimacy.

Critical friends are different. In solidarity work, they are prepared to accept critiques of their own practice and their complicity in oppressions even as they fight in the struggle. They see themselves as part of the problem. Critical friends see themselves as having a greater responsibility to raise the issues and to work for social change and justice. They do not leave it to the oppressed and minoritized. Critical friends start the work by dismantling their own power and privileges. Critical friendship is a mindset that challenges the imperial savior complex (i.e., the "I am going to help them" syndrome). It is a practice that says, "We have to start this" under our leadership and guidance. There is no defensiveness. Critical friends will acknowledge their own complicities and implications in colonial violence using the power of self-determination. Critical friends go out of their way to affirm the legitimacy of Black and Indigenous knowings, philosophies, and perspectives in their own rights as bodies of knowledge. Critical friends do not use Eurocentric lenses to interrogate counter-epistemes. Critical friends acknowledge how ideas have the power to shape political and intellectual practice and serve as the corner-stone under which the individual dignity and collective self-worth of academic scholarship rests.

In our current spaces and geographies, anticolonial work must centre questions of Land, citizenship, and colonization within critical dialogues and practices. Colonialism was not just an interrupter of the Black, racialized, and Indigenous experience. Colonialism means that, as learners, we must continually respond to illegitimate situations and encounters such as racism, sexism, and imperial conquest. For Black, Indigenous, and racialized scholars and learners, we continue to be concerned with problems we have not created ourselves.[35]

In this act of making meanings with our histories and lives, it is critical to remember that knowledge is relational. Black and Indigenous learners are usually under academic scrutiny. But it is productive for us to remember and work with the knowledge that the pursuit of true excellence (both social and academic) will only generate further questions, critiques, and challenges. As we engage in the process of recuperating our devalued and falsely-discredited knowledges, Indigeneity, voice, and experience, it must be remembered: new knowledge should be recovered for pragmatic and subversive—not hegemonic—usage. In effect, while our oppressions may be shared, our individual experiences of these oppressions are unique.

Author's Note

This chapter was initially prepared for two public events: a talk during African Liberation Month, sponsored by the Centre for Integrative Anti-Racism Studies and hosted by the Ontario Institute for Studies in Education, University of Toronto, on March 21, 2018; and the keynote address at the Semi-Annual Spring Conference of the Center for Ethnic Studies at the University of Wisconsin-Parkside on April 5, 2018. I would like to thank the audiences for their comments, which helped strengthen the paper. I also want to acknowledge the comments of Dr. Arlo Kempf. Finally, thanks to Rayshena Vijendran and Alessia Cacciavillani of the University of Toronto for their final read-through.

NOTES

1. The capitalization of *Land* is important as it gestures to a nonanthropocentric meaning. Land is a living thing with its own agencies and subjectivities. This understand departs from the Western understanding, which attributes agency to Land (as well as to Earth, Sea, Sky, and Space) only through *huminitas*.
2. Dei, "Reframing Education."
3. Simpson, "Land as Pedagogy"; Coulthard, *Red Skin, White Masks*; Deloria, "Traditional Technology."
4. See, among many others, Simpson, *Dancing on Our Turtle's Back*; Simpson, "Land as Pegagogy"; Smith, Tuck, and Yang, *Indigenous and Decolonizing Studies*; Styres, "Literacies of Land."
5. For examples, see Simpson, *Dancing on Our Turtle's Back*; Simpson, "Land as Pedagogy." For examples from the African context, see Assié-Lumumba, "Evolving African Attitudes"; Assié-Lumumba, "Harnessing the Empowerment Nexus"; Biraimah, "Moving beyond a Destructive Past"; Ndlovu-Gatsheni, "Decoloniality as the Future."
6. See, among others, Sexton, "Social Life of Social Death"; Sexton, "Unbearable Blackness"; Sexton, "On Black Negativity"; McKittrick, "On Plantations"; McKittrick and Woods, *Black Geographies*; Hudson, "Indigenous & Black Solidarity"; Walcott, *Black Like Who?*; Dumas, "Losing an Arm"; Dumas, "Against the Dark"; Dumas and ross, "Be Real Black"; Adjei, "The (Em)bodiment of Blackness"; Dei, *Reframing Blackness*.
7. Sharpe, *In the Wake*; Dei, *Reframing Blackness*.
8. Césaire, *Discourse on Colonialism*, 9. Césaire noted long ago that colonization is about "thingification," a process that denies Black and African human subjectivity and makes the colonized into slaveable bodies—essentially objects, things without humanity. This process of thingification proceeds along several fronts, culminating in the loss of pride and the development of an inferiority and dependency complex in the colonized.
9. See Oyěwùmí, "Multiculturalism or Multibodism."
10. See Dei, *Anti-Racism Education*.
11. Flores, "Tale of Two Visions," 15.
12. See Leonardo, "The Souls of White Folk"; King, *Black Education*; King, "Anti-Blackness in the Academy."

13. Dei, Karumanchery, and Karumanchery-Luik, *Playing the Race Card*, 91. See also Doyle-Wood, "'Get Out' White Supremacist Projects."
14. Bhabha, *The Location of Culture.*
15. Nyamnjoh, "Potted Plants in Greenhouses."
16. Dei, *Reframing Blackness.*
17. Holmes, *Ancestry of Experience.*
18. Carroll, "Introduction to African-Centered Sociology," 259. See also Adefarakan, "(Re)Conceptualizing 'Indigenous'"; Adefarakan, *The Souls of Yoruba Folk.*
19. Dei, "'Suahunu', the Trialectic Space."
20. Gordon, "Black Issues in Philosophy." See also Dabashi, *Can Non-Europeans Think?*
21. Ani, *Yurugu*; Lynn, "Toward a Critical Race Pedagogy."
22. Hayes, review of Johnson, *Cornell West & Philosophy*, 85.
23. Lynn, "Toward a Critical Race Pedagogy," 610.
24. Wynter, "Towards the Sociogenic Principle."
25. Lynn, "Toward a Critical Race Pedagogy."
26. Perry and Delpit, *Real Ebonics Debate*, 106.
27. See Lynn, "Toward a Critical Race Pedagogy," 608.
28. Ferguson, "C.L.R. James, Marxism," 78.
29. Hayes, review of Johnson, *Cornell West & Philosophy*, 83.
30. Yancy, "Gilbert Haven Jones," 51.
31. Yancy, "Gilbert Haven Jones."
32. Yancy, "Gilbert Haven Jones," 56.
33. Hudson, "Black Indigenous Future."
34. Hudson, "Black Indigenous Future."
35. Biko, *I Write What I Like.*

BIBLIOGRAPHY

Adefarakan, Temitope E. "(Re)Conceptualizing 'Indigenous' from Anti-colonial and Black Feminist Theoretical Perspectives: Living and Imagining Indigeneity Differently." In *Indigenous Philosophies and Critical Education: A Reader,* edited by George J. Sefa Dei, 34–52. New York: Peter Land, 2011.

———. *The Souls of Yoruba Folk: Indigeneity, Race and Critical Spiritual Literacy in the African Diaspora.* New York: Peter Lang, 2015.

Adjei, Paul Banahene. "The (Em)bodiment of Blackness in a Visceral Anti-Black Racism and Ableism Context." *Race and Ethnicity in Education* 21, no. 3 (2018): 1–13.

Ani, Marimba. *Yurugu: An African-Centered Critique of European Cultural Thought and Behavior.* New Jersey: Africa World Press, 1994.

Assié-Lumumba, N'Dri Thérèse. "Evolving African Attitudes to European Education: Resistance, Pervert Effects of the Single System Paradox, and the *Ubuntu* Framework for Renewal." *International Review of Education: Journal of Lifelong Learning* 62 (2016): 1–27.

———. "Harnessing the Empowerment Nexus of Afropolitanism and Higher Education: Purposeful Fusion for Africa's Social Progress in the 21st Century." *Journal of African Transformation* 1, no. 2 (2016): 51–76.

Bhabha, Homi. *The Location of Culture.* London: Routledge, 1994.

Biko, Steve. *I Write What I Like.* New York: Heinemann, 1987.

Biraimah, Karen L. "Moving beyond a Destructive Past to a Decolonised and Inclusive Future: The Role of *Ubuntu*-Style Education in Providing Culturally Relevant Pedagogy for Namibia." *International Review of Education* 62 (2016): 45–62.

Carroll, Karanja Keita. "An Introduction to African-Centered Sociology: Worldview, Epistemology, and Social Theory." *Critical Sociology* 40, no. 2 (2014): 257–70.

Césaire, Aimé. *Discourse on Colonialism*, translated by Joan Pinkham. New York: NYU Press, 2000. First published 1955 in French by Éditions Présence Africaine (Paris).

Coulthard, Glen Sean. *Red Skin, White Masks: Rejecting the Colonial Politics of Recognition*. Minneapolis: University of Minnesota Press, 2014.

Dabashi, Hamid. *Can Non-Europeans Think?* London: Zed Books, 2013.

Dei, George J. Sefa. *Anti-Racism Education in Theory and Practice*. Halifax: Fernwood Publishing, 1996.

———. *Reframing Blackness and Black Solidarities through Anti-Colonial and Decolonial Prisms*. New York: Springer Publishing, 2017.

———. "Reframing Education through Indigenous, Anti-Colonial and Decolonial Prisms." In *The Radical Imagine-Nation*, edited by Peter McLaren and Suzanne Soohoo, 214–35. New York: Peter Lang, 2018.

———. "'Suahunu', The Trialectic Space." *Journal of Black Studies* 43, no. 8 (2012): 823–46.

Dei, George J. Sefa, Leeno Karumanchery, and Nisha Karumanchery-Luik. *Playing the Race Card: Exposing White Power and Privilege*. New York: Peter Lang, 2004.

Deloria, Vine, Jr. "Traditional Technology." In *Power and Place: Indian Education in America*, edited by Vine Deloria Jr. and Daniel Wildcat, 57–66. Golden: Fulcrum Resources, 2001.

Doyle-Wood, Chisani. "'Get Out' White Supremacist Projects: Racialization and Anti-Blackness." Master's thesis, University of Toronto, 2018. TSpace, https://hdl.handle.net/1807/89484.

Dumas, Michael J. "Against the Dark: Antiblackness in Education Policy and Discourse." *Theory into Practice* 55 (2016): 11–19.

———. "'Losing an Arm': Schooling as a Site of Black Suffering." *Race, Ethnicity and Education* 17, no. 1 (2014): 1–29.

Dumas, Michael J., and kihana miraya ross. "'Be Real Black for Me': Imagining BlackCrit in Education." *Urban Education* 51, no. 4 (2016): 415–42.

Ferguson, Steven C. "C.L.R. James, Marxism, and Political Freedom." *APA Newsletters: Newsletter on Philosophy and the Black Experience* 2, no. 2 (2003): 72–82.

Flores, Nelson. "A Tale of Two Visions: Hegemonic Whiteness and Bilingual Education." *Education Policy* 30, no. 1 (2016): 13–38.

Gordon, Lewis. "Black Issues in Philosophy: The African Decolonial Thought of Oyèrónké Oyěwùmí." *Blog of the APA*, May 23, 2018. https://blog.apaonline.org/2018/03/23/black-issues-in-philosophy-the-african-decolonial-thought-of-oyeronke-oyewumi/.

Hayes, Floyd. W., III. Review of *Cornel West and Philosophy: The Quest for Social Justice*, by Clarence Shole Johnson. *APA Newsletters: Newsletter on Philosophy and the Black Experience* 2, no. 2 (2003): 83–85.

Holmes, Leilani. *Ancestry of Experience: A Journey into Hawaiian Ways of Knowing*. Honolulu: University of Hawai'i Press, 2012.

Hudson, Sandra. "Indigenous and Black Solidarity in Practice: #BLMTOTENTCITY." In *New Framings on Anti-Racism and Resistance: Resistance and the New Futurity*, edited by Joanna Newton and Arezou Soltani, 1–16. Rotterdam: Sense Publishers, 2017.

———. "In Search of a Black Indigenous Future: Awakening De/Anti-Colonization." Master's thesis, University of Toronto, 2018. TSpace, https://hdl.handle.net/1807/101596.

King, Joyce E. "Anti-Blackness in the Academy and in Community Activism." Keynote address to Decolonizing Conference, Ontario Institute for Studies in Education, Toronto, ON, November 3–5, 2016.

———. *Black Education: A Transformative Research and Action Agenda for the New Century*. New Jersey: Lawrence Erlbaum Associates Publishers, 2005.

Leonardo, Zeus. "The Souls of White Folk: Critical Pedagogy, Whiteness Studies, and Globalization Discourse." *Race Ethnicity and Education* 5, no. 1 (2002): 1–50.

Lynn, Marvin. "Toward a Critical Race Pedagogy: A Research Note." *Urban Education* 33, no. 5 (1999): 606–26.

McKittrick, Katherine. (2011). "On Plantations, Prisons, and a Black Sense of Place." *Social and Cultural Geography* 12, no. 8 (2011): 947–63.

McKittrick, Katherine, and Clyde Woods, eds. *Black Geographies and the Politics of Place*. Toronto: Between the Lines, 2007.

Ndlovu-Gathsheni, Sabelo J. "Decolonization as the Future of Africa." *History Compass* 13, no. 10 (2015): 485–96.

Nyamnjoh, Francis B. "'Potted Plants in Greenhouses': A Critical Reflection on the Resilience of Colonial Education in Africa." *Journal of Asian and African Studies* 47, no. 2 (2012): 129–54. https://doi.org/10.1177/0021909611417240.

Oyěwùmí, Oyèrónkẹ́. "Multiculturalism or Multibodism: On the Impossible Intersections of Race and Gender in the American White Feminist and Black Nationalist Discourses." *Western Journal of Black Studies* 2, no. 3 (1999): 182–89.

Perry, Theresa, and Lisa Delpit. *The Real Ebonics Debate: Power, Language and the Education of African-American Children*. Boston: Beacon Press, 1998.

Sexton, Jared. "On Black Negativity, or The Affirmation of Nothing: Interview with D. Colucciello Barber." *Society & Space*, September 18, 2017. https://www.societyandspace.org/articles/on-black-negativity-or-the-affirmation-of-nothing.

———. "The Social Life of Social Death: On Afro-Pessimism and Black Optimism." *InTensions Journal* 5 (Fall/Winter 2011): 1–47.

———. "Unbearable Blackness." *Cultural Critique* 90, no. 1 (2015): 159–78.

Sharpe, Christina. *In the Wake: On Blackness and Being*. Durham: Duke University Press, 2016.

Simpson, Leanne. *Dancing on Our Turtle's Back: Stories of Nishnaabeg Re-creation, Resurgence and a New Emergence*. Winnipeg: ARP Books, 2011.

———. "Land as Pedagogy: Nishnaabeg Intelligence and Rebellious Transformation." *Decolonization: Indigeneity, Education & Society* 3, no. 3 (2014): 1–25.

Smith, Linda Tuhiwai, Eve Tuck, and K. Wayne Yang, eds. *Indigenous and Decolonizing Studies in Education: Mapping the Long View*. New York: Routledge, 2019.

Styres, Sandra D. "Literacies of Land: Decolonizing Narratives, Storying, and Literature." In. Smith, Tuck, and Yang, *Indigenous and Decolonizing Studies in Education*, 24–37.

Walcott, Rinaldo. *Black Like Who? Writing Black Canada*. 2nd ed. Toronto: Insomniac Press, 2003.

Wynter, Sylvia. "Towards the Sociogenic Principle: Fanon, Identity, the Puzzle of Conscious Experience, and What It Is Like to Be 'Black'." In *National Identities and Socio-Political Changes in Latin America*, edited by Mercedes F. Durán-Cogan and Antonio Gómez-Moriana, 30–66. New York: Routledge, 2001.

Yancy, George. "Gilbert Haven Jones as an Early Black Philosopher and Educator." *APA Newsletters: Newsletter on Philosophy and the Black Experience* 2, no. 2 (2003): 51–77.

5

LUCY EL-SHERIF
AND MARK SINKE

Some of Us Are More Canadian Than Others

Pedagogies of Citizenship and Learning Racialized Settlerhood

THE CALLS TO ACTION ASSERTED by Canada's 2015 Truth and Reconciliation Commission (TRC) call upon the federal, provincial, territorial, and municipal governments, as well as the parties to the Indian Residential Schools Settlement Agreement and all religious denominations and faith groups, to *"repudiate concepts used to justify European sovereignty over Indigenous lands and peoples* [emphasis added] such as the Doctrine of Discovery and *terra nullius*, and to reform those laws, government policies, and litigation strategies that continue to rely on such concepts."[1]

As highlighted by the TRC's calls, concepts of European sovereignty represent the framework through which white supremacy justifies itself to itself, and its explicit and implicit vestiges remain as organizing principles of Canadian social, economic, political, and cultural life today. In repudiating the concepts used to justify white supremacy, we disturb how white supremacy continues to frame relationships between white and non-white Canadians, and between different non-white Canadian groups, in particular with regard to their relationships to space, place, and land. We unpack how whiteness sets up sociospatial relationships for non-white Canadians, focusing in particular on Muslim Canadians. The word *settler* is often used indiscriminately to describe both white and non-white Canadians whose histories of arrival

81

are not Indigenous to Turtle Island.[2] As a result of this indiscriminate use, the term projects normative notions of belonging to Canada that erase differences in our ways of belonging; we do not all belong in secure and uncontested ways. For example, becoming a settler is a condition of becoming a Canadian citizen. At the same time, the citizenship process attaches different meanings to a person's citizenship based on their race, thereby entwining racialization and colonization together.[3]

Our goal in this chapter is to unsettle the assumption of whiteness in settlerhood, which reinscribes a racial hierarchy. This assumption sets up a normative binary that understands Canadians to be either white settlers or Indigenous people, thus erasing non-white settlers. Canadian settlerhood is constructed on Indigenous land, but it is also constructed on other relationships of oppression—for example slavery, anti-Blackness, war, and orientalism.[4] Thus, being a settler in Canada has different meanings depending on one's race. In this chapter, we trouble normative ideas of Canada and citizenship that understand settlers to all have the same relationship to the nation-state. For all Canadians to take up the TRC's call to "repudiate concepts used to justify European sovereignty over Indigenous lands,"[5] we must foreground the racialized social costs such an oppositional stance carries for non-white Canadians. As we clarify in this chapter, not all settlers have secure relationships to Canada that allow them to object to colonialism without serious consideration of how they are and will be read.

Racialized settlerhood and white settlerhood are neither equivalent nor synonymous. This is clear in the different relationships that we as authors—a Muslimah immigrant woman to Canada and a white Canadian-born male—have to being Canadian. We use race to think through these differing social locations and unpack how racialized settlerhood and white settlerhood are related to nation and land and are internalized in the bodies of racialized and white settlers. By unpacking our different social locations, we race settlerhood and demonstrate that the different ways in which we belong to Canada matter when challenging this colonial present. Our concern is not to excuse non-white Canadians from settler-hood; indeed, we agree that all non-Indigenous, non-Black people on Turtle Island are settlers. Rather, we seek to nuance the ways settler normativity is learned and expressed at the expense of nonnormative citizenship, when both normative and nonnormative Canadian identities depend on Indigenous erasure. We ask, in other words, how it is that we learn a hierarchy of belonging to a place premised on Indigenous removal, erasure, and genocide.

By way of exploring this question, we investigate how the Ottawa Parliament Hill shooting carried out by a Muslim man on October 22, 2014, and the subsequent national grief expressed in the public funeral for the slain white soldier, were representative of the racial configuration of the nation. We argue that state and public responses call forth white and racialized settlerhood. We further argue that the political and social responses to the tragedy teach a message of pervasive settler-colonial domination—a message described by Palestinian writer Mourid Barghouti in the context of the Israeli settler state as "one message all the time and in every way: we are the masters here."[6] Our purpose in focusing on this tragedy is not to argue that this grief was racially motivated, though that may well be true. Rather than unpacking intention, we aim to trace how the public responses to the shooting and the state and public engagement with the funeral worked to educate racially differentiated groups about their place in the social order at an embodied level. We describe this public teaching and learning as "pedagogies of citizenship." We understand pedagogy as relational encounters that seek to alter a person's subjectivity.[7] Citizenship is a "living form of claiming, of being claimed and of feeling within the polity, rather than an act of government conferral."[8] The term *pedagogies of citizenship* represents the intersections of these two ideas. In tracing pedagogies of citizenship, we trace how white and racialized settlerhoods are taught and learned in normative Canadian nationalist practices that may not explicitly refer to Indigeneity at all.

While other tragedies also demonstrate white supremacy and pedagogies of citizenship in Canada—for instance, the 2017 mosque shooting in Québec City—we have chosen to focus on the Parliament Hill tragedy because of the way it illustrates how normative practices of nationalism uphold white supremacy and settler colonialism. The Québec mosque shooting, which was perpetrated by a white Canadian against Muslim Canadians, plays neatly into a national narrative around white supremacy as a problem of a few white-supremacist *individuals*. The shooting on Parliament Hill and the nation's reaction to it, on the other hand, demonstrate the *systemic* nature of Canada's white supremacy problem and its relationship to citizenship and settler identity.

We use a comparative case study approach throughout this chapter to focus on our experiences to understand our respective learnings of October 2014. We therefore follow the leads of Kathleen E. Absolon, Eber Hampton, and Shawn Wilson in acknowledging that the motive and purpose for academic research are necessarily connected to the location of the researcher's self and inform the work from its conception to its completion.[9] We use pedagogies of citizenship to help identify, examine, and understand the differential contours of our positionalities and settler relationships to the Canadian state.

We then historicize the framing of Muslim citizens as Others in Canada. We bring in concepts that help us understand how external social relations are imposed on internal social consciousness, and how social citizenship is always a relational encounter. We bring together these two lines of scholarship to unpack our experiences of the shooting and the funeral procession. By using our inner consciousnesses of our selves in space and in relation to the space around us, we illustrate how pedagogies of citizenship define the options available to Muslim Canadians along a range of subject positions. Significantly, all these subject positions cast Muslim Canadians as Others who are subject to white, Judeo-Christian dominance within Canada. Throughout this chapter, we trace how white supremacy is built on spatial-racial understandings of Canada that simultaneously work to other Muslim Canadians and erase Indigenous land rights—understandings that also work to establish hierarchies of citizenship. We end with a reflection on how white supremacy continues to wreak havoc even within academic discourses that challenge settlerhood.

The Events of October 2014

The national war memorial that stands in Ottawa, Canada's national capital, is a massive bronze and granite structure that has been dedicated to soldiers of Canada's armed forces since it was first erected in 1939. Situated just a few hundred metres from Canada's parliament buildings, it is a destination for the throngs of students and tourists who visit Ottawa daily. As a signifier of national identity that commemorates the battles that Canadians have fought over the last 150 years, the war memorial holds a special place of prominence in the national imaginary.

On Wednesday, October 22, 2014, Corporal Nathan Cirillo was standing ceremonial guard at the National War Memorial and was fatally shot in the back by a then-unknown assailant. The shooter subsequently made his way to the nearby parliament buildings, where Canada's political leaders were in caucus; he was quickly shot and killed by security personnel. Ottawa's downtown core was placed in lockdown while the police searched for co-conspirators, and people across the country sought to understand the developing situation.

The person who committed this attack—Michael Zehaf-Bibeau—was a Canadian citizen who was reportedly struggling with addiction and mental illness.[10] He had converted to Islam ten years prior. As a clearer picture developed about who Zehaf-Bibeau was and what had happened that October morning, members of the public looked to their leaders to help them understand the immense tragedy of the death of Corporal Cirillo and the motivations of Zehaf-Bibeau. Canadian political party leaders began characterizing what the shooting meant along lines consistent with their respective parties' ideologies and in relation to the organizing concept of terrorism.[11] The various leaders attempted to shape public discourses by appealing to tropes of Islamic terror or lone-wolf criminality within the contexts of Canadian multiculturalism and their party perspective. Stephen Harper, prime minister and leader of the Conservative party at the time, described the shooter as a "terrorist" and the attack as a "grim reminder that we are not immune to the types of terrorist attacks we have seen elsewhere around the world."[12] Justin Trudeau, then Liberal party leader, agreed with the RCMP's characterization of the attack as one of terrorism.[13] Tom Mulcair, the left-leaning New Democratic Party leader and leader of the official opposition at the time, described the attack as "an act of hatred and brutality—[a] cowardly act."[14] He later contested describing the event as a "terrorist" attack, but argued that didn't mean it was "any less criminal."[15] The political discourses that prevailed were shaped in relation to the a priori established dominance of the Canadian nation-state that was under attack in some way.[16] The range of meanings ascribed by the state to the Muslim shooter in relation to the killing of the white soldier at the war memorial on Haudenosauneega, Anishinabewaki, Huron-Wendat, and Omamiwininiwak land specifically illustrate our argument in this chapter: that whiteness structures settlerhood for non-Indigenous, non-Black people and produces a differing menu of options for settlers based on their race.

The racialized outsider and enemy have been differently conceived and portrayed in media, histories, and cultural references throughout Canada's history. Military victories over outsider Others are celebrated in monuments and memorials across the country. Originally, the perceived enemy of and dangerous outsider to the settler state was the "savage Native," over whom victory is celebrated through frontier forts.[17] This was progressively followed by perceived victories over other enemies and outsiders throughout history—for example, American republican expansionists in the War of 1812; Métis nationalists under Louis Riel and Gabriel Dumont; Boer citizens of South Africa at the turn of the twentieth century; the imperial expansionists of Germany in the First World War; the fascist axis powers of the Second World War; and Korean and Chinese communists during the Korean War. Most recently, the outsider enemies of the Canadian settler state have been the "covert terrorists" fleeing the Muslim-majority countries of Somalia, Afghanistan, and Syria. We are concerned, here, with this modern incarnation of Canadian identity, constructed in opposition to the Muslim outsider.

As we engage with this story of the Canadian settler state, we choose to focus on the spaces of the war memorial and the state funeral, which belligerently express dominance in the space of the nation. Social relations are produced in part through sets of assumptions about particular geographies (e.g., monuments and funerals)— imaginings that are associated with a particular place and call forth ways of relating to spaces indexed by social and racial markers.[18] Social citizenship can be understood as the social relations inherent in belonging to the nation, and these relations are highlighted in public spectacles that mark out normative, idealized citizens against the violence of an outside, nonnormative citizen.

As we critique this context, however, we ask ourselves: How should we critically engage with the remembrance of a young man's senseless, tragic death? The soldier who was killed was from the authors' city of Hamilton, Ontario. Though we did not know Nathan Cirillo himself, we felt deep personal and collective grief along with many members of our local community. As we write, the significance of his life and death are constantly in our minds. At the same time, we also do the unspeakable: we critique how many characterized the shooter as inhuman. We must not forget that Michael Zehaf-Bibeau was a person who, as his mother described, struggled with mental illness.[19] Public mental health services and social support systems failed him.[20] Engaging with this difficult work, we consider the questions that Audra Simpson asks of herself when examining her own community with important and thoughtful critique: "Can I do this [work of research and writing] and still come home; what am I revealing here and why? Where will this get us?

Who benefits from this and why?"[21] As community members who are also academic researchers, we take a critical stance that seeks to understand how this work can help us relate to the local and broader community in more ethical ways. We also examine how this tragedy was used by the settler state as a pedagogical instrument to further harmful understandings of Canadian citizenship. To do this, we will explicitly position ourselves within our respective roles in relation to the Canadian nation-state.

Positioning the Authors
LUCY AND CANADIAN CITIZENSHIP

I am a Muslimah, white-passing immigrant to Canada with lived experience of being visibly Muslim (i.e., wearing hijab). I am a person for whom state productions of citizenship normativity and in-your-face aggressive nationalism, echoed often in the thirteen years between 2001 and 2014, always evoke the same response: I am not against the national "you," whoever that is—but I will never, ever be with you. I first came to Canada post-9/11 from the United States after the ramifications of that day resulted in threats and a loss of job opportunities for my family, revealing that the aspirational whiteness in which I had been living was an illusion. At that time, Canada was, to me, epitomized in the Arabic song "Baiti El Isgheer" (My Small House) by Lebanese icon Fairuz: "My tiny house in Canada / the horizon is all around us / my door has no key / but I'm not worried."[22] The socioeconomic and political reality sat well with me: Canada took a stand against the war with Iraq and Canadian multiculturalism was far and away better than the 1970s monoculture of Britain, where I had been partly raised.

I began to wear hijab partly as a political protest against being an invisible Muslimah. At first, I did not experience the world any differently; my subjectivity remained intact. However, after a while, when too many experiences did not fit with the world as I had experienced it before, my consciousness changed deeply. From having an expansive sense of space, I went to feeling constricted. From not being conscious of my body unless I wanted to be, I became extremely conscious at all times of its boundaries and what it was doing. Whereas before I was visible as a person and invisible or "stealth" as a Muslimah,[23] now I was often invisible as a person and always hypervisible as a Muslimah.

Significantly, in 2012, after living in Canada for ten years as an untroubled, oblivious settler, I finally understood the similarity between settler colonialism in Canada and Israel. In an instant, everything I knew about settler colonialism in Palestine came to bear on my understanding of my position as a settler on Turtle Island. I began to think more deeply about the similar logics of different systems of oppression. This thinking reflected my process of understanding how racialization works for Black people, which I went through as a white-passing Arab Muslim student in the United States only after I experienced 9/11. Racialization results in dominant society reading the negative acts by one racialized person as a generalizable reflection of the whole community, while positive acts by one racialized person remain specific to that individual. For white people, negative acts by one person are not generalized to the whole community, while positive acts reflect well on white people in general or, more commonly, on a white conception of "humanity."

With hijab, I was out of place in Canada, and processed as lesser: my accent was too good for me; my kids were too cute to be related to me. After some years, I stopped wearing hijab, and the old world came back to me. I could breathe more freely, my consciousness of my body became infinitely smaller, and the places and times where I felt safe expanded exponentially. Ironically, now that I am visible as an individual and no longer a symbol of a faith, I can be as atrocious as I want, and it will only get pegged on me as an individual, not on "all you people."

MARK AND CANADIAN CITIZENSHIP

I was born in Canada as the descendant of European immigrant grandparents who settled in this country after experiencing war and violence in the Netherlands during the Second World War. My hybrid identity as a Dutch-Canadian was partially built upon a conception of Canada as a liberating force for good in the world that welcomed immigrants warmly and openly. Because of these family histories, I developed a dual sense of belonging within the nation both as a child of "hardworking immigrants" and as a potential future "liberator" of others in need. These subjectivities were mapped onto the geographies I freely moved through— schools, museums, Remembrance Day memorials, National Parks, and so on—but hid from me the exclusion and marginalization of Others' bodies and subjectivities. Space was almost always available for me to express myself and feel comfortable. Body consciousness was only required of me if I chose to seek out spaces of marginalization. I am continuing to learn the implications of this exaltation of whiteness that deludes my conceptions of Canadian militarism and multiculturalism, and that requires an exceptionally high cost to maintain. This cost is especially born by Indigenous people whose stories are overwritten with narratives of Canadian settlement and development so that I can presumably belong in Canada without having to engage in any meaningful way with the realities of dispossession and genocide. This reality is not forgotten as we consider in this chapter the exclusion of Muslim bodies from positions of normativity citizenship, precisely because my exaltation in Canadian society requires the denigration of Others who challenge that exaltation with their humanity. When thinking through my experiences of October 2014, I am trying to disentangle the emotional impact of grief and remembrance from the intertwined call to patriotism and continued privileging of white settler subjectivities that leave everybody and every body complicit.

Relationships of Belonging: Space, Place, and Land

If racialized settlerhood has a different relationship of belonging than white settlerhood, how is it that we learn these relationships so differently? And if we want to "repudiate concepts used to justify European sovereignty over Indigenous peoples and lands," as the TRC calls for,[24] how do we identify and unlearn concepts based on *terra nullius* and the Doctrine of Discovery? Here, we highlight seven linked concepts that are helpful in thinking through our relationships to space, place, and land, asserting that these concepts and understandings open up or close down possibilities of subjectivity and meaning. Thinking about these concepts will help us unpack how, precisely, white settlerhood, racialized settlerhood, and their different relationships to belonging are embodied realities.

The first concept, *sovereign/constricted spatiality*, can be defined as an expansiveness/collapsing of subjectivity depending on the relations of power in the spaces where one exists.[25] Literally, figuratively, and physically, a constricted spatiality is often described as a feeling of heaviness on the chest. A tragic, literal example of this is found in the last words uttered by Eric Garner as he was choked to death by police officers in New York City: "I can't breathe."[26] The Black Lives Matter movement found this phrase an apt expression of living in a structurally racist, white-dominated society. By stark contrast, sovereign expansive spatiality can be seen in how European explorer James Cook set out to map and conquer the Pacific: "Not content with the boundaries imposed by gravity, oceans, or ice, Europeans sought possession of all their eyes could see."[27]

To highlight the body further, the second concept, *consciousness of the body's boundaries*, links one's awareness of the previously subconscious movement of one's limbs and body to a recognition of their boundaries, through which one often fumbles.[28] Consider the phenomenon of "man-spreading": how some male subjects take up large amounts of space without considerations for how the boundaries of their bodies impose on the space of others. This contrasts with how female subjects are often raised to be conscious of how they position their limbs.

The third concept, thinking geographically, is *mapping/unmapping*. Mapping explains how particular stories are attached to spaces and places. Unmapping disrupts these stories by revealing other stories attached to the same places that reveal different relations of power.[29] For example, the story of Canada being *terra nullius* until white explorers came to populate it is a story that demonstrates relations of power vis-à-vis the more accurate story: that the Indigenous population was decimated to make way for land grabs.

Fourth, thinking about the body geographically, the concept of *motility/incarceration of the body in space*[30] opens up a question that can be asked about particular bodies: Is this body seen as one that is universally at home anywhere in the world, or as one that is forever discursively emplaced? Consider the contradiction at play in two Canadian experiences: (1) white Canadians being seen as simply Canadian, often regardless of how long they or their family has been in Canada; and (2) Black

Canadians often being asked, "Where are you really from?" Adrienne Shadd, for instance, is asked this question despite being a fifth generation Canadian.[31] The first experience is an example of assumed at-homeness; the second is an example of emplacement. Such experiences of emplacement for people of colour fundamentally shape how they are perceived and limit what they are able to say. This is aptly described by the fifth concept—the *unspeakability of oppositional geographies*[32]—which outlines how expressing one's experience of a place as a minority is an unfathomable opposition to how the dominant group experiences the same place. To speak of these different experiences of place—experiences that directly belie how the dominant group benevolently understands itself—comes with huge social and often material costs. For example, Canada has an idea of itself as a liberal nation, free of structural racism and without a history of slavery. To speak of the ongoing colonization and racism towards Indigenous people in Canada, as Cree member of the opposition Oscar Lathlin in the Manitoba Legislative Assembly did in 1995, is to risk repercussions, such as those Lathlin suffered when he was evicted from the parliament chambers.[33] More recently, the organizers of the Justice for Our Stolen Children camp, a protest against the systemic racism of Saskatchewan's justice and child welfare systems, were arrested, and the camp taken down.[34] This subjugation of which one cannot speak, and which is incomprehensible to those in power, reveals a relation of power that sustains and reproduces itself.

The sixth concept, *uncanny aura of spaces*, proves useful in thinking about our subconscious sense of spatial relations.[35] The ideological aura of a space is the ideology that governs a space through present-absent figures, such as photographs of Elizabeth II in Canadian schools and civic buildings. These images of the Queen provide an ideological haunting of the space with an aura of the sovereign— described as an aura because it is intangible and normalized to many, though it may be extremely visible, corporeal, and material to those who are not in sync with it. The seventh and final concept, *corporeal schema versus racial epidermal schema*,[36] begins to unpack that link between spatial consciousness and representation. By understanding how these schemata work to mark and unmark bodies,[37] we can see the differences between bodies that that are understood to be the actual person present and those that are understood as representations of something insidious. In other words, those experiencing their surroundings through a racial epidermal schema are hypervisible as symbols and less visible as people.

These seven concepts are useful tools for analyzing our experiences of the October 2014 events. We will use them to help us work through the ways these events were pedagogical in nature as they framed and reframed our respective citizenship relationships to the nation. We turn now to unpacking the pedagogical process through which white and racialized settlerhood is learned.

Pedagogies of Citizenship

Pedagogies of citizenship are the relational encounters through which we learn about our social citizenship. These relational encounters of being claimed within or outside of the polity can be traced through differing relationships to Canada imposed on bodies during the events of the Parliament Hill shooting, and those both present and not present at the funeral. From this, a different understanding of relations among "equal" citizens becomes clearer.

The imposition of these social relations is ultimately pedagogical. Following Gaztambide-Fernández and Arráiz Matute, we understand pedagogy to cover varied forms of learning encounters that retain three essential features: they are relational, they are intentional, and they carry an ethical imperative.[38] We engage this understanding of a pedagogical encounter as one where the dominant side of the power relation explicitly seeks to push an altered consciousness on the less dominant side. In the context of the shooting and funeral events, the settler state reveals itself in the blatant narrative of the nation that it pushes—"we are the masters here."[39] When we highlight how learning (non)normative citizenship is fundamentally pedagogical, we are locating the learning in relational encounters—encounters that connect to wider colonial and orientalist patterns, which together make up a symphony of lesser citizenship that is a consistent, cohesive, and coherent message.

The notion of citizenship is often read as the moment of conferral of status by the government to an individual. Audra Simpson, however, describes citizenship as a process, not an event—a constant process of the state imposing its ideology on its citizens.[40] Her work critically highlights that citizenship exists in dialectic relationship, ongoing and relationally constituted between the settler state and the colonized. For us, political and popular responses to events such as the shooting and the funeral reveal who falls within and who falls outside of the polity.

Sunera Thobani argues that the creation of Canada as a nation depended on—and continually depends on—the simultaneous discrimination against and elimination of the Native subject, and the exaltation of a particular Canadian subject and identity. This exaltation is necessary for the formation of a national identity and ethos that is reinscribed in the practices of the nation and its citizens.[41] As Thobani argues, the outsider Other and the insider Self are created simultaneously through dominant discourses of multiculturalism—a view and practice of the good Canadian citizen.[42] In the context of the Parliament Hill shooting, the denigration of the shooter as a symbol of the Muslim outsider occurs at the same time as the exaltation of the fallen soldier as a symbol of the "good Canadian."

Sara Ahmed unpacks how Others, in order to be Others, must first be recognized as such. She argues that this process can happen only because there exists a prior understanding of who is an insider and who is an outsider before the Other is encountered.[43] Capital-O *Other* is an idea of the outsider that is based not on the presence of any particular body but in the mind of the insider. When the insider encounters a new person, they can project Otherness onto this new body to label that person as a stranger and an outsider that is already known prior to their physical arrival. The Other is not a *stranger*, but, as Ahmed demonstrates, *is known to be strange*. The parametres for encounter and relationship are set before the encounter occurs. Thus, when Michael Zehaf-Bibeau shot and killed Nathan Cirillo at the war memorial in Ottawa, his Otherness was already prepared and primed before his arrival, ready to be projected onto him—and projected it was, for example by the politicians whose comments painted him as a terrorist rather than a criminal.

Based on the work of these authors, we trace these relational encounters of ongoing processes of citizenship where white subjects are exalted and invisibilized, and non-white subjects are denigrated and cast into prefigured categories of Otherness. These notions of citizenship are reiterated in multiple ways. Elsewhere, we examine how gaining Canadian citizenship as an immigrant to the country is conditional on swearing allegiance to settler-colonial relations,[44] and how formal schooling educates children towards settler citizenship relationships to the state.[45] All of these overlapping pedagogical experiences shape how settlers and Others understand who belongs as good citizens in Canada. In order to trace these pedagogies of citizenship, we will examine how the citizenship and belonging of Others applied during the events of October 2014. Specifically, we will look at the role that Michael Zehaf-Bibeau stepped into: a Muslim outsider in Canadian society.

Islam as the Other in Canada

In this section, we highlight how colonial and racial relational logics of space and place work in tandem to reject and erase both Canadian Muslims and Indigenous land rights. Entrenching Muslims Otherness can be seen at the institutional level in the story of the Al-Rashid mosque in Edmonton, Alberta. Built in 1938, it was the first purpose-built mosque in Canada. Some fifty years later, a Muslim organization requested to move the mosque within the boundaries of Fort Edmonton Park—a living history museum containing historical structures from different periods of Edmonton's history—during the park's development. The proposed inclusion of the mosque within park boundaries caused a virulent uproar in the media and in public discussions. This uproar was based on the opinion that mosques were part of "other people's cultures" and therefore unsuited to be in a park that was considered to be a "unique expression of our history."[46] The reference to "our history" here implicitly excludes Islam. This metonymic use of Canadian historical authenticity thus slides in for white Judeo-Christianity, revealing how closely related the two are understood to be. In other words, Canada can be seen as essentially Judeo-Christian. From this perspective, the historical mosque was a spatialized anomaly. Objections to its inclusion in the park ejected Muslims from any place of historical longevity in the Canadian landscape and from taking up their normative citizenship rights in establishing places of worship. This contrasts sharply with the understanding afforded to Christian churches built by pioneers, for example.

These disavowals fossilize Muslims as never having had a "real" Canadian presence—a spatialization of race—because the land is imagined as fundamentally belonging to the white Christian settler—a racialization of space. Thus, a historic mosque in Canada is still "other people's cultures,"[47] which means that even if mosques and Muslims are, in fact, a part of Canadian history, some Canadians prefer to erase them from it. And because they are erased from history, mosques are thought to never have had a "real" Canadian presence to begin with. This bizarre circular logic puts Muslims outside Canada, and paints Canada as a non-Muslim space.

All of Canada is built on stolen land, and Edmonton is no exception. It stands on the traditional territory of the Métis, Plains Cree, Woodland Cree, and Tsuu T'ina. Papaschase Cree scholar Dwayne Donald takes up Fort Edmonton Park specifically, interrogating its use as a "historical interpretive park" that is built to demonstrate an understanding of the history of Edmonton.[48] He unpacks how the spatial imaginary of the park, replicated in many other places throughout Canada, is the dominance of one worldview over another, and how forts functioned—and continue to function in their historical remembrance—to convey the separation of Indigenous peoples and Canadians into realms that are physically, temporally, and ontologically binary. These understandings, which position white colonizers as normatively Canadian and Indigenous people as premodern and therefore irrelevant to present-day Canada, demonstrate the public pedagogical function of the park through spatial understandings.

This racialization of space in the historic park—this normative understanding of white, Judeo-Christian, "authentic," "modern," non-Indigenous Canada—was mobilized in opposition to moving the historic mosque. Thus, settler colonialism simultaneously erases Indigeneity and blocks non-White rights, demonstrating Andrea Smith's argument that oppression works in different ways to strengthen white supremacy.[49] This resilient white supremacy multiculturally tolerates Muslims, but responds with a not-in-my-back-yard mentality when they seek to build places of worship even today, with persistent, thinly veiled racist objections to building mosques across Canada.[50] Thinking about how Islam is spatially seen as Other in Canada, when we unpack our individual experiences of Othering and exaltation, we are able to query these experiences in embodied ways. In other words, we ask: How does spatializing Islam as an anomaly in Canada play out on our bodies? In the context of the events of October 2014, the monument and the funeral represent embodied Anglo-Canadian settler dominance and expressions of public pedagogy that work in complementary ways: through the monument, which represents the embodied settler dominance of this land in a static, permanent, etched-in-stone expression of the status quo; and through the funeral, a dynamic and kinetic reassertion of the same settler dominance. In the following sections, we draw from our personal experiences of those days to describe how spatial consciousness was shaped through our embodied experiences as particular types of citizenship were made available to and/or closed off from us.

October 22, 2014: A Monument Attacked and a Soldier Killed
LUCY: STUFFING IN THE UNSPEAKABLE AND REPEATED STORIES THAT
GEOGRAPHICALLY CONFINE AND MAP ME FROM ELSEWHERE

In describing how the Other feels in the space of the nation, Palestinian writer Barghouti says: "He may not rejoice in what makes them happy but he is always afraid when they are afraid. He is always the 'infiltrating element' in demonstrations, even if he never left his house that day."[51] On October 24, 2014, and every time I hear of a shooting or attack, my knee-jerk response is an often unanswered prayer: "Please don't let the perpetrator be Muslim." I scramble to search for any other group I know of that would have similar motivations and tactics—no, it is definitely going to be a Brown or white-passing Muslim male. This uniquely Muslim fear that comes when an attack happens highlights the disjuncture of normative and nonnormative citizenship. In other words, we are all Canadian, but some of us are more Canadian than others.

The first emotion I felt that October day—and the first I feel whenever I hear of an attack—was fear. The second, as always, was the need to shut up. I was thinking unspeakable things, along the lines of Sheila Dawn Gill's unspeakability of oppositional geographies.[52] I was thinking that the attack did not come out of nowhere; rather, it was inextricably linked to a political context. It was unspeakable to posit that there are actual political reasons some Muslim youths sometimes seek to disrupt current political orders. It was unspeakable to name Canada as one of those orders whose racism is hidden under a thin veneer of multiculturalism—where talk of Black Lives Matter Toronto is met with incredulity because "Canada is not like the US," and supporting Palestine is frequently seen as toeing a line of illegality. When and if spoken, these things risk positioning one as an ungrateful immigrant, if not as being entirely unintelligible. And so, similar to 9/11 and countless times since, I stuffed in what needs to be said.

With every attack I wonder: Why is it that the West reads Christianity as a universal religion while Islam is seen as a Middle Eastern one, although both originated in the Middle East? Races or religions that can be incarcerated in space, as Radhika Mohanram explains, stand in stark contrast to the motility of being White.[53] For while Muslims are linked to the Middle East despite the majority of world's Muslims living in Asia, and Black people are linked to Africa despite generations of presence in North America, being White is seen as being at home in vast swaths of the globe, including in places to which they historically immigrated as settlers.[54] It was almost impossible for me to point out the contradictions in "defences" of Muslims that insisted we are good for Canada and guarded against generalizing this terrorist act to all Muslims—defences like the one the Liberal Party leader at the time, Justin Trudeau, offered with great magnanimity. Mapping attaches particular stories to particular spaces.[55] It allows us to see not only how outright racism clearly positions Muslims as Others in Canada, but also how defending Muslims as "good for Canada" similarly maps them as being from elsewhere. To understand the attack as an act of terrorism and not just of criminality, both those who attack and those who defend Muslims are taking up the same racial-spatial story and map of Canada, and both reproduce similar relational positions for Muslims.[56] We are Canadian, but we don't belong here. The soldier and the shooter had geographic stories attached to them, too: the soldier was a son of Hamilton defending the nation; the shooter was a Muslim outsider attacking the nation. Each of those stories is attached to place.

MARK: THE MOTILITY AND AURA OF MONUMENTS

I had just gotten off the commuter bus in downtown Toronto and was walking up University Avenue towards the University of Toronto when I checked my phone and read about the events that were happening in real time in Canada's capital city. The first news reports were focused on the chaos of the unknown situation that was developing in Ottawa as stories came in about shots being fired near the National War Memorial, and then on Parliament Hill. As I followed the story, I noticed once again the monuments that line University Avenue: The Sons of England Memorial, the Canadian Airmen Memorial, and the South African War Memorial. Set up to remind Canadians about the empire that Canada was a part of and the many battles in which Canadian soldiers have fought, the presence of these monuments along my journey forced an altering of my own relationship to them on that specific day, when a similar monument in Ottawa was the site of violence and death. The pedagogical nature of these memorials was forcefully applied to me, as their century-long permanence in that space demonstrated that Canada remembers its colonial past and celebrates it, even when the brutal realities of concentration camps and war crimes perpetrated by soldiers of the British Empire later came to light.[57] In describing the embodiment of monuments with a psychological persona, Derek Hook analyzes how monuments call forth particular subjectivities.[58] Hook draws on Marxist philosopher Henri Lefebvre to understand how a space can embody the personification of a nation, tracing how linguistic tools such as metonymy and metaphor are used in the imbrication of monuments with a national persona.[59] Regarding metonymy, I noticed the materials used in the construction of the many monuments that I passed. Granite and bronze were taken from the ground and reshaped to illustrate colonial power. Along University Avenue, as in Ottawa, these materials have been formed into prominent structures and feature the carved names of the soldiers who died defending the settler state. Regarding metaphoric substitution, Hook identifies two forms of "monumental embodiment": "the literal embodiment of substance, that is, the stand in substitution of a piece of stone for the land, or, for a political order 'intrinsic' to it, and the figurative embodiment of form, the poetic reference, in a figure of colossal stone and the political system that this figure is thought to epitomize."[60] The monument in Ottawa, and others throughout Canada, are the empirical examples of this as spatial examples of empire that are always in interplay with the consciousness of those who visit them.

October 28, 2014: Witnessing a Procession of National Mourning

The attack that occurred at the War Memorial held specific significance for many Canadians, both because it was an attack against a soldier and because it represented an attack on an aspect of Canadian consciousness that is held in high regard as sacred to the nation-state. The soldier was guarding a monument to fallen soldiers that must always be present in our minds. In effect, the shooting became an echo of what the monument stood for. Precisely because the shooting was a disjunctive return of a history that was not supposed to happen, this provoked a national anxiety[61] that was reflected in the heightened security around the subsequent funeral procession—another reminder to normative and nonnormative citizens alike of just who is the master here.

MARK ATTENDING THE FUNERAL PROCESSION: BODY CONSCIOUSNESS IN RESPONSE TO THE EXPLICIT MAPPING OF SOVEREIGNTY INTO MY COMMUNITY

The funeral procession was an astounding affair. I stood outside First Ontario Place, a large municipal arena in Hamilton, and waited with thousands of other people along the sidewalks on either side of the street. Police officers were nearby, watching the crowd and wearing bright yellow reflective vests. Others were watching the crowd as well, and when I looked up at the top of the buildings around me, I saw something that I have never witnessed in my years of living in this neighbourhood: military snipers with scoped weapons at several positions along the nearby rooftops. This was not an ordinary funeral, and this point struck me as I saw the weapons ready, if needed, to kill someone around me. Who were they looking for? Would they think that I am suspicious? I was standing beside a local church pastor who was waving a large Canadian flag. Maybe the snipers would mark my body as patriotic alongside this flag-waver?

The space around me changed when I noticed those snipers, and my body consciousness was altered in response. After some time, the procession itself arrived. I could hear it before I could see it: the uncanny aura of the drums and bagpipes that reached my ears from down Bay Street. When the head of the procession turned the corner and came into view, I saw the uniformed and kilted members of the Argyll and Sutherland Highlanders Regiment of the soldier who had been killed, followed by that fixture of Canadian parades: the pipe band. Pipe bands reestablish the importance of early Scottish settlers to the nation's history as a ghost of the past perpetually informing the present. I had already seen many parades like this before at public events throughout Canada and, because I lived around the corner from this particular regiment's armory, I was accustomed to the Scottish symbols that are part of their uniform. It is not without meaning that the explicit symbolism of Scottish settlers was foregrounded in this funeral procession across the traditional land of the Haudenosaunee and Anishinaabe Nations (where the city of Hamilton now sits). Following the pipe band was a large military vehicle pulling a Second World War gun carriage behind it; on this gun carriage was the flag-draped coffin of Nathan Cirillo. Close behind were family members and a white-robed member of the Anglican clergy. The procession continued for about forty minutes, with many more uniformed soldiers, veterans wearing medals from earlier wars, and young cadets from the army, navy, and air force. Surprisingly, then came members of the red-clad RCMP, followed by rows of police officers and firefighters. It occurred to me at that moment that this was a procession of the uniformed civil service, expressing solidarity with the symbols of Canadian settler identity. I, as a community member, came to grieve with others struck by the death of this local man, but was instead confronted with a procession of power and strength.

LUCY WATCHING THE FUNERAL PROCESSION: UNCANNY AURA AND MY CONSTRICTED SPATIALITY

That day, I decided to watch the funeral on the live stream of the CBC, Canada's public broadcaster. CBC is my default Canadian channel because I find public television more progressive than other Canadian options—less neoliberal and consumerist. So, that day, I did not think twice about where to watch the live stream. In doing so, I experienced the funeral through the same medium as millions of other Canadians: television, or, more specifically, a curated view of events mediated through state channels and offering less sensory experience than being there in person. What I, the hundreds of Hamiltonians in the sports arena who gathered to watch the live stream collectively, and millions of Canadians watching around the country saw was a mix of aerial footage and close-ups of people lining the streets. The aerial shots highlighted how long the procession was, and how many people had come out to pay their respects. We heard the brief comments by the newscasters, who explained the symbolism of what we were seeing: who the Argyles were, who the bagpipe players were, what their caps meant, the signification of their arm positions behind their backs, and other things that were not familiar to me, or likely to many Canadians. The broadcast had little commentary, and the long silences underscored the tragedy and gravity of the shooting. In its curation of what we as viewers saw, and in having such brief commentary, the CBC projected the message the state wanted to convey in uncomplicated ways and broadened the extension of state power.

Above all, what I saw conveyed state power everywhere. State power shut down traffic and work in the Hamilton downtown core and state power kept the people lining the streets in check. The whole scene was that of a city that had been familiar to me for the past twelve years made alien, its normalized and therefore implicit power made explicit and hard to ignore. It was "one message all the time and in every way: we are the masters here."[62] I noticed how the assumed subjectivity of the fallen sentry aligned perfectly with the subjectivity of the state. Would the state have lavished such honour on the soldier had he been Muslim? Would it have held a state funeral in a mosque, or played another instrument not so explicitly Scottish? My identity as a Muslimah Canadian citizen of Arab origin stood in stark contrast to the explicit and normalized Scottish and Christian nature of the funeral projected by the state and amplified in uncomplicated ways.

Downtown Hamilton had an uncanny aura that day, both in its ideological interpellation and its support of the fallen soldier, not as a person but as a symbol; it was not a space for nonnormative citizens like me. I thought of wearing hijab and going, but decided against it. The range of meanings available to me did not include any I wanted to engage with. I could be interpreted as an antagonistic Muslimah, daring to show her face there when she and "her people" are responsible for all this pain and public grief. Or as an apologetic Muslimah, who felt the shooting was tragic and was going to pay respects that were particularly significant coming from someone who was one of "all those people." Or as a loyal Canadian Muslimah, symbolizing Muslim opposition to "terrorism." I could have gone as a white-passing, invisible Muslimah, with no hijab. All of those options felt untrue and fraudulent in one way or another. Had I gone, I likely would have stuffed in what I wanted to say, as I had done in the United States post-9/11—an experience reminiscent of Kathleen M. Kirby's constricted spatiality, which manifests as a very physical, constricted breathing.[63]

I am struck by how I have the privilege to slide between different schemata. On the one hand, when I don't wear a hijab and am white-passing, there's Fanon's corporeal schema in which my consciousness is based on being seen as an individual.[64] On the other hand, when I wear hijab, I am seen through a racial faith schema in which my spatial consciousness is based on being seen through the lens of stories such as this shooting, particularly at the funeral. I felt sad and weary watching the footage and after a while turned it off. Mark and I later talked about our respective experiences. Mark remarked that it was ironic that, although I am Canadian, and Hamilton is my city, I still felt safest not going. I might have had a richer narrative to relay here if I had gone, visibly Muslim or not. But the reasons I felt I could not go also speak to how experiencing the reaction to the shooting at the monument and the subsequent funeral is a response to the one didactic message "all the time and in every way" threading through all state pedagogy that we experience: the message of who, exactly, is master here. For better or for worse, I experienced the procession through the CBC—an experience that gives insight into how spatial consciousness is projected through the media, vastly beyond the people who were there that day.

◀ ▶

Our goal in this chapter has been twofold. We have troubled the notion of whiteness inherent and yet erased in understandings of settlerhood, and we concurrently traced how racialized settlerhood is learned through relationships with space, place, land, and nation—relationships that come to embody subjectivities. Our point of departure was that citizenship, or our relation to nation, frames our settlerhood on this land. Our experiences map out how differences between white settlerhood and racialized settlerhood were apparent in the events of October 2014, and how we are educated on these different citizenships through pedagogical productions of the state. We resisted this by unpacking how white supremacy and racial-spatial understandings of Canada are predicated on the dominance of white settler spatial subjectivity on Turtle Island, taught and reinforced through national monuments and moments of pedagogical reinscription.

We want to highlight again how white settlerhood and racialized settlerhood are not identical, interchangeable, or synonymous, and how the items on the menu of options and possibilities available to white settlers are not all available for racialized settlers. We argue that erasing, conflating, and invisibilizing whiteness in settlerhood reinscribes white supremacy at the expense of people of colour in the short term, and results in a more resilient settler colonialism against Indigenous people in the long term—for if racialized settlers are unable to take up oppositional positions to the state, then they are positioned in dominant multicultural discourses as alibis for the ongoing tolerance of the colonial structure and permission to maintain the status quo.

Throughout this chapter, we have uncovered patterns of spatializing Islam as an Other in Canada on the basis of colonized land. We focused on tracing how the War Memorial, standing in Ottawa on unceded traditional territory of the Algonquin peoples, worked to identify the shooter as a Muslim Other, built on an understanding of the national monument as white Judeo-Christian Canadian authenticity. We are produced through spatial relations as subjects in the nation. Even in an era of "reconciliation," maintaining a national identity in the face of a Muslim Other is maintaining a national identity that is colonial and white. In responding to the TRC calls to action that repudiate concepts of European sovereignty over Indigenous peoples, we urge ourselves and others to also consider how these European concepts insidiously work at establishing Judeo-Christian Anglo dominance over racialized people, and how concepts of white supremacy structure belonging in ways that makes our settlerhoods very different.

Authors' Note

Originally published in a slightly different form as "One Message, All the Time and in Every Way: Spatial Subjectivities and Pedagogies of Citizenship," *Curriculum Inquiry* 48, no. 1 (2018): 35–52, https://doi.org/10.1080/03626784.2017.1409590. Copyright © The Ontario Institute for Studies in Education, University of Toronto, adapted and reprinted with permission from Taylor & Francis Ltd., http://www.tandfonline.com, on behalf of The Ontario Institute for Studies in Education, University of Toronto.

NOTES

1. *Truth and Reconciliation Commission of Canada: Calls to Action*, call 47; see also calls 45.i, 46.ii, and 49. Hereafter cited as TRC calls.
2. Throughout our chapter, we use the name *Turtle Island* to refer to this land, honouring Anishinaabe, Haudenosaunee, and Lenape terms in referring to this land, in contradistinction to Canada, the settler nation state.
3. El-Sherif, "Webs of Relationships."
4. A. Smith, *Heteropatriarchy*.
5. TRC call 47.
6. Barghouti, *I Saw Ramallah*, 141.
7. Gaztambide-Fernández and Matute, "Pushing Against."
8. Simpson, *Mohawk Interruptus*, 43.
9. Absolon, *Kaandossiwin*; Hampton, "Memory Comes Before Knowledge"; Wilson, *Research Is Ceremony*.
10. Friscolanti, "Uncovering a Killer."
11. We recognize that *terrorism* is a heavily contested term. We draw a distinction between *terrorism* and *criminality* here. When dominant society attributes an illegal act to an individual, the act is criminal. When it reads a perpetrator's intent as political or social, the act is one of terrorism. Significantly, the way in which perpetrator intent is read by dominant society falls along racial lines. For example, Alexandre Bissonnette, the Québec mosque shooter who killed six worshippers and injured nineteen others, was charged by the Canadian government as a criminal, not a terrorist. This difference has significant, material consequences. For instance, the victims of that shooting did not receive state compensation because of how Bissonnette was charged.
12. Harper, "PM Speaks," at 1:28.
13. Trudeau, "Liberal Leader Speaks."
14. Mulcair, "Opposition Speaks," transcript para. 1.
15. J. Smith, "Ottawa Shooting Not Terrorism," para. 9.
16. See Gollom, "Ottawa Attack."
17. See Donald, "Forts, Curriculum."
18. Lefebvre, *The Production of Space*.
19. Friscolanti, "Uncovering a Killer."
20. Paperny, "Ottawa Gunman."
21. Simpson, *Mohawk Interruptus*, 111.
22. Fairuz, "Baiti El Isgheer," single, Planet of Performers Production Company, 2005. Our translation.
23. Alsultany, "Stealth Muslim."
24. TRC call 47.
25. Kirby, *Indifferent Boundaries*.
26. Baker, Goodman, and Mueller, "Beyond the Chokehold."
27. Byrd, *The Transit of Empire*, 2.
28. Kirby, *Indifferent Boundaries*.
29. Kirby, *Indifferent Boundaries*.
30. Mohanram, *Black Body*.
31. James and Shadd, *Talking About Identity*, 10.
32. Gill, "The Unspeakability of Racism."
33. Oscar Lathlin, a Cree member of the opposition in the Manitoba Provincial Parliament, was evicted from the parliament chambers when he described the provincial government's policies

towards Indigenous people as systemic racism. For more on this incident, see Gill, "The Unspeakability of Racism."

34. The Justice for Our Stolen Children camp set up on February 28, 2018, to protest the acquittals of those accused of the murders of Tina Fontaine and Colten Boushie, as well as, more broadly, the systemic racism of the justice and child welfare systems against Indigenous children. In June that year, the organizers were arrested and the camp taken down, but protesters set up a larger camp later. The camp was permanently taken down in September after a court order. For a rich recap of the camp events, see Harder, "Thoughts and Images"; see also Regina Leader-Post, "A Look Back."

35. Hook, "Monumental Space."

36. Fanon, *Black Skin, White Masks*.

37. Mohanram, *Black Body*.

38. Gaztambide-Fernández and Matute, "Pushing Against."

39. Barghouti, *I Saw Ramallah*, 141.

40. Simpson, *Mohawk Interruptus*.

41. Thobani, *Exalted Subjects*.

42. Thobani, *Exalted Subjects*. Canadian multiculturalism discourse has been thoroughly critiqued by Thobani and others, as mainstream multiculturalism performs a double move of presenting Canadian subjects as liberal, tolerant, and welcoming while absorbing Indigenous identity into a larger, undifferentiated milieu that is disconnected from land and territory. See also Bannerji, *The Dark Side of the Nation*; Parekh, *Rethinking Multiculturalism*.

43. Ahmed, *Strange Encounters*.

44. El-Sherif, "Webs of Relationships."

45. Sinke, "Learning to Settle."

46. "West Waiver Wrong," 10. See also Karim, "Crescent Dawn," 267.

47. Karim, "Crescent Dawn," 267.

48. Donald, "Forts, Curriculum."

49. A. Smith, "Heteropatriarchy."

50. Isin and Siemiatycki, "Making Space for Mosques."

51. Barghouti, *I Saw Ramallah*, 3.

52. Gill, "The Unspeakability of Racism."

53. Mohanram, *Black Body*.

54. Mohanram, *Black Body*.

55. Razack, *Race, Space, and the Law*.

56. Leader of the opposition Justin Trudeau's exact words on October 22, 2014 were: "Canadians know that acts such as this committed in the name of Islam are an aberration of your faith. Continued mutual cooperation and respect will help prevent the influence of distorted ideological propaganda posing as religion. We will walk forward together not apart." Trudeau, "Liberal Leader Speaks," at 4:23.

57. Boje, *An Imperfect Occupation*.

58. Hook, "Monumental Space."

59. Lefebvre, *The Production of Space*.

60. Hook, "Monumental Space," 696.

61. Hook, "Monumental Space," 696.

62. Barghouti, *I Saw Ramallah*, 141.

63. Kirby, *Indifferent Boundaries*.

64. Fanon, *Black Skin, White Masks*.

BIBLIOGRAPHY

Absolon, Kathleen E. [minogiizhigokwe]. *Kaandossiwin: How We Come to Know*. Winnipeg: Fernwood Publishing, 2011.

Ahmed, Sara. *Strange Encounters: Embodied Others in Post-Coloniality*. London: Routledge, 2000.

Alsultany, Evelyn. "Stealth Muslim." In *Arab & Arab American Feminisms: Gender, Violence, and Belonging*, edited by Rabab Ibrahim Abdulhadi, Evelyn Alsultany, and Nadine Naber, 307–14. Syracuse: Syracuse University Press, 2011.

Baker, Al, J. David Goodman, and Benjamin Mueller. "Beyond the Chokehold: The Path to Eric Garner's Death." *New York Times*, June 13, 2015. https://www.nytimes.com/2015/06/14/nyregion/eric-garner-police-chokehold-staten-island.html.

Bannerji, Himani. *The Dark Side of the Nation: Essays on Multiculturalism, Nationalism, and Gender*. Toronto: Canadian Scholars' Press, 2000.

Barghouti, Mourid. *I Saw Ramallah*. Translated by Ahdaf Soueif. Cairo: American University in Cairo Press, 2002. First published 1974 in Arabic by Dar Al-Hilal (Cairo).

Boje, John. *An Imperfect Occupation: Enduring the South African War*. Urbana: University of Illinois Press, 2015.

Byrd, Jodi A. *The Transit of Empire: Indigenous Critiques of Colonialism*. Minneapolis: University of Minnesota Press, 2011.

Donald, Dwayne. "Forts, Curriculum, and Indigenous Métissage: Imagining Decolonization of Aboriginal-Canadian Relations in Educational Contexts." *First Nations Perspectives* 2, no. 1 (2009): 1–24.

El-Sherif, Lucy. "Webs of Relationships: Pedagogies of Citizenship and Modalities of Settlement for 'Muslims' in Canada." *Lateral* 8, no. 1 (Fall 2019): n.p. https://doi.org/10.25158/L8.2.2.

Fanon, Frantz. *Black Skin, White Masks*. Translated by Richard Philcox. New York: Grove Press, 2008. First published 1952 in French by Éditions de Seuil (Paris).

Friscolanti, Michael. "Uncovering a Killer: Addict, Drifter, Walking Contradiction." *Maclean's*, October 30, 2014. http://www.macleans.ca/news/canada/michael-zehaf-bibeau-addict-drifter-walking-contradiction/.

Gaztambide-Fernández, Rubén A., and Alexandra Arráiz Matute. "Pushing Against." In *Problematizing Public Pedagogy*, edited by Jake Burdick, Jennifer A. Sandlin, and Michael P. O'Malley, 52–64. New York: Routledge, 2013.

Gill, Sheila Dawn. "The Unspeakability of Racism." In Razack, *Race, Space, and the Law*, 157–84.

Gollom, Mark. "Ottawa Attack: Was Michael Zehaf-Bibeau's Attack a Terrorist Act." *CBC News*, October 30, 2014. https://www.cbc.ca/news/canada/ottawa-attack-was-michael-zehaf-bibeau-s-attack-a-terrorist-act-1.2818329.

Hampton, Eber. "Memory Comes Before Knowledge: Research May Improve if Researchers Remember Their Motives." *Canadian Journal of Native Education* 21 (1995 supplement): 46–54.

Harder, Brandon. "Thoughts and Images: The Final Moments of the Justice for Our Stolen Children Camp." *Regina Leader-Post*, September 17, 2018. https://leaderpost.com/feature/thoughts-and-images-the-final-moments-of-the-justice-for-our-stolen-children-camp.

Harper, Stephen. "PM Speaks on Ottawa Shooting." Raw video from Stephen Harper. Recorded October 22, 2014. CBC News video and transcript, 6:56. https://www.cbc.ca/news/politics/ottawa-shooting-harper-mulcair-trudeau-speak-about-attack-1.2809530.

Hook, Derek. "Monumental Space and the Uncanny." *Geoforum* 36, no. 6 (November, 2005): 688–704.

Isin, Engin F., and Myer Siemiatycki. "Making Space for Mosques: Struggles for Urban Citizenship in Diasporic Toronto." In Razack, *Race, Space, and the Law*, 185–209.

James, Carl E., and Adrienne Lynn Shadd, eds. *Talking About Identity: Encounters in Race, Ethnicity and Language*. Toronto: Between the Lines, 2001.

Karim, H. Karim. "Crescent Dawn in the Great White North: Muslim Participation in the Canadian Public Sphere." In *Muslims in the West: From Sojourners to Citizens*, edited by Yvonne Yazbeck Haddad, 262–77. New York: Oxford University Press, 2002.

Kirby, Kathleen M. *Indifferent Boundaries: Spatial Concepts of Human Subjectivity*. New York: Guilford Press, 1996.

Lefebvre, Henri. *The Production of Space*. Translated by Donald Nicholson-Smith. Malden: Blackwell, 1991. First published 1974 in French by Éditions Anthropos (Paris).

Mohanram, Radhika. *Black Body: Women, Colonialism, and Space*. Minneapolis: University of Minnesota Press, 1999.

Mulcair, Tom. "Opposition Speaks about Ottawa Shooting." Raw video from Tom Mulcair. Recorded October 22, 2014. CBC News video and transcript, 5:38. https://www.cbc.ca/news/politics/ottawa-shooting-harper-mulcair-trudeau-speak-about-attack-1.2809530.

Paperny, Anna Mehler. "Why didn't Ottawa Gunman Zehaf-Bibeau Get Treatment 3 Years Ago?" *Global News*, October 30, 2014. http://globalnews.ca/news/1639555/why-didnt-ottawa-gunman-zehaf-bibeau-get-treatment-3-years-ago.

Parekh, Bhikhu. *Rethinking Multiculturalism*. Cambridge: Harvard University Press, 2002.

Razack, Sherene, ed. *Race, Space, and the Law: Unmapping a White Settler Society*. Toronto: Between the Lines, 2002.

Regina Leader-Post. "A Look Back at the Past 197 Days of the Justice For Our Stolen Children Camp." *Regina Leader-Post*, September 12, 2018. https://leaderpost.com/news/local-news/a-look-back-on-the-past-197-days-of-the-justice-for-our-stolen-children-protest-camp.

Simpson, Audra. *Mohawk Interruptus: Political Life across the Borders of Settler States*. Raleigh: Duke University Press, 2014.

Sinke, Mark. "Learning to Settle: Young Student Experiences Learning Indigenous and Canadian Histories in the Figured Worlds of Social Studies Classrooms." PhD diss., University of Toronto, 2020. ProQuest, no. 27994614.

Smith, Andrea. "Heteropatriarchy and the Three Pillars of White Supremacy: Rethinking Women of Color Organizing," in *Color of Violence: The Incite! Anthology*, ed. Incite! Women of Color Against Violence, 65–74. Durham: Duke University Press, 2006.

Smith, Joanna. "Ottawa Shooting Not Terrorism, Says Thomas Mulcair." *Toronto Star: Halifax Edition*, October 29, 2014. https://www.thestar.com/news/canada/2014/10/29/ottawa_shooting_not_terrorism_says_thomas_mulcair.html.

Thobani, Sunera. *Exalted Subjects: Studies in the Making of Race and Nation in Canada*. Toronto: University of Toronto Press, 2007.

Trudeau, Justin. "Liberal Leader Speaks about Ottawa Shooting." Raw video from Justin Trudeau. Recorded October 22, 2014. CBC News video and transcript, https://www.cbc.ca/news/politics/ottawa-shooting-harper-mulcair-trudeau-speak-about-attack-1.2809530.

Truth and Reconciliation Commission of Canada. *Truth and Reconciliation Commission of Canada: Calls to Action*. Winnipeg: National Centre for Truth and Reconciliation, 2015. https://ehprnh2mwo3.exactdn.com/wp-content/uploads/2021/01/Calls_to_Action_English2.pdf.

"West Waiver Wrong." *Edmonton Sun*, June 16, 1989.

Wilson, Shawn. *Research Is Ceremony: Indigenous Research Methods*. Halifax: Fernwood Publishing, 2009.

6

RACHEL YACAA?AŁ
GEORGE

The Performativity
of Reconciliation

Illusory Justice and
the Site C Dam

Change. It's a funny feeling, to empty yourself into efforts towards
the elusive. It's an even funnier feeling when those efforts have been
towards elusive justice. Justice. Not materials, not dreams, not a larger
bank statement, not trinkets, nor personal ventures, but Justice. When
you believe that the right will always prevail and time and time again
it does not happen, you feel a twisting in your chest. A wrestling of the
heart trying not to give up on itself.
> —Helen Knott (Prophet River First Nation),
> "Women, Water, Land: Writing from the Intersections."

As the Truth and Reconciliation Commission of Canada (TRC) wrapped up its
six-year investigation into Indian Residential Schools in 2015 and the country
grappled with its final report and calls to action, it seemed that we were reaching
the height of feel-good reconciliation. One could even go so far as to say that
certain sectors of Canadian society had become obsessed with reconciliation. In
attempting to secure a reconciled state, reconciliation was almost obsessively noted
in ministerial mandate letters, campaign promises, the creation of the Ministry of

Indigenous Relations and Reconciliation in British Columbia, funding packages, Reconciliation Framework Agreements,[1] various arts endeavours, and the list goes on. Reconciliation became a central component of Justin Trudeau's campaign in 2015, and once elected he affirmed this commitment by noting that "no relationship is more important to our government and to Canada than the one with Indigenous peoples."[2] And yet, reconciliation has often been enacted in troubling ways and along uneven lines. Premised on righting relationships, reconciliation in this landscape has frequently been imagined in various state efforts to "close the gap" for Indigenous peoples with improved programs and services. At the same time, despite having fully endorsed the United Nations Declaration on the Rights of Indigenous Peoples (UNDRIP) in 2016 and recently passing Bill C-15, the UNDRIP Act, in 2021, Canada has continued to actively assert its assumed authority over Indigenous lands, waters, and peoples by approving various extractive and exploitative natural resource projects such as the Site C Dam in British Columbia, and violently removing Matriarchs and Indigenous Land Defenders who stand up against this extraction and the invasion of sovereign lands.[3]

Generations of Indigenous activism have connected Indigenous calls for justice with self-determination in all spheres of life, including our relationships with the physical places we call home. The long road to UNDRIP and its implementation is one testament to this. Yet, within the current reconciliation discourse, Indigenous understandings of self-determination as well as our relationships and responsibilities to our territories are often deemphasized or ignored entirely in favour of narrow constructions of justice meted out by and through the state. This upholds the continued neoliberalization of the environment at the expense of complex and vital relationships between Indigenous peoples and their homelands. Woven within this process are the various moves by the settler-colonial state to remake Native lands and waters. This occurs both in the ways that settler-colonial states have laid claims to our territories—through *terra nullius* and the Doctrine of Discovery—and the ways they mark specific places for economic benefit despite the relationships that precede them in those spaces. Settler-colonial violence in our homelands has persisted in the form of what Traci Brynne Voyles termed "wastelanding": a fully colonial process that renders nature extractable, and Indigenous land/seascapes and bodies pollutable and disposable.[4] Yet, due to the intimate and intricate relationships we as Indigenous peoples maintain with our territories—relationships that inform our epistemologies and ontologies—the process of wastelanding also renders our knowledges, like our physical spaces, pollutable and disposable.

While calls for reconciliation have carved out new space for the centring of Indigenous knowledge, particularly in education, we must deeply trouble this in light of concurrency. As settler-colonial violence persists, what does it mean to create space for Indigenous knowledge but not to take its authority and the breadth of our relationality seriously? When Indigenous knowledge is considered dispensable, and Indigenous bodies, lands, and waters are considered disposable, how does reconciliation move towards establishing a "respectful and healthy relationship"?[5] Through an exploration of reconciliation rhetoric around the Site C Dam in British Columbia, this chapter traces settler-colonial society's selective engagement with Indigenous knowledge and authority. I argue that reconciliation and justice cannot be rooted in the performative inclusion of Indigenous knowledge, but instead must manifest in tangible actions that honour and respect Indigenous knowledge, authority, and self-determination.

Trajectories of Reconciliation

Settler-colonial engagement with reconciliation in Canada has seemed to ebb and flow over the years, reaching a peak following the conclusion of the TRC. The affirmation of Indigenous rights in the 1982 Constitution Act marked the beginning of the nation's considerations of reconciliation. Although broadly conceived, section 35 placed a new burden on the federal government and the judiciary to accommodate and respect Indigenous rights and title within their decision-making processes. Despite this, various "successful" Supreme Court rulings for Indigenous peoples have affirmed the fundamentally colonial premise that inherent Indigenous rights "can only exist as long they can be *reconciled with* Crown sovereignty."[6] As a result, Indigenous nations are continually asked to reconcile themselves with the supposed primacy and authority of the Canadian state. In particular, as D'Arcy Vermette argues, the use of reconciliation by the judiciary "illustrates [its] arbitrariness... and the unwillingness of the Court to compromise its colonial mentality"[7] as each particular version of reconciliation employed since the 1990 *R v. Sparrow*[8] decision has sought to restrict Indigenous rights in subtle yet devastating ways.[9]

In the public sphere, considerations of reconciliation were set in motion when the 1996 Royal Commission on Aboriginal Peoples (RCAP) put forward a vision of reconciliation rooted in the treaty principles of mutual respect, reciprocity, and responsibility.[10] Following years of inaction on RCAP's recommendations, the TRC drew reconciliation back into public dialogue when it began its work in 2009. Asserting that Indian residential schools constituted cultural genocide,[11] the TRC released ninety-four calls to action in 2015 aimed at reconciliation[12] and, by extension, justice.[13] The calls to action span a range of program areas including education, child welfare, and health care. Although the TRC did note UNDRIP as the framework for reconciliation,[14] governmental response to the calls to action has more frequently emphasized increased access to and availability of programs and services to "close the gap" for Indigenous peoples, while Indigenous understandings of self-determination—including the inherent right to govern our territories—are marginalized.[15] At the same time, the calls to action sought more diverse inclusion of Indigenous worldviews within Canadian society, attempting to penetrate the core of settler education by adapting curriculum. These calls for inclusion—when considered alongside the refusal to respect Indigenous self-determination evident in the number of incursions to Indigenous sovereignty, such as those on Wet'suwet'en lands in February 2020—seem to indicate an add-and-stir approach wherein reconciliation is understood as the inclusion of Indigenous knowledge within existing structures without requiring structural change to systems that have been complicit in violence.

Over the years, each new emphasis on reconciliation and righting the relationship between Indigenous nations and Canadians has remained tied to illusory rather than substantive justice for Indigenous peoples while reinforcing the hegemonic interests of settlers. In these imaginings of reconciliation by the settler state, there remains a deliberate division and privileging of certain types of Indigenous rights over others. Soft Indigenous rights[16] such as those focused on Indigenous culture, language, and education, have been heavily prioritized by the Canadian state as positively contributing to a multicultural Canadian identity.[17] On the other hand, hard Indigenous rights—those related to governing and maintaining healthy relationships with our territories—have often been either actively silenced or affirmed only when they can be reconciled with Crown sovereignty. Sheryl Lightfoot notes that these rights are termed "hard" to indicate "both the difficulty in negotiation, but also to expose their perceived threat to the 'hard core' of the international system; that is, state territorial sovereignty."[18] This privileging of specific rights within reconciliation discourse removes Indigenous peoples as a challenge to settler access to Indigenous lands and waters.

In seeking redress for colonial violence, Indigenous peoples have found that our right to justice has often been tied to the evolution of a particular kind of reconciliation that seeks to redefine and constrain our relationality, often in ways that are amenable to the objectives of the Canadian settler state to secure unfettered access to lands, waters, and resources. This redefinition of our relationality moves to separate us from our relations with and responsibilities toward the physical places we call home. Our relationships and the responsibilities we hold to our territories inform and generate our knowledges; they are inseparable from our cultural rights. Together they can be understood as our inherent right to self-determination, which entails—as Jeff Corntassel and Cheryl Bryce note—the "unconditional freedom to live one's relational, place-based existence, and practice healthy relationships."[19] To selectively affirm Indigenous knowledges in public forums and create space within education systems for the inclusion of Indigenous knowledges while ignoring or violently prohibiting Indigenous presence on Indigenous lands and waters "is to miss the point entirely."[20] The tensions implicit in this particular entanglement of reconciliation and justice are evident in the utilization of reconciliation rhetoric around the BC Hydro Site C Dam project.

The Site C Dam and Treaty 8 Territory

The Site C Dam is the third planned dam on the Peace River and has been in the works since the 1950s. Under Christie Clark's BC Liberal Government, the project was pushed forward despite ongoing and fierce Indigenous and settler resistance. The over CAD10 billion project will turn an 83-kilometre stretch of the Peace River Valley into a reservoir,[21] flooding "approximately 5,000 hectares of land when the reservoir is finished, and parts of the reservoir will be two to three times the width of current riverbanks."[22] This, of course, does not fully account for residual flooding and impact on the land due to the collapse of "unstable banks."[23] In fact, BC Hydro's modest estimate of the impact is covered only by the "erosion impact line" on their maps, while the potential reshaping of the land is more far-reaching and only partially detailed by the radiating "flood impact line" and "stability impact line" on their maps.[24] The demarcation of the land in this way obscures the beauty and vitality of the region, and silences the interconnected relationships First Nations hold with the vibrant diversity of life within this place.

At various stages of the process, Indigenous communities affected by the proposed Site C Dam have fought to centre their knowledges in state forums such as the spaces created for assessing the project. Under the guidelines established by the Environmental Impact Statement, BC Hydro needed to consult with twenty-nine different First Nations who would be affected by the project,[25] of which twenty-one are Treaty 8 signatories. Out of these twenty-nine communities, only six did not participate in the joint panel that was established to review the Site C Dam (hereafter referred to as the Joint Review Panel), although they did submit information directly to BC Hydro during the pre-panel stage.[26] Indigenous knowledges have filled thousands of pages of documents submitted to these various forums, each detailing the deep connection to and relationships with the land, waters, and more-than-humans[27] in what is now known as the Peace River Valley. It is important to note that Indigenous engagement in these forums cannot be used to indicate the depth or meaningfulness of consultation, nor to evaluate the structures in place for consultation and their ability to achieve free, prior, and informed consent. In spite of the structural flaws in these processes, Indigenous peoples' decisions to engage can be understood as tangible markers of the deep responsibility that these nations have with their kin. At every corner, Indigenous nations have sought to protect and defend their relationships to the lands, waters, and more-than-humans. At every corner, the struggle between protecting kin and resisting colonial processes can be felt deep within Indigenous communities. According to Chief Roland Willson of West Moberly First Nation, "losing the valley to Site C would be like losing an organ from your body...It's like cutting out a kidney. Our connection to the land is spiritual. We're people of the land. You take us off the land and you destroy a piece of who we are."[28]

There is no denying that the Site C project will fundamentally alter the relationships that Treaty 8 First Nations hold with the Peace River Valley given the severe altering of the land outlined by the project. Within the territory, First Nations have identified hundreds of sites in the project flood zone that are sacred or of other cultural or historic significance,[29] including gathering places and burial sites in Bear Flats.[30] Beyond the loss of such vital territory, the environmental impact as a result of the Site C Dam would have devastating consequences on Indigenous communities and their relationships, including the flooding of "a series of small islands where moose take shelter when calving…[and] potentially jeopardiz[ing] migration of an already threatened fish species."[31] It would also cause methylmercury poisoning of fish in the waters,[32] the changing of traditional fish stocks, and the drying of the Peace-Athabasca Delta,[33] to name just a few impacts. In fact, previous extractive resource projects have already produced significant damage to these territories and their relations, and have shed light on the potential damages similar projects may cause in the future. For example, bull trout, a vital food source, became so contaminated with mercury as a result of the Bennett Dam built in 1968 that they exceeded Health Canada's contamination standards.[34] In attempting to bring awareness to the toxicity in the region as a result of extractive industry, Chief Roland Willson held up a Hershey's chocolate kiss on the lawn of the BC Legislature: "the amount of the fish that women of child-bearing age could safely consume about every other day."[35]

Although Indigenous women have, as Kim Anderson notes, been equated with the land, and although "the Euro-constructed image of Native women, therefore, mirrors Western attitudes towards the earth,"[36] there is a tendency to view justice and efforts to protect lands and waters as disconnected from the struggle to protect Indigenous women. In fact, in terms of importance, efforts to protect the land are often placed above the protection of Indigenous women and children. These tendencies fail to conceptualize the ways that Indigenous women and children have been systematically removed from our lands and waters in the attempted complete erasure of Indigenous presence from the landscape. As Helen Knott stresses, the struggles for bodily justice and environmental justice are intrinsically connected: "The ideology that permits the violation of Indigenous bodies is the same one that perpetuates the violation of Indigenous lands."[37]

The explosion of natural resource projects in the northeastern part of what is now British Columbia has fostered environments that lead to violence against women. Indigenous women face particular danger in these spaces, where generations of settler-colonial stories of Indigenous deviance, promiscuity, and dispensability intersect with man camps that breed hypermasculinity and high rates of substance abuse. As Knott notes, these man camps draw individuals "who don't care what happens to the lands [into] our territory. They extend the same mentality to women, both Indigenous and non-Indigenous."[38] In 2016, Amnesty International released their report *Out of Sight, Out of Mind: Gender, Indigenous Rights and Energy Development in Northeast British Columbia, Canada*. The report noted that "in 2014, Fort St. John had the highest per capita crime rate among 31 British Columbia municipalities of 15,000 people or more"; there were numerous indications that this included high rates of violence against Indigenous women and girls.[39] The National Inquiry into Missing and Murdered Indigenous Women and Girls (MMIWG) also noted that "resource extraction projects can drive violence against Indigenous women in several ways, including issues related to transient workers, rotational shift work, substance abuse and addictions, and economic insecurity."[40]

Research on the interconnection between violence against the land and violence against Indigenous peoples continues to point to, as the MMIWG Inquiry has noted, the same conclusion: "federal, provincial, territorial and Indigenous governments, as well as mining and oil and gas companies, should do a more thorough job of considering the safety of Indigenous women and children when making decisions about resource extraction on or near Indigenous territories."[41] Despite this, Amnesty International found that "the assessment of the Site C Dam, in particular, failed to consider the specific impacts on Indigenous women and girls."[42] For many Indigenous peoples, the decision to move forward with these resource extraction projects—despite considerable evidence tracing their connections to violence against Indigenous women, children, and two-spirits—feels like a decision that damns our people to violence and death.

Both the Joint Review Panel and the BC Utilities Commission's Final Report on Site C noted that Indigenous communities were overwhelmingly against the project, many noting how the project violates Treaty 8.[43] In fact, the Joint Review Panel went into detail siding with First Nations on matters related to the detrimental impact of the project on their communities, calling BC Hydro's argument that traditional practices can be reproduced elsewhere "superficial" and unsupported.[44] Despite the obligation to uphold such treaties, which are enshrined in the Canadian Constitution and UNDRIP, there is an evident disregard for the rights and knowledges of Indigenous peoples in the approval and construction of the Site C Dam.[45] In fact, in early 2016, BC Hydro argued against applying UNDRIP to the project, describing the document as "aspirational"[46] and thus not binding. This assertion is a direct parroting of the Conservative federal government's qualified support of UNDRIP as "aspirational" in 2010,[47] and the Liberal federal government's 2016 assertion that UNDRIP's adoption into Canadian law is "unworkable," even after giving the declaration a full endorsement.[48] This qualified engagement with UNDRIP has been affirmed again in the passing of BC provincial Bill 41 (Declaration on the Rights of Indigenous Peoples Act) in 2019, followed by BC Premier John Horgan's assertion that the declaration is "forward looking" and does not apply to current projects such as the Coastal GasLink (CGL) Pipeline through Wet'suwet'en territory.[49] The international community has also weighed in on the violation of Indigenous rights around the Site C Dam. Amnesty International authored a report noting that the project and process have violated Canada's human rights obligations towards Indigenous peoples, and that the impacts to Indigenous peoples rights and well-being cannot be justified.[50] In December 2018, the United Nations Committee on the Elimination of Racial Discrimination instructed Canada to suspend the Site C Dam until the project obtains the "free, prior, and informed consent" of Indigenous peoples following the full and adequate discharge of duty to consult, and gave them until April 8, 2019 to respond.[51] In their interim report submission, Canada deferred a "fulsome response" to the request until a later date.[52]

In describing the effect of the project, the Joint Review Panel explicitly noted that "Site C would be constructed, and virtually all of the physical effects of the Project would occur on land expressly included in Treaty 8."[53] These physical effects, as outlined above, would fundamentally and irreversibly alter the relationships Treaty 8 Nations hold with the lands, waters, and more-than-humans connected deeply in webs of kinship. To make matters even more clear, the Joint Review Panel found that "the Project would significantly affect the current use of land and resources for traditional purposes by Aboriginal peoples...*It would not, however, significantly affect the harvest of fish and wildlife by non-Aboriginal people*" (emphasis added).[54] In advancing a hydropower project as the solution to a supposed energy crisis,[55] these types of projects run, in Kyle Powys Whyte's words, "roughshod over relationships," and reaffirm the harmful relationships between settler states and Indigenous nations.[56]

"150 Years of Disappointment": Reconciliation in British Columbia

The damming of the Peace River has been a hotly contested topic in British Columbia over the last forty years, rivaled only by the Trans Mountain Pipeline Expansion Project and CGL's liquid natural gas (LNG) pipeline through Wet'suwet'en territories. In various forums, Indigenous peoples have documented the ways in which the Site C Dam violates their treaty rights and those rights outlined by UNDRIP. Indigenous knowledge has filled thousands of pages of documents delivered to and in these forums. Despite this, and despite renewed commitments to govern the province in accordance with UNDRIP and to fully embrace "genuine reconciliation,"[57] at a press conference at the BC Legislature on December 11, 2017, Premier John Horgan announced that the Site C Dam would move forward. While stressing that this was "not the project we would have started," Horgan repeated his commitments to the values and best interests of British Columbians.[58] He stated: "We agree that decisions like this must, must, be done in tandem and in concert with Indigenous peoples. *But those challenges have passed*" (emphasis added).[59] Horgan's posturing within this statement sheds important light on the approach being taken towards relationships with Indigenous nations and reconciliation more generally. In one fell swoop, Horgan positioned Indigenous peoples and the legal requirement to consult with self-determining nations as "the challenge" to the rule of law and subsequently to the progress and economic benefit of Canadian society. By emphasizing this oppositional position, Horgan also subtly gestures to longstanding settler-colonial stories of supposed Indigenous deficiency, which suggest that there is something wrong within Indigenous nations particularly when we stand in opposition to what is perceived as the common "best interests" of the settler-colonial nation. These narratives, by extension, suggest that there is something wrong with us rather than with the oppressive structures of power that we push back against.

Selective and superficial settler-colonial engagement with Indigenous knowledge and authority was emphasized again when Indigenous peoples stood in defense of the land and against the encroachment of the CGL pipeline in the winter of 2020. Despite the assertion of Wet'suwet'en sovereignty over their own lands and the United Nations Committee on the Elimination of Racial Discrimination's calls for the immediate halt to construction of the CGL pipeline, the Trans Mountain Pipeline, and the Site C Dam without the free, prior, and informed consent of Indigenous peoples,[60] violence continued through the deployment of RCMP and the invasion of Wet'suwet'en territory in February 2020. On February 10, 2020, the RCMP trespassed on Indigenous lands and tore down the gate across the Morice River Bridge, which had been erected by Wet'suwet'en Land Defenders to protect the community and assert their rights. They battered their way through, destroying reconciliation literally and figuratively, and violently removed Matriarchs and Indigenous Land Defenders in ceremony.

The Horgan government's insistence that resource projects such as the Site C Dam and the CGL pipeline will continue despite Indigenous opposition are alarming not only because of the continued violation of Indigenous rights, but because of the ways in which this government invokes reconciliation while at the same time advancing the destruction of Indigenous life. Only three months prior to his Site C Dam announcement—at the BC Cabinet and First Nations Leaders Gathering in September 2017—Horgan spoke of the vital importance of respecting Indigenous knowledges, noting that

> using traditional understandings of how the land has managed changes is critically important, and I acknowledge Chief Judy Wilson who today reminded us all...that if we are not as a government, as a federal government, as a provincial government, are not going to listen and learn from the experiences of First Nations, and their understanding of the land, we're going to fail again.[61]

Pushing the Site C Dam project forward in the face of resistance by Indigenous nations ignores Indigenous knowledge, which have been recorded in pages and testimony submitted to the Joint Review Panel as well as vocalized at demonstrations against the Site C Dam project. These Indigenous knowledges trace the centrality of relationships and responsibilities to the territory that will be laid to waste by the Site C Dam. By disregarding these knowledges, the Horgan government marks them, and Indigenous rights to self-determination, as unimportant, disconnected from the present, and of lesser value than the supposed best interests of the general population. In these spaces, engagement with Indigenous knowledge and authority becomes performative—invoked as a way to check the boxes of reconciliation and to generate the illusion of justice. Performative reconciliation, without the substantial structural changes necessary for decolonization and respectful relationships, continues to generate settler futurity through the maintenance of settler-colonial power.

The process of marking Indigenous knowledges as marginal and dispensable—a process exemplified in Horgan's "engagement" with and subsequent disregard for Indigenous knowledges around the Site C Dam—also gives cause for concern due to the precedent it establishes. Indigenous scholars have voiced concerns about the selective engagement with Indigenous knowledges within postsecondary institutions, as universities barrel forward to meet the TRC's calls to action by including Indigenous knowledge in a piecemeal fashion, or in ways that are simultaneously additive and disposable. This is most evident in attempts by various institutions to indigenize their programming through the inclusion of Indigenous peoples and various forms of knowledge. Adam Gaudry and Danielle Lorenz critique these strategies in the context of postsecondary institutions, noting that Indigenous inclusion merely seeks to "add Indigenous peoples into pre-existing university structures."[62] In other words, universities believe they "can indigenize without substantial structural change."[63]

In the same way universities have chosen when and how to engage with Indigenous knowledges, Horgan has also asserted authority to uphold or discount Indigenous knowledges when it suits political objectives, thus allowing the performativity of reconciliation to directly benefit settler-colonial power. The depth of Horgan's commitments to Indigenous peoples is made explicit when he states: "When it comes to reconciliation and working with Indigenous leadership, look, there has been over 150 years of disappointment in British Columbia, I'm not the first person to stand before you and disappoint Indigenous people."[64] In expert political double speak, Horgan alludes to the fact that it will be business as usual in the province while crafting an image of himself as the lesser of previous evils due to his commitment to "the more important issues to communities": programs and services for Indigenous peoples.[65] This begs a critical question: How can Indigenous knowledge and authority be honoured and respected[66] while our hard rights, such as Indigenous presence and sovereignty, are positioned as being less important than programs, services, and other soft rights?

As an educator, I believe that education holds an essential role in justice and righting relationships. Settler colonialism is able to persist in part due to the pervasiveness of purposeful ignorance and the normalization of colonial ideologies. However, I fear, as Eve Tuck and K. Wayne Yang do, that a settler move to innocence can be found in focusing on the cultivation of critical consciousness as the only step in decolonization; they note that this allows "*conscientization* to stand in for the more uncomfortable task of relinquishing stolen land."[67] I also agree with them that curriculum, literature, and pedagogy play a vital role in aiding people to identify and understand settler colonialism.[68] And while this can feel like the heavy lifting of change, justice cannot solely be rooted in awareness and critical consciousness without the repatriation of Indigenous land and life. The ways critical consciousness-building can obstruct decolonization is evident in how Premier Horgan upholds and superficially engages with Indigenous knowledge without any tangible respect of Indigenous authority over their relationships in all forms. It cannot be suggested that there is simply a lack of knowledge that is standing in the way of respecting Indigenous refusal of the Site C Dam, or, for that matter, of the CGL pipeline. In fact, as I have already highlighted, Indigenous knowledge has filled thousands of pages of documents delivered to the Joint Review Panel and the BC Utilities Commission regarding the Site C Dam; Indigenous knowledge and experience has been explicitly documented and delivered to the MMIWG Inquiry about the violence experienced as a result of extractive industry projects. The failing here is not a lack of knowledge of Indigenous authority and self-determination; it is fundamentally opposed world-views and an unwillingness to relinquish power.

In order to advance the destruction of vital relationships to place and thus to allow for exploitation and extraction, the colonial process of wastelanding—as Voyles notes—demands that "indigenous ways of knowing landscapes, and their worth must be themselves rendered pollutable, marginal, and unimportant."[69] Indigenous epistemologies and ontologies have always been and will remain deeply informed by our physical and spiritual relationships and presence. Our teachings centre the importance of our relationships to all of creation, and the vibrancy of life in all forms. As Sandra D. Styres asserts: "Land *is* spiritual, emotional, and relational; Land *is* experiential, (re)membered, and storied; Land *is* consciousness—Land *is* sentient."[70] To lose sight of this, to forget its importance, is to lose part of our-selves. In order to oppose the marginalization of our knowledges, we must actively work to (re)story our connection to home, (re)member place, and (re)generate our responsibilities in connection to all of creation. As Linda Tuhiwai Smith argues, "a decolonizing agenda has to help Indigenous peoples to create and revitalize our own frameworks, languages, theories, methodologies and practices."[71] Education can play an important role here as we transition teaching styles from sharing knowledge about abstract topics to motivating action and reflection through critical engage-ment. Our approaches should be rooted in (re)orienting ourselves to the world—in (re)connecting with our responsibilities within our webs of kinship. For nuučaańuł peoples, this is developed from an intimate understanding of *hišukʔišćawaak*—the teaching that everything is one. Centring this teaching requires us to enact our responsibilities to creation in all forms. We are in a constant, active relationship with all life—a relationship that seeks balance based on reciprocity. Justice, as rooted in decolonization and not performative reconciliation, must involve an intimate understanding of the ways our relationships are premised on responsibility and reciprocity; it must involve a reorientation of the settler worldview to emphasize responsibility in an active relationship with the world, alongside the physical presence of Indigenous peoples in our homelands.

Moving Beyond Illusory Justice

The advancement of reconciliation and the justice Indigenous nations hope for and seek through respectful relationships are, when held alongside the continued destruction of Indigenous life and lands, impossible. Under governments that have devoted themselves to the advancement of this version of reconciliation, it has become clear that Indigenous peoples and our knowledges are still marked as dispensable when they do not suit political objectives. Reconciliation's focus on the creation of more programs and services for Indigenous peoples (soft rights) at the expense of Indigenous rights to govern our lands and waters (hard rights) seeks to redefine justice and our relationality in ways that do not honour the breadth of our self-determination. When Indigenous peoples become strictly imagined through the advancement of our soft rights—cultural rights such as those embodied in our languages, songs, prayers, and art—we are no longer imagined as a challenge to settler-colonial access to our territories. What this particular advancement of rights fails to conceptualize is that our culture is deeply tied to our relationality with kin in the physical places we call home.

Given this, reconciliation has more often proceeded along a trajectory marked by performativity and attempts to make Indigeneity commensurate with an image of a unified multicultural state without respect for the existence of plural sovereignties. The superficial engagement with Indigenous knowledge and authority is one facet of this, suggesting a move to check the box of reconciliation without making the structural changes that would make justice possible. Programs and services, and an embracing of our cultural rights are upheld as the fulfillment of reconciliation—and by extension, justice—while the attempted erasure of our physical presence in our homelands proceeds. This is not to say that cultural projects or programs and services should not receive attention, but merely to emphasize that soft rights cannot, and should not, be divorced from hard Indigenous rights; both are integral to our self-determination. The uneven application of reconciliation suggests we are still moving towards what Helen Knott called "elusive justice."[72] As Christi Belcourt has argued,

> What we need is a revolution. A revolution of the mind. We need a revolution of our actions, a revolution of language revitalization... We do not need to bring indigeneity into universities; we need to bring our Indigenous selves out onto the lands to rebuild our ways of learning, to keep this earth and water pure and beautiful for 10,000 more years. We need a revolution that will put our lands back in our control and stop the waters from being polluted.[73]

Indigenous peoples have been resisting the settler-colonial project since first contact, and as Arthur Manuel eloquently affirms, "it is because we have deep feelings for our people and for justice that we struggle in the first place."[74] There is important space for education to involve itself in decolonization, but it must move past superficial inclusion of Indigenous peoples and Indigenous knowledge. Justice and decolonization cannot be imagined without respect for the relationships we hold with each other, with our homelands and homewaters, and with more-than-humans. Our responsibilities and relationships must be understood collectively as our inherent right to self-determination. To separate these rights is to seek to divide us from part of who we are as Indigenous peoples. In order for reconciliation to truly embody justice, it must privilege our understandings of self-determination.

NOTES

1. Arthur Manuel discussed these frameworks in his posthumous book, written in collaboration with Grand Chief Ronald Derrickson, *Reconciliation Manifesto: Recovering the Land, Rebuilding the Economy*. Noting that the overriding objective of settler-colonial governments has always been certainty and unfettered access and control over Indigenous lands and waters, Manuel writes that Reconciliation Framework Agreements are designed as a "new scheme to get us to surrender our title and rights," born of the inconsistency between "the government's business-as-usual political strategy and the effect of the court decisions recognizing our Aboriginal title" (204). The economic uncertainty generated from this has pressured the provincial government to enter into agreements with Indigenous nations on an industry-by-industry basis in order to access lands, waters, and resources without waiting on treaties to be signed. Manuel explicitly notes that "the real problem with the reconciliation agreements is that they relieve pressure on the provincial government and free up our lands for industry, but do not provide any real benefit to Indigenous peoples" (205).
2. Trudeau, "Statement by the Prime Minister," para. 4.
3. Wet'suwet'en hereditary chiefs have stood in opposition to the Coastal GasLink (CGL) liquid natural gas pipeline slated to move through their territory. In response to a court injunction issued by the British Columbia Supreme Court, Wet'suwet'en hereditary chiefs issued an eviction notice to CGL in early January 2020. Just one year earlier, the RCMP invaded Wet'suwet'en lands, arrested fourteen land defenders at Giditmt'en camp, and set up an exclusion zone prohibiting anyone from entering that was not a member of Canadian law enforcement. Following the breakdown of talks between hereditary chiefs and the province of British Columbia—which were called off by CGL because the chiefs continued to refuse to allow CGL workers on their lands—a new raid on Wet'suwet'en lands began. On February 10, 2020, with the world watching, the RCMP violently removed Matriarchs and Indigenous Land Defenders in ceremony upholding Wet'suwet'en law. See Forester, "Hereditary Chiefs"; Unist'ot'en Camp, "Reconciliation Is Dead."
4. Voyles, *Wastelanding*.
5. Reflecting on the definition of reconciliation, the TRC noted that they envisioned reconciliation to focus on "coming to terms with events of the past in a manner that overcomes conflict and establishes a respectful and healthy relationship among people, going forward." Truth and Reconciliation Commission of Canada, *What We Have Learned*, 113.
6. Mackey, *Unsettled Expectations*, 57.
7. Vermette, "Dizzying Dialogue," 57.

8. While it is beyond the scope of this paper to delve into these cases at length, they are important markers for the judicial approach to reconciliation. The Supreme Court of Canada made a precedent-setting decision in 1990 in *R. v. Sparrow*. The case, brought forward following the arrest of Musqueam band member Ronald Sparrow for fishing with a net that was longer than permitted by his fishing licence, recognized that Sparrow had an existing right to fish that was not extinguished prior to the 1982 Constitution Act. In ruling that section 35 of the constitution established that the government could not override or infringe upon those rights without justification, the Supreme Court of Canada established criteria to determine if a right is existing and how the government may be justified in infringing upon it, known today as the "Sparrow Test." See R. v. Sparrow, [1990] 1 S.C.R. 1075, https://scc-csc.lexum.com/scc-csc/scc-csc/en/item/609/index.do. See also Salomons and Hanson, "Sparrow Case."

9. Vermette, "Dizzying Dialogue," 58.

10. Royal Commission on Aboriginal Peoples, *Final Report*, 1:675–97.

11. Truth and Reconciliation Commission of Canada, *Honouring the Truth*, 1.

12. *Truth and Reconciliation Commission of Canada: Calls to Action*.

13. For a more thorough exploration of the connection between conceptions of reconciliation and justice, see George, "Let Us Not Drift."

14. Truth and Reconciliation Commission of Canada, *What We Have Learned*, 3.

15. George, "Let Us Not Drift."

16. Lightfoot, *Global Indigenous Politics*, 13.

17. George, "A Move to Distract."

18. Lightfoot, *Global Indigenous Politics*, 14.

19. Corntassel and Bryce, "Practicing Sustainable Self-Determination," 152.

20. L. Smith, Tuck, and Yang, introduction to *Indigenous and Decolonizing Studies*, 1.

21. Amnesty International, *The Point of No Return*, 3.

22. British Columbia Utilities Commission, *Inquiry Respecting Site C*, 2. Hereafter cited as BCUC inquiry.

23. Sarah Cox notes that, on BC Hydro's map of Site C, engineers have included "unstable banks" that will weaken and collapse, thus expanding the reservoir. See Cox, *Breaching the Peace*, 12.

24. Cox, *Breaching the Peace*, 12–13.

25. Canadian Environmental Assessment Agency and British Columbia Environmental Assessment Agency, *Report of the Joint Review Panel*, 123. Hereafter cited as Joint Review Panel, *Site C*.

26. Joint Review Panel, *Site C*, 124.

27. I deeply recognize the failing of using the term *more-than-human* in discussing our relationships with all of creation. This terminology, along with *other-than-human* and *nonhuman*, continues to emphasize a dichotomy that centres and privileges humans. I do not believe this accurately reflects the nature of our relationships with all of creation—nor, from my own nuučaańuł understanding, of *hišuk?išćawaak*. I believe that so much of this comes from the impossibility of English to truly encapsulate the breadth of how we understand our relationships and responsibilities. My decision to use *more-than-human* comes with this caveat and with the hope that this framing moves, in a small way, to decentre humans and gesture to the importance of all of creation.

28. Chief Ronald Willson, quoted in Cox, *Breaching the Peace*, 94.

29. Amnesty International, *The Point of No Return*, 5.

30. BCUC inquiry, 30.

31. Amnesty International, *The Point of No Return*, 5.

32. BCUC inquiry, 30.

33. Joint Review Panel, *Site C*, 126.

34. Cox, *Breaching the Peace,* 118.
35. Chief Roland Willson, quoted in Cox, *Breaching the Peace,* 116.
36. Anderson, *A Recognition of Being,* 80.
37. Knott, "Violence and Extraction," 152.
38. Knott, "Violence and Extraction," 150.
39. Amnesty International, *Out of Sight, Out of Mind,* 50.
40. National Inquiry into Missing and Murdered Indigenous Women and Girls, 1a:584. Hereafter cited as MMIWG Inquiry report.
41. MMIWG Inquiry report, 1a:584.
42. Amnesty International, *The Point of No Return,* 14.
43. BCUC inquiry, 28–37. See also Joint Review Panel, *Site C.*
44. Joint Review Panel, *Site C,* 96.
45. Amnesty International, *The Point of No Return,* 10.
46. A. Smith, "BC Hydro Argues."
47. Indian and Northern Affairs Canada quoted in Lightfoot, *Global Indigenous Politics,* 108.
48. Former Liberal justice minister Jody Wilson-Raybould addressing the Assembly of First Nations Annual General Assembly in Niagara Falls, July 12, 2016. Quoted in APTN National News,"Justice Minister," para. 3.
49. John Horgan, quoted in APTN National News, "Horgan says," para. 22.
50. Amnesty International, *The Point of No Return,* 15.
51. United Nations Committee on the Elimination of Racial Discrimination to Her Excellency Ms. Rosemary McCarney.
52. Amnesty International, *Canada: Submission to the United Nations,* 5.
53. Joint Review Panel, *Site C,* 124.
54. Joint Review Panel, *Site C,* iv.
55. Various tactics have been used in pushing forward the Site C project, including former BC Premier Christie Clark's fearmongering while campaigning for reelection in 2017. Sarah Cox, in *Breaching the Peace,* specifically draws attention to Clark's declaration that "it was urgent to build Site C 'to literally keep the lights on' for BC families" (23). This construction of a supposed energy crisis was also echoed in documents that were submitted by BC Hydro to the Joint Review Panel, but which the panel found to be baseless. In fact, as Cox notes, "even while Clark raised the spectre of a future electricity shortage so severe that British Columbians might not have enough power to flick on their kitchen lights, BC was swimming in so much extra electricity that hydro customers were paying independent power producers millions of dollars a year not to produce power" (23).
56. Whyte, "It's Too Late for Indigenous Justice," conference presentation.
57. In his opening remarks at the BC Cabinet and First Nations Leaders' Gathering, Horgan spoke of the centrality of governing the province in accordance with UNDRIP, mentioning that it was included in his letters to each of his Ministers. See Horgan, "BC Cabinet and First Nations Leaders' Gathering."
58. Horgan, "Site C Announcement," at 4:27.
59. Horgan, "Site C Announcement," at 3:53.
60. United Nations Committee on the Elimination of Racial Discrimination, *Prevention of Racial Discrimination.*
61. Horgan, "BC Cabinet and First Nations Leaders' Gathering," at 3:35.
62. Gaudry and Lorenz, "Indigenization as Inclusion," 219.
63. Gaudry and Lorenz, "Indigenization as Inclusion," 219.
64. Horgan, "Site C Announcement," at 12:07.

65. Horgan, "Site C Announcement," at 13:05.
66. The TRC highlights honour and respect of Indigenous knowledge and authority as key to their understanding of reconciliation. See TRC, *What We Have Learned*, 113.
67. Tuck and Yang, "Decolonization Is Not a Metaphor," 19.
68. Tuck and Yang, "Decolonization Is Not a Metaphor," 19.
69. Voyles, *Wastelanding*, 11.
70. Styres, "Literacies of Land," 27.
71. L. Smith, Tuck, and Yang, introduction to *Indigenous and Decolonizing Studies*, 7.
72. Knott, "Women, Water, Land," 28.
73. Belcourt, "The Revolution Has Begun," 120.
74. Manuel, "Reserves as Holding Pens," 85.

BIBLIOGRAPHY

Amnesty International. *Canada: Submission to the United Nations Committee on the Elimination of Racial Discrimination*. London: Amnesty International, 2019. https://www.amnesty.org/en/documents/amr20/0110/2019/en/.

———. *Out of Sight, Out of Mind: Gender, Indigenous Rights, and Energy Development in Northeast British Columbia, Canada*. London: Amnesty International, 2016. https://www.amnesty.org/en/documents/amr20/4872/2016/en/.

———. *The Point of No Return: The Human Rights of Indigenous Peoples in Canada Threatened by the Site C Dam*. London: Amnesty International, 2016. https://www.amnesty.org/en/documents/amr20/4281/2016/en/.

Anderson, Kim. *A Recognition of Being: Reconstructing Native Womanhood*. Toronto: Sumach Press, 2000.

APTN National News. "Horgan says 'rule of law applies', LNG pipeline will proceed despite opposition." *APTN National News*, January 13, 2020. https://aptnnews.ca/2020/01/13/horgan-says-rule-of-law-applies-lng-pipeline-will-proceed-despite-opposition/.

———. "Justice Minister Jody Wilson-Raybould Says Adopting UNDRIP into Canadian law 'Unworkable'." *APTN National News*, July 12, 2016. https://aptnnews.ca/2016/07/12/justice-minister-jody-wilson-raybould-says-adopting-undrip-into-canadian-law-unworkable/.

Belcourt, Christi. "The Revolution Has Begun." In *Toward What Justice? Describing Diverse Dreams of Justice in Education*, edited by Eve Tuck and K. Wayne Yang, 113–21. New York: Routledge, 2018.

British Columbia Utilities Commission. *British Columbia Utilities Commission Inquiry Respecting Site C: Final Report to the Government of British Columbia*. November 1, 2017. https://www.bcuc.com/Documents/wp-content/11/11-01-2017-BCUC-Site-C-Inquiry-Final-Report.pdf.

Canadian Environmental Assessment Agency and British Columbia Environmental Assessment Agency. *Report of the Joint Review Panel: Site C Clean Energy Project*, May 1, 2014. https://ceaa-acee.gc.ca/050/documents/p63919/99173E.pdf.

Corntassel, Jeff, and Cheryl Bryce. "Practicing Sustainable Self-Determination: Indigenous Approaches to Cultural Restoration and Revitalization." *Brown Journal of World Affairs* 18, no. 2 (Spring/Summer 2012): 151–62.

Cox, Sarah. *Breaching the Peace: The Site C Dam and a Valley's Stand Against Big Hydro*. Vancouver: UBC Press, 2018.

Forester, Brett. "Hereditary Chiefs Issue Eviction Notice to Pipeline Company in Wet'suwet'en Territory." *APTN National News*, January 5, 2020. https://www.aptnnews.ca/national-news/hereditary-chiefs-issue-eviction-notice-to-pipeline-company-in-wetsuweten-territory/.

Gaudry, Adam, and Danielle Lorenz. "Indigenization as Inclusion, Reconciliation, and Decolonization: Navigating the Different Versions for Indigenizing the Canadian Academy." *AlterNative* 14, no. 3 (2018): 218–27.

George, Rachel yacaaʔał. "Let Us Not Drift: Indigenous Justice in an Age of Reconciliation." PhD Dissertation. University of Victoria, 2021.

———. "A Move to Distract: Mobilizing Truth and Reconciliation in Settler Colonies." In *Pathways to Reconciliation*, edited by Aimee Craft and Paulette Regan, 87–118. Winnipeg: University of Manitoba Press, 2020.

Horgan, John. "BC Cabinet and First Nations Leaders' Gathering Opening Remarks." Vancouver, BC. Recorded September 6, 2017. YouTube video, 43:12. https://www.youtube.com/watch?v=1ZjnLyAW3vs.

———. "Site C Announcement." Victoria, BC. Livestreamed on CBC, December 11, 2017. YouTube Video, 21:08. https://www.youtube.com/watch?v=xOWohJwdZvI.

Justice, Daniel Heath. *Why Indigenous Literatures Matter*. Waterloo: Wilfred Laurier Press, 2018.

Knott, Helen. "Violence and Extraction." In *Keetsahnak: Our Missing and Murdered Indigenous Sisters*, edited by Kim Anderson, Maria Campbell, and Christi Belcourt, 147–59. Edmonton: University of Alberta Press, 2018.

———. "Women, Water, Land: Writing from the Intersections." *Water Rites: Reimagining Water in the West*, edited by Jim Ellis, 25–31. Calgary: University of Calgary Press, 2018.

Lightfoot, Sheryl. *Global Indigenous Politics*. New York: Routledge, 2016.

Mackey, Eva. *Unsettled Expectations: Uncertainty, Land and Settler Decolonization*. Halifax: Fernwood Publishing, 2016.

Manuel, Arthur. "Reserves as Holding Pens." In *The Reconciliation Manifesto: Recovering the Land, Rebuilding the Economy*, by Arthur Manuel and Grand Chief Ronald Derrickson, 82–85. Toronto: Lorimer, 2017.

National Inquiry into Missing and Murdered Indigenous Women and Girls. *Reclaiming Power and Place: The Final Report of the National Inquiry into Missing and Murdered Indigenous Women and Girls*. 2 vols. Ottawa: MMIWG Inquiry, 2019. https://www.mmiwg-ffada.ca/final-report/.

Royal Commission on Aboriginal Peoples. *Report of the Royal Commission on Aboriginal Peoples*. 5 vols. Ottawa: Indian and Northern Affairs Canada, 1996.

Salomons, Tanisha, and Erin Hanson. "Sparrow Case." Indigenous Foundations, First Nations and Indigenous Studies, University of British Columbia. Last updated 2009. https://indigenousfoundations.arts.ubc.ca/sparrow_case/.

Smith, Andrea. "BC Hydro Argues against Applying UNDRIP to Site C Dam Project." *Windspeaker* 34, no. 3 (May 2016): 8.

Smith, Linda Tuhiwai, Eve Tuck, and K. Wayne Yang, eds. *Indigenous and Decolonizing Studies in Education: Mapping the Long View*. New York: Routledge, 2019.

———. Introduction to Smith, Tuck, and Yang, *Indigenous and Decolonizing Studies in Education*, 1–23.

Styres, Sandra D. "Literacies of Land: Decolonizing Narratives, Storying, and Literature." In Smith, Tuck, and Yang, *Indigenous and Decolonizing Studies in Education*, 24–37.

Trudeau, Justin. "Statement by the Prime Minister of Canada on National Aboriginal Day." Prime Minister's Office, June 21, 2016. https://pm.gc.ca/en/news/statements/2016/06/21/statement-prime-minister-canada-national-aboriginal-day.

Truth and Reconciliation Commission of Canada. *Honouring the Truth, Reconciling for the Future: Summary of the Final Report of the Truth and Reconciliation Commission of Canada*. Winnipeg: National Centre for Truth and Reconciliation, 2015. http://www.trc.ca/assets/pdf/Executive_Summary_English_Web.pdf.

———. *Truth and Reconciliation Commission of Canada: Calls to Action*. Winnipeg: National Centre for Truth and Reconciliation, 2015. https://ehprnh2mwo3.exactdn.com/wp-content/uploads/2021/01/Calls_to_Action_English2.pdf.

―――. *What We Have Learned: Principles of Truth and Reconciliation.* Winnipeg: National Centre for Truth and Reconciliation, 2015. https://publications.gc.ca/collections/collection_2015/trc/IR4-6-2015-eng.pdf.

Tuck, Eve, and K. Wayne Yang. "Decolonization Is Not a Metaphor." *Decolonization: Indigeneity, Education, Society* 1, no. 1 (2012): 1–40.

Unist'ot'en Camp. "Reconciliation Is Dead. Revolution Is Alive." Last modified February 13, 2020. http://unistoten.camp/reconciliationisdead/?fbclid=IwAR2t3HL-aN12BhS4Jwlfyt_7wlG6le2g56M5XZD6huEA2UWRh6JxqWf4evs.

United Nations Committee on the Elimination of Racial Discrimination. *Prevention of Racial Discrimination, Including Early Warning and Urgent Action Procedure.* December 13, 2019. https://tbinternet.ohchr.org/Treaties/CERD/Shared%20Documents/CAN/INT_CERD_EWU_CAN_9026_E.pdf.

United Nations Committee on the Elimination of Racial Discrimination to Her Excellency Ms. Rosemary McCarney. December 14, 2018. UN reference locator CERD/EWUAP/Canada-Site C dam/2018/JP/ks. https://tbinternet.ohchr.org/Treaties/CERD/Shared%20Documents/CAN/INT_CERD_ALE_CAN_8818_E.pdf.

Vermette, D'Arcy. "Dizzying Dialogue: Canadian Courts and the Continuing Justification of the Dispossession of Aboriginal People." *Windsor Yearbook of Access to Justice* 29, no. 1 (February 2011): 55–72.

Voyles, Traci Brynne. *Wastelanding: Legacies of Uranium Mining in Navajo Country.* Minnesota: University of Minnesota Press, 2015.

Whyte, Kyle Powys. "It's Too Late for Indigenous Justice: Problems with Urgency in Climate Change Advocacy." Paper presented at the Victoria Colloquium, Victoria, BC, February 8, 2019.

7

TOBY ROLLO

Beyond Curricula

Colonial Pedagogies
in Public Schooling

THE LAST INDIAN RESIDENTIAL SCHOOL
closed in 1996, but as child advocate Cindy Blackstock has argued, the Indian residential school (IRS) system itself did not disappear. Rather, it morphed into the child welfare system.[1] Blackstock points out that many of the colonial functions of the IRS having to do with separating children from their families were transferred to various underfunded and sometimes hostile family services agencies. Has the same thing happened in the domain of education? The Truth and Reconciliation Commission of Canada's (TRC) calls to action have demanded that educational institutions hire more Indigenous teachers and develop a more inclusive curriculum. But while changes to representation and curricula may be welcome, the problem of assimilative *pedagogy* has received very little attention. Curricula and pedagogy are intertwined in educational theory and practice. Education is best understood as reflecting not just the content of the materials but also how the materials are taught and how student learning is assessed. The architects of the IRS system expressed that pedagogy by itself was sufficient to assimilate students. And so, to adequately understand reconciliation in the Canadian context of schooling, the assimilative function of coercive colonial pedagogy must be identified and examined. Only when we come to

terms with the assimilative force of colonial pedagogy as an unbroken continuum extending from the IRS system to public schooling can we attend to the impact of changes to classroom representation or the contents of curricula.

The first call to action listed in the "Education" section of the TRC's calls to action is notable in that it speaks directly to the issue of colonial pedagogy rather than curricula: "We call upon the Government of Canada to repeal section 43 of the *Criminal Code of Canada*."[2] Referred to as the "spanking law," section 43 stipulates that "every schoolteacher, parent or person standing in the place of a parent is justified in using force by way of correction toward a pupil or child, as the case may be, who is under his care, if the force does not exceed what is reasonable under the circumstances."[3] The TRC singled out section 43 in part because it is emblematic of the nonconsensual and often violent "civilizing" approach to schooling that most Indigenous communities in Canada have historically rejected as a colonial imposition. It is this nonconsensual discipline in the service of "the maintenance of order and obedience" that characterized the IRS system no less than the less violent public school system.[4] For the architects of the IRS system, exposing students to a Eurocentric curriculum was of secondary importance to the inculcation of habits of civilized obedience: "From the moment they arrived at residential school, students were taught that discipline and obedience were the two most highly prized virtues they could demonstrate."[5]

I argue in this chapter that the IRS system also transferred many of its assimilative functions to public provincial school systems, to be achieved primarily through colonial pedagogy. I highlight some of the main historical shifts in Canadian colonial pedagogy, beginning with the concerns of early French missionaries that Indigenous parents would not tolerate coercive instruction of children and concluding with the TRC's calls to action, which demonstrate how reconciliation begins by addressing overtly coercive policies and practices in Canadian education. The architects of the IRS system identify pedagogy, not curriculum, as the primary mechanism of assimilation. Indeed, by the mid-twentieth century, officials concluded that a curriculum that includes Indigenous instructors and content, far from challenging Canada's assimilative agenda, would be critical for bringing Indigenous children to accept the influence of nonconsensual colonial pedagogy.[6] Yet today, the focus of Canadian reconciliation in education has been altering the content of curricula. In the final section, I argue that the goal of reconciliation requires that Canada abjure coercive schooling and return the education of Indigenous children and youth to Indigenous communities, allowing those communities to move away from the colonial legacy of controlling and managing children's bodies, imposing metrics and valuations of worth on children, and other cultural habits. In addition to the perennial challenge of underfunding in education, there is a danger that Canada's version of reconciliation will settle for changes in representation and curricular design, leaving the colonial practices of pedagogy and assessment at the heart of Canada's assimilative agenda unchallenged.

Colonial educative practices are rooted in coercion and compulsion rather than the consent of students. The IRS system pursued its civilizing mandate through a program of colonial pedagogy characterized by the control and management of children's bodies that included compulsory attendance,[7] classroom management, and imposed valuations of children's worth such as learning outcomes, standardized assessment, and standardized advancement.[8] Together, these practices comprise a mode of socialization in which strict hierarchies of authority and obedience are normalized and naturalized through the use of disciplinary force (both violent and nonviolent) in the service of "civilizing" human beings. In effect, coercive colonial pedagogy forms the "hidden curriculum" of Indigenous assimilation,[9] the "micro-practices" of compulsory physical and intellectual labour by which Indigenous youth are pressed into the mold of industrious Canadian labourers or transformed into reasonable and responsible Canadian citizens.[10] In this sense, pedagogy itself "teaches" something wholly distinct from the content of curriculum. One can, for example, teach lessons on the importance of consent in a school environment to which the students have not consented. But it is the latter lesson—that children are justifiably coerced and do not have a right to dissent—that makes a more lasting impression than the contents of any textbook or lecture.

Phase I: Dismantling Indigenous Parenting Cultures

The history of colonial education in Canada is a history of adaptations to the resistance of Indigenous children and their parents to colonial pedagogy. Indeed, the IRS system in Canada had to incorporate a number of diverse formats to pursue its goals, most infamously the institutions that held Indigenous youth in residence by force, but also vocational schools, mission schools, industrial schools, on-reserve Indian day schools, partially integrated off-reserve day schools, and fully integrated public schools. Each of these iterations operated with the express goal of assimilating Indigenous peoples into dominant society. The IRS system was characterized by a two-stage, multigenerational strategy that relied first on the residential school format to interrupt the intergenerational transmission of Indigenous parenting cultures before shifting to the much cheaper and more effective day school format, which was designed to complete the integration of children of traumatized residential school survivors into mainstream Canadian society.

From the outset, Indigenous cultures presented deep challenges to European ideals of family and parenting.[11] Early settlers in North America were both puzzled and frustrated by the inclusive and egalitarian structure of families and the reverence for children demonstrated by many Indigenous societies. Whereas women and children were considered peripheral to political life in European cultures, in many Indigenous societies they were venerated as central to the transmission of cultural knowledge, relationships to land, and sovereignty.[12] Accordingly, the dispossession of Indigenous peoples focused first and foremost on the assimilation of women and children into settler society.[13] Settler officials soon realized that the assertion of European sovereignty over Indigenous lands would require both remaking Indigenous family structures to conform to the nuclear family model and removing children from their families so that they could be educated and socialized into habits of industriousness and obedience to authority. A spectrum of strategies were deployed to disrupt the intergenerational reproduction of Indigenous culture and national identity.[14] At first, this work was taken up by churches and religious orders: Catholic in the case of French settler society, and Protestant in the case of English settler society.

The process began taking shape in the seventeenth century and hinged crucially on eliminating the respect afforded to children in Indigenous societies. There was general frustration over the fact that respect for the bodily integrity of Indigenous children was the principal obstacle to the mission's assimilative agendas. In 1620, officials of a Franciscan order, the Récollets, marvelled at the respect afforded to all children in Indigenous societies:

> They love their children dearly, in spite of the doubt that they are really their own, and of the fact that they are for the most part very naughty children, paying little respect, and hardly more obedience; for unhappily, in these lands the young have no respect for the old, nor are children obedient to their parents, and moreover there is no punishment for any fault.[15]

The task was to initiate Indigenous peoples into a world governed by "hierarchy, order, and obedience."[16] Like the Récollets, the Jesuits were convinced of the improvement of all peoples and cultures, including Indigenous peoples, through colonial education in faith and the disciplining effects of agrarian labour.[17] French missionaries soon recognized that Indigenous resistance to assimilative education would require that the children be taken away from these communities: "Since parents were likely to remove their children from school if they believed they were not being well treated, the Jesuits concluded it was best to educate children at a distance from their families."[18] Paul Le Jeune, a notable seventeenth-century Jesuit official who was put in charge of missionary projects in New France, believed that Indigenous peoples afforded an inordinate amount of freedom and respect to their children. He was shocked that the Huron refused to use physical discipline, observing that communities "cannot chastise a child, nor see one chastised," and lamenting how this interfered with the mission of "teaching the young."[19] In the end, Le Jeune concluded that the Huron's family structures and values could only be eroded if children were removed from their parents and communities since "the Savages prevent their instruction; they will not tolerate the chastisement of their children, whatever they may do; they permit only a simple reprimand."[20] Early settlers discovered the same respect for children in virtually every community they encountered.

Nishnaabeg education, for instance, requires that a student openly consent, free from any threat or enticement, to have an adult assist them in their education. As Leanne Betasamosake Simpson describes it, to neglect the fully consensual nature of Nishnaabeg education is to promote the reproduction of colonial habits:

> The word *consensual* here is key because if children learn to normalize dominance and non-consent within the context of education, then non-consent becomes a normalized part of the "tool kit" of those who have and wield power. Within the context of settler colonialism, Indigenous peoples are not seen as worthy recipients of consent, informed or otherwise, and part of being colonized is having to engage in all kinds of processes on a daily basis that, given a choice, we likely wouldn't consent to.[21]

By the early eighteenth century, as French influence waned and the British assumed greater control, the missionary experiment with residential schools in New France concluded.[22] The British Protestant forms of education that followed were secular by comparison and focused more on economic assimilation than on religious conversion. After the American Revolution and the War of 1812, the British were no longer invested in supporting strong Indigenous allies. Following the Bagot Commission's *Report on The Affairs of the Indians in Canada* in 1844,[23] colonial authorities in British North America sought to isolate Indigenous children into schools and settler homes where assimilative education could be guaranteed. But in 1847, Egerton Ryerson, Chief Superintendent of Education in Upper Canada, wrote that religious instruction was still essential to the assimilative education of Indigenous peoples.[24] And so, with the formation of the Canadian state in 1867 and the incorporation of the Indian Act in 1876, jurisdictions within Canada began implementing rudimentary education and social welfare programs, authority over which was initially granted to the religious and missionary organizations that were already embedded in Indigenous communities. It is within this context that the IRS system was devised, predicated on the view that Indigenous traditions, especially the inextricable relationship between women, children, and political life, were holdovers from the past that posed an obstacle to the future of the Canadian settler-colonial project.

The main architects of the IRS system believed that the task of assimilating Indigenous peoples was to be accomplished by promoting western habits of obedience and industriousness. Prime Minister John A. MacDonald described the project as an effort "to do away with the tribal system and assimilate the Indian people in all respects with the inhabitants of the Dominion, as speedily as they are fit for the change."[25] The view held by MacDonald and his secretary of state for the provinces, Hector-Louis Langevin, was that assimilation was a process of habituation altogether distinct from the teaching of facts and figures, reading and writing. This is why residential schools were initially preferred over day schools.

Exposure to traditional Indigenous parenting based on consent and mutual respect compromised the effectiveness of schooling socialization in obedience, resulting in an Indigenous subject who had learned all the correct ideas and skills but none of the correct habits. The TRC final report quotes Langevin as arguing, for instance, that Indigenous students who attended day schools and were therefore permitted to return to their parents in the afternoon "may know how to read and write, but they still remain savages," since partial exposure to colonial pedagogy could not guarantee that children would acquire the essential "habits and tastes...of civilized people."[26] Residence was preferred because an Indigenous boy who excelled in his studies could nevertheless "live like his father by hunting and fishing" and therefore "remain an Indian"[27]—that is, as MacDonald described it before Parliament in 1883, "a savage who can read and write."[28] At least in its beginning stages, then, the necessity of isolating children from the pedagogical influence of communities meant that the education system had to rely on sequestering children for long periods of time in the residential format.

In 1879, MacDonald commissioned Nicholas Flood Davin to write yet another report on the education of Indigenous peoples. Davin's *Report on Industrial Schools for Indians and Half Breeds* confirmed that, in the Canadian context, day schools were ineffective at dissolving Indigenous peoples' "inherent aversion to toil" given that the "influence of the wigwam was stronger than the influence of the school."[29] But from his tours of the United States, Davin had also found that day schools were very effective at providing Indigenous peoples "all reasonable aid in their preparation for citizenship by educating them in industry and in the arts of civilization."[30] Davin had discovered that, in the words of a well-schooled Indigenous leader, "day schools carry no disadvantage [when] the child's home is a civilized home."[31] Residential schools and day schools fulfill different functions at different stages of the assimilative process.

In the Davin Report, then, we find the beginnings of an intergenerational strategy, "a policy that shall look patiently for fruit, not after five or ten years, but after a generation or two."[32] Officials in Canada saw that once residential schools had instilled habits of obedience and industriousness that displaced commitments to consent and community *in the family*, children in those families could be transferred from residential schools to day schools. Residential schools would remain necessary only until the family was sufficiently damaged and could be relied upon to reinforce rather than counteract the civilizing habituation of schooling. And so, in 1879, the IRS system was formally established. Children were placed in residential schools "not to educate them, but primarily to break their link to their culture and identity."[33] It was only once this first phase of assimilation was complete that the children of former residential school survivors could be habituated in the more effective and efficient day school format. The transition was already underway in the United States. As Sandy Grande observes with respect to the Bureau of Indian Affairs in the United States in the early twentieth century, "there were more Indian children in public schools than government (BIA) schools," since public schools were considered by officials to be "the most efficient means by which to train Indians to 'think white'."[34]

Meanwhile, in Canada, the destruction of parenting practices took longer than expected. Indigenous families resisted compulsory attendance and, in particular, the "use of corporal punishment" in schools.[35] In the early twentieth century, the head of Indian Affairs, Duncan Campbell Scott, observed that the content of the curricula was wasted given that attendance was sporadic, and reserves remained bastions of traditional life. Indeed, Scott laments that the most astute graduates of the IRS system, far from being transformed into industrious Canadian farmers or entrepreneurs, would often return to reserves and take up traditional leadership roles: "This relapse actually happened in a large percentage of cases, and most promising pupils were found to have retrograded and to have become leaders in the pagan life of the reserves, instead of contributing to the improvement of their surroundings."[36] In the first few decades of the twentieth century, the failure of the voluntary residential format to interrupt Indigenous consensual parenting practices led to increasingly compulsory approaches to attendance.[37] In 1920, an amendment was made to the Indian Act stipulating compulsory attendance. Parents could be convicted and imprisoned for refusing.[38] Given the increasingly centralized provincial jurisdiction over schooling, many families evaded their reach by returning children to reserves where they fell under federal jurisdiction. In 1935, for example, John Gambler and his wife visited their children at the Desmarais, Alberta, residential school, whereupon "the parents walked away with their children, threatening to shoot whomsoever would endeavour to stop them from taking their children back home."[39] The principal of the school was concerned that, if action were not taken, more parents might follow the Gamblers' example. The federal Indian agent involved, N.P. L'Heureux, revoked the Gamblers' rations (which they did not need), threatened police intervention, and warned of criminal charges under the Indian Act. The children were eventually returned to school.

Eventually, however, the enforcement of compulsory residential schooling orchestrated a devastating interruption in the intergenerational transmission of Indigenous parenting culture.[40] Within a couple of generations, most new Indigenous parents had gone through residential schooling with emerged with limited energy and resources to counter the demands of colonial pedagogy. At this point, government officials determined that the residential format had fulfilled its function and children could, from then on, be gradually transferred to Indian day schools located on or near reserves. The residential schools quickly became the least-used institutions in the IRS system, both in terms of the number of sites and the number of students in attendance. Residential schools became voluntary once again in 1947, after the horrors of the Second World War brought critical attention on practices of genocide. Indigenous attendance was once again a problem. And so, governments shifted the responsibility of assimilating Indigenous children to a more attractive but also more effective format: fully integrated provincial day schools in the public school system.[41] By the

1950s, there were twice as many Indigenous children in day schools as there were in residential schools.[42] Children were transferred out of residential and day schools into provincial schools where they discovered identical practices of nonconsensual attendance, negative reinforcement, restrictions on bodily movement and functions, top-down evaluation and assessment, and hierarchical ranking and certification. In effect, although the last *residential* school closed in 1996 (putting an end to the most egregious examples of abuse), and day schools fell out of use in the post-war period, the IRS system of coercive colonial assimilation continues to function today under the auspices of the public school system.

Today, Indigenous children and youth continue to struggle in these institutions, and they are statistically more inclined to abandon them, leading governments and conservative policy thinktanks such as the Fraser Institute to sound the alarm over low levels of Indigenous attendance and graduation from Canada's public school systems,[43] especially those operated by First Nations. Once again, the worry is that Indigenous peoples are unable or unwilling to properly enforce nonconsenual and assimilative standards. Unfortunately, debates over Indigenous education that play out in the media tend to focus on the absence of evaluative standards and accountability or on inadequate funding and inclusion of culturally relevant content, rather than on any failure to gain the consent of Indigenous children and youth. Public dialogue continues to focus on how to establish clear and objective standards of student learning while also including more Indigenous content and instructors. The hope is that schools will be better equipped to cultivate the literacy and improved wellbeing of Indigenous youth. Moreover, changes in curricula are necessary to expose non-Indigenous students to hitherto neglected Indigenous perspectives, thus promoting the goal of reconciliation.

Phase II: IRS Pedagogies, Curricula, and Next Generations

There is good reason to doubt whether changing the character of school curricula will have the desired decolonial effects. As we've seen, the architects of the IRS system themselves viewed the content of school curricula as playing a minor role relative to pedagogical practices that imbue students with "civilized" habits. Historically, Canadian officials have been much less concerned with preserving a Eurocentric curriculum taught by white teachers as they have with displacing Indigenous parenting traditions of consent and mutual respect. Indeed, once the residential schools were perceived to have successfully interrupted the transmission of Indigenous parenting cultures, Canadian officials began expressing the need to *promote* Indigenous content in the curricula of Canada's public schools. They had made a similar realization south of the border. As early as 1934, for instance, the US secretary of the interior stumbled upon the realization that Indigenous interest in learning English could be improved by ending the prohibition on the use of Indigenous languages in schools.[44] With this development, a new phase of colonial assimilation had begun. As a matter of expedience, as Indian Affairs education official R.A. Hoey concluded in 1940, the residential schools would effectively continue as social welfare housing for "Indian orphan children" and any children suspected of being neglected.[45]

In 1958, the Oblate Fathers in Canada, a group of Catholic educators who oversaw numerous residential schools, met to discuss developments in pedagogy. They were explicit about a number of points that were crucial to the project of Indigenous assimilation. First, the role of the IRS system was not simply to educate but, more importantly, to "acculturate" Indigenous children into productive habits. Second, given the success of the day school format, the only children who needed to remain in residential school were those whose parents had not been civilized enough to permit successful assimilation in day schools. Finally, they discussed how the function of school curricula was not to assimilate Indigenous children directly but to entice them to invest in the assimilation process of schooling.

Inclusive school curricula were identified as important tools of assimilation. The conclusions and recommendations that came out of an Oblate Fathers' workshop on "Indian acculturation" began by clarifying popular misconceptions about the role of curricula in the assimilative process: "Contrary to the layman's opinion, educating canadian [sic] Indians means much more than simply teaching them the three r's or whatever is the basic curriculum in the schools of each province."[46] Acculturation refers to the inculcation of particular habits aside from the cultivation of a particular overt knowledgeability. A child must be understood as "the passive recipient of a training process"[47]—a training process comprised of "imitation of behaviour patterns of adults" within the context of a "reward and punishment system" enforced by parents, institutions such as schools, and often their own peer group.[48] It is within this context that the individual "internalizes and automatizes" civilized habits[49] until eventually, beginning in adolescence, the Indigenous person begins participating obediently and effectively in adult activities such as the "production, processing and distribution of economic goods."[50] These goals can only be secured when the dominant community assimilates youth in a "friendly and sympathetic" manner.[51]

To distinguish curricula from the colonial acculturation process, the Oblate Fathers point out that for the goal of assimilation to be successful, the curricula must actually take Indigenous culture seriously: "Any realistic programme of schooling aimed at acculturating the Indian must be based on respect for his ethnic and cultural background and on the desire to meet his special needs."[52] Curricula must be congenial to Indigenous culture if it is to provide "a frank, pleasant, gradual, and methodical initiation of the Indian to the uses and customs of our canadian society."[53] This the Oblate Fathers refer to as the "principle of accultura-tion."[54] Indigenous children must even be encouraged to develop an "enlightened pride in their ethnic descent," a form of pride that would prove "essential to the resurgence of native leadership."[55] Such leaders could of course be relied upon to promote school attendance and the advantages of graduation. This process of internal colonization through recognition of cultural identity has since been explored at length by the likes of Frantz Fanon and Glen Coulthard.[56]

The Oblate Fathers understood that assimilation would not be successful if based on the rejection of Indigenous culture and identity since this often led to the psychological and spiritual destruction of the individuals themselves. Forcing assimilation through a coercive curriculum tends instead "to take the joy out of life, to produce general feeling of inferiority, and to destroy drive and purpose"—a costly and wasteful result.[57] Assimilation requires a friendly and familiar curriculum to drawn Indigenous peoples in and permit them to "retain their self-respect, their pride of achievement, and their recognition of those elements in their culture which have enduring worth."[58] As one critic explains, these approaches "seek to cut through the resistance Aboriginal children had exhibited in reaction to the more Draconian tactics of the past,"[59] and should therefore invite critical interrogation of the current Canadian focus on promoting Indigenous content.

The Oblate Fathers also understood that acculturation is an intergenerational process that, in the context of the IRS system, required coordination between residential and public school formats to establish colonial habits in young children: "Each generation is exposed to further and deeper contacts, choosing and reinterpreting in relation to what acculturated blend of traditional patterns it has acquired in early childhood."[60] This "law of cultural change" means that participation in schools could only be truly effective once the residential schools had completed their function, ensuring that "the adults who make up the nucleus of the community agree to the changes as inevitable or worthwhile."[61] In short, the only instance in which a non-Indigenous school is suitable for Indigenous children is when their "home and community background" has already been acculturated or when they are "farmed out to white families immediately upon birth."[62] Although the majority of Indigenous children eventually attended day schools, the residential format remained necessary in cases where Indigenous families "either still live a more or less modified native way of life, or have failed to develop, individually or collectively, the socio-economic patterns necessary to successful day-school attendance."[63] They state explicitly that the curricula are secondary: "Indian Education is first and foremost an 'acculturation' responsibility."[64] Failure to acculturate Indigenous children results in them being unable to continue their education, leaving them "totally unfit to earn a decent living or be good citizens and parents, on or off the reserve, eventually becoming a burden on society."[65] The consequences of failed assimilation (or what they euphemistically refer to as "trans-culturation") are that Indigenous children are not prepared to be economically productive, not invested in a Canadian political identity and, most important of all, not disposed to place their children in Canadian schools to be assimilated.

Echoing the concerns of Duncan Campbell Scott, any failure to acculturate those students risks them returning to their traditional ways "with a vengeance."[66] The residential format is key, but so, too, are attempts at reaching adults who managed to escape the residential system. The aim, then, should be to educate the entire community rather than just individuals, so as to secure "the coming generation."[67] Indigenous elders should be invited to give "talks to children on the 'old ways' as well as the necessity to learn 'new ways'."[68] They should be helped to "establish themselves in homes where they can put in practice what they have learned in school."[69] It may seem paradoxical, but for education officials, promoting Indigenous culture and language was considered crucial to ensuring that Indigenous adults "raise their children the 'canadian way'...so that their children will be readier for the canadian school than they themselves were."[70] The Oblate Fathers agreed that the residential format had failed in some instances to perform its function of preparing future Indigenous parents to cultivate the civilized home life necessary for the success of day schools. They attributed this failure to the fact that the program of acculturation initiated by residential schools "stopped at the time it was most needed, namely when school graduates were marrying and bringing-up [sic] children."[71]

The era of the residential school was almost over, but so too was the era of the unintegrated day school. In 1951, the Indian Act was amended in service of this goal, making it easier "to have First Nations children educated in provincial schools."[72] Despite occasional setbacks, the residential format was so successful that it fell out of use by the beginning of the 1960s. In 1961, as part of a special joint committee of the Senate and House of Commons, an Indian Affairs official celebrated and encouraged further expansion of the "move toward education of Indian children in schools which are under the jurisdiction of provinces."[73] By 1964, over 40% of the Indian school population were in integrated school settings.[74] Echoing the Oblate Fathers' conclusions, the residential schools that remained gradually came to "serve as child-welfare institutions," housing only the worst off.[75] Eventually, as Cindy Blackstock observes, this role would fall to child welfare and foster care. At the same time, what would come to be known as the "Sixties Scoop" was removing children to ensure integration into Canadian schools. Indigenous children were often taken from their communities on the pretense that parents had neglected their children's education by not enforcing school attendance. Adoptive parents could be relied upon to fulfill this function.

Phase III: Public School Assimilation and the Circumvention of Indigenous Resistance

In 1963, the Canadian federal government commissioned anthropologist Harry B. Hawthorn to investigate the social and economic state of Indigenous peoples in Canada. The results were published in his report *A Survey of the Contemporary Indians of Canada: Economic, Political, Educational Needs and Policies*. The "Hawthorn Report" mirrored the Oblate Fathers' conclusions, presenting a case for a more benign and effective approach to the assimilation of Indigenous peoples. The report observed that "the most economically depressed bands are the isolated ones in which the majority of adults are illiterate and unschooled."[76] The report was also clear that the purpose of education is to develop the industrious character that can have success in a "large-scale, complex economy that is subject to rapid technological and other changes."[77] Indigenous children must come to see "that an Indian can do other things besides logging, trapping, fishing or small farming."[78] Unfortunately, the progress of Indigenous education was "often marked by retardation and terminated by dropping out."[79] In 1968, as part of the transition, the IRS system was effectively "absorbed into the government's day school system."[80] Indian Affairs "initiated an extensive program through which the majority of First Nations students would be educated in provincial schools."[81] Although Indigenous communities initially supported relocating children to the public school system, they soon found that they "had little ability to influence the provincial schools."[82] Not surprisingly, children in public schools made "faster progress" and became fluent in English much more readily than residential school students.[83] As the TRC report states, "the 1966–67 school year was marked by two significant developments. First, it was in that year that 95% of all school-aged First Nations children were attending school. This result had been achieved largely through integration. Second, it was also the first year in which the number of First Nations students attending provincial schools exceeded the number attending Indian Affairs schools."[84] The multigenerational project of assimilation imagined by Ryerson and other early architects of the IRS system had come to fruition.

Decolonizing Pedagogy

Indigenous parents, children, and communities participate in schooling in Canada for a variety of strategic reasons. For most, graduation provides educational credentials that offer the only path to economic security and wellbeing. For others, there are strategic advantages to studying the political and legal landscape of Canadian Aboriginal policy. Many will go on to be educators themselves in the hopes of improving the communication of Indigenous perspectives to both Indigenous and non-Indigenous youth. However, none of these strategic practices should be interpreted as an endorsement of colonial schooling. As Anishinaabe scholar Leanne Betasamosake Simpson has argued, the system of colonial pedagogy found in "mandatory colonial schooling"[85] and the "institutionalized schooling system" is an immutable feature of all state-run education.[86] Nonconsensual, compulsory schooling has been central to the colonial displacement of numerous Indigenous parenting cultures. As Simpson relates: "Nishnaabeg intelligence has been violently under attack since the beginning days of colonialism through processes that remove Indigenous peoples from our homelands, whether those processes are residential [or] other forms of state run schools."[87]

State-run primary and secondary education systems do not recognize or support land-based pedagogy or curricula. Decolonization of education therefore requires much more than indigenization of the curriculum and teaching staff since such inclusivity has itself been a colonial strategy of promoting Indigenous attendance and success in nonconsensual, assimilative state schooling contexts for almost a century. Rather, decolonization appears to require a troubling of the colonial premise of nonconsensual education entirely—a troubling, that is, of compulsory attendance, classroom management, and imposed assessment, all features of pedagogy that comprise the chief mechanisms of assimilation. The goal of reconciliation, as many have pointed out, entails much more than greater Indigenous representation in public school curricula.[88]

Critics have rightly pointed out that in postsecondary education, strategies of Indigenous inclusion and indigenization ought to be distinguished from the practice of decolonial indigenization, which entails "dismantling the university and building it back up again with a very different role and purpose."[89] Decolonial pedagogy requires an ethos of mutual respect and care,[90] which itself requires a "complete reconceptualization of the social organization of learning in schooling institutions and fundamentally in classrooms."[91] Decolonial pedagogies seek "actions that promote and provoke the fissuring or cracking of the modern/colonial order."[92] This means resisting the public incarnation of the IRS system. Because the formation of colonial subjects in the school system focuses on the registers of both habituation and indoctrination, decolonial pedagogy is distinct from Paulo Freire's more narrowly reflective and intellectual conception of liberation pedagogy, which seeks to make "oppression and its causes objects of reflection by the oppressed, and from that reflection will come their necessary engagement in the struggle for their liberation."[93] To be robustly decolonial, then, reconciliation must include a paradigmatic shift toward full recognition of the dignity and autonomy of the child and, accordingly, repudiation of (1) colonial pedagogies predicated on control and management of children's bodies such as mandatory attendance and classroom management; (2) imposed valuations of children's worth such as learning outcomes, standardized assessment, and standardized advancement; and, more generally, (3) any form of learning that is not directly connected to Indigenous territory and jurisdiction. This is only possible with an education system that is developed and managed by particular Indigenous communities according to their particular traditions and needs.

Finally, it bears noting that resistance takes many forms, including the way youth drop out and communities and families withdraw their children from the public school system. Simpson is careful to note that colonial pedagogy takes different forms, not all of which are overtly violent. In state-run schools, schooling is forced "using the threat of emotional and physical violence," whereas in university the coercion is more subtle: "If you want these credentials, this is what you have to do and this is what you have to endure."[94] Students recognize the hypocrisy of stressing consent in a setting where they are effectively coerced to be in attendance and evaluated according to imposed standards. The sense of hypocrisy is only exacerbated when educators incorporate content on Indigenous practices of consent in these settings. For many racialized and marginalized communities, including Black peoples, the goal is to remove children from contexts in which they will not flourish emotionally or intellectually[95] in an attempt at "protecting them from...whiteness."[96] Decolonial pedagogy proposes "a journey of unlearning, deprogramming, and undoing the generational trauma visited upon our communities" by colonial schooling.[97]

NOTES

1. Blackstock, "Residential Schools."
2. *Truth and Reconciliation Commission of Canada: Calls to Action*, call 6.
3. Criminal Code of Canada, R.S.C. 1985, c. C-4, s. 43.
4. Truth and Reconciliation Commission of Canada, *Final Report*, 1a:517. Hereafter cited as TRC final report.
5. TRC final report, 1a:559.
6. What I am referring to as "colonial pedagogy" connotes elements of both pedagogy and assessment. Confusingly, critical approaches to pedagogy often include issues of curricular contents, while discussions of curriculum often incorporate elements of pedagogy. For instance, as Eve Tuck and K. Wayne Yang note in their introduction to *Indigenous and Decolonizing Studies in Education*, curriculum studies is concerned not only with the content of instruction but with "articulating how the disciplinary procedures in schooling connect to unequal relations of power in society" (xii). For the purposes of this chapter, I distinguish between colonial pedagogy and colonial curricula.
7. Prakash and Esteva, *Escaping Education*.
8. Louie et al., "Applying Indigenizing Principles"; Mahuika, Berryman, and Bishop, "Issues of Culture and Assessment."
9. Giroux and NPenna, "Social Education in the Classroom."
10. Ormiston, "Educating 'Indians'."
11. See Carlson, "Familial Cohesion and Colonial Atomization"; Choate and McKenzie, "Psychometrics in Parenting"; Lindstrom and Choate, "Nistawatsiman"; McKenzie et al., "Aboriginal Grandmothers"; Muir and Bohr, "Contemporary Practice"; Neckoway, Brownlee, and Castellan, "Is Attachment Theory Consistent"; Royal Commission on Aboriginal Peoples, *Summary of the Final Report*, 417, 530 n.415; van de Sande and Menzies, "Native and Mainstream Parenting."
12. Simpson, *Dancing on Our Turtle's Back*, 21.
13. Simpson, "A Homegrown Genocide."
14. Royal Commission on Aboriginal Peoples, *Final Report*, 2:451, 3:406; TRC final report, 6:165.
15. TRC final report, 1:41.
16. TRC final report, 1:42.
17. Arneil, *Domestic Colonies*.
18. TRC final report, 1:43.
19. Le Jeune, "Relation of What Occurred," 219.
20. Le Jeune, "Relation of What Occurred," 195.

21. Simpson, "Land as Pedagogy," 15.
22. TRC final report, 1:46.
23. Bagot, "Report on the Affairs of the Indians in Canada."
24. Ryerson, appendix to *Report of Dr. Ryerson*.
25. John A. MacDonald, quoted in TRC final report, 1b:126.
26. Hector-Louis Langevin, quoted in Truth and Reconciliation Commission of Canada, *What We Have Learned*, 29. Hereafter cited as TRC, *What We Have Learned*.
27. Hector-Louis Langevin, quoted in TRC final report, 1a:159.
28. John A. MacDonald, quoted in TRC, *What We Have Learned*, 6.
29. Davin, *Report on Industrial Schools*, 1–2. Hereafter cited as the Davin Report.
30. Davin Report, 1.
31. Davin Report, 6.
32. Davin Report, 16.
33. TRC final report, 1a:38.
34. Grande, *Red Pedagogy*, 15.
35. TRC final report, 1a:68.
36. Scott, "Indian Affairs: 1867–1912," 615.
37. TRC final report, 1a:266.
38. TRC final report, 1a:279.
39. TRC final report, 1a:286.
40. Ing, "Effects of Residential Schools."
41. Clark and Johnson, "Issues Facing Native Women," 91.
42. TRC final report, 1b:58.
43. Bains, *Myths and Realities*. See also "Quality Education," Indigenous Services Canada, last modified January 25, 2018, https://www.canada.ca/en/indigenous-services-canada/news/2018/01/quality_education.html.
44. Piché, "Indian Acculturation in the U.S.A," 53.
45. TRC final report, 1b:148.
46. Oblate Fathers in Canada, "The Workshop," 13. All instances of the word *canadian* in the Oblate Fathers' publication are lowercase.
47. Renaud, "Acculturation in Theory," 23.
48. Renaud, "Acculturation in Theory," 24.
49. Renaud, "Acculturation in Theory," 25.
50. Renaud, "Acculturation in Theory," 24.
51. Renaud, "Acculturation in Theory," 28.
52. Renaud, "Acculturation in Theory," 13.
53. Renaud, "Acculturation in Theory," 13.
54. Renaud, "Acculturation in Theory," 13.
55. Renaud, "Acculturation in Theory," 14.
56. See Fanon, *Black Skin, White Masks* and Glen Coulthard, *Red Skin, White Masks*.
57. Piché, "Indian Acculturation," 45.
58. Piché, "Indian Acculturation," 45.
59. Ormiston, "Educating 'Indians'," 9.
60. Renaud, "Acculturation in Theory," 28.
61. Renaud, "Acculturation in Theory," 32.
62. Renaud, "Acculturation in Theory," 33.
63. Oblate Fathers in Canada, "The Workshop," 5.
64. Oblate Fathers in Canada, "The Workshop," 5.

65. Oblate Fathers in Canada, "The Workshop," 16.
66. Renaud, "Acculturation in Theory," 34.
67. Renaud, "Acculturation in Theory," 35.
68. Renaud, "Acculturation in Theory," 35.
69. Renaud, "Acculturation in Theory," 35.
70. Renaud, "Acculturation in Theory," 36.
71. Renaud, "Acculturation in Theory," 36.
72. TRC final report, 1a:59.
73. Carney, "The Hawthorn Survey," 618.
74. Carney, "The Hawthorn Survey," 617–18.
75. TRC final report, 1b:148.
76. Hawthorn *Survey of the Contemporary Indians*, 2:102. Hereafter cited as the Hawthorn Report.
77. Hawthorn Report, 1:55.
78. Hawthorn Report, 2:6.
79. Hawthorn Report, 1:5
80. TRC final report, 1b:10.
81. TRC final report, 1b:48.
82. TRC final report, 1b:59.
83. TRC final report, 1b:25
84. TRC final report, 1b:59.
85. Simpson, *Dancing on Our Turtle's Back*, 127.
86. Simpson, "Land as Pedagogy," 8–9.
87. Simpson, "Land as Pedagogy," 13.
88. See Mihesuah and Wilson, *Indigenizing the Academy*.
89. Gaudry and Lorenz, "Indigenization as Inclusion," 223.
90. Lissovoy, "Decolonial Pedagogy."
91. Tejeda, Espinoza, and Gutierrez, "Toward a Decolonizing Pedagogy," 31.
92. Walsh, "Decolonial Pedagogies," 19.
93. Freire, *Pedagogy of the Oppressed*, 48.
94. Simpson, "Land as Pedagogy," 8.
95. Mazama and Lundy, "African American Homeschooling."
96. Richards, "'I Am Protecting Them," at 4:53
97. Romero, "Toward a Critical Unschooling Pedagogy," 67.

BIBLIOGRAPHY

Arneil, Barbara. *Domestic Colonies: The Colonial Turn Inward*. Oxford: Oxford University Press, 2017.

Bagot, Charles. "Report on the Affairs of the Indians in Canada." In *Journals of the Legislative Assembly of the Province of Canada*. Vol. 4., *Session 1844–5*, appendix EEE. Montréal: Rollo Campbell, 1845.

Bains, Ravina. *Myths and Realities of First Nations Education*. Calgary: Fraser Institute, 2014.

Blackstock, Cindy. "Residential Schools: Did They Really Close or Just Morph into Child Welfare?" *Indigenous Law Journal* 6, no. 1 (2007): 71–78.

Carlson, Keith Thor. "Familial Cohesion and Colonial Atomization: Governance and Authority in a Coast Salish Community." *Native Studies Review* 19, no. 2 (2010): 1–42.

Carney, Robert J. "The Hawthorn Survey (1966–1967): Indians and Oblates and Integrated Schooling." *Canadian Catholic Historical Association: Study Sessions* 50 (1983): 609–30. http://www.umanitoba. ca/colleges/st_pauls/ccha/Back Issues/CCHA1983-84/Carney.pdf.

Choate, Peter W., and Amber McKenzie. "Psychometrics in Parenting Capacity Assessments: A Problem for Aboriginal Parents." *First People's Child & Family Review* 10, no. 2 (2015): 31–43.

Clark, Rose L., and Carrie L. Johnson. "Overview of Issues Facing Native Women." In *Sharing Our Stories of Survival: Native Women Surviving Violence*. Edited by Sarah Deer, Bernie Clairmont, Carrie A. Martell, and Maureen L. White Eagle. Lanham: AltaMira Press, 2008.

Coulthard, Glen Sean. *Red Skin White Masks: Rejecting the Colonial Politics of Recognition*. Minneapolis: University of Minnesota Press, 2014.

Davin, Nicholas Flood. *Report on Industrial Schools for Indians and Half Breeds*. [Ottawa?]: [1879?]. Microfilm.

Fanon, Frantz. *Black Skin, White Masks*. London: Paladin, 1970.

Freire, Paulo. *Pedagogy of the Oppressed*. 3rd ed. New York: Continuum, 1970.

Gaudry, Adam, and Danielle Lorenz. "Indigenization as Inclusion, Reconciliation, and Decolonization: Navigating the Different Visions for Indigenizing the Canadian Academy." *AlterNative* 14, no. 3 (2018): 218–27.

Giroux, Henry A., and Anthony N. Penna. "Social Education in the Classroom: The Dynamics of the Hidden Curriculum." *Theory and Research in Social Education* 7 (Spring 1979): 21–41. https://doi.org/10.1080/00933104.1980.10506070.

Grande, Sandy. *Red Pedagogy: Native American Social and Political Thought*. New York: Rowman and Littlefield, 2004.

Hawthorn, H.B., ed. *A Survey of the Contemporary Indians of Canada: Economic, Political, Educational Needs and Policies*. 2 vols. Ottawa: Indian Affairs Branch, 1967.

Ing, Rosalyn N. "The Effects of Residential Schools on Native Child-Rearing Patterns." Master's thesis, University of British Columbia, 1990. UBC Open Collections. https://doi.org/10.14288/1.0102443.

Le Jeune, Paul. "Relation of What Occurred in New France in the Year 1633." In *The Jesuit Relations and Allied Documents: Travels and Explorations of the Jesuit Missionaries in New France, 1610–1791*. Vol. 5, *Québec: 1632–1633*, edited by Reuben Gold Thwaites, translated by John Cutler Covert, 83–267. Cleavland: The Burrows Brothers Company, 1897.

Lindstrom, Gabrielle, and Peter W. Choate. "Nistawatsiman: Rethinking Assessment of Aboriginal Parents for Child Welfare Following the Truth and Reconciliation Commission." *First People's Child & Family Review* 11, no. 2 (2016): 45–59.

Lissovoy, Noah D. "Decolonial Pedagogy and the Ethics of the Global." *Discourse: Studies in the Cultural Politics of Education* 31, no. 3 (2010): 279–93.

Louie, Dustin William, Yvonne Poitras Pratt, Aubrey Jean Hanson, and Jacqueline Ottmann. "Applying Indigenizing Principles of Decolonizing Methodologies in University Classrooms." *Canadian Journal of Higher Education* 47, no. 3 (2017): 16–33.

Mahuika, Rangimarie, Mere Berryman, and Russell Bishop. "Issues of Culture and Assessment in New Zealand Education Pertaining to Māori Students." *Assessment Matters* 3, no. 11 (2011): 183–98.

Mazama, Anna, and Garvey Lundy. "African American Homeschooling as Racial Protectionism." *Journal of Black Studies* 43, no. 7 (2012): 723–48.

McKenzie, Holly A., Carrie Bourassa, Wendee Kubik, Kerrie Strathy, and Betty McKenna. "Aboriginal Grandmothers Caring for Grandchildren: Located in a Policy Gap." *Indigenous Policy Journal* 21, no. 4 (2010): 1–18.

Mihesuah, Devon Abbott, and Angela Cavender Wilson, eds. *Indigenizing the Academy: Transforming Scholarship and Empowering Communities*. Lincoln: University of Nebraska Press, 2004.

Muir, Nicole, and Yvonne Bohr. "Contemporary Practice of Traditional Aboriginal Child Rearing: A Review." *First Peoples Child & Family Review* 9, no. 1 (2014): 66–79.

Neckoway, Raymond, Keith Brownlee, and Bruno Castellan. "Is Attachment Theory Consistent with Aboriginal Parenting Realities?" *First Peoples Child & Family Review* 3, no. 2, (2007): 65–74.

Oblate Fathers in Canada, eds. *Residential Education for Indian Acculturation*. Ottawa: Indian and Eskimo Welfare Commission, 1958.

———. "The Workshop." In Oblate Fathers in Canada, *Residential Education for Indian Acculturation*, 4–16.

Ormiston, Alice. "Educating 'Indians': Practices of Becoming Canadian." *The Canadian Journal of Native Studies* 22, no. 1 (2002): 1–22.

Piché, Paul. "Indian Acculturation in the U.S.A." In Oblate Fathers in Canada, *Residential Education for Indian Acculturation*, 45–56.

Prakash, Madhu Suri, and Gustavo Esteva. *Escaping Education: Living as Learning Within Grassroots Cultures*. 2nd ed. New York: Peter Lang, 2008.

Renaud, P.A. "Acculturation in Theory." In Oblate Fathers in Canada, *Residential Education for Indian Acculturation* 17–36.

Richards, Akila. "'I Am Protecting Them from Whiteness': Why This Mom Chose to Take Her Kids out of Public School." Interview with Piya Chattopadhyay. *Out in the Open*, CBC Radio, April 15, 2018. https://www.cbc.ca/radio/outintheopen/protection-1.4608124/i-am-protecting-them-from-whiteness-why-this-mom-chose-to-take-her-kids-out-of-public-school-1.4609054.

Romero, Noah. "Toward a Critical Unschooling Pedagogy." *Journal of Unschooling and Alternative Learning* 12, no. 23 (2018): 56–71.

Royal Commission on Aboriginal Peoples. *Report of the Royal Commission on Aboriginal Peoples*. 5 vols. Ottawa: Indian and Northern Affairs Canada, 1996.

———. *Summary of the Final Report*. Ottawa: Indian and Northern Affairs Canada, 1997.

Ryerson, Egerton. Appendix to *Report of Dr. Ryerson on Industrial Schools with Dr. Ryerson's Report of 1847 Attached*. Ottawa: Government Print Bureau, 1898.

Scott, Duncan Campbell. "Indian Affairs: 1867–1912." In *Canada and its Provinces*. Vol. 7. Edited by Adam Shortt and Arthur G. Doughty. Toronto: University of Edinburgh Press, 1913.

Simpson, Leanne. *Dancing on Our Turtle's Back*. Peterborough: ARP Books, 2011.

Simpson, Leanne Betasamosake. "A Homegrown Genocide." *Briarpatch Magazine*, July 23, 2012. https://briarpatchmagazine.com/articles/view/honour-the-apology.

———. "Land as Pedagogy: Nishnaabeg Intelligence and Rebellious Transformation." *Decolonization: Indigeneity, Education & Society* 3, no. 33 (2014): 1–25. http://decolonization.org/index.php/des/article/view/22170.

Tejeda, Carlos, Manuel Espinoza, and Kris Gutierrez. "Toward a Decolonizing Pedagogy: Social Justice Reconsidered." In *Pedagogies of Difference: Rethinking Education for Social Justice*, edited by Peter Pericles Trifonas, 9–37. New York: Routledge, 2002.

Truth and Reconciliation Commission of Canada. *The Final Report of the Truth and Reconciliation Commision of Canada*. 6 vols. Montréal: McGill-Queens University Press, 2015.

———. *Truth and Reconciliation Commission of Canada: Calls to Action*. Winnipeg: National Centre for Truth and Reconciliation, 2015. https://ehprnh2mwo3.exactdn.com/wp-content/uploads/2021/01/Calls_to_Action_English2.pdf.

———. *What We Have Learned: Principles of Truth and Reconciliation*. Winnipeg: National Centre for Truth and Reconciliation, 2015.

Tuck, Eve, and K. Wayne Yang. Series editors' introduction to *Indigenous and Decolonizing Studies in Education: Mapping the Long View*, edited by Linda Tuhiwai Smith, Eve Tuck, and K. Wayne Yang, x–xxi. New York: Routledge, 2019.

van de Sande, Adje, and Peter Menzies. "Native and Mainstream Parenting: A Comparative Study." *Native Social Work Journal* 4, no. 1 (2003): 126–39.

Walsh, Catherine E. "Decolonial Pedagogies Walking and Asking. Notes to Paulo Freire from AbyaYala." *International Journal of Lifelong Education* 34, no. 1 (2015): 9–21.

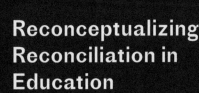

Reconceptualizing Reconciliation in Education

Teaching and Learning in Right Relation

8

SANDRA D. STYRES
AND ARLO KEMPF

Reconciliation and Relational Ethics in Education

Setting the Context

Since the release of the Truth and Reconciliation Commission of Canada's (TRC) report in 2015, many subsequent events, including the 2021 unearthing of the mass grave at the former Kamloops Indian residential school (IRS) and the multiple unmarked graves at Marieval IRS, have shocked Canadians and brought a differently heightened focus to the "reconciliation project." Survivors of the IRS system have been speaking about mass and unmarked graves at IRSs for many decades, and it is highly likely that many more will be found. The troubling concept of reconciliation can no longer be seen as an abstract, tacit, or benign notion with no current political and social implications. These graves are glaring and unmistakable evidence of the violence perpetuated against our children in the name of education. The Honourable Murray Sinclair (former Chair of the TRC) has stated that "education got us into this mess...and education is the key to reconciliation."[1] The TRC report identified education as a critical site for reconciliatory efforts with ministries of education and school boards pushing for teachers to implement its calls to action in their classrooms. The province of Ontario echoes the TRC's focus on education as a "key component" of reconciliation.[2] In this fragile political climate where reconciliation remains high on the national agenda, current scholarship shows that many educational institutions are still falling far short of implementing the TRC and promoting relational ethics within universities. Many institutional actors report that they do not know what to do, how to do it, what it is supposed to look like, who to talk to, or appropriate ways or places to seek information.

Colonialism continues to be an ongoing process that shapes both the structure and quality of relationships between non-Indigenous settler Canadians and Indigenous peoples. Emma Lowman and Adam Barker write that settler identities do not erase the diverse stories of how non-Indigenous people came to be here.[3] The term *settler* for non-Indigenous Canadians (regardless of their stories of arrival) reinforce uncomfortable realities that they may very much like to turn away from: their own historical and contemporary complicity in the tangled colonial relationships with Indigenous Peoples and these lands. While there is at least some effort in this post-TRC era to acknowledge colonialism as a historic reality, there remains a settler Canadian tendency to lean into the three D's—deny, deflect, and defend—when addressing their own complicity in the ways colonialism continues to operate systemically and structurally through networks and relations of power, privilege, and patriarchy. They deny their own complicity in the legacy of settler colonialism, deflect from the discomfort of unsettling colonial narratives, and defend settler futurities. While there can be no one definition of settler identity, there are shared attributes that characterize settler colonialism. These shared attributes relate to ethics of positionality (how and in what ways one positions oneself in relation to Indigenous lands) and relationality (how and in what ways one is or is not in relationship to Indigenous Peoples and lands). One can uncover their positionalities and relationalities by asking themselves five key questions: (1) Whose traditional lands am I on? (2) How have I come to be in this place? (3) What is my relationship to the Indigenous land I am situated on and the Indigenous People of this land? (4) What do these questions mean to me? (5) Why are these questions important?

Whether we choose to acknowledge it or not, we now exist in relationship with each other and to this land—a land that has and still does exist first and foremost in relationship to Indigenous people. To be in good relationship with one another requires an acknowledgement of whose traditional lands we are now on as well as the historical and contemporary realities of those relationships. To that end, we will explore Indigenous-settler reconciliation and relational ethics by first examining the ethics of positionality. We will move to a discussion on coloniality and Indigenous anticolonial resistance. We will then delve into the ethics of relationality and conclude with a conversation about Indigenous futurities in education.

Ethics of Positionality

The ethics of positionality are closely related to issues of identity that are often complex and shifting. Lowman and Barker tell us that "the words we use to name ourselves are important" as they tell us who we are, both individually and as a collective.[4] From a reconciliation perspective, an ethics of positionality is an acknowledgement of individual culpability in national narratives informed by networks and relations of power and privilege, which in turn maintain and reinforce colonialism and structural racism in the Canadian context. Rauna Kuokkanen writes that critical engagement is "helpful in its insistence that we pay attention to the exclusions and the silences in narratives."[5] It is also helpful, due to its inherent reflexive criticism, in leading us to examine the ways we are intimately complicit participants in the topics and/or issues we engage. The ethics of positionality complicate complicity and disrupt taken-for-granted embodiments of what it means to be "Canadian." If reconciliation is to be more than a token attempt at another colonial feel-good project, the ethics of positionality demand an acknowledgement that settler Canadians' existence, both as individuals and as a nation, is predicated upon a nation that "violently displaces others for its own wants and desires, breaks treaties, and uses police and starvation to clear the land."[6] Seeing ourselves "for who we are, not just who we claim to be" is key to any authentic truth-telling and reconciliation.[7] Ethics of positionality shift rhetoric that reinforce "claims to settler futurity"[8] and the "fantasies of settler entitlement"[9] toward those discourses that critically examine the ways settler Canadians and all those who now call Canada home (regardless of their arrival stories) are in relationship to the lands, waterways, and Indigenous Peoples. In colonial contexts, land and water rights are always sites of contestation and resistance where disparate worldviews collide, engage, and polarize each other. Ethics of positionality in reconciliation engage Indigenous claims to land, water, and treaty rights as the original and host peoples of these lands. As authors, we seek to model an ethics of positionality by clearly outlining who we are in relation to kinship ties and to our places.

SANDRA'S BACKGROUND

Our stories are sacred, they are spirit, they are ceremony, and they are medicine. Our stories ground our understandings of our relationships and responsibilities to our places. They also guide our ways of being in the world and heal our soul wounds. As such, I want to share my story with you and how that story informs the work I do.

I am privileged to be a member of the Six Nations of the Grand River community through marriage to my husband, who is Kanien'kehá:ka, Turtle Clan. The Six Nations community gave me a place to belong when I did not have a place. I have been living in the Six Nations community for over 20 years, raising my family and taking great care to live out the five *R*'s—relationship, responsibility, relevance, respect, and reciprocity—in serving my community.[10]

My own Indigenous heritage is not grounded in the Six Nations community, but rather finds its roots in what was once known as the upper Mohawk Valley in Southern Québec. Those roots, and thereby my story, were fractured by long-ago events.

I was born in Tiohtiá:ke tsi ionhwéntsare (Montréal, Québec) and lived there until I was 16 years of age, when my family moved to Oniatariio' (Ontario). I am of Kanien'kehá:ka (Mohawk), and mixed Euro-Canadian descent. My First Nations heritage comes from my connection to my ancestors through my father's lineage (Kanien'kehá:ka and French). My mother's lineage connects me to my English and Welsh ancestors from Europe.

Québec has had and continues to have a very contentious relationship with the Indigenous Peoples who reside within its borders. The loss of my connections to place and to my people came about as a result of colonialism, racism, assimilationist political policies, and the governments' continued attempts to divide and conquer the Haudenosaunee people by severing the connections to their matrilineage. This led to many Haudenosaunee women and their children losing their connections to their place, their lineage, and their authority as Clan Mothers. Many of us, including myself, have lost connections to people and place in this way and are now working to repatriate those connections. This also speaks to our strength and resiliency as Indigenous people. These stories of loss, displacement, and the labour of repatriation mean that many of us have complex relationships to our places as a result of the ongoing legacy of colonialism.

Locating oneself in relation to everything one does is a key foundational principle in Indigeneity. The only place from which any of us can write or speak with any degree of certainty is from the position of who we are in relation to what we know. In this way, I am accountable for my own cultural location that situates me in relation to my community at home and at large, as well as within this writing. Locating oneself is a relational, respectful, and reciprocal process that is a key element of Indigenous philosophies and relational ethics. As an educator, I am always aware that I am intimately connected to the very systems I criticize. I am also always conscious of the fact that, as an Indigenous person of First Nations and mixed Euro-Canadian ancestry within academia, I must consistently embrace the messy fluidity of an insider-outsider perspective. I am at once privileged and complicit in so many tangled ways, yet simultaneously marginalized and erased within the very system to which I am intimately connected and of which I am critical. This necessitates that I participate in and negotiate multiple discourses that at times contradict, erase, or marginalize the Other within myself. This also necessitates that I participate in and navigate challenging dichotomous lines of thought while simultaneously opening up spaces of possibility.

ARLO'S BACKGROUND

I am a White, first-generation settler Canadian who rarely gets asked where he's from, and never where he's *from* from. On my father's side, my ancestors came to North America from what is now Germany. On my mother's side, our people come from Oklahoma. After searching through a series of adoption records, stories, lies, and aspirations, as best I can tell, my maternal ancestors were likely Scottish and Cherokee. I'll never be sure; no one has made any claims to or been claimed by one group or another. Others read me as White and I read myself as White. I was born on Kanien'kehá:ka land in Tiohtiá:ke (commonly known as Montréal). My parents were recent immigrants from the United States. We later moved to Treaty 13 territory. I grew up there, in the territory of the Mississaugas of the New Credit—what is commonly known as Toronto—where I work and live today.

Upon beginning this writing together, Sandra and I felt part of the significance of the two of us sharing a discursive space was that we are coming from different places. We recognize that while we share a great many understandings of reconciliation, we operate with and from different truths at times. Acknowledging that where we have come from (and are coming from) informs where we are, Sandra and I are writing from different places. As a settler Canadian, reconciliation has in many ways been offered to me (by my government, my media, and my academic spaces) as another Canadian accomplishment: a moment of our creation and of which we can be proud, an eagle's feather in the already full cap of Canadian multicultural achievements. Popular (mis)conceptions of the TRC offer a reading that suggest that it closes a chapter in Canadian history. In fact, it marks a call to co-construct a future of walking in intentional right relation.

In my experience as a settler Canadian, a key marker of settlerhood is that I and other settler Canadians can usually choose to ignore all conversations, considerations, and complications associated with reconciliation. In fact, as is the case for many Canadians, the release of the TRC report in 2015 was far easier to overlook than Canada 150 sesquicentennial celebrations in 2017. Colonial momentum is a river into which Canadian settlers are born or into which they migrate, and for many of us the TRC has not necessarily been disruptive to this flow. Stepping out of the water requires first noticing its ceaseless movement—the way it flows around bends, breaks over rocks and through low-hanging brush. Once noticed, it takes some doing to get out of its rushing waters. I am not there yet, but I am working to find, at the very least, the shallows on the margins of the river from which to catch my breath and step out of the flow. In these moments, I see that colonial tide and remember that all that flows must eventually ebb. I write from this space of privilege, complication, and humility—a positionality that informs my work as a scholar and my actions as a citizen, family member, descendant, and human.

Coloniality in Context

> The essence of the American character is to explore new horizons and to tame new frontiers...When it comes to defending America, it is not enough to merely have an American presence in space, we must have an American dominance in space.
> —Former US president Donald Trump[11]

> Too bad the kid died but he got what he deserved.
> —Words attributed to an unnamed RCMP Officer commenting on the not-guilty verdict of Gerald Stanley, a White farmer, who shot and killed Colten Boushie, a young Indigenous man[12]

We offer these two distinct but related sentiments to frame the context in which we take up questions of decolonization and reconciliation. Former US president Trump's vision of dominating and taming the unknown (space) is also a call to dominate and tame the known. Here, space is a metaphorical representation of a general and total object that will come to exist (i.e., cease to be merely an abstract frontier) through the process of be(com)ing dominated and tamed by American empire. Space, a potentially infinite thing, can be neither tamed nor conquered, but that's okay—colonialism is more significant as a direction than as a destination. Colonialism need never arrive; it must simply continue. We see this, too, in the offerings of the anonymous RCMP officer credited above. The mountie and the former US president share an instinct and offer us two sides of the same coin.

The story of the death of Colten Boushie offers a powerful illustration of an ecosystem of White supremacy in Canada that revolves around power and land. Boushie, a 22-year-old Nêhiyawak (Cree) man, was shot to death by Gerald Stanley, a White farmer in Saskatchewan, when Boushie and his friends pulled into Stanley's farm with a flat tire on August 9, 2016. Whether the gun went off accidentally, as Stanley's defence claimed, or whether Stanley sought to kill Boushie for being on his property, it was Stanley's acquittal by an all-White jury that was perhaps the more powerful injustice. The killing was an individual act—a death resulting from a dispute over notions of land, place, and trespass. The acquittal (one of numerous cases in which all-White juries have pronounced the innocence of White people who have killed Indigenous people) was a systemic act—one that also centred on notions of land, place, and trespass. Put another way, the killing was one Canadian's action, while the acquittal was a Canadian action. The pedagogy of the killing is thus twofold, offering lessons for both White farmers with guns and Indigenous kids with flat tires.

Stanley's actions, and his acquittal, happened on Treaty 6 territory. Signed by British officials and Indigenous inhabitants of the area, Treaty 6 covers much of central Alberta and Saskatchewan. It was enacted in 1876, alongside the Indian

Act. That same year, the intercontinental railway was completed. As would follow so many treaty signings, the colonial signatories would fail to honour many of their obligations—most notably the Medicine Chest clause, which guaranteed health-care for Indigenous inhabitants. Canadian courts soon decided that Canada no longer had this and other obligations. Rather than a reciprocal agreement, treaties were often treated by Euro-Canada as evidence of passive surrender by Indigenous nations: surrender of land, culture, resources, agency, autonomy, and the right to self-determination. Ironically, the few obligations actually fulfilled (although only partially) by Euro-Canada, such as tax exemptions and federal funding for some services, often form the basis of popular White-supremacist stereotypes of lazy and dependent Indigenous peoples.

Indigenous peoples are, of course, forcibly subjected to (and subject to) Canada's legal systems, and this is not working in their favour. (A quick internet search for Bradley Barton Raymond Cormier will flesh out more of the history of White juries acquitting White folks accused of killing Indigenous folks.) More broadly, estimates suggest that up to 2 million Indigenous people have died as a result of Euro-Canadian colonial policies.[13] Nationally in Canada, Indigenous people are roughly twice as likely to die from avoidable causes as non-Indigenous people,[14] while the deaths of over 4000 Indigenous women and girls continue to go unsolved. CTV News reports that "Indigenous people are 10 times more likely than [W]hite people to have been shot and killed by police in Canada."[15] Indigenous people are also more likely than non-Indigenous people to be wrongfully convicted in Canadian courts.[16]

At the time of Boushie's death in 2016, of the 265 most powerful positions in Saskatchewan education, business, law, and government, fewer than 5% were occupied by Indigenous peoples.[17] Among the provinces' 101 judges, two were Indigenous. Meanwhile, over 80% of prisoners in provincial jails were Indigenous, although only 16% of Saskatchewan's population is Indigenous.[18] In 2016, the on-reserve rate of high school completion for Indigenous people was 70% in British Columbia and 36% in Manitoba (the country's highest and lowest respectively)—rates that, while improving, will take 35 years to reach parity with those of non-Indigenous Canadians.[19] On top of this, Cindy Blackstock has reported that, nation-ally, there are "three times the number of First Nations children in foster care today than there were at the height of the residential schools and the problem is getting worse in many parts of the country."[20] These are among hundreds of contemporary statistical illustrations of a Canadian White-supremacist ecosystem. Such facts and figures are ultimately the sum of countless parts, including micro- and macro-aggressions at the individual level, prejudice and discrimination at the institutional level, and trends and policies at the systemic level—three spaces that are mutually productive and sustaining.

While many Canadians are deeply invested in a distinction between the United States and Canada, the colonial instincts and behaviours of the two nations are often very much on the same page. Trump's imagined conquest of infinity (i.e., of space) offers a contemporary *terra nullius* for twenty-first-century imperialism. It is no more American than it is Canadian, French, British, Portuguese, Spanish, Russian, or any other colonial nationality. Just who Trump will be taming and/or conquering is less important than a priori imperial ontology—the possessive and totalizing nature of colonial being.

About 600 kilometres west of Stanley's farm, in the traditional territory of the Stoney Nakota Peoples, lies Banff National Park. The town of Banff, a shiny patrician Disneyland, was built by Canadian prisoners of war during the First World War. These prisoners were forced to labour year-round in dangerous conditions to create a tourist outpost in the heart of the Rockies. Canada had violently removed the Indigenous folks from the area by then, and systematically denied them hunting rights and other access to the land in breach of treaty obligations. Beginning in the late 1800s, however, Banff introduced Indian Days, which granted Indigenous people access to Banff as part of a spectacle for tourists—a practice that ended in 1978. Today, Banff and nearby Canadian national parks are the centres of a global tourist attraction that has people from around the world visiting the region's "unspoiled" and majestic sites. The product being sold is the discovery of clean/empty/pure land: *terra nullius* for the masses.

At the foot of Lake Louise, around which a resort town playground for the wealthy has sprung up, stands a sign posted by Parks Canada that reads, in part: "This world-famous lake is protected for all time in Banff National Park...The need to protect this special place was recognized from the early days of tourism." Preservation and protection in this narrative are Canadian offerings, while the phrase "for all time" offers a Canadian version of the conquest of the infinite, the implication being that Banff National Park will be here for all time as an extension of a nation that will *also* be here for all time.

Most of the land in Banff National Park, the "empty" playground/discovery zone that lies at the western edge of Treaty 6, is protected from people establishing permanent residence. This is preservation. Meanwhile, concentrated populations of historically displaced Stoney Nakota peoples living in relatively tiny reservations nearby do not benefit from the tourist dollars from Vancouver, Toronto, Montréal, France, China, or Australia. This is part of what contemporary Canadian "protection and preservation" includes, but the complications don't end there. Only a few days before former US president Trump announced the US space odyssey, Canadian Prime Minister Justin Trudeau fought to save the controversial Trans Mountain Pipeline expansion by purchasing the project, which runs through Treaty 6 territory, from US oil giant Kinder Morgan for CAD4.5 billion. While the global environmental impact of the pipeline is unclear, multiple Indigenous nations object to the building of the dangerous pipeline on their lands.

Despite perhaps significant differences of intent, the colonial project and the resultant ecosystems of White supremacy are manifest in these highly distinct moments of Boushie, of the perpetual conquest of space, and of the claims to national park spaces/lands for all time (on Boushie's treaty territory, no less). Underpinned by the statistics offered above, these phenomena give a variegated sketch of North American colonial ontology in motion—the river mentioned in Arlo's introduction. This river has no regard for national borders. Settler colonialism has always been transnational in character and operation. On the same day Gerald Stanley shot Colten Boushie to death, at least fourteen people were killed by Saudi-led, US-backed coalition airstrikes that hit a food factory in Yemen's capital Sana'a, while the US occupation of Iraq was in full swing—acts of taming, conquest, and dominance. In framing the context of this discussion, we suggest the colonial is thus multifaceted, complex, and multidimensional—operating across space and time. So too, it should be noted, is resistance to settler colonialism, or what we may term anticolonialism.

Indigenous Anticolonial Resistance

> I speak partly for the record, but mostly in memory of the kindly and well-intentioned men and women and their descendants—perhaps some of us here in this chamber—whose remarkable works, good deeds and historical tales in the residential schools go unacknowledged for the most part.
> —Former Canadian senator Lynn Beyak[21]

> Reconciliation seems to be us forgiving them…I would forgive anyone for standing on my feet if they got off…They're still squarely on our feet.
> —Lee Maracle, Stó:lō traditional teacher and writer[22]

As the quote from former senator Beyak above portends, simple truths such as "residential schooling was horrible" are often up for debate in Canada. This illustrates Lee Maracle's point that reconciliation cannot really begin when colonialism persists. There is also a degree of inherent incommensurability in the notion of a colonial operation (Canada) engaging in reconciliatory (or even conciliatory) discourse around relationships with Indigenous peoples. Canada—the country, the project, the idea—is an ongoing response to the Indigenous peoples of Turtle Island. As stated previously, whether we choose to acknowledge it or not, we all exist in relationship with each other and to this land—a land that has and still does exist first and foremost in relationship to Indigenous people in Canada. As such, there is no Canada without Indigenous people, as Canadian identity in its original form and vision is an alternative to Indigeneity—a colonial response to the culture, nations, organizations, and peoples of Turtle Island. The contemporary ecosystems of White supremacy continue the colonial conversation upon which Canada was founded and through which it is maintained and reproduced. Although early encounters between Indigenous People and Europeans on Turtle Island were sometimes violent, we do well to remember that contact was a series of ongoing negotiations in which Indigenous peoples "consciously decided to share" land.[23] Still, conscious choice or not, these moments cannot be taken as freeze-frames of finality in which colonialism started, the Europeans won, and we moved on from there.

Such conversations have defined Canadian discourse since its beginnings. According to Roberta Jamieson, President and CEO of the Indigenous education organization Indspire, John A. MacDonald, Canada's first prime minister, contended in 1887 that "Providence has been pleased to provide us with one nation, unbroken from sea to sea, to be peopled by one people with one common heritage and a common religion."[24] MacDonald further suggested that "the great aim of our legislation has been to do away with the tribal system and assimilate the Indian people in all respects with the other inhabitants of the Dominion as speedily as they are fit to change."[25] That same year, Wilfrid Laurier, Liberal Party leader and future Canadian prime minister, justified taking land from "savages" by arguing that a Canada ruled by Indigenous people would "forever have remained barren and unproductive," while under "civilized" rule it "would afford homes and happiness to teeming millions."[26] Laurier's racist understanding of Indigenous people is still with many Canadians today—normalized and embedded in taken-for-granted national narratives. Making the case for mandatory residential schooling for Indigenous children a generation later, Duncan Campbell Scott, the official in charge of the IRS system, contended:

> I want to get rid of the Indian problem. I do not think as a matter of fact, that the country ought to continuously protect a class of people who are able to stand alone...Our objective is to continue until there is not a single Indian in Canada that has not been absorbed into the body politic and there is no Indian question, and no Indian Department, that is the whole object of this Bill.[27]

Just as colonialism itself has never stopped, neither have various forms of resistances. Euro-Canadian colonialism is a failed conquest. Canadian White-supremacist ecosystems are contested spaces. To be clear, the Canadian colonial project has failed despite the best efforts of Canada. Canada is not the all-White, all-Christian country that the first prime minister aspired to make of it. Duncan Campbell Scott's plan to absorb all Indigenous folks into the Canadian body politic has, despite the Canadian IRS system's intergenerational impacts on Indigenous people across the country, never been fully realized. These failures of conquest are attributable to constant and unrelenting resistance by Indigenous peoples from the time of contact to colonial domination.

In addition to individual acts and refusals (both active and passive), Indigenous peoples have consistently resisted colonial subjugation and exploitation at every turn through active resistances, treaty violations, and diplomacy and warfare as early as the 1600s and 1700s. Through ongoing assertions of rights in the 1800s despite attempts by the government to quash all forms of resistance and assertion of rights by enacting the Indian Act, which essentially legalized treaty violations and cultural genocide. Through armed rebellions on the prairies (including the Red River Rebellion) and the refusals of Indigenous families to send their children to residential schools. Through preserving languages and cultural practices despite Canada's determination of illegality. Through "Pan-Indian" movements, including the National Indian Brotherhood and the Assembly of First Nations, and Red Power movements toward self-determination and sovereignty. Through the Kanesatahke, Ipperwash, Idle No More, Caledonia, and Standing Rock resistances. Through ongoing and outstanding contemporary land-claims negotiations processes, including Trans Mountain Pipeline protestors and Wet'suwet'en Land defenders. There are countless more examples within all sectors of society across Turtle Island. We also note the important roles of both scholarly and community voices of refusal that have informed and been informed by these resistances—voices that constitute important spokes on the anticolonial wheel.[28]

The context for our discussion of reconciliation and the ethics of relationality thus emerges from this complicated historical present—this contested archaeology of the present. Eva Mackey writes that settler fantasy is the belief that Canada's colonial history is one of peaceful settlement rather than acts of genocide, legislated assimilation, and the dispossession of lands.[29] We have come to realize that in any movement toward reconciliation, the conversations need to shift from colonial/anticolonial or even decolonizing frameworks—those that remain fixed in colonial relationships of power and privilege and attempts to reinforce the mythology of settler claims and entitlement—to frameworks based on the ethics of relationality. The 2015 TRC report states that "reconciliation is about establishing and maintaining a mutually respectful relationship" and that "there are no easy shortcuts to reconciliation."[30]

Toward a New Ethics of Relationality

Given the context we have attempted to sketch above, we begin with a heuristic: Is reconciliation between the Canadian state and Indigenous Nations on Turtle Island truly conceivable? Is Canada—itself a concept and set of mechanisms designed for Indigenous displacement and genocide—ontologically capable of being in a reconciliatory relationship with Indigenous peoples?

We suggest reconciliation may indeed be inconceivable. The persistent Canadian colonial violence and inequity described in the previous sections are not bracketed phenomena. Rather, they are evidence of the Canadian state doing what it was designed to do: conduct a multifaceted, settler-colonial siege against Indigenous peoples. Canadian Prime Minister Justin Trudeau (a legacy candidate of Canadian twentieth and twenty-first century colonial-golden-era fantasy) illustrated the limits of progressive settler-colonial governance with the firing and silencing of the first Indigenous and first female Attorney General of Canada, Jody Wilson-Raybould (a Kwakwaka'wakw member of Canadian Parliament). As a clear indication of the limits of possibility regarding Indigenous and national Canadian relations, Prime Minister Trudeau removed Wilson-Raybould from her top governmental post and subsequently expelled her from the Liberal Party of Canada in January 2019. Wilson-Raybould, it appears, was removed for doing her job to the letter of the law and for challenging implicit instructions to engage in ethically questionable behaviour. This, alongside broken promises on clean water, pipelines, education, and other aspects of treaty relations between Canada and Indigenous Nations, suggests that even at its most progressive, the Canadian state cannot walk in right relationship any more than a fish can breathe air.

Despite our pessimism about Canada, we are still on Indigenous lands, on Turtle Island, living together, and living apart. Recognizing that the dismantling of the Canadian state may have to wait and that we need to exist in the meantime, how do we move forward? In the context of this contested notion of reconciliation, an ethics of relationality is required that involves authentic truth-telling of the realities of a colonial history—a truth-telling that is not constantly up for debate. Reconciliation cannot happen while it remains a colonial project steeped in the structural racism that continues to inform Canada's relationship with Indigenous peoples. Arthur Manuel tells us that what is broken is not simply a set of behaviours: Canada cannot fix this by simply smiling and playing nice, assuming then that all will be well.[31] In a colonial context, it is the original and enduring rights of Indigenous peoples that are broken. These fundamental rights are treaty and sovereignty rights. What is required to repair and restore the relationship between Indigenous peoples and Canada as a whole is not empty rhetoric, token "apologies and hugs," but "recognition and restitution."[32] Canada must recognize the constitutionally protected lands and treaty rights that belong to Indigenous peoples as sovereign peoples rather than constantly looking for ways to extinguish those rights—must give restitution for a legacy of colonialism cloaked in cultural genocide, land theft, displacement, stolen children, legislative extinction, and third-world living conditions. Mackey writes that "treaty is a participatory verb."[33] It is a process of engaging in relationships ethically and responsibly. Responsibility in the ethics of relationality is mindful, reciprocal, and respectful.

Reconciliation and Relationality in Education

The ethics of relationality involved in reconciling treaty and sovereignty rights is an ethics that understands these rights as an ongoing process of critical social action. In her article "Reconcili*action*: Reconciling Contestation in the Academy," Styres writes that reconciliation is a complex and challenging endeavour and that there is no easy pathway around the messy and challenging process of reconciling the long history of colonial relationships between Canadians and Indigenous peoples. She further states that "with the national spotlight currently shining on the 'reconciliation' project, Indigenous scholars have been consistently highlighting the importance of addressing treaty rights in any reconciliatory efforts, particularly in education."[34] One fundamental right is the right to a quality, culturally relevant education that is based on the ethics of respectful relationships. Indeed, the TRC's final report and calls to action identified education as a key site for reconciliation. To that end, ministries of education and school boards have been exerting consistent pressure on teachers to implement the TRC's calls to action in their classrooms. The government of Ontario, in line with the TRC, has itself named education a "key component" of reconciliation.[35]

There are four big systems in society: political, educational, martial, and judicial. Linda Tuhiwai Smith says that big systems are human systems: they were created by humans and as such can be changed by humans.[36] An education system that remains rooted in colonialism and structural racism will only reinforce any reconciliatory efforts as a colonial project framed in colonial narratives. Styres tells us that reconcili*action*—engaging reconciliation as a complex process of critical social action—is the way forward.[37] It shifts colonial narratives and structures by dismantling the myth of "settler claims to futurities"[38] and the ways those myths inform how education is currently delivered. The question often asked is, How do we Indigenize education? We would say that one cannot Indigenize education or any other big system that remains structurally and systemically grounded in colonial ideologies.

With education in mind, we consider the words of Audre Lorde, a Caribbean-American writer and political activist who argues that "the master's tools will never dismantle the master's house."[39] Many of our educational systems are continuing to use the same tools, blue prints, and building materials as were used in earlier periods of colonial reproduction. As we note above, the TRC locates education at the centre of its calls to action, suggesting that without it, there is no way forward into right relation. We, the authors of this chapter, have both been guided by these calls in our classrooms, in interactions with students, and in our administrative work in university graduate, undergraduate, and teacher education programs. During the course of our work, we have had the tragic privilege of understanding the powerful disconnect between the colonial university structure (a colonial present) and the framework suggested by reconciliation, which requires a still-absent cessation of settler-colonial activity on the part of Canada at all levels of government, in its various big systems, and in their related institutions. All of these remain steeped in colonial relations of power and privilege, and universities are no exception. They have always been and continue to be colonial spaces.

As a collection of systems that produce and reproduce colonial epistemology and logic, education is today very much a project of settler futurity.[40] The temporal logics of colonialism have long been theorized by anticolonial scholars. As Glenn Coulthard argues, "Indigenous peoples' individual and collective resentment—expressed as an angry and vigilant unwillingness to forgive—ought to be seen as an affective indication that we care deeply about ourselves, about our land and cultural communities, and about the rights and obligations we hold as First Peoples."[41] Writing fifty years earlier, anticolonial theorist Frantz Fanon (whose work inspired the title of Coulthard's *Red Skin, White Masks*) stated that "colonialism is not satisfied with holding a people in its grip and emptying the native's brain of all form and content. By a kind of perverted logic, it turns to the past of the oppressed people, and distorts, disfigures and destroys it. This work of devaluing colonial history takes on a dialectical significance today."[42] Linda Tuhiwai Smith, writing on resistance and decolonization almost thirty years before Coulthard in her seminal text on decolonizing methodologies, similarly argued that "the intellectual project of decolonizing has to set out ways to proceed through a colonizing world. It needs a radical compassion that reaches out, that seeks collaboration, and that is open to possibilities that can only be imagined as other things fall into place."[43] All of this holds true more than a generation later. We suggest that a relational ethics may work with Smith's notions of radical compassion and collaboration, as well as with resistance to coloniality, as part of a way of moving forward in right relation.

A Way Forward

Coulthard's, Fanon's, and Smith's arguments have proven to be both astute and prescient. The phenomena they describe continue today in K to 12 classrooms as well as in postsecondary education, particularly in the ways we teach teachers to be teachers. Education, although often antiquated in method, is ultimately a project of imagining and designing futures.[44] Our schools and our universities are still very much designed to produce colonial futures. They are living embodiments of settler futurity—institutions that, in James Baldwin's words, render the future "knowable through specific practices (i.e., calculation, imagination, and performance)."[45] Schooling often engages these very tasks and activities. In order to make reconciliation conceivable (to address our earlier heuristic), perhaps we need to imagine and enact Indigenous futurity in schooling by engaging an ethics of relationality and a supplanting of settler-colonial logic, epistemology, and futurity—that is, by taking aim at the domains of calculation, imagination, and performance, as Baldwin's work suggests.

Reconciliation is a complex and challenging endeavour that necessitates first identifying the effects of settler colonialism on educational practices and then finding ways to begin decolonizing those practices.[46] Indigenous scholars are calling for an approach to education (at all levels) that goes beyond the use of compulsory Indigenous content courses as the check mark for reconciliatory efforts in education.[47] A key way forward would be to implement an Indigenous-led and -driven education that has a core foundation of Indigenous land-centred philosophies. In order to accomplish this, Wildcat and colleagues suggest that we "find ways of reinserting people into relationships with and on the land as a mode of decolonizing education,"[48] and argue that we need to move from talking about the land within classrooms to critically engaging in dialogue with and on the land in physical, social, and spiritual contexts.

For Indigenous people, education is a relational construct that is philosophically underpinned by Land.[49] Wildcat and colleagues tell us that "land-based education, in resurging and sustaining Indigenous life and knowledge, acts in direct contestation to settler colonialism and its drive to eliminate Indigenous life and Indigenous claims to land."[50] Land-centred education embeds students, instructors, and community in the ethics of relationality within land-based pedagogies and practices, which are the impetus for respectful reconciliation education. While land-centred educational opportunities may be open to all students, it is important that all instructors and leaders of such opportunities be Indigenous. This is echoed by other Indigenous scholars who assert the importance of land-centred education coming from "within our intellectual traditions, through the land, in an Indigenous context using Indigenous processes and should also be Indigenous led and controlled. Being present on the land provides powerful ways of seeing one's relationships to the land and other-than-humans, as well as new ways in contesting settler colonialism and its sense making mechanisms."[51] Land-centred education is fundamentally grounded in Indigenous philosophies that are based on intimate and sacred connections to our places, governances, histories, stories, ceremonies, and languages. It finds its expression in the principles of relevance, respect, responsibility, reciprocity, and relationality.[52] It is through land-centred education that we can imagine a shared tomorrow based on respectful relations and reimagine Indigenous futurities grounded in Indigenous leadership and Indigenous intellectualism. This reimagining opens opportunities for engaging with educational spaces in deep and profound ways as we immerse ourselves in natural, spiritual, and built worlds.

NOTES

1. Sinclair, "Murray Sinclair Interview," at 9:33.
2. Government of Ontario, *The Journey Together*, 19.
3. Lowman and Barker, *Settler*, 19.
4. Lowman and Barker, *Settler*, 1.
5. Kuokkanen, *Reshaping the University*, xiv.
6. Kuokkanen, *Reshaping the University*, 1.
7. Lowman and Barker, *Settler*, 1.
8. Tuck and Yang, "Decolonization Is Not a Metaphor," 3.

9. Mackey, *Unsettled Expectations*, 9.
10. For more thorough discussions of these five *R*'s, see Kirkness and Barnhardt, "First Nations and Higher Education"; Styres and Zinga, "Community-First Land-Centred Research Method."
11. Donald Trump, quoted in Lewin, "Trump Orders Space Force," para. 3.
12. Unnamed RCMP officer, quoted in Trimble, "'Appalling' Facebook Comment," para. 6.
13. Palmater, *Beyond Blood*.
14. Park et al., "Avoidable Mortality," 12.
15. Flanagan, "Likely to Be Shot," para. 1.
16. Cecco, "National Travesty."
17. Macdonald, "Saskatchewan: A Special Report."
18. Macdonald, "Saskatchewan: A Special Report."
19. *Aboriginal Population Profile, 2016 Census*.
20. Blackstock, *Reconciliation Means*, 2.
21. Lynn Beyak, quoted in Tasker, "Conservative Senator Defends," para. 2.
22. Lee Maracle, recorded in St. John, *Colonization Road*, at 39:38
23. Jamieson, "Canada's Original Promise," at 2:48.
24. Jamieson, "Canada's Original Promise," at 12:35.
25. John A. MacDonald, quoted in Beazley, "Decolonizing the Indian Act," para. 5.
26. Wilfrid Laurier, quoted in Hopper, "Sure, John A. Macdonald," First Nations People sec., para. 3.
27. Duncan Campbell Scott, quoted in Titley, *A Narrow Vision*, 50.
28. See Grande, "Refusing the University"; McCarty and Grande, "Indigenous Elsewheres"; Coulthard, *Red Skin, White Masks*; Tuck and Yang, "Unbecoming Claims"; Simpson, "On Ethnographic Refusal."
29. Mackey, *Unsettled Expectations*.
30. Truth and Reconciliation Commission of Canada, *Honouring the Truth*, 6, 15.
31. Manuel, in Manuel and Derrickson, *Reconciliation Manifesto*.
32. Manuel, in Manuel and Derrickson, *The Reconciliation Manifesto*, 57.
33. Mackey, *Unsettled Expectations*, 141.
34. Styres, "Reconcili*action*," 2.
35. Government of Ontario, *The Journey Together*, 19.
36. Smith, "SSHRC Research Panel."
37. Styres, "Reconcili*action*."
38. Tuck and Yang, "Decolonization Is Not a Metaphor," 1.
39. Lorde, "The Master's Tools," 98.
40. See Tuck and Gaztambide-Fernández, "Curriculum, Replacement, and Settler Futurity"; Tuck and Yang, "Decolonization Is Not a Metaphor"; Baldwin, "Whiteness and Futurity."
41. Coulthard, *Red Skin, White Masks*, 126.
42. Fanon, *Wretched of the Earth*, 210.
43. Smith, *Decolonizing Methodologies*, 288.
44. See Dei and Kempf, "Katrina."
45. James Baldwin, quoted in Tuck and Gaztambide-Fernández, "Curriculum, Replacement," 80.
46. See Styres, "Reconcili*action*."
47. See, e.g., Anderson, Chiarotto, and Comay, *Natural Curiosity*; Cajete, *Look to the Mountain*; Four Arrows, *Teaching Truly*; Goodyear-Ka'öpua, *The Seeds We Planted*; Kermoal and Altamirano-Jiménez, *Living on the Land*; Madden, "Pedagogical Pathways."
48. Wildcat et al., "Learning from the Land," ii.
49. For a discussion of the concept of Land, see Styres, *Pathways for Remembering*. See also Wildcat et al., "Learning from the Land."

50. Wildcat et al., "Learning from the Land," iii.
51. Wildcat et al., "Learning from the Land," v.
52. Styres and Zinga, "Community-First Land-Centred Research Method." See also Kirkness and Barnhardt, "First Nations and Higher Education."

BIBLIOGRAPHY

Aboriginal Population Profile, 2016 Census. Statistics Canada Catalogue no. 98-510-X2016001, updated July 18, 2018. https://www12.statcan.gc.ca/census-recensement/2016/dp-pd/abpopprof/index.cfm?Lang=E.

Anderson, Doug, Lorraine Chiarotto, and Julie Comay. *Natural Curiosity: A Resource for Educators— The Importance of Indigenous Perspectives in Children's Environmental Inquiry.* 2nd ed. Toronto: Dr. Eric Jackman Institute of Child Study Ontario Institute for Studies in Education, 2017.

Baldwin, Andrew. "Whiteness and Futurity: Towards a Research Agenda." *Progress in Human Geography* 36, no. 2 (2012): 172–87.

Beazley, Doug. "Decolonizing the Indian Act." *National Magazine,* December 18, 2017. https://www.nationalmagazine.ca/en-ca/articles/law/in-depth/2017/decolonizing-the-indian-act.

Blackstock, Cindy. *Reconciliation Means Not Saying Sorry Twice: How Inequities in Federal Government Child Welfare Funding, and Benefit, on Reserves Drives First Nations Children into Foster Care.* Ottawa: First Nations Child and Family Caring Society of Canada, 2015. https://fncaringsociety.com/sites/default/files/fnwitness/FNCFCS-submission-status-of-women.pdf.

Cajete, Gregory. *Look to the Mountain: An Ecology of Indigenous Education.* Skyland: Kivaki Press, 1994.

Cecco, Leyland. "'National Travesty': Report Shows One Third of Canada's Prisoners are Indigenous." *The Guardian,* January 22, 2020. https://www.theguardian.com/world/2020/jan/22/one-third-canada-prisoners-indigenous-report.

Coulthard, Glen Sean. *Red Skin, White Masks: Rejecting the Colonial Politics of Recognition.* Minneapolis: University of Minnesota Press, 2014.

Dei, George J. Sefa, and Arlo Kempf. "Katrina, Cronulla Beach and France on Fire: An Anti-Colonial Critique of Empire in 2006." *Journal of Contemporary Issues in Education* 1, no. 2 (2007): 4–25.

Fanon, Frantz. *The Wretched of the Earth.* Translated by Constance Farrington. New York: Grove Press, 1963.

Flanagan, Ryan. "Why Are Indigenous People in Canada So Much More Likely to Be Shot and Killed by Police?" *CTV News,* June 19, 2020. www.ctvnews.ca/canada/why-are-indigenous-people-in-canada-so-much-more-likely-to-be-shot-and-killed-by-police-1.4989864.

Four Arrows. *Teaching Truly: A Curriculum to Indigenize Mainstream Education.* New York: Peter Lang Publishing, 2013.

Goodyear-Ka'ōpua, Noelani. *The Seeds We Planted: Portraits of a Native Hawaiian Charter School.* Minneapolis: University of Minnesota Press, 2013.

Government of Ontario. *The Journey Together: Ontario's Commitment to Reconciliation with Indigenous Peoples.* Ottawa: Queen's Printer for Ontario, 2016. https://files.ontario.ca/trc_report_web_mar17_en_1.pdf.

Grande, Sandy. "Refusing the University." In *Toward What Justice? Describing Diverse Dreams of Justice in Education,* edited by Eve Tuck and K. Wayne Yang, 47–65. New York: Routledge, 2018.

Hopper, Tristin. "Sure, John A. Macdonald was a Racist, Colonizer and Misogynist—But So Were Most Canadians Back Then." *National Post,* January 10, 2015. https://nationalpost.com/news/canada/sure-john-a-macdonald-was-was-a-racist-colonizer-and-misogynist-but-so-were-most-canadians-back-then.

Jamieson, Roberta. "Canada's Original Promise: Still Waiting to Be Realized." In *Ideas,* hosted by Paul Kennedy, produced by CBC Radio, June 30, 2017. Podcast, MP3 audio, 53:59. https://www.cbc.ca/radio/ideas/canada-s-original-promise-still-waiting-to-be-realized-1.4185851.

Kermoal, Natalie, and Isobel Altamirano-Jiménez. *Living on the Land: Indigenous Women's Understanding of Place*. Edmonton: Athabasca University Press, 2016.

Kirkness, Verna J., and Ray Barnhardt. "First Nations and Higher Education: The Four *R*'s—Respect, Relevance, Reciprocity, Responsibility." *Journal of American Indian Education* 30, no. 3 (2001): 1–15. http://www.jstor.org/stable/24397980.

Kuokkanen, Rauna. *Reshaping the University: Responsibility, Indigenous Epistems, and the Logic of the Gift*. Vancouver: UBC Press, 2007.

Lewin, Sarah. "Trump Orders Space Force for 'American Dominance', Signs Space-Traffic Policy." *Space*, June 18, 2018. https://www.space.com/40921-trump-space-traffic-policy-american-leadership.html.

Lorde, Audre. "The Master's Tools Will Never Dismantle the Master's House." In *This Bridge Called My Back*, edited by Cherríe Moraga and Gloria Anzaldúa, 98–101. Watertown: Persephone Press, 1981.

Lowman, Emma, and Adam Barker. *Settler Identity and Colonialism in 21st Century Canada*. Winnipeg: Fernwood Publishing, 2016.

Macdonald, Nancy. "Saskatchewan: A Special Report on Race and Power." *MacLean's*, July 29, 2016. https://www.macleans.ca/news/canada/saskatchewan-a-special-report-on-race-and-power/.

Mackey, Eva. *Unsettled Expectations: Uncertainty, Land and Settler Decolonization*. Winnipeg: Fernwood Publishing, 2016.

Madden, Brooke. "Pedagogical Pathways for Indigenous Education with/in Teacher Education." *Teaching and Teacher Education* 51 (2015): 1–15.

Manuel, Arthur, and Grand Chief Ronald Derrickson. *The Reconciliation Manifesto: Recovering the Land, Rebuilding the Economy*. Toronto: Lorimer Press, 2017.

McCarty, Teresa, and Sandy Grande. "Indigenous Elsewheres: Refusal and Re-membering in Education Research, Policy, and Praxis." *International Journal of Qualitative Studies in Education* 31, no. 3 (2018): 165–67.

Palmater, Pamela. *Beyond Blood: Rethinking Indigenous Identity*. Vancouver: UBC Press, 2015.

Park, Jungwee, Michael Tjepkema, Neil Goedhuis, and Jennifer Pennock. "Avoidable Mortality among First Nations Adults in Canada: A Cohort Analysis." *Health Reports* 26, no. 8 (August 2015): 10–16.

Simpson, Audra. "On Ethnographic Refusal: Indigeneity, 'Voice' and Colonial Citizenship." *Junctures* 9 (December 2007): 67–80.

Sinclair, Murray. "Murray Sinclair Interview." By Peter Mansbridge. *The National*, June 1, 2015. https://www.cbc.ca/news/thenational/murray-sinclair-interview-1.3096341.

Smith, Linda Tuhiwai. *Decolonizing Methodologies: Research and Indigenous Peoples*. London: Zed Publishers, 1991.

———. "SSHRC Research Panel." Unlisted panel discussion at the Annual Conference of the Canadian Society for the Study of Education, Regina, SK, May 2018.

St. John, Michelle, dir. *Colonization Road*. Produced by Michelle St. John, Jordan O'Connor, Shane Belcourt, and Brendan Brady. Canada: Decolonization Road Productions Inc., 2016.

Styres, Sandra D. *Pathways for Remembering and Recognizing Indigenous Thought in Education: Philosophies of Iethi'nihsténha Ohwentsia'kékha (Land)*. Toronto: University of Toronto Press, 2017.

———. "Reconciliaction: Reconciling Contestation in the Academy." *Power and Education* 12, no. 2 (2020): 157–72. https://doi.org/10.1177/1757743820916845.

Styres, Sandra D., and Dawn Zinga. "The Community-First Land-Centred Research Method: Bringing a 'Good Mind' to Indigenous Education Research." *Canadian Journal of Education* 36, no. 2 (2013): 284–313.

Tasker, John Paul. "Conservative Senator Defends 'Well-Intentioned' Residential School System." *CBC News*, March 8, 2017. https://www.cbc.ca/news/politics/residential-school-system-well-intentioned-conservative-senator-1.4015115.

Titley, E. Brian. *A Narrow Vision: Duncan Campbell Scott and the Administration of Indian Affairs in Canada.* Vancouver: UBC Press, 1986.

Trimble, Ken. "'Appalling' Facebook comment on Colten Boushie's Death Leads to RCMP Conduct Probe." *National Post*, February 16, 2018. https://nationalpost.com/news/canada/appalling-comment-on-saskatchewan-indigenous-mans-death-probed-by-rcmp.

Truth and Reconciliation Commission of Canada. *Honouring the Truth, Reconciling for the Future: Summary of the Final Report of the Truth and Reconciliation Commission of Canada.* Winnipeg: National Centre for Truth and Reconciliation, 2015. http://www.trc.ca/assets/pdf/Executive_Summary_English_Web.pdf.

Tuck, Eve, and Rubén A. Gaztambide-Fernández. "Curriculum, Replacement, and Settler Futurity." *Journal of Curriculum Theorizing* 29, no. 1 (2013): 72–89.

Tuck, Eve, and K. Wayne Yang. "Decolonization Is Not a Metaphor." *Decolonization: Indigeneity, Education & Society* 1, no. 1 (2012): 1–40.

———. "Unbecoming Claims: Pedagogies of Refusal in Qualitative Research." *Qualitative Inquiry* 20, no. 6 (July 2014): 811–18. https://doi.org/10.1177/1077800414530265.

Wildcat, Matthew, Mandee McDonald, Stephanie Irlbacher-Fox, and Glen Coulthard. "Learning from the Land: Indigenous Land Based Pedagogy and Decolonization." *Decolonization: Indigeneity, Education & Society* 3, no. 3 (2014): i–xv.

9

LYNNE WILTSE

Exploring Tensions in Taking Up the Call for Reconciliation in Teacher Education

It's about the stories we tell, and the stories others tell about us.
It's about how stories can either strengthen, wound, or seemingly
erase our shared connections, and how our stories are expressed or
repressed, shared or hidden, recognized or dismissed...When absent,
they leave gaps that communicate as surely as the presences.
—Daniel Heath Justice, *Why Indigenous Literatures Matter*

Daniel Heath Justice describes *Why Indigenous Literatures Matter* as a book about stories—specifically, how and why they matter. Needless to say, Justice is referring to the stories Indigenous peoples tell.[1] He explains that, in the past, these stories have too often been repressed, hidden, or dismissed. As for the stories others tell about Indigenous people, they have too often been the wounding kind. In her book *Unsettling the Settler Within*, Paulette Regan depicts settler stories as "counter-narratives that create decolonizing space" and "require us to risk revealing ourselves as vulnerable 'not-knowers' who are willing to examine our dual positions as colonizer-perpetrators and colonizer-allies."[2] In writing this chapter, I have become more aware of the depth of my "not knowing." In the introduction to her book *Pathways for Remembering and Recognizing Indigenous Thought in Education,* Sandra D. Styres explains: "Locating ourselves in relation to everything we do is one of the key foundational principles of Indigeneity. The only place from which any of us can write or speak with some degree of certainty is from the position of who we are in relation to what we know."[3] I am a settler teacher educator who teaches courses in children's literature and in language and literacy in an elementary curriculum department. Before carrying on with this chapter, I acknowledge Treaty 6 territory, the traditional lands of the Cree, Dene, Blackfoot, Saulteaux, Nakota Sioux, and Métis, on which I currently live and work. I also respectfully acknowledge Tk'emlups te Secwepemc territory, where the research study of which I speak in this chapter took place, and the traditional territories of the Ulkatcho, 'Namgis and Tseshaht First Nations, on whose lands the schools in which I taught were located. The calls to action of the Truth and Reconciliation Commission of Canada (TRC), in particular those related to education for reconciliation,[4] have caused me to reflect on my career as a teacher and teacher educator with, for the most part, Indigenous school-aged students and settler pre- and in-service teachers. My hope is that the story I tell in this chapter will create space for ongoing study and thoughtful conversations on the troubling issues of truth and reconciliation in teacher education and K to 12 classrooms.

My Story

It wasn't until I began my first teaching position in a small First Nations community in the interior of British Columbia that I realized how inadequately my teacher education program had prepared me for teaching Indigenous students. I felt that lack from the day I arrived, when a group of students arrived at my teacherage to greet me. Based on their language use, I thought something was wrong with the children. In time, I learned that these children were speaking a dialect of English known variously (depending on context) as Indian, Aboriginal, Indigenous, or First Nations English. My students spoke a variety of English influenced by their mother tongue, Carrier. Given colonial histories, there is a bias towards settler varieties of English; so-called nonstandard varieties have long been considered deficient by educators.[5] At the time, though, the deficiency was mine, as I had learned nothing about Indigenous English, and precious little about Indigenous peoples, during my B.Ed. degree.[6] Although the lack I experienced as a teacher of Indigenous students was multifaceted, I highlight the language issue here because it later became the impetus for my academic scholarship and has relevance to this chapter.

The school was well equipped (in terms of a gym and a library), but for the most part, the resources were neither culturally relevant nor locally developed. Moreover, relationships between home and school were poor. Few family members visited the school or attended parent-teacher interviews; at the same time, the teaching staff rarely, if ever, set foot on the reserve. I had a sense that the lack of interaction between the school and the community negatively impacted the students, but it wasn't until I'd lived through subsequent teaching experiences that I understood this more fully. As a beginning teacher, the learning curve was steep. This inaugural teaching experience had a profound impact on me as a teacher and later as a teacher educator. Before furthering my career, I took some time off to travel and reflect.

My next teaching positions were in band-operated schools on the west coast of Vancouver Island, in Alert Bay with the Nimpkish Band and outside Port Alberni with the Nuu Chah Nulth Tribal Council. Due to funding issues, both of these schools were housed in former residential school buildings. One of the classrooms in which I taught had been a dormitory at the Alberni Indian Residential School. The many grim stories I heard about the residential school from family members gave me a glimpse into the legacy of residential schooling. The band-operated schools provided an alternative to public schools. Underresourced and housed as they were in old residential school buildings, they had neither gyms nor libraries (new schools with both of these amenities have long since been built in both locations). They were, however, in the students' communities. They taught Indigenous language and culture, developed local resources, and maintained strong school-home relationships. For me, the involvement of family and community members in all aspects of school was the most dramatic difference. For example, participation at parent-teacher interviews was close to 100%, family members came to school functions and volunteered on field trips, and so forth. The expectation that teachers be involved in the community was another difference. In Alert Bay, we attended beginner dance and language classes. In both communities, we were invited to Potlatches and other ceremonies. For the students, closer school-community-home relationships resulted in increased student engagement with and achievement in school. And, unlike in my first teaching position, as a non-Indigenous teacher I felt I was providing an education worth caring about.[7] During these years, though, I was troubled by negative comments others made regarding Indigenous students and their families. Justice's words resonated: "Many of the stories of Indigenous peoples are toxic, and to my mind the most corrosive of all is the story of Indigenous deficiency."[8] These toxic stories contrasted sharply with the children and families I worked with. It would be years before I became familiar with Gerald Vizenor's notion of "survivance," which describes the ways in which Indigenous narratives reflect not only survival, but also resistance, in challenging the persistence of settler colonialism.[9] In retrospect, though, I was witnessing this in the communities in which I taught.

After teaching for a decade in these First Nations communities, I left British Columbia for graduate studies at the University of Alberta. Graduate school proved to be a profound learning experience, and at the same time most unsettling. During a graduate seminar on global education, I was introduced to the term *white privilege* for the first time in Peggy McIntosh's article of the same name.[10] Although the term was new, I was able, due to my earlier teaching experiences, to situate myself in the concept and recognize the regular advantages of white privilege in my life. For example, once during my time in Albert Bay, I travelled with three of my Indigenous colleagues to Victoria for an education conference. We stopped at a café in Campbell River for lunch. The waitress treated me differently than my colleagues—with more attention and politeness. I recall being surprised and uncomfortable at the time. In Alert Bay, as a non-Indigenous person in a minority position, I hadn't experienced anything similar. When I read McIntosh's article, this memory came back to me as an apt example of what I could take for granted as a white person. Graduate studies provided an opportunity for me to explore the academic literature and theories that informed my teaching in First Nations communities, albeit in retrospect.

This discomfort and learning accompanied me through graduate school and into my first position in teacher education at a small university in the interior of British Columbia. I had completed a master's thesis on Indigenous language loss and revival. The data, gathered in an urban school, pointed to the importance of a language of identity for students who spoke a variety of English influenced by their ancestral language, rather than the ancestral language itself, due to the legacy of residential schooling. I had also completed doctoral research on minority language learners, conducting an ethnographic case study of community practices in a multilingual urban classroom. Study contributions pointed to the value of using hybrid language practices, with particular attention to academic discourse, to develop English literacy and improve the academic achievement of refugee and immigrant youth. The first major funded study I applied for in my new teaching position—the study that I discuss in this chapter—comprised key learnings from my teaching and graduate student experiences (i.e., who I was then in relation to what I knew[11]). Motivated by my teaching experiences in First Nations communities, the study was situated in a framework that identified "societal power relations and their reflection in educational structures and interactions as a primary cause of underachievement among English language learners and students from marginalized social groups."[12] Within this broader framework, my particular focus as a language and literacy researcher was on the implications of deficit views of language variation in school: teachers often view English language variation as an impediment to students acquiring literacy skills. As a settler teacher educator, and given the gaps in my own B.Ed. program, my priority in this study was finding ways to support pre- and in-service teachers in their explorations of instructional practices that enable students to draw on their multilingual repertoires to develop academic language.

Study Details

My three-year school-university collaborative research project investigated how minority language students' linguistic and cultural resources from home and community networks may provide these students with access to academic literacies.

Within a broad sociocultural framework, the study drew on "third space theory" in conjunction with the concept of "funds of knowledge."[13] Because these approaches view diversity as a resource rather than a deficit,[14] they consider linguistic and cultural diversity as resources that can be used as scaffolds for new learning. The research was a qualitative study, drawing on the work of educational researchers who have used ethnographic studies to understand children's language and literacy practices, both in school[15] and out of school.[16] Within a broad ethnographic case study design, my research used a students-as-researchers approach.[17] The project involved three interconnected groups of research participants: (1) a teacher-researcher study group of teachers who taught at the intermediate grade level (Grades 4 to 7); (2) students from the participating teachers' classes, some of whom were Indigenous; and (3) preservice teachers in my language and literacy curriculum classes who were partnered with students in participating teachers' classes. Data sources included field notes from classroom observations, artifacts, students' assignments, transcripts from audiotaped teacher-researcher meetings, and semistructured interviews of select school students and preservice teachers. The teacher-researcher and preservice teacher quotations throughout this chapter are drawn from this data, collected over the course of the study between 2008 and 2011. The names of all participants, schools, and locations used here are pseudonyms. The selected excerpts were chosen because of their promise to trouble truth and reconciliation in Canadian education. I begin with the teachers' story.

The Story of Settler Discomfort: Teachers

> The question of who is learning what and how much is essentially a
> question of what conversations they are a part of, and this question is
> a subset of the more powerful question of what conversations are to be
> had in a given culture.
> —Ray McDermott, "The Acquisition of a Child
> by a Learning Disability"

The teacher-researcher group was comprised of six teachers who taught Grades 4 to 7. Three of the teachers taught at Wolfwood School, operated by the local First Nations band; the other three taught at "inner-city" public schools with significant (but not majority) numbers of Indigenous students. Of the Wolfwood School teachers, Gayle and Carol were First Nations (though only Gayle was from the local community), and Terry was non-Indigenous. Of the teachers who taught at public schools within the district, two were non-Indigenous (Les and Eleanor). The third teacher was from the local First Nation, but left the study early for a maternity leave.

Based on my experience—first as a teacher with no access to the academic literature, and then as a graduate student with no students—I budgeted for teacher release time in my research proposal; the time to talk proved invaluable. We met monthly to discuss sociocultural perspectives on minority language education and related classroom practice. The principal at Wolfwood School offered us the library as a meeting space. The school followed the provincial Ministry of Education curriculum in addition to offering programming in the local Indigenous language, history, and culture. The school was situated next to a former residential school, which now houses band offices and a museum on the history of residential schooling. Many students had relatives who had attended the residential school. Study findings suggested that teachers generally had insufficient time to read research literature that could improve their practice; they further found that the value of providing teachers with time to do this research could not be overestimated.[18] The readings and subsequent conversations allowed teachers to think about issues such as language, culture, class, power, and privilege in ways they had not considered before. The time we spent listening to each other over the three years of the study also contributed to "the building of respectful relationships between Indigenous and settler populations."[19]

For Terry, the non-Indigenous teacher from Wolfwood school, the main takeaway of the project had been "that teachers truly have to be reflective and open to change. I come away from one of our meetings with an idea, and then you give us another reading and I change my idea again." One of the readings that caused Terry to reconsider her views was Gloria Ladson-Billings's "It's Not the Culture of Poverty, It's the Poverty of Culture," which focuses on the "ways prospective and novice teachers simultaneously construct culture as both the problem and the answer to their struggles with students different from themselves."[20] The teachers with whom Ladson-Billings works teach in large, urban, American schools—contexts that vary significantly from the schools in my study. However, parallels can be made. Terry provided an example of how the reading had provoked change in her: "Well, because of the preconceived ideas. I kind of changed my mind that maybe I don't need to know everything about the students in advance so that I can make the curriculum fit the students. It made me think I have to get to know the students within the classroom in each particular year."

Terry's comment was situated within a larger discussion about expectations of Indigenous students, prompting her to step back from the notion that teaching and learning problems reside in the traits of students or their families; it is crucial to get to know students' backgrounds, but not to make premature assumptions based on ethnicity, race, class, and so forth. The remark also fit within the study's funds-of-knowledge perspective. Elizabeth Marshall and Kelleen Toohey note that a funds-of-knowledge perspective "acknowledges that minority children, like their majority classmates, have participated in social practices in their families and communities, and...urges schools and teachers to connect school learning to children's out-of-school learning."[21] However, as Marshall and Toohey also note, many schools and educators know so little about the out-of-school lives of their minority students that they find it difficult to build on funds of knowledge from children's homes and communities.

This reality was a factor in my research project. Over the course of the study, it became clear that the type of schools in which the teachers taught, as well as the backgrounds of the teachers, determined to a considerable degree how successful they were in integrating children's funds of knowledge into the school curriculum. Study findings showed that, because Wolfwood School was a band-operated school in its students' community, the distance between out-of-school lives and in-school learning was relatively narrow for many of the students. This was seldom the case for the Indigenous students who attended the other schools in the study. For example, during one of our monthly meetings, Les, who taught at one of the public schools, identified the "disconnect between home for students and parents and the school community as a key issue" and "finding ways to bridge that gap as absolutely critical." During the same meeting, Eleanor, who taught at another public school, made an earnest acknowledgement to the Wolfwood School teachers: "I think I should send all my First Nations children to your school, as they're getting short-changed with me. You use who the students are in your teaching and I think they would learn much better that way. I think they're in the wrong place with me." In response, Terry spoke to an aspect of what this meant for the students at Wolfwood School: "I think something that our school does very well is give our students pride in who they are. When they go to high school, if they experience racism or have difficulties, they have some strength in being proud of who they are as a First Nations person." Terry's comment corresponds with the claim that the "effects of racism in the wider society can be significantly ameliorated when the school implements instruction that affirms students' identities and challenges the devaluation of students and communities in the wider society."[22] However, Terry found that, as a non-Indigenous teacher, maximizing the possibilities for her students had not come easily: "When I first came to Wolfwood, I was so willing to and wanted to learn the First Nations way, 'cause I was in a First Nations school, right? I thought I knew something about it, but when I got there, I realized how much I didn't know. I haven't lived it. And I was uncomfortable to ask questions."

Not long before she made this comment, Terry had had her teaching evaluated. She explained that the person conducting the evaluation "challenged me to be more aware that I am non–First Nations in a First Nations school. He wants to see how I'm making the classroom experience more relevant to my students' culture. So, I'm nervous because I thought I was doing pretty good." Still, she was aware of the lack: "When I don't understand something, I don't hide it. I usually come to Gayle. But when Gayle and I talk about what we're doing in our classrooms is very different." Part of the reason for the difference is that Gayle grew up in the community the school served and was a member of the local First Nations band; she knew the students and their families. Terry frequently consulted with Gayle, in part because of Gayle's insider knowledge of the community, but also because she had previously taught Terry's students (Gayle taught the Grade 5 class; Terry taught Grade 6/7). Terry elaborated, "I still haven't had an Elder come in if I'm going to be teaching about First Nations history. I don't have the resource base that Gayle has being from the community—that's not available to me unless I seek it out. People have said, 'Well, if you want that person to come in, go over and talk to them and pass them tobacco.' I haven't done that because I'm uncomfortable."

The topic of home visits or attending community events triggered teacher discomfort. Ladson-Billings speaks about teacher discomfort in her article, which is structured around "critical incidents" drawn from interviews, journals, and electronic portfolios, that describe preservice and novice teachers' understandings of their work. One of these incidents features teachers from a suburban school who invite Ladson-Billings to talk with them about a "problem" they are experiencing: "They cannot get the African American and Hmong parents to come to school."[23] Rather than giving a pat answer, Ladson-Billings asked the teachers questions about what efforts the school had made to be a presence in the communities from which the students come—for example, attending community events. None of the teachers had. Parallels could be made to my study. The teachers in the public schools identified lack of family involvement as an issue. Of more concern was the public school teachers' reluctance to venture into the community. For example, Les noted that "it's really hard to get the First Nations parents into our school" while simultaneously acknowledging that "I'm nervous to attend community functions and do home visits in our neighbourhood." Terry expressed similar anxiety: "Something else that I'm nervous to do is home visits; I haven't done any. So, that's another challenge for me." It was at this point in the conversation that Gayle mentioned she had taken Terry to a wake when a student's grandmother had passed: "I just said, I'll take you to the wake. There were a few of us, but it was like that changed everything in that child's life." This prompted Terry to tell us about a previous time when her discomfort inhibited her from attending a wake: "There had been a death in someone's family prior that I didn't go to, but once I had gone to that wake with you, I really wished that I had. Why didn't I jump out of my box, my comfort zone and go to the service for this other child's grandmother?"

While Terry's narrative is unique, her fears reflect a discomfort shared by many settler teachers. Her teaching experience resonates with the notion of a "pedagogy of discomfort." As Megan Boler and Michalinos Zembylas define it, a pedagogy of discomfort is a framework for understanding people's reluctance to move out of their comfort zones.[24] These pedagogies recognize and problematize our daily habits and routines that are largely shaped by dominant values and assumptions. They also highlight gaps and absences in current curricular practices. Drawing on Deborah Britzman, Boler and Zembylas explain that "discourses include the silences as much as they include the spoken and written words...For instance, in the organization of the subject matter, what is *not* included in the school curriculum can be as telling as that which is included."[25] This is consistent with Susan Dion's point that while teachers are being encouraged to include Aboriginal content across the curriculum, most teachers, "like the majority of Canadians, know little about Aboriginal people, history, and culture."[26] Dion's comment describes well the non-Indigenous teachers in my study; they were very insecure about teaching Indigenous content and Indigenous students. Boler and Zembylas speak to this uncomfortable positioning: "Inhabiting this ambiguity can be very discomforting and demands substantial negative emotional labor such as vulnerability, anger, and suffering."[27] It took time and trust before the teachers were ready to dwell in that difficult place; through their willingness to do so, however, they were able to "expand the borders of comfort zones."[28] Terry, for example, was no longer comfortable *not* acting in her students' best interest. Teacher discomfort, which has the potential to "function as white discourse...that sustains whiteness as a system of supremacy"[29] should not be used as an excuse to avoid the difficult work.

These anecdotes from my study (of which I have only been able to provide a small selection) take me back to my own, contrasting teaching experiences in First Nations communities at public and band-operated schools. I know experientially the difference it can make to students, teachers, and community if close school-home relationships have been developed; research confirms this.[30] As well, for a funds-of-knowledge approach to be maximized, it is helpful for teachers to know the communities in which they work, as Gayle did. That is, however, not the reality for many teachers, who "find themselves teaching in neighbourhoods where they themselves are strangers."[31] In large part, the conversations the teacher-researchers were part of enabled this change—conversations that were usually not to be had in their teacher culture.

The literature that informed the study (i.e., sociocultural theory) also framed our conversations. Our readings led to rich discussions about how the teachers' students could "construct identities of competence that fuel academic engagement."[32] In retrospect, I acknowledge that the works of Indigenous and non-Indigenous scholars who critically interrogate reconciliation should have had a more central place in the study than they did. The conversations did, however, centre Indigenous leadership, following Gregory Cajete's words: "Gone are the days of our being marginalized; Indigenous teachers must now take a leading role in effecting educational change."[33] In the context of our teacher-research group, it was Gayle who led the change. Although I cannot do justice to Gayle's prominent role in this short summary, I want to acknowledge that Gayle increasingly became the group member to whom we all turned for Indigenous knowledge and guidance about teaching Indigenous students. Looking back, and in relation to Celia Haig-Brown's paper *Taking Indigenous Thought Seriously,* I realize that through Gayle, a community-based knowledge keeper, we had opportunities to consider Indigenous thought; through our conversations, she introduced us to a "new/old way of being in and with the world."[34]

The Story of Settler Disruption: Preservice Teachers

As with the teacher-researcher group, my teaching experiences also informed the preservice teacher component of the study. The research proposal was grounded in a situated and participatory approach to teacher education, with a plan to involve preservice teachers in inquiry-based projects investigating learning and teaching in minority students' communities.[35] During the first year of the study, I was teaching two classes of preservice teachers, all of whom were also participating in the study. During the fall term of the study, the teacher-researcher group made plans for the collaborative projects that would take place, beginning in the winter term, between our respective students, with the teachers choosing the nature of the collaborations. The preservice teachers were placed in literacy partnerships with two members of the teacher-researcher group who requested to participate in this stage of the study: Eleanor, who taught in a public school, and Gayle, who taught at Wolfwood School. Both teachers taught Grade 5. Eleanor chose to have her partnerships centre around her students' science fair, while Gayle's partnerships were to focus on her school's heritage fair. Both fairs were relevant to the study's academic literacy focus, specifically in the area of content literacy. For the purposes of this chapter, I will focus on Gayle's heritage fair partnerships.

Each year, all students in Grades 4 to 7 at Wolfwood School participated in the Heritage Fair Program, a multimedia educational initiative developed to increase awareness and interest in community and/or family culture and Canadian history. The program involved family and community participation, with the heritage fair itself being a school-wide undertaking. The preservice teachers in the project were paired with students as part of a case study assignment; the partnerships centred around the children's projects for heritage fair. My preservice teachers and I visited the school during our course time so that partners could meet. Through the one-on-one mentorship, the students received support from their preservice teacher partners with research, data collection, writing, and visual representation. Gayle was keen for her students to have one-on-one support and a chance to work with a university student. Involvement in the research study would enable my B.Ed. students to learn about children's language and literacy practices through a situated approach and offer them an opportunity to begin to understand how "learning to teach means coming to terms with particular orientations toward knowledge, power and identity."[36]

Study findings suggested that, for many of my B.Ed. students, coming to such terms was not easy. Here, I return to the story of Indigenous deficiency, according to which "Indigenous peoples are in a constant state of lack."[37] Justice notes that "we've all heard this story, in one form or another,"[38] and my students were no exception. For example, Marilyn, one of the older preservice teachers in the study, explained how her personal biography left her with preconceived notions about Aboriginal people: "Being from northern Saskatchewan, I grew up with that idea that Aboriginal people are poor, and they're less educated. My grandmother was a foster mom and she took in a lot of Aboriginal children. I had the idea they were abandoned, and that many of them had fetal alcohol syndrome. So, that was always my perspective because that's what I had been exposed to." In a feature issue of *Maclean's* on Canada's problem with racism directed towards Indigenous people, Nancy Macdonald reports that "one in three Prairie residents believe that many racial stereotypes are accurate"—a higher rate than reported elsewhere in Canada.[39] Marylin could be encompassed in these Prairie statistics.

It should be noted, though, that while rates may be lower elsewhere in Canada, my study findings yielded no shortage of evidence of racial stereotyping in British Columbia, where the study was conducted. In the following interview excerpt, Susan, another preservice teacher, speaks to her experience: "I wish that I'd known more because it would have made me more sensitive to seeing stories in the media or hearing, 'Oh that's another drunk on the road.' I don't like that, but that's what's out there. And, it's not comfortable. And I listen to other people say similar things and I struggle because that's how we were brought up. If you don't know the other side of the story, it's just that you're ignorant." Clearly, much of "what's out there" is misinformed, as well as racist. Such perceptions, whether they were *owned*, as with Marilyn, or *heard*, as with Susan, likely influenced their thoughts about and interactions with Indigenous students. Marilyn was a case in point, given her preconceived ideas about Indigenous people: "I thought that going to Wolfwood School would bring me face to face with students who were sheltered and disadvantaged. Unfortunately, that inhibited my idea of who Aboriginal children were." Another preservice teacher, Melanie, had her preconceptions disrupted by her student partner, Pippa: "Pippa literally showed this to be false when she opened her scrapbook and showed me all the marvellous places she has been. She was well versed; she didn't have a language barrier." Pippa also had strong family support. Her father was very involved in the heritage fair project; he gave the class a lesson on how to add images downloaded from the internet to their projects and accompanied Pippa in the field as she conducted research.

Family support of this nature challenged many of the preservice teachers' prior expectations of Indigenous parents. Carolyn, for example, was challenged. Students were expected to conduct an interview as part of their heritage fair project. Carolyn's student partner Phillipa interviewed her paternal and maternal grandmothers about their experiences in two different residential schools in the interior of British Columbia. Phillipa's project was poignantly entitled *Locked Up Indians*. Carolyn explained: "The past stereotypes that I've heard, Philippa was not a part of them at all." She elaborated: "Her parents are very, very involved in her education and she said they were always asking about homework. Philippa was proud that her dad was one of the managers for natural resources. They were always asking questions like, "What are you doing? What are you reading about?" And it made a difference...Also, Philippa's larger family group was involved, both grandmas and her aunt, in addition to her parents." I wanted my preservice teachers to know stories other than those of

Indigenous deficiency; the heritage fair collaborations (although flawed) were providing stories of Indigenous competency.[40]

In his discussion on the damaging effects of stories of Indigenous deficiency, Justice says: "This isn't to say that there aren't profound and challenging social and political problems. Indigenous peoples are vastly overrepresented in all negative social indicators in Canada, the US, and other settler states, and grossly underrepresented in the positive ones."[41] On this note, there were children at Wolfwood School whose lives were noticeably impacted by the intergenerational effects of residential school. Some were living in poverty. Others had family members who struggled with substance abuse. Educators needed to be aware of the impacts of colonization. Through the partnerships, some of the preservice teachers came to recognize their white privilege. A case in point is preservice teacher Nancy, partnered with student Cheryl. Cheryl's heritage fair project was on the Echo Mask that had been in her grandfather's family before being confiscated during a Potlatch in 1921 and exhibited at the Canadian Museum of Civilization. Nancy explained that Cheryl wanted to interview her grandfather for her project, but had neither a phone nor the money for a calling card. So, Nancy helped her write a letter and get a stamp. "In my middle-class world, long distance phone calls, envelopes, and stamps are part of everyday life. At this point, I was seeing this student through my white middle-class lens," she said.

But knowledge of contemporary difficult realities is not enough, as Justice makes clear: "We can't acknowledge these problems without also directly acknowledging the colonial violence in which they're embedded."[42] Nancy was also beginning to recognize the connections between her white privilege and colonialism: "I have only recently begun to understand the horrors that white society inflicted on Aboriginal peoples. I feel very sorry, and although I personally was not responsible, I carry some of the guilt of white people." As Regan notes, "for settlers, coming to grips with the IRS [Indian residential school] experience involves thinking about and working through the difficult emotions associated with the various ways in which we are implicated."[43] Similarly, preservice teacher Susan explained the impact of her newfound knowledge of residential schooling: "I'm disappointed that it wasn't part of my education, 'cause I feel it could have been a little bit different, understanding where their families would be coming from in terms of residential schools...I feel so badly I didn't know about this before."

Susan's anecdote calls to mind Dion's video lecture "Introducing and Disrupting the 'Perfect Stranger'."[44] Dion explains that when teachers invite her into their classrooms to speak to their students, many of them tell her that they know nothing about Aboriginal people. This sounds very much like Susan, my preservice teacher, who described the partnership at Wolfwood School as her "first experience with Aboriginal people," adding, "Growing up, I didn't have any friends or classmates who were Aboriginal." Dion wondered why so many teachers (and Canadians in general) desire to position themselves as distant from Aboriginal people. After some thought, she came up with the expression *the perfect stranger*: a positioning that, Dion argues, lets Canadians avoid any responsibility. To disrupt that positioning, Dion designed a learning experience that asks teachers to investigate the biography of their relationship with Aboriginal peoples. They must ask themselves: What do I know about Aboriginal people? What informs my knowing? Susan expanded on both questions: "I had the very general stereotype of how Aboriginal people or First Nations chose not to be part of our community, and to live on reserve land, all of those claims that were more about how we came in and took over." Although beyond the scope of this chapter, Susan's reference to stolen land is at the core of conflictual setter-Indigenous relations, and redress of these lands is fundamental to remediating justice between Indigenous peoples and settler society.[45] Through their partnerships, in conjunction with a course on the history of education in which they were learning about residential schooling, the preservice teachers were coming to understand that "problems facing Indigenous communities originate with us."[46] As Roger Epp notes, "the subject is not the 'Indian problem' but the 'settler' problem."[47]

Troubling My Story

Writing this chapter has caused me to reflect more deeply on this research study and on my teaching experiences in First Nations communities. They are troubled reflections. The first revisits Peggy McIntosh's article "White Privilege." Not surprisingly, time, experience, and critiques of her work cause me to read this article differently today than I did when I was a graduate student. One difference is my positioning as a language and literacy teacher educator rather than as a graduate student in a foundations department. Christina Berchini makes the point that there is very little research around whiteness in English and literacy education, and argues for the need to move beyond the paradox of white privilege to prepare teachers to engage in more critical analyses of context and power.[48] Research on white teacher identity often draws from the tenets of McIntosh's white privilege / invisible knapsack activity.[49] For example, Timothy Lensmire and colleagues from the Midwest Critical Whiteness Collective contend that McIntosh's seminal article acts as a synecdoche (or stand-in) for all antiracist work done in teacher education, and that this limits possibilities for anti-racist action.[50] Ini conversation, Mary Lee-Nichols—also a member of the Critical Whiteness Collective and a teacher who led a required multicultural education class in a small, predominantly white university—explained to me that, prior to reading the work of Peggy McIntosh and others, she had not considered what it meant to be white, nor had she recognized the privileges associated with race. Years later, as a teacher educator, she tried to direct her preservice teachers toward a pedagogy of social justice through class readings, writings, and activities. I can see myself reflected in Mary's teaching anecdote. I had similar goals for the preservice teachers in my study, though. As I was teaching a language and literacy course, the readings I assigned prior to my preservice teachers' student partnerships were selected to disrupt deficit views of English language variation in students' acquisition of literacy skills and to support the inclusion of previously excluded forms of knowledge, languages, and literacies in school.

The Midwest Critical Whiteness Collective's description of students' "confessions" (ritual testimonies associated with taking up the McIntosh article in classes) also caught my attention. They explain that confessions can be used to "prove" that one is antiracist, or, as in Mary's story, to show that something positive is happening in our teacher education courses. For example, Mary was encouraged when students confessed privilege, as with one student who claimed that the course literally changed her whole perspective. I recognize myself (and some of my students) in this description, as well—this time with more discomfort. For example, Marilyn's views had changed, sparked by her partnership with Pippa: "It will change my perspective and my teaching as well because I will not come into the classroom with such a low expectation or a low understanding of Aboriginal students." Given Tasha Riley and Charles Ungerleider's study as to how preservice teachers' discriminatory judgments and low expectations can negatively affect the academic achievement and opportunities of Aboriginal students,[51] in addition to personal experience that confirms this, I was encouraged by the change in Marilyn's views. I wanted my preservice teachers to have their discriminatory views disrupted before they became teachers. As Lisa Korteweg and Tesa Fiddler note, however, "teacher education-as-reconciliation does not serve Indigenous children and families/ communities if it repels or defeats new teachers from engaging in the real transformative work of relationship-building and relational teaching."[52] Margaret Kovach stresses this concern: "The transformative potential for academia in welcoming diverse knowledges is significant, but at what cost to Indigenous peoples?"[53]

Korteweg's and Fiddler's collaborative Indigenous-settler teacher education partnership resulted in their specialized B.Ed. course Indigenizing Perspectives and Practices in Education. This course was researched and redesigned over the six years it was taught to five cohorts of settler teacher candidates. My research study was situated in a required language and literacy course in which I was also responsible for teaching preservice teachers how to teach children the six strands of language arts (reading, writing, listening, speaking, viewing, and representing). There are some similarities between Korteweg and Fiddler's teacher education course and my own. In particular, we all sought to disrupt settler preservice teachers' ignorance of Indigenous peoples while aiming to improve education for Indigenous students and their families.[54] However, in contrast to Korteweg's and Fiddler's course, the ways in which the transformative potential of my study fell short are obvious. Although my students would have opportunities to further their learning in a subsequent required course (Teaching First Nations Children), I recognize that I did not adequately prepare my preservice teachers for the necessary relational work with students. I agree with Jennifer Tupper that the "creation of discomfort/disruption in teacher education spaces should be viewed as not only an essential condition for (white) preservice teachers, but also for teacher educators."[55] Regrettably, I did not do justice to working alongside my students "to reveal and unpack settler identities."[56]

My second major reflection has led me to think about the students' heritage fair projects differently. While not the focus of this chapter, they were an integral part of the study. What I have learned in this regard has been humbling. Shortly after completing the study research, an article, "Creepy White Gaze: Rethinking the Diorama as a Pedagogical Activity," caught my attention. In it, authors Andrea Sterzuk and Valerie Mulholland critique a heritage fair entry entitled "Great Plains Indians." Their analysis centres on a photograph, which appeared in a Saskatchewan provincial teachers' newsletter, of a "White settler child and two White settler educators gathered around the student's heritage fair entry."[57] In their introduction, the authors note that while the photograph could be seen as innocuous and inclusive, it was "actually a snapshot of the educational community's role in the discursive production of the colonized and the colonizer."[58] As a white settler educator whose research involved Indigenous students' heritage projects, the article certainly provoked a strong measure of discomfort in me. What Sterzuk and Mulholland had to say about museums, in particular, caused me to query the projects: "Most heritage fair displays mimic traditional forms of representation developed and practiced in Western museums from the 18th century forward."[59] Reading this critique made me question the appropriateness of this form of representation, in particular for Indigenous students. In some respects, my research participants' projects were typical of what Jo-ann Archibald refers to as the museum-and-history approach in elementary classrooms.[60] I rationalized, however, that my study was different as it involved Indigenous students examining the cultural and linguistic practices that were part of their lives in their homes and communities. For example, in addition to the topics mentioned in the study overview, one student researched the appropriation of her First Nations band's land by the provincial hydroelectric company; another, a powwow dancer, completed her project on jingle dress dancing; and a young boy investigated familial hunting practices. These projects were characterized by valuable learning for the students. Given the key role of literacy in academic achievement, the academic literacies component of the research was significant. Canadian statistics (albeit gathered according to white, "settlerstream" standards)[61] show an increasing literacy gap between First Nations, Métis, Inuit, and other Canadians.[62] Nevertheless, I have come to reexamine my line of reasoning.

In his book *Indigenous Community: Rekindling the Teaching of the Seventh Fire*, Indigenous scholar and science educator Gregory Cajete explains that for "Indigenous Peoples, modern education continues to reflect the deeply wounding processes of colonization. Traditional forms of knowing and educating have never been given credence in the objectified world of modern 'scientifically' administered education."[63] Cajete's words helped me to understand that, while the projects drew on students' funds of knowledge, they were grounded in Western traditions of education and were not reflective of Indigenous worldviews. Accomplishing change necessitates a project that will "interrupt the dominant discourse and offer teachers and students alternative ways of knowing."[64] Unlike Cajete, who over time came to reconcile conflicts about his training as a science teacher and his own experiences as an Indigenous person, allowing him to move in the "direction of culturally-based education,"[65] I grasped that what I had considered culturally appropriate education—the heritage projects, but also my years of teaching in band-operated schools—was grounded in a mainstream philosophy of education. As Styres explains, "colonial relations have disrupted traditional pedagogies, imposing dominant Western systems of power and privilege into learning processes."[66] Decolonization means challenging the dominance of Western thought and restoring traditional teachings. Willie Ermine suggests that reconciling Indigenous and Western worldviews "is the fundamental problem of cultural encounters."[67] Acknowledging this deep dilemma emphasizes the gaps in my own understanding regarding Indigeneity and what is needed to decolonize reconciliation in education.

A third reflection—the last I will touch on here—has led me to revisit a comment I made earlier regarding my teaching at band-operated schools in First Nations communities: that I felt I was providing an education worth caring about. During my last year of teaching before leaving for graduate school, I saw a television adaptation of a Canadian play about a young woman who, rather than marrying her boyfriend, chose to become a nun and went to teach at a residential school. The young nun believed she was "called" to do this work—she had good intentions, and initially thought what she was doing was right. In time, she becomes disillusioned, as she realizes the role she has played in forcefully stripping the children of their language, customs, and religion. This, in turn, shatters her faith.

At the time, the story had a profound effect on me. I wondered: Had I been a teacher at an earlier time, could I have worked at a residential school, like the nun in the movie? Could I have believed that what I was doing was right? Needless to say, this was a most unsettling thought. It shook my faith. But, because I was teaching in schools that were situated in students' communities—schools that offered Indigenous language, art, and dance programs in an attempt to restore what had been damaged during residential school and its aftermath, and that had locally developed resources and community members who I could draw on in my teaching—I felt that I was teaching in a better place and time for Indigenous students. Still, over the years, thoughts of the young nun returned from time to time. Once I started working on this chapter, I felt compelled to revisit the film, but could not recall the name. With persistence, I finally tracked down its source: *Sisters*, a play by Wendy Lill. I was able to get a copy. Published in 1991, *Sisters* was first performed in 1989 at the Ship's Company in Parrsboro, Nova Scotia. The television adaptation I saw earned Lill a Gemini Award in 1992. Set in 1969 rural Nova Scotia, with flashbacks to 1950 and the years in between, *Sisters* provides a tough look at a convent-run Indian residential school. The description on the back of the play notes that while the play chronicles in graphic detail the by now well documented agenda of cultural genocide which motivated the establishment of Native residential schools in Canada, the daring triumph of this play is that it reveals the far less well documented cultural infrastructure and values of the society which created those schools—the church and the state of white, colonial, paternalistic Canada.[68]

With the TRC and their calls to action, these policies are also now well documented. Reading the play in relation to what I know now shattered my faith. As a teacher, I had good intentions. Of course, good intentions are not enough. Celia Haig-Brown's and David Nock's book *With Good Intentions* examines the efforts of educators, lawyers, and activists of European ancestry who worked with and on behalf of Indigenous peoples when colonization was at its height.[69] Despite good intentions, they were still implicated in the colonialist project (i.e., the Christianization and "civilization" of Canada's First Peoples). I need to reexamine my past teaching in Indigenous communities and my current work in teacher education "not only as [they relate] to residential schools but to the whole colonial project…[and] how the broken treaties, unresolved land claims, and conflicts over traditional lands and resource rights have a detrimental impact today."[70]

Over the course of writing this chapter, I have developed greater awareness as to the depth of my "not knowing." The place from which I write is much less certain than I initially thought it was. With its focus on Indigenous-settler relations situated within teacher education and school contexts, my chapter is meant to contribute to the dialogue around reconceptualizing reconciliation in education.

Among the TRC's calls to action in the area of education for reconciliation are the calls to "make age-appropriate curriculum on residential schools, Treaties, and Aboriginal peoples' historical and contemporary contributions to Canada a mandatory education requirement for Kindergarten to Grade Twelve students" and to "educate teachers on how to integrate Indigenous knowledge and teaching methods into classrooms."[71] The expectation is that settler teachers and teacher educators will have an important role in developing and implementing curriculum that is historically accurate, that is respectful of Indigenous knowledge systems, and that incorporates Indigenous pedagogy. But the story I told in this chapter, despite its potential to inform teacher education, is troubled. In troubling my story, I have come to realize that reconciliation (in education) is in trouble. Even as I acknowledge this, many of the pre- and in-service teachers with whom I currently work, who are tasked with taking up the TRC calls to action with their students, come to mind. As a settler teacher educator, I am not sure how to best support these teachers, who very much resemble the settler teachers in my study—caring and committed, unknowing and uncertain. Teachers will need support in confronting the colonizing practices that continue to impact education. As Lorenzo Cherubini notes, "it takes enormous courage to question how one perceives and relates to one's own epistemic values and traditions, particularly when these ideologies are substantially different to the principles of Indigenous Knowledge and thought."[72] Haig-Brown notes that it is "never too late to start somewhere in our quest for better questions and better stories to give meaning to our scholarship."[73] Perhaps Regan's question provides a place to start. She asks: "How can we, as non-Indigenous people, unsettle ourselves...not just in words but by our actions, as we confront the history of colonization, violence, racism, and injustice that remains part of the IRS legacy today?"[74] I hope that the lessons about settler colonialism offered in this chapter can contribute to the ways in which settler educators respond to this question as we begin to create a better story for reconciliation in education.

NOTES

1. Terminology has been problematic in this chapter, in part because language usage has shifted over the close to four decades encompassed in the chapter. While I increasingly use the term *Indigenous*, I have also used the term *Aboriginal*, in which I include the Inuit, First Nations, and Métis peoples in Canada, as this is the terminology used in policy documents published by Alberta Education and other sources (see, e.g., "New Standards to Help Build More Inclusive Schools," Alberta Education, last updated February 7, 2018, https://www.alberta.ca/release. cfm?xID=523706BE2FD5C-04C2-AE72-8C01F26C8A1F2DDB). At other times, I use the term that is most appropriate for the particular context (i.e., *First Nations* or *Indian*), based on the published literature, media, or interview excerpts to which I am referring.
2. Regan, *Unsettling the Settler*, 28.
3. Styres, *Pathways for Remembering*, 7.
4. *Truth and Reconciliation Commission of Canada: Calls to Action*, calls 62–65. Hereafter cited as TRC calls.
5. Sterzuk, *Struggle for Legitimacy*.
6. Wiltse, "But My Students All Speak English."
7. Oskineegish, "Are You Providing an Education."
8. Justice, *Why Indigenous Literatures Matter*, 2.
9. Vizenor, "Aesthetics of Survivance."
10. McIntosh, "White Privilege."
11. Styres. *Pathways for Remembering*, 7.
12. Cummins et al., "Identity Texts and Academic Achievement," 559.
13. Moje et al., "Funds of Knowledge."
14. Cummins, Chow, and Schecter, "Community as Curriculum."
15. See Comber, *Literacy, Place, and Pedagogies*.

16. Schultz and Hull, *School's Out!*

17. Egan-Robertson and Bloome, *Students as Researchers*.

18. Toohey and Waterstone, "Negotiating Expertise in an Action Research Community," 307–08.

19. Kapyrka and Dockstator, "Indigenous Knowledges," 98–99.

20. Ladson-Billings, "Not the Culture of Poverty," 104.

21. Marshall and Toohey, "Representing Family," 221–22.

22. Cummins et al., "Identity Texts," 563.

23. Ladson-Billings, "Not the Culture of Poverty," 108.

24. Boler and Zembylas, "Discomforting Truths."

25. Boler and Zembylas, "Discomforting Truths," 120.

26. Dion, *Braiding Histories*, 330.

27. Boler and Zembylas, "Discomforting Truths," 129.

28. Boler and Zembylas, "Discomforting Truths," 133.

29. Blaisdell, "Beyond Discomfort?" 1.

30. See Aquash, "First Nations Control of Education"; Comber, "Schools as Meeting Places."

31. Comber, *Literacy, Place, and Pedagogies*, 361.

32. Cummins et al., "Identity Texts," 559.

33. Cajete, *Indigenous Community*, 21.

34. Haig-Brown, "Taking Indigenous Thought Seriously," 19.

35. See Pease-Alvarez and Schecter, *Learning, Teaching, and Community*; Schecter and Cummins, *Multilingual Education in Practice*.

36. Britzman, *Practice Makes Practice*, 33.

37. Justice, *Why Indigenous Literatures Matter*, 2.

38. Justice, *Why Indigenous Literatures Matter*, 2.

39. Macdonald, "Welcome to Winnipeg," 19.

40. See Wiltse, "Not Just 'Sunny Days'"; Wiltse, "Leaning Over the Fence."

41. Justice, *Why Indigenous Literatures Matter*, 3.

42. Justice, *Why Indigenous Literatures Matter*, 4.

43. Regan, *Unsettling the Settler*, 176.

44. Dion, "Introducing and Disrupting the 'Perfect Stranger'."

45. See Alfred, "Restitution Is the Real Pathway"; Corntassel, Chaw-win-is, and T'lakwadzi, "Indigenous Storytelling"; Tuck and Yang, "Decolonization Is Not a Metaphor."

46. Lowman and Barker, *Settler*, 6.

47. Epp, *We Are All Treaty People*, 126.

48. Berchini, "Reconceptualizing Whiteness."

49. McIntosh, "White Privilege."

50. Lensmire et al., "McIntosh as Synecdoche."

51. Riley and Ungerleider, "Pre-Service Teachers' Discriminatory Judgments."

52. Korteweg and Fiddler, "Unlearning Colonial Identities," 270.

53. Kovach, *Indigenous Methodologies*, 12.

54. Korteweg and Fiddler, "Unlearning Colonial Identities."

55. Tupper, "Disrupting Ignorance and Settler Identities," 49–50.

56. Tupper, "Disrupting Ignorance," 50.

57. Sterzuk and Mullholland, "Creepy White Gaze," 16.

58. Sterzuk and Mullholland, "Creepy White Gaze," 17.

59. Sterzuk and Mullholland, "Creepy White Gaze," 22.

60. Jo-ann Archibald, *Indigenous Storywork*.

61. Korteweg and Bissell, "Complexities of Researching Youth," 15.

Exploring Tensions in Taking Up the Call for Reconciliation in Teacher Education

62. See Canadian Council on Learning, *Report on Learning in Canada, 2007*; Canadian Council on Learning, *Improving Literacy Levels Among Aboriginal Canadians*.
63. Cajete, *Indigenous Community*, 8.
64. Dion, *Braiding Histories*, 64. Dion offers her Braiding Histories Stories project, a pedagogy of possibility, as an example of an alternative way of knowing.
65. Cajete, *Indigenous Community*, 8.
66. Styres, *Pathways for Remembering*, 94.
67. Ermine, "Ethical Space of Engagement," 201.
68. Back cover of Lill, *Sisters*. Copy by Talonbooks.
69. Haig-Brown and Nock, *With Good Intentions*.
70. Regan, *Unsettling the Settler*, 230.
71. TRC calls 62.i and 62.ii.
72. Cherubini, "'Taking Haig-Brown Seriously," 14.
73. Haig-Brown, "Taking Indigenous Thought Seriously," 11.
74. Regan, *Unsettling the Settler Within*, 11.

BIBLIOGRAPHY

Alfred, Taiaiake. "Restitution Is the Real Pathway to Justice for Indigenous Peoples." In *Response, Responsibility, and Renewal: Canada's Truth and Reconciliation Journey*, edited by Gregory Younging, Jonathon Dewar, and Mike DeGagné, 179–87. Ottawa: Aboriginal Healing Foundation, 2009.

Aquash, Mark. "First Nations Control of Education: One Community's Experience." *Canadian Journal of Native Education* 36, no. 1 (2013): 59–76.

Archibald, Jo-ann [Q'um Q'um Xiiem]. *Indigenous Storywork: Educating the Heart, Mind, Body, and Spirit*. Vancouver: UBC Press, 2014.

Berchini, Christina. "Reconceptualizing Whiteness in English Education: Failure, Fraughtness, and Accounting for Context." *English Education* 51, no. 2 (2019): 151–81.

Blaisdell, Benjamin. "Beyond Discomfort? Equity Coaching to Disrupt Whiteness." *Whiteness and Education* 3, no. 1 (2019): 162–81. https://doi.org/10.1080/23793406.2019.1569477.

Boler, Megan, and Michalinos Zembylas. "Discomforting Truths: The Emotional Terrain of Understanding Difference." In *Pedagogies of Difference: Rethinking Education for Social Change*, edited by Peter Trifonas, 110–36. New York: RoutledgeFalmer, 2002.

Britzman, Deborah P. *Practice Makes Practice: A Critical Study of Learning to Teach*. Albany: SUNY, 2003.

Cajete, Gregory. *Indigenous Community: Rekindling the Teaching of the Seventh Fire*. St. Paul: Living Justice Press, 2015.

Canadian Council on Learning. *Improving Literacy Levels Among Aboriginal Canadians* Ottawa: Canadian Council on Learning, 2008.

———. *Report on Learning in Canada 2007: Redefining How Success Is Measured in First Nation, Inuit, and Métis Learning*. Ottawa: Canadian Council on Learning, 2007. https://www.afn.ca/uploads/files/ education/5._2007_redefining_how_success_is_measured_en.pdf.

Cherubini, Lorenzo. "'Taking Haig-Brown Seriously': Implications of Indigenous Thought on Ontario Educators." *Journal of the Canadian Association for Curriculum Studies* 7, no. 1 (2009): 6–23.

Cochran-Smith, Marilyn. *Walking the Road: Race, Diversity, and Social Justice in Teacher Education*. New York: Teachers' College Press, 2004.

Comber, Barbara. *Literacy, Place, and Pedagogies of Possibility*. London: Routledge, 2016.

———. "Schools as Meeting Places: Critical and Inclusive Literacies in Changing Local Environments." *Language Arts* 90, no. 5 (2013): 361–71.

Corntassel, Jeff, Chaw-win-is, and T'lakwadzi. "Indigenous Storytelling, Truth-Telling, and Community Approaches to Reconciliation." *ESC: English Studies in Canada* 35, no. 1 (2019): 137–59.

Cummins, Jim, Patricia Chow, and Sandra Schecter. "Community as Curriculum." *Language Arts* 83, no. 4 (2006): 297–307.

Cummins, Jim, Shirley Hu, Paula Markus, and Kristiina M. Montero. "Identity Texts and Academic Achievement: Connecting the Dots in Multilingual School Contexts." *TESOL Quarterly* 49, no. 3 (2015): 555–81.

Curry, Mary Jane. "Drawing on Funds of Knowledge and Creating Third Spaces to Engage Students with Academic Literacies." *Journal of Applied Linguistics* 4, no. 1 (2007): 125–29.

Dion, Susan D. *Braiding Histories: Learning from Aboriginal Peoples Experiences and Perspectives.* Vancouver: UBC Press, 2009.

———. "Introducing and Disrupting the 'Perfect Stranger'." Recorded 2013. Vimeo video, 5:09, https://vimeo.com/59543958.

Egan-Robertson, Ann, and David Bloome, eds. *Students as Researchers of Culture and Language in Their Own Communities.* Cresskill: Hampton Press, 1998.

Epp, Roger. *We Are All Treaty People: Prairie Essays.* Edmonton: University of Alberta Press, 2008.

Ermine, Willie. "The Ethical Space of Engagement." *Indigenous Law Journal* 6, no. 1 (2007): 193–203.

Haig-Brown, Celia, and David Nock, eds. *With Good Intentions: Euro-Canadian and Aboriginal Relations in Colonial Canada.* Vancouver: UBC Press, 2011.

Justice, Daniel Heath. *Why Indigenous Literatures Matter.* Waterloo: Wilfrid Laurier University Press, 2018.

Kapyrka, Julie, and Mark Dockstator. "Indigenous Knowledges and Western Knowledges in Environmental Education: Acknowledging the Tensions for the Benefits of a 'Two-Worlds' Approach." *Canadian Journal of Environmental Education* 17 (2012): 97–112.

Korteweg, Lisa, and Alex Bissell. "The Complexities of Researching Youth Civic Engagement in Canada with/by Indigenous Youth: Settler-Colonial Challenges for Tikkun Olam Pedagogies of Repair and Reconciliation." *Citizenship Education Research Journal* 5, no. 2 (2015): 14–26.

Korteweg, Lisa, and Tesa Fiddler. "Unlearning Colonial Identities While Engaging in Relationality: Settler Teachers' Education-as-Reconciliation." *McGill Journal of Education* 53, no. 2 (2018): 254–75.

Kovach, Margaret. *Indigenous Methodologies: Characteristics, Conversations, and Contexts.* Toronto: University of Toronto Press, 2009.

Ladson-Billings, Gloria. "It's Not the Culture of Poverty, It's the Poverty of Culture: The Problem with Teacher Education." *Anthropology & Education Quarterly* 37, no. 2 (2006): 104–09.

Lensmire, Timothy, Shannon McManimon, Jessica Tierney, Mary Lee-Nichols, Casey Zachary, Audrey Lensmire, and Bryan Davis. "McIntosh as Synecdoche: How Teacher Education's Focus on White Privilege Undermines Antiracism." *Harvard Educational Review* 83, no. 3 (2013): 410–30.

Lill, Wendy. *Sisters.* Vancouver: Talonbooks, 1991.

Lowman, Emma Battle, and Adam J. Barker. *Settler: Identity and Colonialism in 21st Century Canada.* Halifax: Fernwood Publishing, 2015.

Macdonald, Nancy. "Welcome to Winnipeg: Where Canada's Racism Problem Is at Its Worst." *Maclean's* 128, no. 4 (2015): 16–24.

Marshall, Elizabeth, and Kelleen Toohey. "Representing Family: Community Funds of Knowledge, Bilingualism, and Multimodality." *Harvard Education Review* 80, no. 2 (2010): 221–41.

McIntosh, Peggy. "White Privilege: Unpacking the Invisible Knapsack." In *Race, Class, and Gender in the United States: An Integrated Study.* 4th ed., edited by Paula S. Rothernburg, 165–69. New York: St. Martin's Press, 1988.

Moje, Elizabeth, Kathryn Ciechanowski, Katherine Kramer, Lindsay Ellis, Rosario Carrillo, and Tehani Collazo. "Working Toward Third Space in Content Area Literacy: An Examination of Everyday Funds of Knowledge and Discourse." *Reading Research Quarterly* 39, no. 1 (2004): 38–70.

Moll, Luis C., Cathy Amanti, Deborah Neff, and Norma Gonzales. "Funds of Knowledge for Teaching: Using a Qualitative Approach to Connect Homes and Classrooms." *Theory into Practice* 31, no. 2, (1992): 132–41.

Mujawamariya, Donatille, and Gada Mahrouse. "Multicultural Education in Canadian Preservice Programs: Teacher Candidates' Perspectives." *Alberta Journal of Educational Research* 50, no. 4 (2004): 336–53.

Oskineegish, Melissa. "Are You Providing an Education That is Worth Caring About? Advice to Non-Native Teachers in Northern First Nations Communities." *Canadian Journal of Education* 38, no. 3 (2015): 1–25.

Pease-Alvarez, Lucinda, and Sandra Schecter, eds. *Learning, Teaching, and Community: Contributions of Situated and Participatory Approaches to Educational Innovation.* Mahwah: Lawrence Erlbaum Associates, 2005.

Regan, Paulette. *Unsettling the Settler Within: Indian Residential Schools, Truth Telling, and Reconciliation in Canada.* Vancouver: UBC Press, 2014.

Riley, Tasha, and Charles Ungerleider. "Pre-Service Teachers' Discriminatory Judgments." *The Alberta Journal of Educational Research* 54, no. 4 (2008): 378–87.

Schecter, Sandra, and Jim Cummins. *Multilingual Education in Practice: Using Diversity as a Resource.* Portsmouth: Heinemann, 2003.

Schultz, Katherine, and Glynda A. Hull, eds. *School's Out! Bridging Out-of-School Literacies with Classroom Practice.* New York: Teachers College Press, 2002.

Sterzuk, Andrea. *The Struggle for Legitimacy: Indigenized Englishes in Settler Schools.* Toronto: Multilingual Matters, 2011.

Sterzuk, Andrea, and Valerie Mulholland. "Creepy White Gaze: Rethinking the Diorama as a Pedagogical Activity." *Alberta Journal of Educational Research* 57, no. 1 (2011): 16–27.

Styres, Sandra D. *Pathways for Remembering and Recognizing Indigenous Thought in Education: Philosophies of Iethi'nihsténha Ohwentsia'k ékha (Land).* Toronto: University of Toronto Press, 2017.

Toohey, Kelleen, and Bonnie Waterstone. "Negotiating Expertise in an Action Research Community." In *Critical Pedagogies and Language Learning,* edited by Bonny Waterstone and Kelleen Toohey, 291–310. Cambridge: Cambridge University Press, 2004.

Truth and Reconciliation Commission of Canada. *Truth and Reconciliation Commission of Canada: Calls to Action.* Winnipeg: National Centre for Truth and Reconciliation, 2015. https://ehprnh2mwo3. exactdn.com/wp-content/uploads/2021/01/Calls_to_Action_English2.pdf.

Tuck, Eve, and K. Wayne Yang. "Decolonization Is Not a Metaphor." *Decolonization: Indigeneity, Education & Society* 1, no. 1 (2012): 1–40, https://jps.library.utoronto.ca/index.php/des/article/view/18630.

Tupper, Jennifer. "Disrupting Ignorance and Settler Identities: The Challenges of Preparing Beginning Teachers for Treaty Education." *In Education* 17, no. 3 (2011): 38–55.

Vizenor, Gerald. "Aesthetics of Survivance." In *Survivance: Narratives of Native Presence,* edited by Gerald Vizenor, 1–24. Lincoln: University of Nebraska Press, 2008.

Wallace, Catherine. "Conversations around the Literacy Hour in a Multilingual London Primary School." *Language and Education* 19, no. 4 (2005): 146–61.

Wiltse, Lynne. "'But My Students All Speak English': Ethical Research Issues of Aboriginal English." *TESL Canada Journal* 28, no. 5 (2011): 53–71.

———. "Leaning Over the Fence: Heritage Fair Projects as 'Funds of Knowledge'." *Alberta Journal of Educational Research* 60, no. 2 (2014): 361–76.

———. "Not Just 'Sunny Days': Aboriginal Students Connect Out-of-School Literacy Resources with School Literacy Practices." *Literacy* 49, no. 2 (2015): 60–68.

10

**DANIELA BASCUÑÁN,
MARK SINKE,
SHAWNA M. CARROLL,
AND JEAN-PAUL
RESTOULE**

Troubling Trespass

Moving Settler Teachers
Toward Decolonization

THIS CHAPTER WAS BORN FROM a larger study that sought to understand the strategies that current and former teachers and teacher candidates have employed as they teach or taught about Indigenous perspectives and epistemologies. The study also looked at the aspects of their work that participants found constraining, and those they found liberating. In this chapter, we focus on how settler teachers in our study negotiated their many hesitancies and the ways that they were apprehensive about "trespassing" into areas that are not theirs to claim. We understand these hesitancies to be enacted through "moves to innocence." As explained by Eve Tuck and K. Wayne Yang, moves to innocence are ways that settlers aim to reconcile their guilt and complicity in settler colonialism, as well as to rescue settler futurity and remain innocent. We draw on these moves to innocence to think through these questions and acknowledge that they "need not, and perhaps cannot, be answered in order for decolonization to exist as a framework."[1] These moves to innocence are nested within the complex ways that settler teachers are always already trespassing on Indigenous lands through absorption, erasure, and eliding difference. We examine the importance of and opportunities for educators to thoughtfully and critically move towards the integration of Indigenous epistemologies in classrooms rather than reproduce the status quo. We trouble teachers' approaches and performances that can also be seen as tokenism, appropriation, and cultural tourism, all of which maintain colonial power. We disturb settler teachers' engagement in this work—work that is both necessary and problematic as they/we continue to trespass on stolen lands.

Background

Understanding Indigenous peoples' histories and worldviews is relevant to all educators in Canada. Its importance has been recognized in a myriad of policy documents, including the final report of the Royal Commission on Aboriginal Peoples in 1996, Ontario's *First Nations, Métis, and Inuit Education Policy Framework* in 2007, and the Association of Canadian Deans of Education's *Accord on Indigenous Education* in 2010. Furthermore, the calls to action of the Truth and Reconciliation Commission of Canada (TRC) include a number of recommendations for educators in Canadian public schools who teach about Indigenous histories and wish to move towards more thoughtful engagement of Indigenous epistemologies.[2] While higher education institutions have begun to take up this important work in their teacher training programs, there is a limited academic understanding about how effectively these changes are improving the knowledge that educators in Ontario have about the histories, perspectives, and epistemologies of First Nations, Métis, and Inuit peoples.[3] It is within this context that we completed this research project.

Theoretical Approach

At the root of our theoretical approach is the notion that the land currently referred to as Canada was stolen: through military conquest, genocide, treaty processes that included force, willful misleading, nondelivery of promises, and through processes of resource extraction and land enclosure. Furthermore, we recognize that the process of stealing Indigenous lands is an ongoing process that is perpetuated through settler-colonial processes.[4] We see acts of the reinscription of settler-colonial ideologies within the education system as part of the settler-colonial process of erasure. We aim to subvert these ideologies by centring Indigenous epistemologies within education.

Trespass is the term we use to examine how educators enact hesitancies and to explain their specific apprehensions when teaching with Indigenous epistemologies. At its foundation, we see trespass as the literal wrongful intrusion onto land. White settlers were not invited into ownership of Indigenous lands, yet they continue to enact trespass in ongoing global structures of colonialism, imperialism, displacement, and forced removal of Indigenous bodies from their lands. On these lands, we understand trespass as a by-product of the work of teaching with Indigenous epistemologies and perspectives at the centre of educators' work. Although trespass is a constant apprehension of many teachers, an understanding of and critical reflection on it is also necessary for settler teachers to engage "in a good way." Halting education due to worries is not an option.

On this stolen land, we understand settlers as having many different positionalities and responsibilities in the processes of teaching and enacting treaty relationships. As explained by Eve Tuck and Karyn Recollet, "Settlers are different than migrants, immigrants, or other newcomers because they bring their own laws and worldviews, and enforce them in a new land. Settlers clear land of Indigenous peoples, often through genocide but also through forced removals, residential schooling, blood quantum policies, and other policies designed to diminish Indigenous peoples' claims to land."[5] Following Tuck and Recollet, we understand that all non-Indigenous educators are settlers on this land, but also that each person's story of arrival differs. In other words, we wish to highlight the complex relationships and responsibilities that settlers of colour have with the colonial government, social structures, and value systems. As Corey Snelgrove, Rita Kaur Dhamoon, and Jeff Corntassel explain, "everyone is 'structurally implicated' in the dispossession of Indigenous lands. Everyone is differentially structurally implicated."[6]

Through these acts of settler colonialism that continue today, certain epistemologies and knowledges are seen as valid and are upheld in the education system and in society as a whole. Our research project asked educators to reflect on their use of Indigenous ways of knowing in their teaching practices to understand what successes and barriers exist for educators in the current context.

Indigenous worldviews refer to interdependent, holistic systems and understandings about humanity and embody many things all at once.[7] To clarify, we turn to Kathleen Absolon's use of the term *Indigenous epistemologies* to refer to multiple systems of knowledge and relationships, including cultures, cosmovisions, spiritualities, worldviews, traditional stories, and histories.[8] These epistemologies can be understood in relation to ontologies, which refer to the nature of realities; both concepts are underpinned by notions of relationality.[9] Indigenous standpoints customarily centre notions of interconnectivity and relationships.[10] Wilson explains that Indigenous relationships to knowledge and to other people are directly derived from relationships to their land.[11] Significantly, Indigenous notions of being, knowing, relating, and doing cannot be separated from axiological principles. All these aspects are to be carried out "in a good way," which, in an Anishinaabe worldview, means striving for balance and harmony of all life: *mino-bimaatisiwin*.[12] We strive to engage in the research following the ethics of the Anishinaabe seven sacred teachings: respect, love, wisdom, bravery, humility, honesty, and truth in all actions, including research, knowing, and relating.[13] Anishinaabe teachings and values were used by the Indigenous and non-Indigenous research team as guides, helping to ensure ethical conduct throughout all processes.[14]

Methodology

The data on which this chapter relies were collected as part of a larger research study examining the reflections and practices of settler and Indigenous teachers around Indigenous perspectives in the classroom. This segment of the larger study focused on stories from 130 current teachers and teachers-in-training who opted in to one of four research sessions at a one-day conference held in 2017. We explain these research sessions below. The conference was created as part of the research project, and was called *Kimaacihtoomin e-Anishinaabek kikinoo'amaakewin*: Beginning to Teach in an Indigenous Way. It was mounted as a professional development opportunity for teachers who were seeking it, and as a way to create a participant pool that shared a concern for doing Indigenous pedagogy well in mainstream classrooms. While these spaces are crucial, it is important to note that a one-day conference can only start a conversation about these complex issues and histories. Still, we hope that it could act as a fuel to an important fire of action in the classroom. This research project follows a narrative inquiry methodological approach,[15] which allowed for an understanding of the importance of relationships between the participants and researchers and the productive nature of sharing stories. As storytelling is viewed as an Indigenous method of knowing that shares the ethics of the sacred teachings, and narrative inquiry focuses on stories we tell each other as educators, the methods chosen are complementary.

Participants who contributed to the study's data each shared their stories and perspectives in one of four research groups that were part of the one-day conference. Each of the four research groups was framed around a different way of sharing stories: individual guided narrative writing, dramatic storytelling, collaborative visual arts relational mapping, and a talking circle that was led by our research partner who is a member of the Dokis First Nation. Participants in each group were asked to examine three areas of their teaching practice: (1) the multiple ways in which they incorporate Indigenous perspectives and knowledges into their teaching practices; (2) the successes they have had in this area; and (3) the barriers they have faced along the way. Having participants focus on these three areas and tell their stories through writing, artwork, drama, and oral sharing allowed for "meaning making through the shaping or ordering of experience."[16]

The four storytelling research groups produced various data sources that were later analyzed by members of the research team. The research team analyzed transcripts from the drama, sharing circle, and visual mapping groups, as well as the written responses from the guided writing group, using an emergent coding process that highlighted the significant themes and concepts that became evident in how the participants described their teaching experiences.[17] Using our theoretical framework—that decolonization is not a metaphor,[18] and that all settlers are implicated, though differently, in the colonial project—allowed us to actively seek an understanding of the participants' experiences by prioritizing possibilities that exist and examining these through compassionate and critical approaches.

Indigenous participants in the research groups contributed their stories and experiences along with non-Indigenous participants. While these responses have helped shape our understanding of the research context, this chapter focuses on the data provided by non-Indigenous participants. At the same time, we understand the importance of decentring settlerhood, which we understand as the de facto ideological and material existence of any person living in a settler-colonial society.

Analysis

Our analysis works to divest from settlerhood by learning more about how it operates. We have chosen to focus on the settler stories specifically, while attending to the notion that settler educators are attempting to do the right thing by engaging with Indigenous education. In this chapter, we focus on the themes of "hesitancy" and "trespass," both of which were identified by our emergent coding process.

Our theoretical framing of settler colonialism and Indigenous epistemologies allows us to understand the participants' hesitancies and trespass in specific ways. We see hesitancies as (1) spaces for productivity and (2) spaces for anxiety, which show teachers' moves to innocence.[19] An examination of this first framing— hesitancies as productive pauses—allows for a compassionate and critical understanding of the pauses and silences in participant conversations. It allows space for these pauses, which, in this work, are necessary for self-reflection, learning, growing, and collaborating. It also highlights that time can be understood beyond the linear colonial conception of time by which the school system is currently bound. We understand the colonial and neoliberal understandings of time as key to the settler-colonial process of erasure. As Riyad Shahjahan explains, the learning process in the current colonial system is understood through a capitalist production lens, where results are quantified, compared, and improved for production. We further draw on Shahjahan's work to remind us to "slow down" in order to remember the importance of real, embodied ways of knowing and to understand that taking our time is key to an anticolonial framework in the classroom.[20] So, when settler teacher participants described "productive" pauses, we saw the potential for those teachers to learn and grow within these times and spaces of reflection.

The second way we understand hesitancies is as spaces for anxiety. These occur when educators pause due to their worries of trespass. They halt their teaching by refusing to teach a history or epistemology that is not familiar to them because they are anxious about appropriating, stereotyping, offending others, or not having the right knowledge or terminology.

As mentioned above, there are explicit educational directives for the inclusion of Indigenous epistemologies.[21] When done superficially, this "inclusion" can be harmful and it is important to note that inclusion is still practiced within a settler-colonial education system and curriculum. Throughout the data, we found that teachers' anxiety in trespass could lead to both the productive (based on learning) and nonproductive (based on anxiety) hesitancies. Their worries of trespass could lead to moves to innocence. Through our data, we conclude that settler educators are making some of these moves to innocence, although perhaps unknowingly. One way we found this is through fantasizing adoption. Fantasizing adoption occurs when settlers take on Indigenous practices and knowledge, becoming "indigenized," asking Indigenous peoples to give their "land, [their] claim to the land, [their] very Indian-ness to the settler for safe-keeping."[22] This adoption of Indigenous culture becomes part of the settler's aim to rid themselves of their guilt and "anxiety of settler un-belonging."[23] In the data, settler teachers shared stories in which they described feeling pained by their involvement in situations where they felt that they had to teach culture. Rather than become responsible for claiming Indigenous knowledge and sharing it, the settler teacher is advised to teach the histories, politics, and social effects of relations with Canada. Alternately, the settler teacher can establish and foster relationships with Indigenous people and communities to provide opportunities for their students to learn directly from Indigenous people about relationship to land, songs, stories, ceremonies, and those things that are more appropriately shared by Indigenous people.

The guilt settler teachers felt when learning about harms done to Indigenous people and their struggles against those harms caused the settler teachers to feel caught up in those same struggles. While this feeling has the potential to build allyship and encourage working together to counter oppression, it also carries the risk that settler teachers may equivocate the pain and oppression experienced by Indigenous people with their own pain, essentially seeing themselves as oppressed rather than as beneficiaries of oppression. Settler teachers spoke of the issue of decolonization as "our" issue, a turn of phrase that secures a settler future. As educators begin to include Indigenous perspectives in their classrooms, they may reproduce unequal relationships and secure their settler futurity by becoming more expert in Indigeneity than Indigenous people. Settler educators must reflect on their own positionalities, the reality of their trespass, and their responsibilities to land and treaties. They must refocus their energies away from "solving the Indian problem" to rid themselves of guilt, and ask instead, "How do we solve the settler problem?"[24] Until they do this, they will continue to be trespassing.

Another way in which we saw the settler participants' moves to innocence was through colonial equivocation, in which experiences of oppression are all equated under the banner of colonization. Embedded in these ideas is the "at risk-ing / asterisk-ing"[25] of Indigenous peoples—that is, seeing Indigenous peoples as "at risk" or simply as a small minority among other minorities. In our research data, we observed this asterisking within teacher attempts to be more inclusive of many types of difference in their classrooms, with Indigenous experience being subsumed within multiculturalism. For example, one participant explained:

> As cliché as it might sound, I am most inspired by the possibility of change. I think that for too long our society has "othered" or "hidden" the perspectives, cultures and "ways of knowing" of so many groups of people. As a teacher, I believe I have been afforded a position in which I can help to change that, to make even the slightest difference! I feel that by including those who have been excluded we stand to gain so much more as a society—we stand to gain "wholesomeness."[26]

While inclusion can be seen as a positive motivation, the annexation of Indigenous perspectives as simply one more diversity requirement risks going down an unintentionally harmful path on which settlers remain invested in their own futurity and ignore the ongoing colonization of stolen land. Sharing Indigenous knowledge, power, and importance in the settler education system becomes a requirement, but inclusion is on the terms of the settler. When settler educators bring Indigenous perspectives into their classrooms within the frame of general inclusion, they simply fit one more different or Other perspective into the settler-colonial curriculum, thereby ensuring the colonial curriculum itself remains intact. These moves to innocence directly relate to settler educator attempts to avoid trespass, which appear in the data as attempts to absorb, erase, and elide settler differences with Indigenous histories and perspectives. These actions are explained in detail in the next section.

We understand that trespass can often be an aspect of moves to innocence. These moves to innocence ensure a future for settlers in which settlers can get rid of their guilt and reconcile their complicity in settler colonialism with the goal of "moving on."[27] Through this framework, we understand there is much that is irreconcilable within the structure of settler colonialism and the unproductive pauses of settler teachers. When avoiding discussion of Indigenous content because of anxiety about doing it wrong, or trespassing into knowledge terrains uncomfortable to them, the settler teacher, already a trespasser, in effect delays the possibility of social change through reproducing the status quo with their inaction. The pause or hesitancy thus has the effect of maintaining unchallenged settler legitimacy and ongoing colonialism. Teachers are always already trespassing and should begin the conversation of how to teach Indigenous histories and epistemologies with this in mind.

Our readings of Tuck and Yang and of Shahjahan help us understand the need for teachers to move beyond moves to innocence and anxieties of trespass, and move instead into the possibilities of productive hesitancies and certain trespasses.[28] Settler teachers cannot be absolved of teaching Indigenous histories and epistemologies simply because they are not Indigenous. Failing to do this work is too often a fallback on Eurocentric ways of knowing, which exclude non-European ways of knowing in general and Indigenous epistemologies in particular, thereby recreating systems of oppression. Defaulting to what has already been naturalized in schools is not an option.

Trespass as Absorption, Erasure, and Elision of Difference

Participants often voiced their intention to "rebuild and replace knowledge that was lost and subjugated in the past"[29] as a way of engaging with the reality of trespass. Teachers were hesitant to trespass, so some chose to pause and reflect. This was not pausing as inaction, but rather as the creation of the space necessary to learn more about Indigenous-Canadian relations and histories, sit in their discomfort, and contemplate the complexities of the issues before making important decisions in their classrooms. Because of this, teachers were able to find openings to discuss important issues and make amends with the past in many subject areas. We suggest that some teachers have begun to understand this personal sense of trespass because they have learned to historicize their teaching contexts and recognize the ongoing treaty relationships that encompass all people on Turtle Island.

Many of the educators in the study had not learned about Indigenous histories or perspectives until they began engaging with Indigenous activists and educators in light of conversations around reconciliation, Indigenous movements like Idle No More, and the Standing Rock resistance. The TRC's calls to action created national discourses about the need to bring these conversations into the classroom.[30] Teachers felt as though their new learning required a response. This growing understanding showed that teachers were more aware of their temporal and spatial locations, and their positionalities with respect to these histories and issues. Specifically, respondents commented on more substantial incorporation of Indigenous histories within their practicum placements. They noticed that the ways in which Indigenous issues and concerns were taught in practice were not commensurate with their growing knowledge and awareness. Many teachers explained that they felt committed to bringing Indigenous histories into their future classrooms. Although we agree that this sentiment is positive, it should be enacted with care as these actions come with warnings to reflect upon, dangers to avoid, and complexities to navigate. Some of these complexities obviously reflect issues common to the profession in general. Here, we take up two specific examples, which we found in teachers' descriptions of the spaces of anxiety, and which reveal the work of trespass: (1) attempts to absorb and/or erase Indigenous experiences and (2) attempts to elide Indigenous differences. These practices result in the extraction of Indigenous voices, contributing to the literal and metaphorical trespass of settler teachers teaching Indigenous content on Indigenous lands.

ABSORPTION THROUGH THE "AFFORDANCE" OF SPACE

We noted that many teacher practitioners unwittingly leaned into practices that *actively engage in trespass* on Indigenous lands. Specifically, the data were illustrative of teachers trespassing by creating the illusion of *affording spaces* for Indigenous worldviews, histories, and wisdom teachings in their classrooms. These inadvertent practices enact Indigenous erasure through absorption or assimilation.

As noted earlier, many participant teachers were developing awareness of structural inequities about settler-colonial structures on and ensuing devastation of Indigenous communities. Emerging understandings of "asymmetrical" settler-Indigenous relations on Turtle Island led teachers to address these inequalities by attempting to marry Indigenous content to Education Ministry mandates and the TRC's calls to action. Many of the teachers understood many of the effects of genocidal practices against Indigenous Nations. These important starting points were enriched by teachers' experiences of compulsory components of their preservice programs that asked them to incorporate Indigenous content in their classes using an inclusion-based lens. This study highlighted common practices of compensating through inclusion, like in the earlier example of the research participant who described inclusion as a route to "wholesomeness." This additive inclusion ignores the genocidal history and ongoing practices of colonization and understands inclusion as a retribution or an offering of space for Indigenous content within the otherwise unchanged and unchallenged settler curriculum. This inclusion gave specific time slots for Indigenous content in an additive, superficial way that ignored the ways in which these messages and important teachings are erased and ignored through the remainder of the curriculum. It was contemplated as a space to be shared through an act of bestowing: the settler teacher giving space to teach the vastness that is Indigenous content. These understandings of "giving" space for Indigenous perspectives were prevalent in several cross-sections of data. Many participants described Indigenous content as an attachment or appendage to other curricular or classroom practices without reflecting on the continual trespass of settlers on stolen land. Two participant comments epitomize this idea:

> Through my courses in [my teacher education program] as well
> as workshops and readings I have done for personal interest,
> something that stands out to me the most is the importance of
> *giving* the Indigenous cultures a place in the classroom. This can
> be done through *incorporating* their perspectives in different subject
> areas rather than teaching solely from the government-settler
> perspective. (emphasis added)[31]

> Since I am going to be an educator in a Canadian classroom,
> part of "being Canadian" is knowing about the Indigenous side
> of "Canadian-ness."[32]

Participants' opinions were well-meaning and did not come from a place of purposefully causing harm. They were born of a genuine personal desire and a newfound responsibility to do well and take action in teachers' own sites of practice. However, the idea of continually *making space* for Indigenous perspectives—merely adding them on to current curriculum—might not have the same impact as a holistic infusion of Indigenous perspectives through all aspects of curriculum. What can be added can also be taken away. By contrast, a starting point that situates teachings within land relationships is more diffuse. It involves changing the space itself, not just making room for the content. By changing the space, the content can be embedded in such a way that it cannot be easily taken away. Any move that sees Indigeneity as a part of Canadianness and not as a thing in itself that predates the notion of Canada is a move toward erasure. It makes of Indigeneity an appendage rather than allowing it to be its own being.

As noted above, teachers spoke a great deal about *expanding spaces* to be *shared with* Indigenous wisdom teachings, histories, and contributions. However well-informed some pedagogical choices might seem, they may still cause harm through erasure. As teachers are working within the structured setting of settler-colonial schooling, we understand the normativity of the school system wherein teachers are implicated in reproducing harm. Absorption and erasure in this context refer to a marked settler-colonial reinscription—or settler futurity—visible in curriculum, with symbolic and material dispossession as the outcome.[33] Essentially, then, the underlying messages, values, and structures of state curricula have been used to exert settler-colonial hegemony in schooling contexts. In this way, the curriculum field is predisposed to upholding and maintaining settler futurity through Indigenous erasure and replacement.[34] Settler colonialism continues to recursively and normatively operate in educational spaces. Often unwittingly, teachers teach curriculum that fortifies ideologies of dispossession through the "colonial fort logics" of exclusion and difference.[35] Although teachers may actively challenge these ideas through inclusionary efforts, their actions may instead unwittingly normalize the colonial beliefs and values encoded in the curriculum. Indeed, they may find that their own personal worldviews become compromised in the process, contributing to even greater anxiety about the work of Indigenizing classrooms. Even if we choose to divest from harm, we still risk contributing to erasure through absorption by enacting our desires to be inclusive.[36] In other words, when teachers enact an illusory sense of affordance to create spaces for Indigenous content, they are in fact actors of invasion; they are practicing elements of trespass. This is characterized by the wish to share a pedagogical space with historically marginalized Others and for the benefit of Others. However, it is also constructed as a space to alleviate their guilt as trespassing settlers. Keeping paternalism and intrusion in check is one of the many ongoing challenges and obligations for the settler teacher. When one teaches *for* the Other, there is no space for working with and walking alongside the Other—in this case, Indigenous communities. Having Indigenous Others stand on our settler shoulders is more ethically productive than voicing their concerns *for* them.

Eliding Difference

Teaching Indigenous knowledges can constitute trespass when it elides difference. Our study notes that it was characteristic for teachers, particularly teachers of colour, to elide difference and call attention to an assumed shared oppression and history of exclusion. The following respondent illustrates the elision of difference:

> I first began learning about how to integrate Indigenous perspectives in my teaching during my [initial teacher education] program at [Faculty of Education]. As a visible minority myself, I think that what resonated with me the most was the critical need our society has to create inclusive spaces in which our children can learn and grow. I didn't always have that growing up—neither did my mother, brother, cousins, et cetera. And so for me, being able to make a positive change in which children feel welcome, celebrated, represented, and considered is crucial—being able to include other ways of thinking, knowing, and doing is crucial.[37]

Highlighting a shared experience of exclusion when teaching Indigenous content is a common practice in the elision of difference. Of course, this is not to negate racialized people's experiences of oppression; however, when students and teachers who are marginalized are learning about genocidal histories of Turtle Island, they should analyze their experiences of oppression through their own histories while recognizing the histories of Turtle Island.[38] Finding connection between one's marginal status and experiences of Indigenous marginalization could be beneficial, but only if used as an entry point into a conversation, not a personal platform to find sameness and ignore the complicated realities of trespass on stolen land.

In educational discourses, the main umbrella of equity and inclusion often merges Indigenous rights into a common discussion of injustice, which erases contextualized, unique, and necessary differences. Seeking proximity to the experiences of oppression and exclusion that Indigenous peoples have faced carries a couple of risks or cautions. The first caution is the important reality that all settler teachers including settlers of colour have inherited responsibilities within the treaties governing the lands where they live and work. One's rights and responsibilities to the land are inextricably linked to the treaties, proclamations, histories, and relationships peoples had with the land before any settlers arrived. Even settlers of colour are treaty beneficiaries and have responsibilities as settlers.[39] Settler educators must also be cautious about equating experiences of marginalization with one another. If those who are marginalized equate their experiences with Indigenous experiences, it ignores the importance of the treaties and of declarations that, by centring not race but occupancy, have established the rights of Indigenous peoples within Canadian law. Thus, if settler teachers equate all experiences of marginalization and exclusion with those of Indigenous peoples, they actually diminish the importance and reality of Indigenous rights held under treaties. This, of course, is not to say they do not experience exclusionary practices and marginalization in the settler context; however, we must recognize Indigenous peoples' special statuses and protections, which the treaties are meant to protect.[40] Finding common ground is an important pedagogical step for building awareness among teachers and students. It is about understanding shared exclusion, marginalization, and experiences of racism—and that is a great starting point. However, teachers must also move on to the next fundamental step: demonstrating how the relationship of Indigenous people to the land and to all subsequent newcomers is a distinct relationship, both historically and contemporarily, and must be entered into as such.

As teachers attempt to address historical asymmetries in a context where educational mandates increasingly encourage the integration of Indigenous epistemologies, it is not enough to have good intentions. Even those teachers who strive to teach through a social-justice lens may, in fact, be enacting forms of trespass by reproducing erasure, absorption, and elision. Teachers can mitigate these risks by always questioning their own actions and motives, and by striving to inculcate the same self-awareness in their students.

The Inevitability of Trespass

As one begins to recognize their guilt and complicity in acts of trespass, it is understandable that some settler teachers may respond with moves to innocence. As settler teachers and other settlers encounter a deeper understanding of oppressive settler structures, they aim to separate themselves from these structures through moves to innocence. It is important to remember that these moves to innocence will not absolve settler educators, so long as colonial relations remain in place. Trespass is ultimately inevitable: settlers are on Indigenous lands. Although settler teachers may aim to avoid trespass, they cannot. They must acknowledge this reality so that they can begin to move forward "in a good way." The original peoples of this land had their own languages, social structures, traditions, beliefs, and stories. Settlers aimed to assert their own languages, social structures, traditions, and beliefs upon the people and territories as though the land were empty upon their arrival and not already under the governance of others. This is trespassing. The settlement of Canada was enacted through the genocidal practices that aimed to disappear the Indigenous peoples who lived on the land, and these ongoing practices of erasure continue these trespassing legacies on stolen land. Indigenous writers have highlighted the many ways that their personal and collective lives have been trespassed upon by settler policies and practices. One stark example is the establishment of the Indian Act. Others include residential schools, stealing children from Indigenous communities, the destruction of Indigenous lands and resources, the banning of languages and traditions—and the list goes on.[41] Although settler teachers aim to prove that they are innocent of these settler practices, it is necessary to reflect on the ways that all settlers, and the education systems created by and for settlers, have been enabled precisely *because of* these settler practices. The education system is not outside of settler policies. Indeed, it is one of the main tools of reproducing settler-colonial ideologies, while at the same time restricting access to Indigenous knowledges through the historical and continual erasure of Indigenous languages, which ultimately allows for English dominance. It is evident that all settlers are complicit in settler-colonial practices of trespassing.

It is important at this point to reiterate that settler trespass is complicated and includes settler arrivals that are not part of the white settler conquest. Settlers who came to the land because of global systems of oppression and exploitation are still complicit in settler-colonial processes, albeit differently. These conversations of complicated complicity are shown through the seminal work of Bonita Lawrence and Enakshi Dua, and in more recent work such as that of Martin Cannon. These scholars explain the importance of naming the differences between settler colonial-ists and those who have arrived here due to exploitation, such as people who were stolen and sold in the slave trade, those who laboured on the trans-Canada railway, and others exploited through more recent policies (e.g., the Live-in Caregiver Program and its exploitation of Filipina caregivers).[42] We want to call attention to these crucial differences, as settlers of colour should have necessarily different responses to Indigenous erasure than white settlers. We could speak at length about this important issue, but due to space constraints we will simply say this: Everyone living on Turtle Island has a responsibility to recognize the histories of Indigenous erasure and live in accordance with their land's treaties and Indigenous commu-nities' knowledges. Whether coming to this stolen land by choice or because of complicated global systems of oppression, it is clear that all settlers are trespassing on Indigenous lands. With this knowledge, we encourage settler educators and preservice teachers to move beyond innocence and recognize the ways in which they trespass through intentional reflection. If settler educators use their efforts to "remain innocent," much of this important task is lost. Of course, this space of recognition is not simple and requires both reflection and learning about the histories and present-day practices of Indigenous erasure.

The Necessity and Possibility of This Work

Even with self-reflection and in-depth knowledges of the histories of this land, this type of curriculum work will always move dangerously close to the appropriation and tokenism of Indigenous histories and knowledges. In this chapter, we have highlighted ways in which settler teachers engage in trespass while seeking to follow a path towards Indigenous inclusion and incorporation. Teachers undergird the progress of settler futurity through absorption and erasure of Indigeneity while eliding differences that are essential to furthering Indigenous epistemologies. With the contradictions of this work, we must ask how settler educators can do this work without reproducing settler structures. First, along with understanding the inevitability of trespass, settler teachers must acknowledge and name the conditions that have led them to take up Indigenous education and name what they are choosing to do about it. Settler teachers are on a spectrum of sorts with respect to different levels of engagement in their sites of practice and how they address settler-Indigenous relationships and Indigenous knowledges. This spectrum is impinged upon by many factors, including our individual subject positions; our individual settlerhoods are shaped by a multitude of factors.[43] Teacher subjectivities shift to situate their experiences and positionalities on this land according to their desires to reconcile history, address institutional mandates, and/or take personal journeys. All of these reasons are tempered by the knowledge that their teaching often constitutes moves to innocence: reconciling history has less to do with restitution with Indigenous people than it does with resolving teachers' own historical complicities.[44] Furthering the institutional mandates for Indigenous inclusion that pay tribute to Indigenous relations through land acknowledgement and content offerings must be mitigated carefully so that they are not enacted in a consumptive manner. As this research has demonstrated, teachers' personal journeys of social justice, even when carefully undertaken, can reflect moves to innocence.

Though there are many obstacles, we believe it is still possible for settler educators to engage with Indigenous epistemologies in decolonial ways. As settler teachers continue to trespass on Indigenous lands, it is important to pay attention to hopeful and critical opportunities in this work. We suggest educators can do this by becoming knowledgeable about existing treaty teachings and creating real relationships with their Indigenous communities. Only then should educators plan their curricula and pedagogy. This requires a level of care that can only be actualized by moving in at least one of two directions—preferably both. The first is grounding teacher practice in perspectives that honour Indigenous wisdom teachings. These practices must unequivocally be centred around the land and its people. This means centring teachings that have been set by Indigenous peoples themselves. The second is engaging in practices that interrogate the structures that further the normalcy of settler colonialism. Teachers must teach students about treaties, the Indian Act, and other laws and policies that make the existence of settlerhood appear normal and innocent, or that excuse actions that lead to Indigenous erasure and marginalization. The goal is for settlers to find and enact responsibility in dismantling these forms of power. By seeking possibilities through these acts of decolonization, teachers will, in fact, be moving forward the futures of Indigenous peoples.

In Canadian public school contexts, some teachers have played central roles in cultivating civil deliberation in the search for equitable outcomes for their school communities and in response to the national conversations surrounding reconciliation. Mainstream reconciliation discourses are insufficient for determining how successful these deliberations have been in adequately addressing the past-present responsibilities that come with teaching in the wake of Indigenous genocide. This study has provided insight into the complexities of teaching Indigenous histories and worldviews, the barriers and motivations for their inclusion, and the practice of working through unsettling discomfort and troubling settler educators' trespass. We have offered an important beginning to a conversation about the need for settler teachers to self-reflection on their roles and responsibilities on stolen land and their complicity in settler-colonial processes and trespass. Our study has illuminated the complexities of settler teachers prioritization of Indigenous histories and perspectives by highlighting the problematics of doing so while confronting the fact that doing nothing does not absolve them of their trespass. We reiterate the importance of teaching curriculum through a treaty-based lens and with Indigenous collaboration and consultation. Although we understand the difficulty of this work for settler educators' continual trespass and complicity in settler processes, we urge educators to continue to self-reflect, bring treaty-based curriculum and Indigenous communities' authentic collaboration into their classrooms, and trouble their trespass on stolen lands.

Authors' Note

We would like to acknowledge the contribution of a SSHRC Insight Grant, which funded this research project.

NOTES

1. Tuck and Yang, "Decolonization Is Not a Metaphor," 35.
2. Truth and Reconciliation Commission of Canada, *Calls to Action.* Hereafter cited as TRC calls.
3. Mashford-Pringle and Nardozi, "Aboriginal Knowledge Infusion"; Vetter and Blimkie, "Learning to Teach"; den Heyer, "Sticky Points"; Tanaka, "Transforming Perspectives."
4. Tupper, "Possibilities for Reconciliation."
5. Tuck and Recollet, "Introduction to Native Feminist Texts," 17.
6. Snelgrove, Dhamoon, and Corntassel. "Unsettling Settler Colonialism," 25.
7. Corntassel, Chaw-win-is, and T'lakwadzi, "Indigenous Storytelling."
8. Absolon, *Kaandossiwin.*
9. Wilson, *Research Is Ceremony.*
10. Absolon, *Kaandossiwin*; Cajete, "Indigenous Knowledge"; Wilson, *Research Is Ceremony.*
11. Wilson, *Research Is Ceremony.*
12. LaDuke, "Indigenous Environmental Perspectives."
13. Benton-Binai, *The Mishomis Book.*
14. Absolon, *Kaandossiwin*; Castellano, "Ethics of Aboriginal Research"; Wilson, *Research Is Ceremony.*
15. Chase, "Narrative Inquiry"; Clandinin, *Handbook of Narrative Inquiry*; Clandinin and Caine, "Narrative Inquiry."
16. Chase, "Narrative Inquiry," 56.

17. Strauss and Corbin, *Basics of Qualitative Research*; Glaser, *Basics of Grounded Theory Analysis*; Stemler, "An Overview of Content Analysis."
18. Tuck and Yang, "Decolonization Is Not a Metaphor."
19. Tuck and Yang, "Decolonization Is Not a Metaphor."
20. Shahjahan, "Being 'Lazy'."
21. TRC calls.
22. Tuck and Yang, "Decolonization Is Not a Metaphor," 14.
23. Tuck and Yang, "Decolonization Is Not a Metaphor," 15.
24. Regan, *Unsettling the Settler*, 11.
25. Tuck and Yang, "Decolonization Is Not a Metaphor," 4.
26. Guided writing participant, April 20, 2017.
27. Tuck and Yang, "Decolonization is Not a Metaphor."
28. Tuck and Yang, "Decolonization Is Not a Metaphor"; Shahjahan, "Being 'Lazy'."
29. Guided writing participant, April 20, 2017.
30. See especially TRC calls 62 and 63.
31. Talking circle participant, April 20, 2017.
32. Talking circle participant, April 20, 2017.
33. Tuck and Gaztambide-Fernández, "Curriculum, Replacement."
34. Tuck and Gaztambide-Fernández, "Curriculum, Replacement."
35. Donald, "The Pedagogy of the Fort."
36. Eve Tuck, "Suspending Damage."
37. Talking circle participant, April 20, 2017.
38. Haig-Brown, "Decolonizing Diaspora."
39. See Aboriginal Education Office, *Education Policy Framework*; Sehdev, "People of Colour in Treaty"; Alfred and Rollo, "Resetting and Restoring the Relationship; Rollo, "I Am Canadian!"
40. Rollo, "I Am Canadian!"
41. See Royal Commission on Aboriginal Peoples, *Report*; Truth and Reconciliation Commission, *Honouring the Truth*; Imai, *Annual Annotated Indian Act*; Hill, *500 Years of Resistance*; Kulchyski, *The Red Indians*.
42. Lawrence and Dua, "Decolonizing Antiracism"; Cannon, "Changing the Subject." See also Tungohan et al., "After the Live-In Caregiver Program."
43. Haig-Brown, "Decolonizing Diaspora"; Cannon, "Changing the Subject."
44. Corntassel, Chaw-win-is, and T'lakwadzi, "Indigenous Storytelling."

BIBLIOGRAPHY

Aboriginal Education Office. *Ontario First Nation, Métis, and Inuit Education Policy Framework*. Ministry of Education, Government of Ontario, 2007. http://www.edu.gov.on.ca/eng/aboriginal/fnmiFramework.pdf.

Absolon, Kathleen E. [minogiizhigokwe]. *Kaandossiwin: How We Come to Know*. Black Point: Fernwood Publishing, 2011.

Alfred, Taiaiake, and Tobold Rollo. "Resetting and Restoring the Relationship between Indigenous Peoples and Canada." In *The Winter We Danced: Voices from the Past, the Future, and the Idle No More Movement*, edited by The Kino-nda-niimi Collective, 314–15. Winnipeg: ARP Books, 2014.

Association of Canadian Deans of Education. *ACDE's Accord on Indigenous Education: Progress Report*, 2010. https://www.twu.ca/sites/default/files/accord-for-indigenous-education-progress-report.pdf.

Benton-Binai, Edward. *The Mishomis Book: The Voice of the Ojibway*. Minneapolis: University of Minnesota Press, 1988.

Cajete, Gregory. "Indigenous Knowledge and Western Science: Contrasts and Similarities." Banff Centre Talks, Banff, AB, recorded September 2014. YouTube video, 29:04. https://youtu.be/nFeNIOgIbzw.

Cannon, Martin. "Changing the Subject in Teacher Education: Centering Indigenous, Diasporic, and Settler Colonial Relations." *Cultural and Pedagogical Inquiry* 4, no. 2 (2013): 21–37.

Carleton, Sean. "Decolonizing Cottage Country: Anishinaabe Art Intervenes in Canada's Wild Rice War." *Canadian Dimension*, September 15, 2016. https://canadiandimension.com/articles/view/decolonizing-cottage-country-anishinaabe-art-intervenes-in-canadas-wild-ric.

Carroll, Shawna M., Daniela Bascuñán, Mark Sinke, and Jean-Paul Restoule. "How Discomfort Reproduces Settler Structures: Moving Beyond Fear and Becoming Imperfect Accomplices," *Journal of Curriculum and Teaching* 9, no. 2 (2020): 9–19.

Castellano, Marlene Brant. "Ethics of Aboriginal Research." *International Journal of Indigenous Health* 1, no. 1 (2004): 98–114.

Chase, Susan E. "Narrative Inquiry: Still a Field in the Making." In *Collecting and Interpreting Qualitative Materials*. 4th ed., edited by Norman K. Denzin and Yvonna S. Lincoln, 55–84. Los Angeles: SAGE, 2013.

Clandinin, Jean D., ed. *Handbook of Narrative Inquiry: Mapping a Methodology*. Thousand Oaks: SAGE, 2006.

Clandinin, Jean D., and Vera Caine. "Narrative Inquiry." In *The SAGE Encyclopedia of Qualitative Research Methods,* edited by L.M. Given, 542–44. Thousand Oaks: SAGE, 2008. https://doi.org/10.4135/9781412963909.n275.

Corntassel, Jeff, Chaw-win-is, and T'lakwadzi. "Indigenous Storytelling, Truth-Telling, and Community Approaches to Reconciliation." *ESC: English Studies in Canada* 35, no. 1 (2009): 137–59.

Dei, George J. Sefa. "The Denial of Difference: Reframing Anti-Racist Praxis." *Race Ethnicity and Education* 2, no. 1 (2011): 17–38.

den Heyer, Kent. "Sticky Points: Teacher Educators Re-examine their Practice in Light of a New Alberta Social Studies Program and Its Inclusion of Aboriginal Perspectives." *Teaching Education* 20, no. 4 (2009): 343–55.

Donald, Dwayne Trevor. "The Pedagogy of the Fort: Curriculum, Aboriginal-Canadian Relations, and Indigenous Métissage." PhD diss., University of Alberta, 2009.

Glaser, Barney G. *Basics of Grounded Theory Analysis: Emergence Versus Forcing.* Mill Valley: Sociology Press, 1992.

Haig-Brown, Celia. "Decolonizing Diaspora: Whose Traditional Land Are We On?" *Cultural and Pedagogical Inquiry* 1, no. 1 (2009): 4–21.

Hill, Gord. *The 500 Years of Resistance Comic Book.* Vancouver: Arsenal Pulp Press, 2010.

Imai, Shin. *Annual Annotated Indian Act and Aboriginal Constitutional Provisions.* Toronto: Carswell, 2015.

Kapryka, Julie. "For the Love of Manoominikewin." *Anishinabek News*, November 18, 2015. http://anishinabeknews.ca/2015/11/18/for-the-love-of-manoominikewin/.

Kovach, Margaret. *Indigenous Methodologies: Characteristics, Conversations and Contexts.* Toronto: University of Toronto Press, 2009.

Kulchyski, Peter Keith. *The Red Indians: An Episodic Informal Collection of Tales from the History of Aboriginal Peoples' Struggles in Canada.* Winnipeg: ARP Books, 2007.

LaDuke, Winona. "Indigenous Environmental Perspectives: A North American Primer." *Akwe:Kon Journal* 9, no. 2 (1992): 52–71.

Lawrence, Bonita, and Enakshi Dua. "Decolonizing Antiracism." *Social Justice* 32, no. 4 (2005): 120–43.

Mashford-Pringle, Angela, and Angela Nardozi. "Aboriginal Knowledge Infusion in Initial Teacher Education at the Ontario Institute for Studies in Education at the University of Toronto." *International Indigenous Policy Journal* 4, no. 4 (2013): 1–19.

Regan, Paulette. *Unsettling the Settler Within: Indian Residential Schools, Truth Telling, and Reconciliation in Canada*. Vancouver: UBC Press, 2010.

Rollo, Tobold. "I Am Canadian! (Because of Treaties with Indigenous Nations)." In *The Winter We Danced: Voices from the Past, the Future, and the Idle no More Movement*, edited by Kino-nda-niimi Collective, 226–29. Winnipeg: ARP Books, 2014.

Royal Commission on Aboriginal Peoples. *Report of the Royal Commission on Aboriginal Peoples*. 5 vols. Ottawa: Indian and Northern Affairs Canada, 1996.

Sehdev, Robinder Kaur. "People of Colour in Treaty." In *Cultivating Canada: Reconciliation through the Lens of Cultural Diversity*. Rev. ed., edited by Ashok Mathur, Mike DeGagné, and Jonathan Dewar, 265–74. Ottawa: Aboriginal Healing Foundation, 2011.

Shahjahan, Riyad A. "Being 'Lazy' and Slowing Down: Toward Decolonizing Time, Our Body, and Pedagogy." *Educational Philosophy and Theory* 47, no. 5 (2015): 488–501.

Snelgrove, Corey, Rita Kaur Dhamoon, and Jeff Corntassel. "Unsettling Settler Colonialism: The Discourse and Politics of Settlers, and Solidarity with Indigenous Nations." *Decolonization: Indigeneity, Education & Society* 3, no. 2 (2014): 1–32.

Stemler, Steve. "An Overview of Content Analysis." *Practical Assessment, Research & Evaluation* 7, (2001): 137–46.

Strauss, Anselm, and Juliet Corbin. *Basics of Qualitative Research*. 2nd ed. Thousand Oaks: SAGE, 1998.

Tanaka, Michele Therese Duke. "Transforming Perspectives: The Immersion of Student Teachers in Indigenous Ways of Knowing." PhD diss., University of Victoria, 2009. UVicSpace. http://hdl.handle.net/1828/1664.

Truth and Reconciliation Commission of Canada. *Honouring the Truth, Reconciling for the Future: Summary of the Final Report of the Truth and Reconciliation Commission of Canada*. Winnipeg: National Centre for Truth and Reconciliation, 2015. http://www.trc.ca/assets/pdf/ Honouring_the_Truth_Reconciling_for_the_Future_July_232015.pdf.

———. *Truth and Reconciliation Commission of Canada: Calls to Action*. Winnipeg: National Centre for Truth and Reconciliation, 2015. https://ehprnh2mwo3.exactdn.com/wp-content/ uploads/2021/01/Calls_to_Action_English2.pdf.

Tuck, Eve. "Suspending Damage: A Letter to Communities." *Harvard Educational Review* 79, no. 3 (2009): 409–27.

Tuck, Eve, and Rubén A. Gaztambide-Fernández. "Curriculum, Replacement, and Settler Futurity." *Journal of Curriculum Theorizing* 29, no. 1 (2013): 72–89.

Tuck, Eve, and Karyn Recollet. "Introduction to Native Feminist Texts." *English Journal* 106, no. 1 (2016): 16–22.

Tuck, Eve, and K. Wayne Yang. "Decolonization Is Not a Metaphor." *Decolonization: Indigeneity, Education, Society* 1, no. 1 (2012): 1–40.

Tungohan, Ethal, Rupa Banerjee, Wayne Chu, Petronila Cleto, Conely de Leon, Mila Garcia, Philip Kelly, Marco Luciano, Cynthia Palmaria, and Christopher Sorio. "After the Live-In Caregiver Program: Filipina Caregivers' Experiences of Graduated and Uneven Citizenship." *Canadian Ethnic Studies* 47 no.1 (2015): 87–105.

Tupper, Jennifer Anne. "The Possibilities for Reconciliation through Difficult Dialogues: Treaty Education as Peacebuilding." *Curriculum Inquiry* 44, no. 4 (2014): 469–88.

Vetter, Diane M., and Melissa Blimkie. "Learning to Teach in Culturally Responsive and Respectful Ways: The First Steps in Creating a First Nation, Métis and Inuit Education Infusion in a Mainstream Teacher Education Program." *Canadian Journal of Native Studies* 31, no. 2 (2011): 173–85.

Whitney, Kaitlin Stack. "Manoomin: The Taming of Wild Rice in the Great Lakes Region." *Arcadia* 2, https://doi.org/10.5282/rcc/6830.

Wilson, Shawn. *Research Is Ceremony: Indigenous Research Methods*. Halifax: Fernwood Publishing, 2008.

11

**CELIA HAIG-BROWN
AND RUTH GREEN**

Talking It Through, Talking Through It

A Dialogue on
Indigenizing Education

SKE:NON AND HELLO! DO COME INTO our conversation; it is one we have been having over the past few years. We write this chapter as friends, co-conspirators, and "academics." We strive for a conversational tone to give you the feel of what it is like when we speak with each other and, now, turn to speak with you. We want to include you in our conversation. Even though we are the speakers, we invite you to sit with us and we hope you can hear what we are saying to each other. We position ourselves as Indigenous and non-Indigenous people who are personally and professionally committed to working toward the Indigenization of academia via the dream of decolonization! At the same time, we always recognize the contradiction inherent in imagining western institutions can do such work. Before we begin, let us introduce ourselves.

Introductions
We met on the traditional territory of the Anishnaabe and Haudenosaunee Confederacies and the historic homelands of the Huron-Wendat. We have built our relationship in the territory that is covered by the Dish With One Spoon Wampum

Belt. We live and work on the territory that is currently care taken by the Mississauga of the Credit First Nation. This place is known as Tkaronto. We both work at York University.

RUTH GREEN

Kanien'kehá:ka niwakonhwentsiò:ten.
I am a Mohawk.
Wakeniáhten.
I am a Turtle.

Introducing myself in my mother's mother's language is new for me. I want to tell you who I am but I wish that I could do so in Kanien'kehá:ka. Maybe someday, or maybe my children will be able to do so.

I am the product of colonization. I am an Indigenous person who has gone through pain but has also reasserted my Indigeneity. Unlike previous generations, I am not ashamed. "Worse" yet, I am proud. I remind myself on a daily basis: "It is always a good day to be Indigenous" and "I am the daughter of the Indian they could not kill." I am resistance.

I was born in Toronto to an "Indian" mother and a Celtic father. I am the third child (and second daughter) of four children. Even though my parents had relationships with Indigenous artists, we were raised apart from culture. I do not blame my mother for not passing the teachings on to me. She did not have the teachings passed to her. The ruptures caused by colonization impacted our family and lineage. My Indigeneity has never been something that I questioned. It would have been impossible for me to pass as a white-coded person. Even with my fairer skin, whenever my mother entered the room, I was outed. Truth be told, I have only been picking up teachings for the past eighteen years of my life. It all started when I went back to school.

I have been at York University for the past six years. This is my first full-time academic job. I defended my doctoral work, "Understanding Your Education," about Guest responses to Indigenous education, in January of 2016.[1] Both my undergraduate and my master's degrees are in social work, a professional program. This is now the field that I teach in. Prior to returning to school, I worked as a Chef in fine Italian restaurants.

I am a parent to two wonderful little people on this earth and one that has returned to the Spirit World. The children who call me Ista ("mother" in Mohawk) are a huge driving force in my work. I want to leave this place better for them and the faces that have yet to come.

CELIA HAIG-BROWN

Yes, I am a settler. My father came from England when he was 18; my mother from Seattle, where I was born. She went home to her mum to give birth. Before moving west, her family was made up of generations of settlers in northeastern North America. My father's people are river people, storytellers, and educators. On Vancouver Island, my parents taught me my deep connection with rivers. It began with one river, the Campbell, that constantly called to me just across the orchard below our house. They also taught me respect for the people whose traditional land we occupied. I knew that the canoe bay where we parked our cedar-ribbed freight canoe had originally been the site where the Kwakwaka'wakw people had parked their canoes. I did not yet know how to ask where they had gone. But their ghostly presence lodged in my young mind as I met the children and grandchildren of those very people. Since that time, I have given birth to three children in Secwepemc territory. Three of my six grandchildren were born here in Tkaronto, where we are writing, and the other three were born in Secwepemc territory where I still have a cabin in the bush and where I go to restore my soul.

That river that raised me gave me an unwavering sense of curiosity, of the meaning of home, and it revealed to me the incredible complexity, persistence, and ever-changing face and body of its endless flow.

As a small child, I accompanied my father to the Line Fence Pool (the one located where the fence that kept the sheep in check came down to the river bank). For hours, I played on the edge and watched the waving river weeds, the caddice fly larvae with their jointed black legs gesturing crazily out of the pebble and stick encasings they constructed from their parts of the river. I picked and ate the salmon berries—some were the vibrant orangey-pink of salmon eggs and some a richer red mixed with yellow. Always the same green, serrated-edged leaves. I have a botanical print of the salmon berry on the wall of my kitchen in Toronto now. It was my mother's and it reminds me daily of who I am and where I come from.

This initial understanding of my connection to Land, and to rivers in particular, has served me well in my relationships with Land and rivers over time in a number of areas of Canada.[2] In terms of my work with Indigenous peoples (and others) who live within and/or understand about these interrelationships, my upbringing has given us some common ground, so to speak, for starting and then continuing our conversations.

In the fall of 1976—a few months after you, Ruth, were born—I began work as the coordinator for the University of British Columbia's Native Indian Teacher Education Program (NITEP). For the next ten years, I worked with Indigenous student teachers, who were often turning to the university after other careers, as they became elementary teachers in the schools of British Columbia—not specifically in reserve schools, but as fully qualified teachers who could choose where they wanted to work. My formal education in all things Indigenous really began there with them and their patience, and sometimes lack of patience, with me.

203

On the bookshelf of our classroom in the former Kamloops Indian Residential School sat a thin document entitled *Indian Control of Indian Education*.³ Although now seen as a historical document—when it is remembered at all—it actually articulates a sound beginning to our dialogue with its call for local control.

Now you know something of who we are.

A good place for us to begin.

In this chapter we engage with three distinct but interrelated topics. They have come to each of us in varied and distinct ways. Within our relationship, we have talked through our understandings of some of their intricacies and we want to share our conversations with you. First, we engage with two A words: *appropriation* and *ally*. We move from there into the central discussion of the chapter, where Celia introduces an iterative model responding to the Truth and Reconciliation's calls to action and other recent calls. This model describes a cyclical process which can be seen to simply rehearse systemic changes we know are needed and yet still need to act on. While obvious to some, the calls are also worth reiterating. Ruth provides her thoughts and comments on the model. In doing so, she provides an Indigenous response. Finally, we take up the very difficult epistemological and ontological responses to the calls. We call these responses Indigenization: centring Indigenous knowledge in courses, curricula, and throughout the academy.

Then it will be your turn to do some work in response to the calls to action.

Conversation
DECOLONIZATION VERSUS DECOLONIZING

Celia: First, a moment to talk about decolonizing. I prefer to use the gerund form of the word. For those of you who may not have been subjected to learning grammar and parts of speech, it is the *-ing* form of a verb that functions as a noun. This form implies an action in progress, one that is on-going. I do this because I wish to indicate that we are engaged in a process and that while decoloniza*tion* may be a long-term goal, for the moment, it is the process—the decolonizi*ng*—that requires attention. If we are to take seriously the idea of decolonizing, then we need to know at least a little something about the form of colonization that hit Canada and the world 150 years and more ago.

Ruth: I feel that decolonizing is the work to be done, but the approach that we, in universities, have been taking is not as disruptive as it needs to be to the colonial structures. We are Indigenizing spaces. We are bringing in knowledges and pedagogies, but we are not dismantling the power and privilege that colonial structures provide to non-Indigenous people.

SETTLER VERSUS NON-INDIGENOUS

Ruth: We want to give you some thoughts on the term *non-Indigenous*. In other work, I have articulated the distinctions that I make between non-Indigenous individuals who are settling or settlers on these Lands and those I consider Guests. I talk about a movement between a settler to a Guest as they take up learning and responsibilities over dominant constructs of rights-based frameworks.[4] Celia and I have also decided that we want to use the term *non-Indigenous* instead of *settler* here as we feel that there is a distinction. We recognize that being a settler is a privilege and wish to disrupt the notion that all people who are non-Indigenous have the same access to that privilege. Colonization has had global impacts. We are very much aware of this and do not equate all experiences of being on this Land as the same.

Celia: While I can definitely identify as a settler, I prefer to use the term *non-Indigenous* for two reasons; there are at least two pieces of work the term does that are worth preserving. First of all, it refers to all those who are not Indigenous as something nameless—as *non*entities. In many Indigenous languages, the term for the Nations themselves can be translated as "the people." All others exist outside of the immediate relationship of being "the people." I find this a good reminder to people who are not Indigenous to this land. The second thing the term *non-Indigenous* does is to ensure that we are not just speaking of those who chose to settle on Indigenous lands. Many people have arrived on Indigenous lands enslaved, as indentured labourers, as victims of sex trafficking, and not as people who planned the voyage or wanted to stay in the places where they landed. I worry that the term *settler* may sometimes erase difference and obfuscate inequity.

APPROPRIATION

Following on, we see a couple of other terms as major hurdles to Indigenizing and decolonizing. We call them the A words. The first is the problem of appropriation.

Celia: I have written elsewhere about appropriation, starting with the definitions that range from theft to learning.[5] Simply put, I see the problem of appropriation for non-Indigenous scholars manifested in three ways.

First, people (academics) take up aspects of a culture without appropriate respect or context, without a sense of responsibility, and without acknowledging the source of their teachings. That's theft. Jo-ann Archibald writes of this lack of respect making her stomach churn: "If non-Indigenous teachers and Indigenous teachers are to use and tell Indigenous stories, they must begin a cultural sensitivity learning process that includes gaining knowledge of storytelling protocol and the nature of these stories."[6]

Ruth: I believe that the appropriation of Indigenous knowledges can be much more damaging than the complete erasure of Indigenous topics in education. First, appropriation is colonial violence when Indigenous knowledges, ways of knowing, and being become commodities that are disembodied from the Land and the People. Worse than theft, the *rush to reconciliation* has non-Indigenous people "performing" as Indigenous without having taken the time or respect necessary to struggle to understand what it means to be Indigenous in a society that outlawed the very aspects that are now being appropriated. In many spaces and places, there is now an expectation that Indigenous knowledges will be included in courses, gatherings, and conferences. I struggle with this as sometimes it is a non-Indigenous person or settler group organizing "solidarity," and in that rush to reconciliation, the inclusion or "performance" does not include Indigenous people. Appropriation is picking and choosing the trappings one wants from Indigenous ways of being while not having to live with the collective trauma that is the result of generations of genocidal policies.

Second, in a reductionist reaction to the insensitive and disrespectful taking up of Indigenous knowledges (read as appropriative), people (academics) reprimand those who have actually taken the time to learn and be taught respectfully and responsibly when they dare to express their teachings. My good friend and mentor Lee Maracle taught me a word for non-Indigenous people that take on responsibilities. She talked about the responsibility to learn, to disrupt, and to (re)teach. Lee called these people "Indigenist." As I have explained elsewhere, an Indigenist is not Indigenous, but is able to forge friendships and relations with Indigenous people that respect Indigenous worldview, autonomy, and protocols.[7]

Celia: Did I ever tell you that Lee and I figured out we probably played together when we were kids and my dad visited her family at various times? Her aunt said, "He always had that little girl with him."

Ruth: I love that story. It makes so much sense knowing the both of you!
Indigenists are people who have done the work to learn from Indigenous people, be they knowledge keepers, Elders, or children.

They respect not only Indigenous knowledges but also Indigenous Peoples, communities, and Nations. They hold their teachings close to the heart and know that it is not their role to position themselves as knowledge keepers. As Lee forcefully argued in her public speeches, "It is time to get out of the Knower's Chair." That is when learning and that is when Indigenizing might begin within the universities. An Indigenist person will never claim that they are Indigenous. They will probably start every introduction articulating their non-Indigeneity. Too often, it is assumed that they are Indigenous because they work in or with Indigenous people. I have even told Celia clearly that every chance she gets she needs to "out" herself as white. And we laugh together at that command.

I have been fortunate enough to be mentored by a few non-Indigenous individuals who have spent years quietly learning from Elders and knowledge keepers. These people speak up when needed, know protocols, and support Indigenous peoples without ever stepping in front of them.

Celia: The third problem of appropriation comes when, perhaps fearful of making a mistake or being reprimanded, those non-Indigenous people who have taken the time to listen and learn from Indigenous teachers remain silent, shirking their responsibility to pass on what they have learned despite the hours their teachers have invested in them.

Ruth: This is the point where I see that appropriation is theft! At a recent gathering, I noticed something telling. As the Eagle Feather went around the room, Indigenous person after Indigenous person apologized for not knowing their culture, their language, or all of their teachings. We, as Indigenous people, have had these stolen from us via colonization. Note that I refuse to say that, as Indigenous peoples, we have "lost" our culture, our languages, or our teachings. I am not irresponsible. I did not simply misplace or drop my language. It is not lost. It was stolen. That being said, if an Indigenous knowledge keeper has invested in a non-Indigenous person, that person has a moral obligation to uphold those teachings and responsibilities even though they have been denied to so many Indigenous people. It is theft of a particular kind to listen to and actually hear those teachings—that is, to be given responsibilities—but not do anything with them. This does not mean that the non-Indigenous person starts to explain the teachings in a way that belittles Indigenous people for not knowing, but that they humbly share the knowledge that they have been gifted. I have heard many non-Indigenous people say, "As I was taught by _____..." or "I heard a knowledge keeper from _____ Nation explain..."

Celia: But those expressions must always be done tentatively. Recognizing what Ruth articulated above, we non-Indigenous people have not experienced the generations of genocidal policies and practices that have impacted so many Indigenous Peoples globally. Let me say up front that I do believe it is possible for all people (even white ones) to learn—that it is possible, with good teachers, to have Indigenous knowledge/teachings/theory become part of our understandings of the world no matter what our origins. But our histories will never be the same. Let me also say that, even while I acknowledge that there are aspects of languages that are incommensurable, I firmly believe that even the English language can be pushed to take up Indigenous knowledge in respectful and appropriate ways. But probably never fully. As my friend and colleague Susan Ehrlich says, language is not a strait jacket. And, of course, I relish the title of the Gloria Bird's and Joy Harjo's edited collection, *Re-inventing the Enemy's Language.*

ALLY

The second *A* word, after *appropriation*, is *ally*.

Celia: Let me say that *ally* is not a word that I have often used for myself. (I thought I had never used it, but then, while rereading an old article of mine the other day, there it was: *ally*.) In many ways, the word feels presumptuous: Whose ally? When? Under what conditions? Who gets to decide? These are the questions of someone who has been thinking about decolonizing and reconciliation for some time and now (thank you, Hon. Murray Sinclair). I wanted to see what people have written about the word *ally*. The internet, my usual starting point these days, yielded references primarily to those First Nations who served as allies with Canada in the War of 1812. That was before they became wards of the state and then veterans of two great wars in Europe. My next thought was to look through Lynne Davis's edited collection *Alliances: Re/Envisioning Indigenous-non-Indigenous Relationships*, which I will discuss in more detail below. Beyond Davis's work, the main source I encountered related directly to the work of self-described Pākehā scholar Jen Margaret. She came to North America to study "allies" in order to think about the role of allies in Aotearoa, particularly in relation to the Treaty of Waitangi. And her first and most impressive stop was to learn from Professor Lynne Davis. Margaret's research led her to the word *coalition* as a way to address the relationships she was exploring. For me, her most important insight is that "being an ally is a practice and a process—not an identity."[8]

In her book *Unsettling the Settler Within*, Paulette Regan takes up the term *settler-ally* in a way that resonates with this understanding.

She writes, "Historically and into the present, we remain obsessed with solving the Indian problem even as we deflect attention from the settler problem. As a settler-ally, I must continuously confront the colonizer-perpetrator in myself, interrogating my own position as a beneficiary of colonial injustice."[9] Lynne Davis's work deepens the discussion in terms of her recognition that the way people name their work together matters: coalitions, alliances, partnerships—and I would add collaborations and conspiracies. Davis writes: "They have their own theories and languages for talking about these relationships."[10] Most importantly, power relationships based in persisting colonialism circulate through all these connections: they must be and are constantly negotiated and renegotiated even when they are not explicitly named. Krista Johnston, in her examination of whiteness and allies, quotes Audrey Thomson's work: "The entire white identity model is organized around individuals getting to feel good about being white in nonracist ways... Functionally, the most important value is being and feeling like a good white person; political action takes second place to personal integrity."[11] And there was the issue that was concerning me: a positionality such as white ally "must be opened up to anti-colonial critique."[12] No room for salvation or even self-congratulation here.

Ruth: I think I prefer the term *co-conspirators* to *allies*. If Indigenous thought and worldviews are to find a place shoulder-to-shoulder with western (and other) forms of thought, we do not really need allies or people who position themselves as such. We need co-conspirators! We need people who are willing to resist the academic canon as the sole source of legitimate knowledge. We need people who are willing to give up the dominant ways of knowing, to unlearn, and to move to a relearning stance. We need non-Indigenous people who are willing to speak up when it is not safe for Indigenous people. We need people who are not afraid!

I have been taught the Seven Grandparent teachings. I have had many traditional knowledge keepers teach me about the Grandparents, and have read a text version, which is available in Edward Benton-Banai's *Mishomis Book*, originally published in 1988. One of the teachings is Bravery. It has been told to me that Bravery exists only in relation to fear; an act is not brave one unless you are afraid. There are many times that I feel that fear in the pit of my stomach: I think, "I cannot do this!" but then I remember to be brave. It might be scary for non-Indigenous people to take a step towards Indigenization. Don't let that hold you back! Be brave! I am thinking about how a Guest is the one who knows how to move between their world as a disrupter of colonial discourse and the Indigenous world as a constant learner. Even though you, Celia, tell us that in the fall of 1976, you took up a role as NITEP Coordinator, you know that your understanding of Indigeneity is still as an outsider. Yet you have been doing this work since before I could sit up! Here is a point where we can name the difference between BEING Indigenous and supporting the work of Indigenous Peoples. It is not about the number of ceremonies one attends, it is not about who counts you as a friend, it is not about the hours, weeks, months, and years of commitment, it is about LIVED reality of BEING Indigenous.

Responding to All the Calls

So, on that note, on to the second focus of this chapter: responding to the calls. By this we mean *all* the calls: the Truth and Reconciliation Commission of Canada's (TRC) calls to action for education that arise from this context, this time and place; calls that echo out of and across the Land; long-ago calls from the old, rounded mountains and the open plains; calls that ripple across the lakes, streams, and river waters; calls that swirl into our ears as they circle around us once again, resonating with the layers and layers of Indigenous calls to action related to schools and education over the years, the decades, the centuries.

Like water on rock, Indigenous peoples have been arguing for holistic and truthful education and schools for what has indeed become centuries. Here are only a few examples of where these arguments can be found: The 1918 League of Indians of Canada; the Special Joint Committee established to examine the Indian Act in the late 1940s; the National Indian Brotherhood's *Indian Control of Indian Education*; the Royal Commission on Aboriginal Peoples; and now the TRC.[13] Any opportunity to speak to governments about the importance of good education for children and adults alike has been, and continues to be, taken: the words are there in so many documents. And within those documents there are so many resonances and yet so little response or action arising from the pleas. But now, with the TRC in our hearts and minds and, yes, the media, we are perfectly positioned to listen and, perhaps this time, really hear and act on these calls.

"Who is this we?" you might ask, considering all that the people who are reading this—you—have done and continue to do. This we still includes you. It includes us—all of us. The needs and demands continue; there is more to be done and the momentum is growing. It is led by the many highly accomplished and well-educated Indigenous knowledge keepers in the universities: Indigenous people such as Dale Turner's "word warriors": people in government, in the arts, and in positions of knowledge and authority in rural and urban Indigenous communities and all the places in between.[14]

We can use this time of awareness to once again call ourselves, our colleagues, and our institutions to account for the continuing limited presence of Indigenous thinkers, faculty, and students on our campuses, in our programs, and in the curricula that guide us. In spite of all the accomplishments and changes over the last few decades, we have a long way to go. But let us be clear: we are not really in a position to speak to each reader's situation, but we do know that our institution, York University, only began to seriously address its shortcomings in this regard in 2019. Lack of knowledge and even of active resistance on the part of various colleagues and administrators have been problems in this context and in others over the years.

Considering the work of accelerating various forms of Indigenous success within the academy, we turn to one of our favourite articles on the topic: Verna Kirkness and Ray Barnhardt's pivotal piece "First Nations and Higher Education: the Four *R*'s—Respect, Relevance, Reciprocity and Responsibility."

Ruth: OHHHH I LOVE THIS ARTICLE! It continues to serve as a sound starting place for those seeking to transform the university (and is readily available on the internet).

Celia: Keeping that work in mind, I pushed myself to create a schematic that represents some of the work that I have been doing over the years within the academy. I hope it may serve as something of a guide for others.

I started with the NITEP and its clear goal of having we non-Indigenous people work our way out of a job so that Indigenous people would assume full control; this has remained a touchstone over the years. (Remember *Indian Control of Indian Education*, the document I saw sitting on the shelf when I arrived to work with NITEP?) Although I have never again applied for or worked in a position explicitly involving Indigeneity, one of my primary goals within the academy is opening up the space for Indigenous scholars and scholarship. Another goal is to ensure that I work to infuse Indigenous authors and my version of Indigenous thought into every course I teach. After all, everything we do in Canada starts with the Land and Indigenous people—history, education, medicine, and so on. Maybe that is an argument for another day, but we challenge you to take it up in your own work.

THE ITERATIVE MODEL

Celia's iterative model provides one approach to responding to the calls. Simply put, the model proposes the following phases: raise awareness, create space, get out of the way, and be available. The iterative aspect comes with the need to constantly repeat. Jump into the flow at any point and realize the interconnectedness of the phases— never linear, always cycling. While we acknowledge that non-Indigenous peoples arrive and have arrived in the country called Canada from many places, many experiences, and over many years, every non-Indigenous person has a responsibility

Talking It Through, Talking Through It

Figure 1. Responding to the Calls.
Adapted from graphic design by Ryan Koelwyn,
concept by Celia Haig-Brown (2019).

to be cognizant of the traditional territories we have come to occupy.[15] For the model that follows, we have loosely attached Verna's and Ray's four *R*'s to organize the four phases, but it should be noted that each *R* in fact speaks to each phase.

Phase 1: Raise Awareness
Raise awareness, your own and others'. You can't be useful if you don't know anything. We associate this phase with relevance, one of Verna's and Ray's *R*'s.

Celia: Can you imagine that when I first encountered *Indian Control of Indian Education*, that slim document on the book shelf in the Kamloops NITEP Centre, I didn't read it because I thought that if I referred to it I would be appropriating? My students soon set me right. As Judit Moschkovich wrote years ago, while she does not hold us "responsible for the roots of this ignorance about other cultures," she does hold us responsible for "the *transformation* of this ignorance."[16] Stay abreast of recent scholarly and policy debates. Read the news. Watch the films. Listen to the music. See the art. Do not assume that something that has First Nations or Indigenous in the headlines or title does not pertain to you. It does! Read Indigenous scholars. And when there is the opportunity or, more importantly, the need to speak to Indigeneity—never for or over Indigenous peoples—take the risk and do so. Note the gaping holes in the conversations and the planning and insert references to Indigeneity every chance you get.

Ruth: This is the point where non-Indigenous people really need to take the role of learner! There needs to be a learning to HEAR! As one of my favourite Elders, Joanne Dallaire, has taught me, I have two ears, two eyes, and only one mouth. I need to master the ears and eyes before I can use my mouth. It is not the responsibility of Indigenous people to educate non-Indigenous people. We are writing and producing works that are advancing us. We welcome you to read our works, to attend our talks— but please do not be first up at the microphone to tell us you are a "good" person and then ask, "What can I do to help?" That responsibility lies with you. Leave the space in front of the mic so that Indigenous people, especially those who are advancing on their own academic journey, can ask deeper, more informed questions. Enroll in our courses. When you do enroll, please do not assume that we can teach you everything you need to know! The average university course is three hours a week for twelve weeks, and that translates to one and a half days of your life! Thirty-six hours!

Phase 2: Create Space

Create space for Indigenous scholars and students. Learn to listen and listen well. Use your position whenever possible. Invite resource people from local communities or organizations into your classrooms and contexts (and pay them well). We see this as being in line with Verna's and Ray's concept of responsibility.

Ruth: But please ensure that when you bring in a speaker you follow a few simple rules! First, have your students do their homework beforehand. What have you assigned for readings? What discussions have you had with them to ensure that the Indigenous person can speak from their expertise without having to walk your students through Colonization 101? Second, build your own relationships with the individuals that you want to bring in. Do your own homework. Do not turn to your overstretched Indigenous colleagues asking them to recommend a speaker for you! My friends are smart, engaged, and mostly funny, but are also so tired of being tapped by me to speak in an underprepared classroom. If you are bringing in an Elder, please make sure that the class will respect the knowledge that the Elder brings. I always say, "I love my granny: I would never put her under the bus!"

Celia: Join search and recruitment committees in your school and in your faculty. Become graduate program director, associate dean, associate vice president—and then lobby to be replaced by Indigenous faculty. Insist that the merit review of Indigenous research that SSHRC has developed become familiar to all review committees from research to admissions to awards and searches. If there are too few Indigenous faculty members to meet all the demands, invite community-based scholars to be part of committees. Recognize their expertise (pay them) and, again, listen. Never stop lobbying for Indigenous student recruitment and Indigenous faculty hires. Agree to review grant proposals, review articles, review tenure and promotion cases,review programs—even when you don't have time. Keep learning about the best way to read proposals that may stretch your understanding of what Indigenous scholarship is. Work on admissions committees to ensure that strong Indigenous students are admitted. Learn to recognize the many forms that strength can take. Offer courses, create clubs and programs, lobby every chance you get. Be prepared to fight when the need arises. Oh, and by the way, do not assume that every Indigenous student or faculty member wants to focus on Indigeneity or Indigenous studies. Some want to be chemical engineers or mathematicians or music educators.

Ruth: And recognize their power and fight so that Indigenous knowledges are embedded in programs for chemical engineers, mathematicians, and music educators. There are Indigenous people who want to be in each of these fields and should have access to relevant and holistic education. Indigenous knowledges have something to say to each and every discipline. Use your place of power to ensure that these "non-Indigenized" programs are unsettled from solely western-focused knowledges.

Phase 3: Get Out of the Way!

Get out of the way! Or, in Verna's and Ray's model, practice reciprocity. Remember the need for caucus of specific groups away from the general crowd. Don't take offence. Know that sometimes, there is a need for a time and space for particular people to be together where, as Bernice Johnson Reagon put it, "you can sift out what people are saying about you and decide who you really are...where you can act out community."[17] Know also that there may be strong resentment about the existence of a non-Indigenous person whose level of privilege may have allowed them to acquire Indigenous knowledge or to have had experiences in Indigenous contexts. Such a reaction is not a moment to take offence; rather, it is a time to consider what has allowed some people to have knowledge and others never to have been exposed to it. Get over yourself. Remember colonialism is alive and well and we are all implicated.

Ruth: Dr. Lynn Gehl's "Ally Bill of Responsibilities": Read it! Learn it! It is important.[18]

In the winter of 2012–2013, Indigenous and non-Indigenous people took to the streets of cities across North America to raise awareness, to hold hands, and to DANCE! Theresa Spence, the chief from Attawapiskat

First Nation, sat in ceremony in a Tipi on Victoria Island in the Ottawa River. We, both Indigenous and non-Indigenous, stated that we would be Idle No More against the colonial structures. Dr. Gehl watched all of this and responded by drafting her "Ally Bill," in which she outlined sixteen ways to ensure that one is being a responsible ally/Guest. In rereading the responsibilities, I see that Dr. Gehl covers much of what Celia and I have discussed. I really encourage you to read them, print them out, tape them to the fridge (at home and in the staff kitchen), and live them!

Phase 4: Be Available
Being available is linked to Verna's and Ray's points about respect. There is still space and a need for allies—well we would rather friends, colleagues, and co-conspirators. Build respectful relationships!

Celia: Surprise, surprise, there are not always enough Indigenous faculty members to go around to do all that needs to be done. Even while working to change that, be an advocate. Support Indigenous students who may be working in an area aligned with your work. Find time to connect with others working in the area, especially new hires and new students. Find appropriate ways to welcome them. Sharing food is good. And, as a person working on decolonizing, feel in the ensuing conversations the amazing, reciprocal space where you, too, do not have to work so hard to have a conversation because it starts from a place where so much is commonly understood.

Ruth: And please be a safer space for Indigenous folks to talk about how hard it can be to live and work within academia. Do not assume that Indigenous scholars will trust you: show them that you have learned enough so they can come to know that they can trust you! Once we know that you know something of the complexities of our positions, we might open up to you. This comes from a place of pleading with tears in my eyes. I have been told so often that I am so strong, I forget that I am allowed to be hurt and cry. If I do open up, please know that I am probably in a very vulnerable space. Please just listen to me, let me cry, and then remind me that I am my ancestors' best dream. When a young scholar asks for your support, respect their confidences! Do not brag that so and so asked for advice, support, or letters of reference. Keep the heartache and struggles confidential and always ask what you can share before you do. If we trust you with our vulnerabilities please take it as an honour and never use it against us, even if differences arise later!

And there you have it. The four phases: raise awareness, create space, get out of the way, and be available.

Epistemological and Ontological Responses:
The Rightful Place of Indigenous Knowledges in the Academy

This section brings us to the third and final part of the chapter. For us, it is most exciting and most challenging part in terms of both the TRC's calls to action and the work to be done within the academy. We focus on three of the TRC's calls that relate to education (somewhat paraphrased and with our own glosses):

1. Develop culturally appropriate curricula.
2. Protect the right to Aboriginal languages, including teaching credit courses. Develop programs and courses in the languages (this because within the language lies the worldview, the concepts, and the meanings of Indigenous knowledge).
3. Educate teachers (and, we add, professors, professionals, and administrators) on how to integrate and support the integration of Indigenous knowledge and teaching methods into classrooms (and their workplaces).[19]

Herein lies one of the biggest challenges facing us as we respond to the TRC: How do we work toward the re-creation of the university in a way that takes seriously Indigenous knowledges as a legitimate worldview deserving of full recognition within the academy?

Celia: When I think of this goal, I am reminded of two past situations in my life. First situation: An Indigenous colleague asks me what I am thinking about her theorizing in an article she is writing for a refereed journal. She is incorporating traditional teachings throughout and using them as a frame for her work. I am enthusiastic as I see the theory and the rest of the narrative beautifully interwoven. She says that other scholars have told her there is no theory in the paper and she *must theorize* her work. I now wonder: Did this paper get published? What did her "peers" think? And who got to be counted as her "peers"?

Second situation: I am preparing a research grant proposal and sharing it for feedback with one of my non-Indigenous colleagues. Throughout the proposal, I have been drawing on my understandings of Indigenous thought, using it as theoretical framing and proposed analysis. My colleague says, "You need to have a theoretical framework. The theory is missing." I am stymied. I point out that Indigenous thought is the theoretical framework. His response: "Thought is first order thinking and theory is third order thinking. You need theory. And anyway, who are you to use Indigenous thought?" I ignore his advice and his warning and the grant application is successful.

Ruth: Have I told you about my pot of soup? As I travel between the worlds of academic and authentic Indian, I sometimes find myself caught in trying to explain what I am doing. And no matter how many times I tell my story or show myself, I find that there can be a place where I am embodying Indigenous theory yet others see me as untheoretical. This means that before I speak and act I have to walk others through a space of confusion: their lack of understanding of Indigenous thought.

A few years ago, I was teaching an undergraduate course on identity and antidiscrimination. "Aboriginality" was one of the weekly topics. I had assigned a reading by Bonnie Freeman in which she talks about making soup for the students as a way to build community and create a learning space.[20] As this brilliant scholar and I are cousins, I mentioned in my Facebook status that I was teaching her chapter. She immediately asked me if I was making soup for the students. I understood what she was asking me. She was not asking: "Are you being a nice person and making food as a good 'Indian'?" Rather, she was pushing me theoretically to ask if I was willing and able, as teacher, to be a strong Host who would take the responsibility seriously. She was asking: "Are you setting up the relationships between Host and Guest as the wampum and teachings explain?"

Bringing this scenario into the conversation is not a way to set myself up as "authentic" or show off the ways I bring traditional teachings into a dominant space; nor is it a way to claim I am demonstrating that dominant discourse and ways of teaching, engaging, and creating knowledge are problematic. Rather, I want to show that even something as critical of dominant thought as poststructuralism can, in the same breath, reduce this challenge—making soup—to a nice gesture and raise the warning that I am in danger of essentializing myself and replicating a dated cultural competence model. Even as poststructuralism allows for thinking outside the dominant box, it remains a theoretical framework focused on the dominant: its main purpose is to challenge the "box." In stark contrast, Indigenous theory is neither the box nor a rejection of the box. Indigenous theory exists on a plane distinct from any box. It exists on a plane that is multidimensional, circular, and never invested in the rejection or the upholding of dominant theory. It exists as its own set of theories, ideologies, and methodologies that are incommensurable with others.

With this example of making soup, I want to show you that such activity is not a matter of being nice. I am not presenting an understanding of what it means to teach with an Indigenous lens. I am not looking at the dominant from a space of being deficient or different. I am really not even looking at the dominant. I am situated in understanding responsibilities and relationships that are grounded in Indigenous theory: Onkwehonwe theory that has spoken for itself and to itself since time immemorial. I am embodying that theory and I am continuing the conversation.

ASSERTING INDIGENOUS KNOWLEDGE INTO THE ACADEMY

On that note, we turn to the prescient work of Rauna Kuokkanen in her 2007 text *Reshaping the University: Responsibility, Indigenous Epistemes and the Logic of the Gift.* Professor Kuokkanen presents the problem: "It has become apparent to me that Indigenous discourses are allowed to exist in the university, but only in marginal spaces or within clearly defined parametres established by the dominant discourse, which is grounded in certain assumptions, values, conceptions of knowledge and views of the world."[21] She adds that "as an institution, the academy supports and reproduces certain systems of thought and knowledge, and certain structures and conventions, that rarely reflect or represent Indigenous worldviews."[22]

What does it look and sound like when Indigenous thought informs the academy? Ruth has shown one example and here we present another. In 2015, a panel of Indigenous scholars responded to a talk that Native American scholar Brenda Child gave at York University. One of those scholars, Canada Research Chair Deborah McGregor, cross-appointed to York's Osgoode Hall Law School and Faculty of Environmental Studies, spoke of justice. Environmental justice. She asked us, in a sense, to consider what justice means to us. Responses from attendees focused on being decent to fellow human beings and ensuring fair and equitable treatment. Nods all around. "Well," she said, "for Anishinaabe, justice means fair and equitable treatment for all our relations: the rocks, rivers, and trees, all things animate and inanimate, all of Creation."[23]

In one of her publications, Dr. McGregor acknowledges that justice is "most certainly about power relationships among people and between people and various institutions of colonization," and notes that "justice from an Aboriginal perspective is about justice for all beings of Creation, not only because threats to their existence threaten ours but because from an Aboriginal perspective justice among beings of Creation is life-affirming."[24] She concludes the chapter by addressing the responsibilities that come with the goal of justice.

Celia: Even now as I reread these words, I find my brain doing a little dance working to grasp the significance of our "interfering with other beings"— the river's ability to renew and contribute to the cycle of water that sustains Creation. What a profound way to address what some scientists might call sustainability. It shifts understanding.

Another sign of things shifting in terms of recognition of Indigenous thought is the following guideline from SSHRC. As York's Associate Vice President Research

(Celia) and Chair of the Indigenous Council (Ruth), we circulated the text to all faculty and administrators at York:

> The Guidelines for the Merit Review of Indigenous Research ensure that Indigenous research incorporating Indigenous knowledge systems (including ontologies, epistemologies and methodologies) is recognized as a scholarly contribution and meets SSHRC's standards of excellence. The guidelines are also designed to encourage that Indigenous research be conducted with sensitivity, and only after consideration about who conducts the research and why and how it is conducted.[25]

It has been too easy for non-Indigenous people in particular to tell themselves that this work has nothing to do with them. It all happened long ago and times have moved on. When that temptation arises, the words of Peter Kulchyski remind us all of the work to be done:

> In the minutiae of quotidian life, in the presuppositions of service providers, in the structures of State actions and inactions, in the continuing struggles over land use, in a whole trajectory of policies and plans, the work of the conquest is being completed here and now. By our generation. It is our descendants, a hundred years from now, who will protest that they were not here when land claims were being negotiated, when Aboriginal rights were distorted beyond recognition, when the final acts of the great historical drama of conquest were performed. You who remain silent while this injustice continues, you are responsible. Here. And now.
>   But then again, so am I.[26]

There is our challenge. We have the guidance. We have the responsibility. We have the knowledge of what has happened and what is continuing to happen in terms of inequities and unaddressed treaty rights and other legal violations. Some of us have the privileges that have accrued from the lands and resources that form the basis of Canada: lands and resources that were integral to Indigenous lives and cultures since time immemorial and whose care must become integral to all our lives.

We conclude with some encouraging words from Marie Battiste in her book *Decolonizing Education*, which make most clear both the work to be done in our post-secondary institutions and schools and the best ways for each of us to approach this work. She writes: "It is Indigenous people who must provide the standards, principles, and protections that accompany the centring of Indigenous knowledge."[27] She goes on to say that Indigenous people's goals of sovereignty and self-determination "must not be an agenda for Indigenous people alone, as so many have been complicit in their subordination, and beneficiaries of the relationships that enabled land to be used, bought, taken or misused."[28] Citing the work of Len Findlay, she proposes instead that "non-Indigenous scholars can...develop a connective critical stand from their location to the Indigenous agenda, noting, promoting, activating, defusing, infusing, complicating, and in general putting the Indigenous agenda firmly in the present."[29]

The calls are out. The directives are there. Read, listen, and learn. Let us begin the next phase of this long overdue work. And remember, the Trickster is always present and playing.

NOTES

1. Koleszar-Green, "Understanding Your Education."
2. I borrow the term *Land* and its meaning from Styres, *Pathways for Remembering*.
3. National Indian Brotherhood, *Indian Control*.
4. Koleszar-Green, "Understanding Your Education."
5. Haig-Brown, "Indigenous Thought."
6. Archibald [Q'um Q'um Xiiem], *Indigenous Storywork*, 46.
7. Maracle, personal communication, October 6, 2013; Koleszar-Green, "Understanding Your Education."
8. Margaret, *Working as Allies*, 12.
9. Regan, *Unsettling the Settler*, 236.
10. Lynne Davis, introduction to *Alliances*, 7.
11. Johnston, "Unsettling Citizenship," 234.
12. Johnston, "Unsettling Citizenship," 179.
13. Dyck and Sadik, "Indigenous Political Organization"; Special Joint Committee of the Senate and House of Commons Appointed to Examine and Consider the Indian Act, *Minutes of Proceedings and Evidence*, 430–31; National Indian Brotherhood, *Indian Control*; Royal Commission on Aboriginal Peoples, *Highlights*; Truth and Reconciliation Commission of Canada, *Honouring the Truth*.
14. Turner, *This Is Not a Peace Pipe*.
15. See Haig-Brown, "Decolonizing Diaspora."
16. Moschkovich, "But I Know You," 83.
17. Reagon, "Coalition Politics," 345.
18. Gehl, "Ally Bill," https://www.lynngehl.com/ally-bill-of-responsibilities.html.
19. *Truth and Reconciliation Commission of Canada: Calls to Action*, calls 10.iii, 10.iv, and 62.ii.
20. Freeman, "Indigenous Pathways."
21. Kuokkanen, *Reshaping the University*, xviii.
22. Kuokkanen, *Reshaping the University*, 1.
23. Deborah McGregor's response to Brenda Child, "Remembering Colonialism: the Boarding School as a Metaphor," (guest lecture, York Centre for Education and Community, Toronto, ON, October 19. 2015).
24. McGregor, "Honouring Our Relations," 27.
25. SSHRC, "Guidelines for the Merit Review," Context sec., para. 3.

26. Kulchyski, *Like the Sound of a Drum*, 3.
27. Battiste, *Decolonizing Education*, 73.
28. Battiste, *Decolonizing Education*, 74.
29. Battiste, *Decolonizing Education*, 74.

BIBLIOGRAPHY

Archibald, Jo-ann [Q'um Q'um Xiiem]. *Indigenous Storywork: Educating the Heart, Mind, Body, and Spirit.* Vancouver: UBC Press, 2008.

Battiste, Marie. *Decolonizing Education: Nourishing the Learning Spirit.* Saskatoon: Purich Publishing, 2013.

Benton-Banai, Edward. *The Mishomis Book: The Voice of the Ojibway.* Minneapolis: University of Minnesota, 2010.

Davis, Lynne. Introduction to *Alliances: Re/Envisioning Indigenous-non-Indigenous Relationships*, edited by Lynne Davis, 1–12. Toronto: University of Toronto Press, 2010.

Dyck, Noel, and Tonio Sadik. "Indigenous Political Organization and Activism in Canada," last modified April 15, 2016. In *The Canadian Encyclopedia*, edited by Bronwyn Graves. Toronto: Historica Foundation. Last updated February 11, 2021. https://www.thecanadianencyclopedia.ca/en/article/aboriginal-people-political-organization-and-activism.

Freeman, Bonnie. "Indigenous Pathways to Anti-oppressive Practice." In *Doing Anti-oppressive Practice: Building Transformative Politicized Social Work.* 2nd ed., edited by Deborah Baines, 116–132. Halifax: Fernwood Publishing, 2011.

Gehl, Lynn. "Ally Bill of Responsibilities." Accessed July 20, 2021, https://www.lynngehl.com/ally-bill-of-responsibilities.html.

Haig-Brown, Celia. "Decolonizing Diaspora: Whose Traditional Land Are We On?" *Cultural and Pedagogical Inquiry* 1, no. 2 (2009): 4–21.

———. "Indigenous Thought, Appropriation and Non-Aboriginal People." *Canadian Journal of Education* 33, no. 4 (2010): 925–50.

Harjo, Joy, and Gloria Bird (eds.) with Beth Cuthand, Valerie Martinez, and Patricia Blanco. *Reinventing the Enemy's Language: Contemporary Native Women's Writings of North America.* New York: W.W. Norton & Company, 1998.

Johnston, Krista. "Unsettling Citizenship: Movements for Indigenous Sovereignty and Migrant Justice in a Settler City." PhD diss., York University, 2015. CORE. https://core.ac.uk/display/77105016.

Kirkness, Verna J., and Ray Barnhardt. "First Nations and Higher Education: The Four *R*'s—Respect, Relevance, Reciprocity, Responsibility." *Journal of American Indian Education* 30, no. 3 (2001): 1–15. http://www.jstor.org/stable/24397980.

Koleszar-Green, Ruth. "Understanding Your Education: Onkwehonwe and Guests Responsibilities to Peace, Friendship and Mutual Respect." PhD diss., University of Toronto, 2016. TSpace. http://hdl.handle.net/1807/73051.

Kulchyski, Peter. *Like the Sound of a Drum: Aboriginal Cultural Politics in Denendeh and Nunavut.* Winnipeg: University of Manitoba Press, 2005.

Kuokkanen, Rauna. *Reshaping the University: Responsibility, Indigenous Epistemes, and the Logic of the Gift.* Vancouver: UBC Press, 2007.

Margaret, Jen. *Working as Allies.* Winston Churchill Memorial Trust Fellowship Report, August 2010. http://www.awea.org.nz/sites/awea.org.nz/files/Jen%20Margaret%20Winston%20Churchill%20Report%202010.pdf.

McGregor, Deborah. "Honouring Our Relations: An Anishnaabe Perspective on Environmental Justice." In *Speaking for Ourselves: Environmental Justice in Canada*, edited by Julian Agyeman, Peter Cole, Randolph Haluza-DeLay, and Pat O'Riley. Vancouver: UBC Press, 2009.

Moschkovich, Judit. "—But I Know You, American Woman." In *This Bridge Called My Back: Writings by Radical Women of Color*, edited by Cherríe Moraga and Gloria Anzaldúa, 83. Berkeley: Third Woman Press, 2002. First published 1981 by Persephone Press (Watertown).

National Indian Brotherhood. *Indian Control of Indian Education*. Ottawa: Assembly of First Nations, 1972.

Reagon, Bernice Johnson. "Coalition Politics: Turning the Century." In *Home Girls: A Black Feminist Anthology*, edited by Barbara Smith, 356–68. New York: Kitchen Table Press, 1983.

Regan, Paulette. *Unsettling the Settler Within: Indian Residential Schools, Truth Telling, and Reconciliation in Canada*. Vancouver: UBC Press, 2010.

Royal Commission on Aboriginal Peoples. *People to People, Nation to Nation: Highlights from the Report of the Royal Commission on Aboriginal Peoples*. Ottawa: The Commission, 1996.

Special Joint Committee of the Senate and House of Commons Appointed to Examine and Consider the Indian Act. *Minutes of Proceedings and Evidence*. Ottawa: Special Joint Committee, 1946.

SSHRC [Social Sciences and Humanities Research Council]. "Guidelines for the Merit Review of Indigenous Research." Last updated June 18, 2019. http://www.sshrc-crsh.gc.ca/funding-financement/merit_review-evaluation_du_merite/guidelines_research-lignes_directrices_recherche-eng.aspx.

Styres, Sandra D. *Pathways for Remembering and Recognizing Indigenous Thought in Education: Philosophies of Iethi'nihsténha Ohwentsia'kékha (Land)*. Toronto: University of Toronto Press, 2017.

Truth and Reconciliation Commission of Canada. *Honouring the Truth, Reconciling for the Future: Summary of the Final Report of the Truth and Reconciliation Commission of Canada*. Winnipeg: National Centre for Truth and Reconciliation, 2015. http://www.trc.ca/assets/pdf/Honouring_the_Truth_Reconciling_for_the_Future_July_232015.pdf.

———. *Truth and Reconciliation Commission of Canada: Calls to Action*. Winnipeg: National Centre for Truth and Reconciliation, 2015. https://ehprnh2mwo3.exactdn.com/wp-content/uploads/2021/01/Calls_to_Action_English2.pdf.

Turner, Dale. *This is Not a Peace Pipe: Towards a Critical Indigenous Philosophy*. Toronto: University of Toronto Press, 2006.

12

JENNIFER BRANT

Recalling the Spirit and Intent of Indigenous Literatures

The foundational basis of any relationship is an exchange of stories.
— Rebecca Thomas, "Etuaptmumk: Two-Eyed Seeing,"
TEDx Talk

We must share our stories and we must learn to listen to stories
other than our own…Our knowledges lives in our stories.
— Elder Albert Marshall, Mi'kmaw, "Learning Together"

By listening to your story, my story can change. By listening to your
story, I can change.
— Anonymous participant quoted in Truth and
Reconciliation Commission, *Honouring the Truth*

I begin with the above phrases to draw attention to the power of stories. The first shared by Rebecca Thomas in her TEDx talk entitled *Etuaptmumk: Two-Eyed Seeing* and the second by Elder Albert Marshall who brought forward the idea of Etuaptmumk (two-eyed seeing) as a guiding principle for co-learning. He describes it as "the gift of

223

multiple perspectives, which is treasured by the Mi'kmaw people."[1] The third phrase was published in the introduction of the summary of the final report of the Truth and Reconciliation Commission of Canada (TRC). It was spoken by a non-Indigenous woman who participated in one of the Commission's public Sharing Circles to discuss truth-telling and reconciliation. Her contribution speaks to the transformative power of sharing our truths.

As this chapter's epigraphs suggest, stories indeed have a particularly important role to play in advancing the TRC's calls to action, especially those that centre on education. As educators grapple with what it means to teach in post-TRC Canada, it seems that many are turning to Indigenous literatures. To this end, recent shifts in education indicate a commitment to becoming more inclusive of Indigenous texts. A prominent example of this is the revised Indigenous literature course that has been adopted by some Ontario school boards as a mandatory part of Grade 11 English instruction. With these shifts, it is critical that educators be prepared to teach the texts in ways that honour the spirit and intent of the authors. Attention to process and pedagogy is essential.

Contemporary Indigenous-settler relations are rooted in a messy and complicated history of treaty negotiations that paved the way for expansion and settlement across the nation. Although largely erased from history texts, it is well documented that the spirit and intent of original treaty negotiations have not been honoured. In fact, some Indigenous and non-Indigenous legal scholars refer to the treaty-making process as a coerced and organized takeover. It has been argued that the true spirit and intent of early treaty negotiations promised in verbal transla- tion and symbolically codified in wampum belts was never reflected in the written documentation.[2] In *Spirit & Intent: A Collection of Short Stories and Other Writings*, Sara General writes about the importance of "honour[ing] the living spirit and intent of the Treaties" and aligns this principle with honouring the truth of stories.[3] The notion of spirit and intent is echoed in Susan Dion's work *Braiding Histories: Learning from Aboriginal Peoples' Experiences and Perspectives*. Dion's book is based on the Braiding Histories Stories that she wrote with her brother to examine the ways teachers brought Indigenous curriculum into their own classrooms.[4] Dion notes that the Braiding Histories Stories were written with particular attention to honouring the stories' subjects through a process of retelling that created harmony within the stories. Dion writes, "We can never be sure that we know the intention of our subjects. Our hope is to recognize the singularity of the individual and to do so in such a way that the story subjects would recognize themselves in our stories."[5] I extend the principle of spirit and intent in this chapter to call upon educators to honour the intention of authors/storytellers in ways that are both reconciliatory and transfor- mative. By attending to the spirit and intent of Indigenous literatures, educators are likely to experience a deeper awareness of the transformative power of stories.

This chapter will consider the valuable role Indigenous literatures play in decolonizing and reconciliatory frameworks while noting the pedagogical work that must accompany Indigenous stories. I present this work as a call for educators to reflect on their personal relationships to reconciliation, examine their willingness to listen and learn from multiple perspectives, and consider decolonizing and reconciliatory approaches to bringing Indigenous literatures into their own classrooms. I begin by highlighting the express commitment of Indigenous authors to have their work included in mainstream classrooms. Next, I advance the work of Indigenous literatures to trouble settler educational space. I then outline my approach to enacting Indigenous Maternal Pedagogies to teach Indigenous literatures in transformative ways. In response to the momentum of reconciliation, I present Indigenous Maternal Pedagogies as a responsive pedagogical approach to working with stories in ways that do not undermine reconciliatory efforts but rather invoke the spirit and intent of Indigenous literatures. This is followed by a discussion on how Indigenous literatures can effectively serve as a catalyst for social change and transformative engagement. To come full circle, I present the experiences of Indigenous learners who journeyed with Indigenous literatures in a course in which I enacted Indigenous Maternal Pedagogies. I interweave their narratives with the spirit and intent of Indigenous literatures by drawing attention to the healing nature of truth-telling. This chapter serves as an important starting place for teachers by providing valuable insights into the intricacies of Indigenous stories and highlighting the unique pedagogical strategies that attend to the spirit and intent of Indigenous literatures.

A Commitment to Share Indigenous Literatures

The commitment to sharing Indigenous stories for reconciliatory education has been expressed by Indigenous authors who want to get their work into classrooms despite the lack of government funding for Indigenous resources. In July 2018, Doug Ford's Ontario Progressive Conservative government cancelled the TRC curriculum writing sessions that were intended to ensure the inclusion of Indigenous content in Ontario classrooms. In response, several Indigenous authors offered schools free copies of their books. Prompted by Cherie Dimaline, who offered to send twenty free copies of *The Marrow Thieves* to interested educators, Kateri Akiwenzie-Damm, Monique Gray Smith, Tracey Lindberg, and Chelsea Vowel also offered to provide free copies of their recent books for classroom use.

The push for the inclusion of Indigenous literatures throughout the education system can be further and more widely understood in terms of the momentum to honour the work of the TRC. Following the approval of the Indian Residential Schools Settlement Agreement, the TRC formally commenced in June 2008. Between 2009 and 2014, over 6750 residential school survivor and witness statements were collected during the TRC's statement-gathering process. In response to Canada's colonial history, the legacy of residential schools, and the ongoing colonial processes that filter through all sectors of Canadian society, the TRC released a series of educational documents including ninety-four calls to action, some of which are directly aimed at postsecondary institutions. These calls to action reinforce the role of education in advancing reconciliation by highlighting the immediate need to redress the intergenerational effects of the Indian residential school system and the ongoing colonialization that permeates public education. For example, calls 24 and 63 together refer to the needs for the following changes in postsecondary programs for Indigenous and non-Indigenous learners:

- Incorporating Indigenous teachings and content related to residential schools, treaties, and Indigenous rights
- Building students' intercultural competency, conflict resolution skills, and commitments to human rights and antiracism
- Enhancing students' capacity for intercultural understandings, empathy, and mutual respect[6]

Indeed, educators hold an integral role when it comes to advancing reconciliation. Indigenous literatures can serve as valuable tools toward meaningful engagement with truth and reconciliation. It is critical, however, that educators ensure they are effectively working with and through these stories in ways that are reconciliatory by pairing them with lessons that attend to the truths of Indigenous-settler relations.

In this post-TRC Canada, educators are rushing to engage in reconciliation in the classroom, and a conversation about educational pathways to advance reconciliation is necessary. As Yvonne Poitras Pratt and Patricia J. Danyluk explain, "moving towards reconciliation cannot be accomplished by simply changing the curriculum, inviting in an Elder for a one-time talk, or...gathering additional learning resources. Instead, it is vital that educators examine their positionality and perspectives, and...understand where their responsibilities lie in this work."[7] Moreover, reconciliation must be understood as a timely and ongoing process that is unfolding individually and collectively. Individually, it involves an examination of one's own positionality as it relates to reconciliation and a willingness to listen and learn. Collectively, reconciliation must be understood as something that is "not optional; rather, reconciliation is framed on the recognition of inherent rights of Indigenous peoples that can, and must be, recognized as legal rights that make the case for mandatory inclusion in our classrooms."[8] This is where the mandatory inclusion of Indigenous literatures and the need for reconciliatory process and pedagogy comes in. The editors of this collection highlight the importance of troubling mainstream discourses of reconciliation. Alongside this, we must trouble the ways in which Indigenous texts are suddenly being taken up in classrooms. Specifically, we must ensure these texts are accompanied with lessons that foster transformative learning.

Advancing Indigenous Literatures to Trouble Settler Educational Spaces

Aubrey Jean Hanson posits that bringing Indigenous literatures into settler educational spaces raises pedagogical challenges as these "are often institutional spaces that include a large proportion of non-Indigenous students, a non-Indigenous instructor, and an epistemological framework largely rooted in Eurocentric traditions."[9] Teachers have been taught through "a biased version of history and a deliberate silencing of the Indigenous perspective by colonial powerholders."[10] The resulting "lack of understanding and awareness of Indigenous issues also limits the ability of novice and practicing teachers to break the cycle of discrimination."[11] As Jennifer Hardwick notes, students who have gone through a colonial education will read Indigenous literature through a colonial lens: "Even our brightest and most engaged students have gone through an education system that teaches them to accept and perpetuate colonization."[12] The challenge, then, is to ensure these literatures are not being presented in ways that are harmful, disrespectful, or racist against Indigenous peoples and Indigenous Knowledge systems by adopting pedagogical strategies to ensure students are not interpreting the material in colonial or damaging ways. Hardwick writes: "Decolonizing narratives can be misread as colonial if readers do not have the knowledge-base to engage with them...It is not enough to introduce Canadians to decolonizing narratives; decolonization needs to begin with a process of unlearning and re-learning."[13] This process of unlearning and relearning must begin prior to reading Indigenous literatures. As Hardwick explains:

> Indigenous literature's capacity to engage in this kind of decoloniza-
> tion makes it an excellent social and pedagogical tool, particularly in
> a university setting where sustained dialogue and analysis can coax
> reluctant settler readers to engage. However, the process of using
> Indigenous literature to tackle denial, paternalism, and racism in a
> classroom setting can be frustrating and damaging for Indigenous
> and settler students alike, and for professors. Students are often
> resistant and confused, and their misconceptions can foster unhealthy
> environments for learners who are more aware of Indigenous histories,
> cultures, and life-ways. I contend that this resistance and confusion
> manifests in part because Indigenous literature is all-too-often used to
> counteract colonial narratives before colonial narratives are properly
> dismantled and understood.[14]

Moreover, Hardwick suggested that Indigenous literatures "be paired with lessons on treaties, and dialogue about the impact of assimilationist policies and the importance of Indigenous sovereignty."[15] Likewise, Hanson cautions that is not enough to simply include Indigenous literatures; educators must also work intentionally with them through "the process and the pedagogy."[16] Troubling settler educational spaces through Indigenous literatures, then, involves pedagogical strategies for teacher preparedness to combat what Susan Dion refers to as the "perfect stranger": a position that many teachers claim to describe their lack of knowledge about Indigenous peoples.[17] Dion offers a "pedagogy of remembrance" so that the teacher candidates she works with will come to know, remember, and interrogate their relationship to Indigenous peoples in Canada.[18] As Dion explains, access to a wide range of Indigenous literatures, when accompanied by in-class discussions, can foster these points of remembrance and affect change by dismantling the reproduction of dominant ways of knowing about Indigenous peoples.

Troubling settler educational spaces and engaging in reconciliatory pedagogy encompasses a decolonizing understanding of reconciliation that connects reason and emotion. As Paulette Regan explains, this involves a personal commitment of educators to unsettle, disrupt, and unlearn how the past has been understood, and to consider how this connects to contemporary Indigenous-settler relations.[19] It involves embracing feelings of discomfort and confronting the connection between past and present. Extending this, if the purpose of engaging with Indigenous literatures is to respond to truth and reconciliation in Canada, then the personal surely becomes political and teachers must move students beyond passive empathy towards ethical responses and action. Regan describes passive empathy as a neutral response to injustices rather than a response that prompts students to consider their own positionality as beneficiaries of historical and social injustices, and then to reflect on their responsibilities to enact change. Within the context of settler educational spaces, students and educators must engage with Indigenous literatures in ways that are transformative and offer pathways for engaging students in social change.

Extending the intentional process and pedagogy noted above, Indigenous literatures must, importantly, be paired with consideration of the assurances in place in the educational environment to safeguard against cultural appropriation and to ensure the cultural safety of Indigenous learners. In this context, cultural safety can be understood as an environment where individuals feel respected, safe, and free to express their cultural identities without discrimination.[20] Moreover, it is important for the trend of celebrating Indigenous cultures to not become a showcase of monolithic identities trapped in the past—a phenomenon referred to as "cheap reconciliation."[21] Instead, important lessons that unpack a deep history of settler colonialism need to be taken up alongside the texts. Thus, educators must commit to implementing Indigenous material in ways that align with a decolonizing and reconciliatory pedagogy. Without the intentional process and pedagogy, teaching Indigenous literatures within a colonial setting may be done in ways that are not only detrimental to cultural safety, but are inherently racist, harmful, and disrespectful. Thus, "it takes good intentions on the part of teachers and educational authorities to engage with Indigenous texts in open-minded ways."[22] Important considerations include how stories are introduced, positioned, and interpreted, as well as the meaning that is advanced within the context of reconciliation. Educators also must take the time to reflect on how they can move forward in ways that attend to the cultural identities of Indigenous learners who have suddenly gone from being invisible to being highly visible in classroom spaces. As Hanson cautions, "a great deal of learning is required...to develop responsive relationships with this work."[23] Below, I describe my own pedagogical approach—Indigenous Maternal Pedagogies— to showcase how one might attend to the spirit and intent of this work.

Indigenous Maternal Pedagogies

In my own teaching, I enact Indigenous Maternal Pedagogies as a decolonizing and reconciliatory approach to working with Indigenous literatures. I present this as an antiracist framework that intentionally centres the spirit and intent of Indigenous literatures throughout my lessons. Indigenous Maternal Pedagogies draw from the field of Maternal Pedagogies and Indigenous worldviews to embrace the "whole student" and establish a teaching and learning environment that speaks to the hearts and minds of learners.[24] This environment is intended to offer a safe classroom environment where students can be their whole authentic selves, and where their realities and lived experiences are positioned as strengths[25] and key assets to establishing an ethical space[26] for cross-cultural and antiracist dialogue.[27] Such dialogue is essential to decolonizing education for all learners.[28] I present Indigenous Maternal Pedagogies as an environment that resists the "keeper current"—which, according to Battiste, is embedded in mainstream education[29]—and reclaims Indigenous women-centred worldviews that are nurturing and nourishing for all learners. Thus, Indigenous Maternal Pedagogies offer a decolonizing space for "actively resisting colonial paradigms" and "reject[ing] colonial curricula that [offer] students a fragmented and distorted picture of Indigenous peoples, and [instead] offer students a critical perspective of the historical context that created that fragmentation."[30] As learners begin their journeys of unpacking educational experiences characterized by colonial curricula, the movement forward within an Indigenizing space centres Indigenous worldviews, knowledges, and connections to land, place, and territory.[31]

I developed this pedagogical approach in order to promote the cultural identity development of students, encourage ethical dialogue, and foster agency, advocacy, and activism through shared Indigenous maternal teachings. Activism is an integral element that must be brought into settler education spaces to move learners beyond passive empathy to political theorizing and action. The value of Indigenous Maternal Pedagogies is documented more fully in my dissertation "Journeying Toward a Praxis of Indigenous Maternal Pedagogies: Lessons From Our Sweetgrass Baskets." There, I articulate it as a decolonizing and Indigenizing framework intended to nourish the learning spirit and counteract the harmful effects of Eurocentrism that devalue and delegitimize Indigenous knowledges. Three theoretical frameworks are braided together to enact Indigenous Maternal Pedagogies: cultural identity development, Homeplace, and Maternal Essence, the latter of which is found within Indigenous cultural teachings and literatures.[32] I align Indigenous Maternal Pedagogies with Hardwick's call to dismantle colonial narratives before working with Indigenous literatures and Hanson's call to work with Indigenous literatures with "good intentions."[33] To explain how the process and the pedagogy work, I will outline some of the pedagogical underpinnings of my approach to teaching Indigenous literatures. I will do this by describing how I enacted Indigenous Maternal Pedagogies in an undergraduate course, Reclaiming Indigenous Women's Literature, that I developed and taught for several years as a doctoral student. A full discussion of this course as it relates to cultural identity and community wellbeing is documented in "Rebirth and Renewal: Finding Empowerment through Indigenous Women's Literature."[34]

ENACTING INDIGENOUS MATERNAL PEDAGOGIES THROUGH CULTURAL IDENTITY THEORIES

I designed and delivered the Reclaiming Indigenous Women's Literature course by attending to Kim Anderson's theory of cultural identity theory for Indigenous women.[35] Anderson presents her theory of identity formation by extending the Medicine Wheel teachings to include four components: resistance, reclamation, construction, and action. Anderson describes this as "a process of self-definition" through which Indigenous women engage in "resisting negative definitions of being; reclaiming Aboriginal tradition; constructing a positive identity by translating tradition into the contemporary context; and acting on that identity in a way that nourishes the overall well-being of our communities."[36] The course introduced students to Anderson's theory during the first class by connecting the students to concrete personal and political realities of Indigenous women, some of which are my own realities. I then prompted students to explore the ways in which Anderson's theory applies to their own lives through small-group discussions. The goal is for Indigenous and non-Indigenous students to commune over the injustices and take steps together towards action. Even if their positionality involves inaction, walking them through this framework deepens their understanding of how their own experience is rooted in the experiences of others. My hope is that this moves all students toward political theorizing and action. Anderson's theory is then used to structure the entire course into four sections to align with the four phases: resist, reclaim, construct, and act. Lessons that take place during the resist phase of the course serve as a foundation for the "unlearning" of colonial histories and provide students with a decolonial lens for reading Indigenous literatures.

I began the course with material that highlights the points of settler contact and colonial policies that Indigenous women have resisted, as well as the negative stereotypes that continue to perpetuate social inequities for Indigenous women. As an example, Janice Acoose-Miswonigeesikokwe's *Iskwewak Kah'Ki Yaw Ni Wahkomakanak: Neither Indian Princesses nor Easy Squaws*, provides an opportunity for the students to learn about what Acoose-Miswonigeesikokwe referred to as white-eurocanadian-christian patriarchy.[37] Acoose-Miswonigeesikokwe writes about her points of contact with white-eurocanadian-christian patriarchy throughout her life and connects these institutions to the negative images of Indigenous women that have been expressed and maintained throughout mainstream Canadian literature. According to Acoose-Miswonigeesikokwe, literary representations describing Indigenous women as lewd, licentious, dissolute, dangerous, or promiscuous, alongside those that lean more towards the polar-opposite "Indian Princess" representation, trap Indigenous women in a Squaw/Princess binary.[38] Students learn that these representations are not only upheld by white-eurocanadian-christian-patriarchal institutions, but they have been used to justify many of the legally sanctioned policies that have targeted Indigenous women, such as the eugenics movement, the pass system, and the Sixties Scoop. This trend of targeting Indigenous women continues today and is reflected in the overrepresentation of Indigenous children in child protective services. The extent of the harm done by this binary is seen in the tragic and disheartening reality of the horrific numbers of Indigenous women, girls, trans people, and two-spirit people who go missing or are murdered. Amnesty International's *Stolen Sisters* report formally documented the cases and issued a call for immediate action. A central slogan in their media campaign, "silence is violence," powerfully captured the reality at play. Many of the students I taught prior to the launch of the National Inquiry into Missing and Murdered Indigenous Women (MMIWG) had not heard of the *Stolen Sisters* report or the MMIWG awareness campaigns that have taken place across Turtle Island for decades.

The slogan "silence is violence" took on a deeper meaning for the students who reflected, with my urging, on the silencing of Indigenous women. I encouraged students to think critically about the Indigenous leaders that have been written about or documented more widely throughout history; names like Sitting Bull and Crazy Horse usually came to mind. I then asked students to consider the names of historical figures who are Indigenous women. Typically, only one woman came to mind: Pocahontas. Students were prompted to consider this in light of the valuable and very powerful role Indigenous women had in traditional, matriarchal, egalitarian societies. Despite this, few stories are known of Indigenous women leaders throughout history. To extend my argument and connect it to the Squaw/Princess binary described above, the story of Pocahontas that was most familiar to my students was one in which she is presented as the young, virginal, yet highly sexualized princess. By drawing on the Squaw/Princess binary that imprisons Indigenous women, I conveyed the importance of literatures that are written by Indigenous women: they are expressions of traditional and contemporary identities that provide true representations of Indigenous womanhood. For example, instead of the Pocahontas story familiar to my students, I presented Beth Brant's version, "Grandmothers of a New World," in which she describes Pocahontas as a woman of authority who fought for her Nation until her final days.[39] These initial lessons set a tone for the course's reclamation, construction, and action phases that followed.

PEDAGOGICAL CHALLENGES AND ETHICAL SPACE

As an Indigenous scholar, I find that Anderson's four-phase framework— resist, reclaim, construct, and act—provides a seamless and necessary way for me to deliver a course on Indigenous women's literature. More than simply theorize, it allows me to make profound personal and political connections with the intention of fostering the desire to move beyond passive empathy to action. It is likely that a settler educator will need to consider other frameworks to attend to an effective reconciliatory process and pedagogy for teaching courses on Indigenous literatures. This must involve the processes of unlearning and relearning, as well as deep reflection on one's positionality as it relates to reconciliation and truth-telling. I offer my own experiences with Anderson's framework because it holds valuable lessons that might prompt pathways for settler educators to work with these texts in ways that foster transformative learning.

I first began teaching Indigenous literatures in the Gidayaamin program, an Indigenous women's university access program that was mostly comprised of Indigenous learners. I encouraged students to bring their whole selves into the learning environment with attention to the ways in which they might identify and relate to the literature. The intimate class size offered a safe space for expressing vulnerabilities and engaging in emotional discussions. The classroom dynamic shifted when this course became cross-listed with other departments and enrolment became predominantly non-Indigenous. With this shift, I became more aware of the importance of creating a safe space for ethical engagement as Indigenous and non-Indigenous learners journeyed through the literature together. As Hanson notes, "such mixed spaces offer pedagogical challenges for reading Indigenous literatures."[40]

To give a sense of the pedagogical challenges that can arise with these topics, I recall a conversation that took place between two students in my first year of teaching the Reclaiming Indigenous Women's Literature course. A non-Indigenous student shared her struggle with the difficult nature of the stories, expressing the desire for authors to provide happy endings. In response, an Indigenous student powerfully replied: "There is no happy ending, sister!" As a class we discussed the notion of the "happy ending," and how perhaps this might conflict with the storyteller's purpose and the overall authenticity of Indigenous literatures. During these teachable moments, it is important to connect these difficult truths to everyday realities in ways that prompt desire to move from thought to action so that students consider the politics of social change. I assign powerful autobiographies including Maria Campbell's *Half-Breed* and Morningstar Mercredi's *Morningstar: A Warrior's Spirit*. These two books showcase the life stories of the authors, both of whom overcame oppressive forces that led them to prostitution and addictions. We read about their journeys toward recovery, which brought them to their vocations as writers, mentors, and frontline workers. Beatrice Culleton's *In Search of April Raintree* and *Come Walk With Me* offer powerful narratives that highlight hardships to which many Indigenous women can relate. They also inspire hopes and dreams through examples of perseverance. But as the above interaction taught me, these powerful stories must be taught alongside lessons that extend passive empathy to action. Indeed, this cannot be done without attention to the development of an ethical space.

To create ethical spaces, I begin my courses by working with the students to draft a set of classroom ethics that will govern student conduct. The ethical space of engagement is implemented in my class by sharing the Haudenosaunee teaching of Ka'nikonhrí:io, which emphasizes the importance of bringing a "good mind" to all that we do. From an Anishinaabe perspective, this understanding is also encouraged through Mino-biimaadiziwinan, which is a belief in living "the good life" through a good mind that involves a harmonious balance of the mind, body, and spirit.[41] Extending the "good mind" teachings to the classroom encourages students to come to class with a good mind and to be respectful of one another's worldviews and ways of being. I explain that it is okay to disagree, but there is a need to respect everyone's contributions, understand that everyone has a voice and also has the right to be silent, and understand that everyone contributes to the safe and ethical space that we all co-create. Students are reminded of these classroom ethics as difficult and emotionally charged conversations arise throughout the course.

I am now teaching mandatory Indigenous content courses in teacher education. The classroom dynamic is different than it was when I taught courses offered as Indigenous studies electives. In these mandatory courses, some students express a willingness and eagerness to learn while others express strong resistances to course material and lessons. To combat the "cheap reconciliation that is the hallmark of denial,"[42] my approach involves a commitment to dismantling colonial narratives that manifest "indoctrinated ignorance" and "historical amnesia" alongside intentional work with Indigenous literatures. This is not an easy task. I extend the work of Elder Albert Marshall and of Rebecca Thomas on Etuaptmumk, discussed at the beginning of this chapter, to highlight the importance of under-standing multiple perspectives. The stories shared in classroom discussions tend to stir up mixed emotions, as I discuss in the next section. The stories trouble the notions of Canada being a "fair country" by exposing human rights violations and social injustices. This is challenging for many preservice teachers who take great pride in the image of Canada as a peacekeeping nation. As students journey with Indigenous literatures, they come to understand a different narrative and are prompted to think critically about their roles in enacting social change.

Indigenous Literatures: A Catalyst for Social Change

In "Truth, Reconciliation, and Amnesia: Porcupines and China Dolls and the Canadian Conscience," Keavy Martin writes:

> If we bracket the frantic desire for closure, or catharsis, which too often accompanies the reading or hearing of Aboriginal stories, we create the possibility that the telling of such stories be about filling in—rather than widening—the gaps in our national history. This is part of the importance of residential school literature, and—ironically—of storytelling initiatives like the Truth and Reconciliation Commission. Although ostensibly directed toward healing and closure, they in fact function to ensure scars remain visible—that historical wounds continue to seep.[43]

These words highlight the importance of stories and truth-telling in making visible the social injustices of the past. Truth-telling can serve as a catalyst for social change if we share the stories that expose social injustices and connect these works to the colonial, sociocultural, and political realities of the everyday. This sentiment is echoed by Lisa Monchalin, who begins her book *The Colonial Problem: An Indigenous Perspective on Crime and Injustice in Canada* with the following "Note to Instructors":

> For non-Indigenous peoples, learning about injustices can produce feelings of guilt, anger, and shame. Some people will resist learning about the violent, brutal, and heinous policies and practices of the cultural annihilation, European domination, subjugation, and exploitation of Indigenous peoples. This story challenges the Canadian identity, the country's view of itself "as a nation of benevolent peacemakers." Learning about these aforementioned realities not only brings students' conceptual understandings into dispute but also challenges students at an emotional level.[44]

Sharing these difficult stories can be challenging. One tension I have had to grapple with is how to effectively engage my class in emotionally charged dialogue while ensuring a nurturing classroom environment. I position my classroom as a safe space for exposing social injustices, and this is where I extend the ethical space of engagement noted earlier. While difficult stories cause discomfort, the greater harm is in not telling these stories. Angelique Nixon reaffirms my stance on the importance of emotionally charged dialogue: "We need public language and new (our) voices to talk about issues of race, gender, class, sexuality, and other aspects of difference. We need honesty and real dirty talk. We need people to be able to express their anger in useful ways and channel these energies into change."[45]

I understand "dirty talk" to be politically and emotionally charged dialogue that challenges preconceived notions and understandings of histories and contemporary realities; that confronts the intersectionalities of oppression, as well as the dominant systems of privilege that sustain and are sustained by the oppression of others; and that reveals the difficult issues of slavery, eugenics, residential schools, and so on that have built what Acoose-Miswonigeesikokwe refers to as the "white-eurocentric-christian patriarchy."[46] Nixon's message about the necessity of difficult classroom conversations resonates with the words of Julie Kaomea, who articulates the importance of uncomfortable dialogue for change.[47] Consider also the words Morningstar Mercredi expressed during her keynote at the Missing and Murdered Indigenous Women's Conference: "The issues we talk about make some people uncomfortable. Well, I'll tell you what—Get uncomfortable!"[48] Mercredi continued by unapologetically sharing her story—one that is deeply rooted in intergenerational trauma, violence, and abuse. Her intention was not to share a story that would comfort her audience but rather one that will perhaps disrupt their understandings of settler violence and prompt them to consider their relationship to past and present colonial injustices that have led and lead to violence against Indigenous women and girls in Canada. I further understand her words as an acknowledgement that transformation takes place in a space of vulnerability where one is willing to "get uncomfortable."

The challenges described above are not to be misunderstood as a detriment to a safe space for ethical engagement. A safe and ethical environment is necessary to walk students through uncomfortable material. Indeed, as Monchalin expresses, there is a need for students to move out of their comfort zones, as "stepping outside of one's comfort zone can serve as a catalyst for engaging in constructive critical dialogue."[49] Monchalin also notes the need to engage in uncomfortable dialogue by establishing a safe classroom environment. She highlights the importance of truth-telling through storytelling and ceremony. As she notes, this can be done within classroom spaces by bringing in Elders and Traditional Knowledge Keepers, and by conducting ceremony such as smudging. These steps to create a space for Indigenous Maternal Pedagogies are part of a larger movement of Indigenizing the academy by centring Indigenous worldviews.[50]

While my work in Indigenous educational spaces has largely focused on the connection between cultural identity and wellbeing, my role teaching mandatory Indigenous content courses in teacher education focuses on walking teacher candidates through the messy decolonial processes of unlearning and relearning. The students searching for the "happy ending" in Indigenous stories mirror those who are looking for an easy "how to guide" for incorporating Indigenous perspectives in their classrooms. This is a sentiment often expressed by many of the teacher candidates throughout my course. The process of unlearning is new to many of them and can surely be frustrating in a fast-paced program. The structure of these mandatory Indigenous content courses in teacher education is a critical area for further study. These courses cover a lot of difficult material that challenges students in intellectual and emotional ways. Arguably, there is not enough time to cover all this material in one course. This, however, is the reality of a messy and dark colonial history that must be confronted, especially in teacher education. The mandatory Indigenous content course is only a small component of their teacher education certification. This is, indeed, problematic for individuals who will go on to teach our future generations. I must engage in this work in a way that propels teacher candidates on an ongoing journey of intellectual and emotional reconciliatory work—that is, I must propel them to continue this work even after they leave my class.

My focus on cultural identity and wellbeing centres antiracist education through truth-telling. Verna St. Denis asserts that antiracist education involves moving beyond cultural identity to include racial identity. As she points out, it is important to understand racial identity and the processes of racialization because it helps bring understanding to the way "race has been used and is continually used to justify inequality and oppression."[51] Her article, published over ten years ago, calls for "the widespread offering of a critical anti-racist education as a requirement at all universities across Canada" because Indigenous peoples are far too often called upon to challenge "deeply entrenched racist ideology without the time and resources to adequately do so."[52] Her call to Canadian universities is echoed in the TRC's aforementioned calls to action, which focus on both intercultural under-standings and antiracist education. For St. Denis, a focus on cultural revitalization without antiracist education tends to blame Indigenous peoples for their own loss of language and cultural identity instead of troubling the colonial processes and racialized legislations that continually justify the ongoing oppression and inequality of Indigenous peoples. Moreover, narrowly focusing on cultural revitalization places the responsibility to enact that revitalization solely on Indigenous people while ignoring the role non-Indigenous people play in the ongoing colonization that permeates all facets of Canadian society, especially education.

I noted above that my pedagogical approach aligns with the TRC's calls to action. Indeed, through the lesson plan described above and other class activities, I am working to advance the processes of reconciliation by promoting "culturally appropriate curricula"[53] for "building student capacity for intercultural understand-ing, empathy, and mutual respect."[54] Indigenous Maternal Pedagogies provide a safe space for dialogue on contemporary issues such as racialized, sexualized, and gender-based violence in Canada and the current suicide epidemics in Northern communities. Through classroom conversations and activities, national responses to these issues will be troubled and participants will be prompted to reflect on their own worldviews and consider issues of power and privilege. This work is intended to inspire compassion and empathy through transformative and cross-cultural understandings that encourage all to become part of an informed dialogue as we advance equity, justice, and action.

THE HEALING POWER OF TRUTH-TELLING

One component that is being largely swept under the rug in the collective rush to reconcile is the need for the healing that accompanies the truth-telling process. As residential school survivor Evelyn Brockwood eloquently reminded TRC commissioners:

> When this came out at the beginning, I believe it was 1990, about residential schools, people coming out with their stories, and…I thought the term, the words they were using, were truth, healing and reconciliation. But somehow it seems like we are going from truth telling to reconciliation, to reconcile with our white brothers and sisters. My brothers and sisters, we have a lot of work to do in the middle. We should really lift up the word healing.[55]

Healing can be a painful process. Part of that work "in the middle" involves having difficult conversations that confront the past, revealing the hard truths, and working through those stories. Healing cannot take place until these truths are acknowledged and confronted. The sort of "cheap reconciliation" that tends to brush over the difficult material can move us away from healing and lead to "further error and injustice,"[56] and frustration, as evidenced in my former student's response noted above: "There is no happy ending, sister!" As educators, it is our role to honour the spirit and intent of Indigenous literatures by embracing the hard truths and difficult realities and propelling them forward to promote social justice. These stories will move students out of their comfort zones and into zones that open up space for critical dialogue as a catalyst for change. This is the kind of change that fosters a place for healing through the process of truth-telling.

The healing power of stories was clearly expressed by Indigenous women who participated in my doctoral research and journeyed with Indigenous literatures. In this section, I share some of their words to showcase their personal connections to Indigenous literatures as it relates to healing. One of the books that I assign in my class is Marlene Carvell's *Sweetgrass Basket*, a story that gently and eloquently offers a glimpse into the residential school experience through the fictional voices of two sisters. The women who participated in my research made such profound connections to this book as it related to their journeys with Indigenous literature. I discussed this with the Elder, Grandmother Shirley, who guided my doctoral research and she encouraged me to work with the sweetgrass basket teachings. As I document more fully in my dissertation, the research process itself became an extension of the sweetgrass basket teachings.[57] Setting out, I had no idea that sweetgrass teachings would play such a prominent role in my journey towards the praxis of Indigenous Maternal Pedagogies. I continue to assign the book *Sweetgrass Basket* in the mandatory Indigenous courses I teach in teacher education to help guide the unit on residential schools and use it as a starting place to introduce students to ethical and relational practices in education. The powerful connections that Indigenous and non-Indigenous students continue to make with this book demonstrate the power of Indigenous women's literatures and the effect they can have on shaping classroom lessons in meaningful ways.

My course introduced other books that document intergenerational trauma and contemporary experiences related to racialized, sexualized, and gender-based violence. One such book is Helen Knott's memoir *In My Own Mocassins: A Memoir of Resilience*. In the book's introduction, Knott shares that her story comes from a lived space. She writes: "I have lived this story. I had to pull this story out of body, out of bone, out of a place so deep that it does not have a name."[58] Knott cautions that her novel was not written for a non-Indigenous reader to bring their "pity and their judgment," though it does invite them to enter and read with an open heart. Knott says she wrote her novel for Indigenous women in the spirit of healing and self-love, noting that "as Indigenous women, we sometimes unapologetically write for ourselves."[59] The Indigenous women participants in my doctoral research described literature written by and for Indigenous women as a profound source of empowerment and healing. They found it important to not only see themselves reflected in the stories, but to see that these stories offered authentic reflections of the everyday realities to which they were connected. For some, this literature helped them to feel safe with their own feelings and experiences, prompting them to share their own personal stories with the class. As one participant, Sabrina, explained, "I learned the importance of telling your story and the importance of being able to listen to other women's stories."[60] The importance of "telling your story" was also expressed by Sherry, who commented on the empowerment she found upon reading Morningstar Mercredi's book *Morningstar: A Warrior's Spirit*:

> In that book there's a lot of truth. There's a lot of things that happen and I don't even know how she found the courage to write it herself... *resilience*, like reading, getting through the book, getting through the hard parts, and seeing how she went through all of that and still was able to say yes this happened to me but it doesn't define me and who I am. Reading that book, for me, I was like in awe of her and her strength.[61]

As I stated earlier, I also assign Beatrice Culleton's *In Search of April Raintree*. Culleton expresses the sentiment of "liv[ing] powerfully or succumb[ing] to victimhood."[62] The book takes readers through a powerful story of overcoming a life of victimization to move toward personal triumph as the main characters, April and Cheryl, pivot back and forth between cultural shame and pride. When I first encountered the book, I fervently read it in two days and immediately knew it was essential for the Indigenous women's literature course. I consider the book a must-read for all Canadians as it takes readers down some of the dark roads of Canada's past and provides a sociocultural understanding of contemporary Indigenous realities. To demonstrate the healing power of this text, I share excerpts from two of the Indigenous women who participated in my doctoral research, Jessica and Sherry:

> In Search of April Raintree was one of the readings that I really enjoyed but also learned a lot from because…you're not holding anything back in that book it's like out there. It's kind of like…it's hard to face reality sometimes but then you realize what Indigenous women went through back throughout the years. That was my kind of experience. Just learning about who we were and how we overcame things.[63]

> In Search of April Raintree, the very first book that we read in that course I had read previously, my sister had read it and she said you have to read this, and I remember reading it and being locked in my room…I remember I was crying and sobbing and angry but I had to go through the emotions because for the most part I relate to it and [connect it to] stuff that had happened to me in the past.[64]

The personal connections Jessica and Sherry described were shared by other students as well. The women noted the importance of having these stories to help them come to terms with the intergenerational traumas in their own families but also how to overcome and work though those hardships. For others, reading the book became a journey of wholeness. As Sabrina noted, personal connections to the story helped her become safe with her feelings and her own experiences. This was also fostered by classroom conversations that followed this text as students found deeper connections with other Indigenous women in the stories and throughout the course. Sabrina explained, "It's really like a collective experience…It's kind of comforting to be able to identify your experiences that you go through in life and know that you're not alone."[65] She elaborated further:

> In Search of April Raintree and the Sweetgrass Basket, those are sad stories and I know they're reality because I face that in my family, like that's my family…so they weren't really shocking to me, they didn't have that shocking effect, it was kind of like well it's out there now like and other aspects like where I would never be able or I would never consider telling my story in that kind of context but because it was out there it kind of made me feel a little bit more safe with my feelings, my own feelings.[66]

All of these comments showcase the personal connections that Indigenous women find within Indigenous literatures—especially those that are unapologetically Indigenous. As evidenced in Sabrina's comment, the personal connection was indeed healing and the expression of becoming safe with her own feelings prompted a sense of wholeness. The women who journeyed with Indigenous women's literature showcase the value of bringing this material into educational settings as it relates to truth-telling, healing, and reconciliation. It is important to note, however, that the sharing of personal stories may rarely take place in settler educational spaces and should not be expected or urged. It may be that personal connections to the stories are shared in reflective journaling and all students should be prompted to consider the meaning these stories hold for personal and collective reconciliation. Reflective journaling and effective discussions offer a powerful strategy for attending to the need to consider social injustices and promote transformative learning. I share these personal accounts from my doctoral research to highlight the healing power of Indigenous literatures and encourage classroom conversations to take place cautiously in an effort to foster ethical reconciliation.

I've shared the healing power of Indigenous women's literatures as expressed by Indigenous women who participated in my doctoral research. I intentionally centre their experiences as lessons for teachers and issue a call to attend to the spirit and intent of Indigenous literatures. I challenge teachers to consider what it means to work with intention and to move beyond cheap reconciliation so that non-Indigenous students are presented with this material in ways that effectively respond to the TRC's calls to action. This work rests in the pedagogical commitments of individual teachers to bring Indigenous literatures into their classrooms with the intent of unpacking material that exposes the truths that are often not shared in educational settings. These ways of teaching should challenge students intellectually and emotionally through critical reading and reflective applications. Indigenous literatures should be presented in ways that prompt students to move beyond passive empathy and make deeper connections to contemporary social justice and human rights issues.

    Indigenous literatures can serve as both windows and mirrors.[67] For Indigenous readers who find personal connections in these works, the literatures can serve as mirrors that reflect their own realities, from the hardships and the violences to the strength and creative acts of resistance. The mirrors offer reflections of resilience and personal triumphs; this has been described as healing and empowering by former students. For non-Indigenous readers, the stories are incredibly eye-opening; they offer insights—windows—into the lives of the authors that are strikingly different from the stories that have historically dominated (and arguably continue to dominate) mainstream classrooms. The windows alone might allow a clear view to promote empathy, compassion, and cross-cultural understanding.

Coupled with attention to process and pedagogy, the windows offer a pedagogical space that can move students beyond passive empathy toward transformative learning and social action. To come full circle and attend to the spirit and intent of Indigenous literatures, I end this chapter with a closing thought from Daniel Heath Justice:

> [Indigenous literatures] reflect the truths of our survival and our own special beauty in the world to which we belong. They don't hide the traumas or the shadows; they don't make everything neat and tidy, or presume that the horrors of colonialism will be easily put to rest— like zombies, vampires, and ungentled ghosts, settler colonialism is nothing if not persistent. But our literatures remind us that our histories are more than tragedy, more than suffering, more than the stories of degradation and deficiency that settler colonialism would have us believe. They remind us that we're the inheritors of heavy, painful legacies, but also of hope and possibility, of a responsibility to make the world a better place for those yet to come.[68]

NOTES

1. Marshall, "Learning Together," 6.
2. Monchalin, *The Colonial Problem.*
3. General, *Spirit & Intent,* 10
4. See Dion, *Braiding Histories,* Appendix A: "The Braiding Histories Stories as Distributed for Classroom Use."
5. Dion, *Braiding Histories,* 91.
6. *Truth and Reconciliation Commission of Canada: Calls to Action,* calls 24 and 63. Hereafter cited as TRC calls.
7. Pratt and Danyluk, "Exploring Reconciliatory Pedagogy," 4.
8. Pratt and Danyluk, "Exploring Reconciliatory Pedagogy," 5.
9. Hanson, "Reading for Reconciliation," 76.
10. Pratt and Danyluk, "Learning What Schooling Left Out," 7.
11. Pratt and Danyluk, "Learning What Schooling Left Out," 7.
12. Hardwick, "Dismantling Narratives," 114.
13. Hardwick, "Dismantling Narratives," 102.
14. Hardwick, "Dismantling Narratives," 112.
15. Hardwick, "Dismantling Narrative," 114.
16. Hanson, "Reading for Reconciliation," 77.
17. Dion, "Disrupting Molded Images."
18. Dion, "Disrupting Molded Images," 331.
19. Regan, *Unsettling the Settler.*

20. See Bennett and Salonen, "Intercultural Communication"; Fernando and Bennett, "Culturally Safe Space"; Hunt, "Cultural Safety."
21. Regan, *Unsettling the Settler*, 185.
22. Hanson, "Reading for Reconciliation," 77.
23. Hanson, "Reading for Reconciliation," 69–70.
24. See O'Reilly, *Maternal Theory*.
25. See Bernal, "Critical Race Theory"; Yosso, "Whose Culture."
26. Ermine, "Ethical Space of Engagement."
27. See St. Denis, "Aboriginal Education."
28. See Battiste, *Decolonizing Education*.
29. Battiste, *Decolonizing Education*, 107.
30. Battiste, *Decolonizing Education*, 186.
31. See Battiste, *Decolonizing Education*; Smith, *Decolonizing Methodologies*.
32. For cultural identity development, see Anderson, *Recognition of Being*. Regarding Homeplace, see hooks, "Homeplace"; J. Brant, "Finding Homeplace." For Maternal Essence in Indigenous cultural contexts, see J. Brant and Anderson, "In the Scholarly Way." See also J. Brant, "Journeying Toward a Praxis."
33. Hardwick, "Dismantling Narratives"; Hanson, "Reading for Reconciliation," 77.
34. J. Brant, "Rebirth and Renewal."
35. Anderson, *Recognition of Being*.
36. Anderson, *Recognition of Being*, 15.
37. To align with Acoose-Miswonigeesikokwe, I have intentionally lowercased each word.
38. Acoose-Miswonigeesikokwe, *Iskwewak Kah'Ki Yaw Ni Wahkomakanak*.
39. B. Brant, *Writing as Witness*, 83–103.
40. Hanson, "Reading for Reconciliation," 76.
41. See Anderson, "Minobimadziwin"; Newhouse and FitzMaurice, introduction to *Well-Being in the Urban Aboriginal Community*.
42. Regan, *Unsettling the Settler*, 185.
43. Martin, "Truth, Reconciliation, and Amnesia," 62.
44. Monchalin, *The Colonial Problem*, xxv.
45. Nixon, "The Magic and Fury," para. 10.
46. Acoose-Miswonigeesikokwe, *Iskwewak Kah'Ki Yaw Ni Wahkomakanak*, 14.
47. Kaomea, "Dilemmas of an Indigenous Academic."
48. Mercredi, keynote address.
49. Monchalin, *The Colonial Problem*, xxv.
50. See Battiste, *Decolonizing Education*; Smith, *Decolonizing Methodologies*; Kovach, *Indigenous Methodologies*.
51. St. Denis, "Aboriginal Education," 1071.
52. St. Denis, "Aboriginal Education," 1083.
53. TRC call 10.iii.
54. TRC call 63.iii.
55. Evelyn Brockwood, quoted in Truth and Reconciliation Commission of Canada, *Honouring the Truth*, 16.
56. Martin, "Truth, Reconciliation, and Amnesia," 62.
57. J. Brant, "Journeying Toward a Praxis."
58. Knott, *In My Own Moccasins*, xiii.
59. Knott, *In My Own Moccasins*, xvi.

60. Sabrina, quoted in J. Brant, "Journeying Toward a Praxis," 169. All study participants requested to have their real names used.
61. Sherry, quoted in J. Brant, "Journeying Toward a Praxis," 179.
62. Culleton, *April Raintree*, 237.
63. Jessica, quoted in J. Brant, "Journeying Toward a Praxis," 178.
64. Sherry, quoted in J. Brant, "Journeying Toward a Praxis," 179.
65. Sabrina, quoted in J. Brant, "Journeying Toward a Praxis," 180.
66. Sabrina, quoted in J. Brant, "Journeying Toward a Praxis," 180.
67. See Bishop, "Windows and Mirrors."
68. Justice, *Why Indigenous Literatures Matter*, 210.

BIBLIOGRAPHY

Acoose-Miswonigeesikokwe, Janice. *Iskwewak Kah'Ki Yaw Ni Wahkomakanak: Neither Indian Princesses nor Easy Squaws*. 2nd ed. Toronto: Women's Press, 2016.

Amnesty International. *Stolen Sisters: A Human Rights Response to Discrimination and Violence against Aboriginal Women in Canada*. Ottawa: Amnesty International Canada, 2004.

Anderson, Kim. "Minobimadziwin: The Good Life for Aboriginal Women." *Centre of Excellence for Women's Health Research Bulletin* 4, no. 2 (2005): 8–9.

———. *A Recognition of Being: Reconstructing Native Womanhood*. 2nd ed. Toronto: Sumach Press, 2016.

Battiste, Marie. *Decolonizing Education: Nourishing the Learning Spirit*. Saskatoon: Purich Books, 2013.

Bennett, Janet M., and Riikka Salonen. "Intercultural Communication and the New American Campus." *Change: The Magazine of Higher Learning* 39, no. 2 (2007): 46–50. https://doi.org/10.3200/CHNG.39.2.46-C4.

Bernal, Dolores Delgado. "Critical Race Theory, LatCrit Theory and Critical Race-Gendered Epistemologies: Recognizing Students of Colour as Holders and Creators of Knowledge." *Qualitative Inquiry* 8 (2002): 105–26.

Bishop, R.S. "Windows and Mirrors: Children's Books and Parallel Cultures." In *California State University, San Bernardino Reading Conference: 14th Annual Conference Proceedings*, edited by Margaret Atwell and Adria Klein, 3–12. San Bernardino: CSUSB Reading Conference, 1990.

Brant, Beth. *Writing as Witness: Essay and Talk*. Toronto: Women's Press, 1994.

Brant, Jennifer. "Finding Homeplace within Indigenous Literatures: A Pedagogical Juncture of bell hooks' Feminist Theory and Indigenous Maternal Pedagogies." *Hypatia* (forthcoming).

———. "Journeying Toward a Praxis of Indigenous Maternal Pedagogies: Lessons from Our Sweetgrass Baskets." PhD diss., Brock University, 2017. http://hdl.handle.net/10464/13126.

———. "Rebirth and Renewal: Finding Empowerment through Indigenous Women's Literature." In *Mothers of the Nations: Indigenous Mothering as Global Resistance, Reclaiming, and Recovery*, edited by Dawn Memee Lavell-Harvard and Kim Anderson, 207–28. Toronto: Demeter Press, 2014.

Brant, Jennifer, and Kim Anderson. "In the Scholarly Way: Marking Generations of Inroads to Empowered Indigenous Mothering." In *What Do Mothers Need? Motherhood Activists and Scholars Speak Out on Maternal Empowerment for the 21st Century*, edited by Andrea O'Reilly, 203–08. Toronto: Demeter Press, 2012.

Campbell, Maria. *Half-Breed*. Halifax: Goodread Biographies, 1973.

Carvell, Marlene. *Sweetgrass Basket*. New York: Dutton Children's Books, 2005.

Culleton, Beatrice. *Come Walk with Me: A Memoir*. Winnipeg: Highwater Press, 2009.

———. *In Search of April Raintree*. Winnipeg: Pemmican Press, 1983.

Dion, Susan. *Braiding Histories: Learning from Aboriginal Peoples' Experiences and Perspectives*. Vancouver: UBC Press, 2009.

———. "Disrupting Molded Images: Identities, Responsibilities and Relationships—Teachers and Indigenous Subject Material." *Teaching Education* 18, no. 4 (2007): 329–42.

Ermine, Willie. "The Ethical Space of Engagement." *Indigenous Law Journal* 6, no. 1 (2007): 193–203.

Fernando, Terrina, and Bindi Bennett. "Creating a Culturally Safe Space When Teaching Aboriginal Content in Social Work: A Scoping Review." *Australian Social Work* 72, no.1 (2019): 47–61. https://doi.org/10.1080/0312407X.2018.1518467.

General, Sara. *Spirit & Intent: A Collection of Short Stories and other Writings*. Self-published, 2015.

Hanson, Aubrey Jean. "Reading for Reconciliation? Indigenous Literatures in a Post-TRC Canada." *English Studies in Canada* 43, no. 2/3 (2017): 69–90.

Hardwick, Jennifer. "Dismantling Narratives: Settler Ignorance, Indigenous Literature and the Development of a Decolonizing Discourse." *Topia* 33 (2015): 100–17.

hooks, bell. "Homeplace: A Site of Resistance." In *Maternal Theory: Essential* Readings, edited by Andrea O'Reilly, 761–81. Toronto: Demeter Press, 2007.

Hunt, Elena. "Cultural Safety in University Teaching and Learning." *Procedia: Social and Behavioral Sciences* 106 (December 2013): 767–76.

Justice, Daniel Heath. *Why Indigenous Literatures Matter*. Waterloo: Wilfrid Laurier University Press, 2018.

Kaomea, Julie. "Dilemmas of an Indigenous Academic: A Native Hawaiian Story." In *Decolonizing Research in Cross-Cultural Contexts: Critical Personal Narratives*, edited by Kagendo Mutua and Beth Blue Swadener, 27–44. Albany: SUNY, 2004.

Knott, Helen. *In My Own Moccasins: A Memoir of Resilience*. Regina: University of Regina Press.

Kovach, Margaret. *Indigenous Methodologies: Characteristics, Conversations, and Contexts*. Toronto: University of Toronto Press, 2009.

Marshall, Albert. "Learning Together by Learning to Listen to Each Other." *Education Canada* 58, no. 2 (2018): 6–7.

Martin, Keavy. "Truth, Reconciliation, and Amnesia: Porcupines and China Dolls and the Canadian Conscience." *English Studies in Canada* 35, no. 1 (March 2009): 47–65.

Mercredi, Morningstar. Keynote address at the Missing Indigenous Women Conference "Missing Women: Decolonization, Third Wave Feminisms, and Indigenous People of Canada and Mexico," Regina, SK, August 2008.

———. *Morningstar: A Warrior's Spirit*. Regina: Coteau Books, 2006.

Monchalin, Lisa. *The Colonial Problem: An Indigenous Perspective on Crime and Injustice in Canada*. Toronto: University of Toronto Press, 2016.

Newhouse, David, and Kevin FitzMaurice. Introduction to *Well-Being in the Urban Aboriginal Community*, edited by David Newhouse, Kevin FitzMaurice, Tricia McGuire-Adams, and Daniel Jetté. Toronto: Thompson Educational Publishing, 2012.

Nixon, Angelique V. "The Magic and Fury of Audre Lorde: Feminist Praxis and Pedagogy." *The Feminist Wire* (blog), February 24, 2014. https://thefeministwire.com/2014/02/the-magic-and-fury-of-audre-lorde-feminist-praxis-and-pedagogy/.

O'Reilly, Andrea, ed. *Maternal Theory: Essential Readings*. Toronto: Demeter Press, 2007.

Pratt, Yvonne Poitras, and Patricia J. Danyluk. "Exploring Reconciliatory Pedagogy and Its Possibilities through Educator-Led Praxis." *The Canadian Journal for the Scholarship of Teaching and Learning* 10, no. 3 (2019): article 8. https://doi.org/10.5206/cjsotl-rcacea.2019.3.9479.

———. "Learning what Schooling Left Out: Making an Indigenous Case for Critical Service-Learning and Reconciliatory Pedagogy within Teacher Education." *Canadian Journal of Education* 40, no. 1 (March 2017): 1–29.

Regan, Paulette. *Unsettling the Settler Within: Indian Residential Schools, Truth Telling, and Reconciliation in Canada*. Vancouver: UBC Press, 2011.

Smith, Linda Tuhiwai. *Decolonizing Methodologies: Research and Indigenous Peoples*. London: Zed Books, 1999.

St. Denis, Verna. "Aboriginal Education with Anti-Racist Education: Building Alliances across Cultural and Racial Identity Politics." *Canadian Journal of Education* 30, no. 4 (December 2007): 1068–92. https://doi.org/10.2307/20466679.

Thomas, Rebecca. "Etuaptmumk: Two-Eyed Seeing." Filmed May 26, 2016, at TEDxNSCCWaterfront, Dartmouth, NS. YouTube video, 14:22. https://www.youtube.com/watch?v=bA9EwcFbVfg.

Truth and Reconciliation Commission of Canada. *Honouring the Truth, Reconciling for the Future: Summary of the Final Report of the Truth and Reconciliation Commission of Canada*. Winnipeg: National Centre for Truth and Reconciliation, 2015. http://www.trc.ca/assets/pdf/Executive_Summary_English_Web.pdf.

———. *Truth and Reconciliation Commission of Canada: Calls to Action*. Winnipeg: National Centre for Truth and Reconciliation, 2015. https://ehprnh2mwo3.exactdn.com/wp-content/uploads/2021/01/Calls_to_Action_English2.pdf.

Yosso, Tara J. "Whose Culture Has Capital? A Critical Race Theory Discussion of Community Cultural Wealth." *Race Ethnicity and Education* 8 (2005): 69–91. https://doi.org/10.1080/1361332052000341006.

13

**DAVID NEWHOUSE
AND ROBIN QUANTICK**

Teaching Indigenous Studies in a Time of Reconciliation

An Anticolonial Approach
Toward Postcolonial
Awareness

TEACHING ABOUT RECONCILIATION
requires teaching about a troubled relationship and imagining a new world. It requires that we challenge the world that many of our students grew up in. We must also challenge our students' understandings of how the world works and their positions, often of privilege, in it. Teaching about reconciliation means that we create trouble for our students who then go on to create trouble for their parents and at some point, we hope, create trouble for the country in which they live, challenging it to live up to its ideals. Teaching about reconciliation means creating trouble particularly when we take an anticolonial or decolonizing approach. Paulette Regan argues that a significant part of the reconciliation journey requires that the settler be unsettled.[1] Arthur Manuel and Ronald M. Derrickson similarly argue that Canada itself must be unsettled.[2] Teaching about reconciliation means unsettling, which spells trouble.

First-year university students taking an Indigenous credit requirement course at Trent University in 2017 spoke of the trouble that they encountered. The statements of two non-Indigenous students follow:

It was hard to be part of the lectures. As a non-Indigenous person, I felt disconnected from everything. It was like this course was designed for Indigenous people and if you weren't part of that group then it was a privilege to be there. I didn't like how it seemed like everything was my fault because my ancestors were settlers. I was born here, this is my home. It was not something that was taken from anyone when I was born. I am not a settler and the use of the word settler directed against me was not appreciated. Yes, I know I am privileged and things happened in the past, but this is my home just as much as anyone else. I am not a settler.

I ended up learning a lot more than I originally thought in this course. I entered this course with a somewhat negative mindset, expecting to be largely uninterested in the course material. Despite this, I actually found a number of lectures, readings, and videos quite interesting and the course tied in well to my history courses...On the grand scheme, this course has changed my perspective of the situation of the Indigenous peoples in Canada. I now have a better understanding of their history, culture, their position in Canadian society, and the struggles they have faced at the hands of colonialism.[3]

An Indigenous student responded:

Overall, the course was very informative, but I felt it was tailored for non-Indigenous [students] that did not know or have previous knowledge. I also felt my emotional state when going out of lecture was depressive or somewhat angering. I was a little tired of being told what happened to our people after knowing about Indigenous history in Canada.

As a prelude to moving forward and creating a new relationship between Indigenous peoples and Canadians, we need to be aware of Canada's history with Indigenous peoples. We need to know what happened and why. Murray Sinclair, who served as Chair of the Truth and Reconciliation Commission (TRC), is often quoted as saying that "education got us into this mess...But education is the key to reconciliation."[4] Universities are beginning to institute Indigenous content requirements (ICRs) across their curricula—but what does this mean for Indigenous studies programs and professors, as the burden of Indigenous education at the university level falls largely upon them? This chapter documents our experiences as two professors (one Indigenous, one non-Indigenous) at Trent University as we prepared, piloted, and delivered two new ICR courses. The chapter describes and analyzes Indigenous Studies at Trent University and the context for the ICR, the framing of the course in anticolonial terms, and the role of the course in creating postcolonial consciousness. It also presents some lessons for instructors who are embarking on a similar journey.

ICRs emerged in Canadian universities as part of their response to the TRC's 2015 calls to action and report.[5] They are usually framed through the lens of Indigenization.[6] An ICR requires students to take a course that provides them with a backgrounder on colonization and its impact upon Indigenous peoples, and helps them to understand the cultural foundations of Indigenous peoples. ICRs are intended to provide students with the foundational knowledge that will enable them to act as more effective allies for Indigenous peoples in the quest for justice. ICRs, along with Indigenization more generally, have been the subject of considerable controversy. Gaudry and Lorez discusses Indigenization as existing along a spectrum from "Indigenous inclusion" to "decolonial Indigenization," with "reconciliation Indigenization" occupying a middle space between the two.[7] Indigenous inclusion asks Indigenous peoples to adapt to the academy. Decolonial Indigenization calls for radical transformation of the academy and a reorientation of the knowledge production system. Reconciliation Indigenization focuses on creating a common ground between Indigenous and Western intellectual traditions. Our efforts at Trent occupy a space firmly in the middle. Our work as a university has been guided by our Indigenous Education Council for more than thirty years. More recently, the university has formed an Indigenous Knowledge Keepers Council comprised of local Elders who provide advice on land and cultural matters. The recognition of Elders and Indigenous Knowledge as integral parts of our academic mission is foundational to Trent. In April 2010, the university Senate and Board of Governors adopted the following resolution: "We foster an environment where Indigenous knowledges are respected and recognized as valid means by which to understand the world." The resolution was incorporated into the university's vision statement in 2011.[8]

As a political project, reconciliation is a complex reimagining of the relationship between Indigenous peoples, Canadians, and the Canadian state. We are asked to reimagine the relationship, which is one of Canadian power over Indigenous peoples, as a relationship between disparate sovereignties. It aims to reimagine Canada. Reconciliation "consists of remedial efforts designed to close quality-of-life gaps and improve the relationship between Indigenous and other peoples within Canada and governance actions intended to bring Indigenous peoples and their institutions into the structures and processes established for Canada. Part of this undertaking is a critical examination of Canada itself, and this requires an understanding of the political goals of Indigenous peoples."[9] Reconciliation is also about reimagining the power relationship between Indigenous peoples and the Canadian state and examining the foundations of Canadian sovereignty. Reconciliation, then, has a practical aspect and a philosophical aspect: it is intended to improve the life circumstances of Indigenous peoples in the short term and ultimately tackle the constitutional foundation of Canada. Reconciliation is pursued through the actions of individuals and institutions and is highly complex and contentious. A guide map to institutional change has been provided by the TRC's ninety-four calls to action. A key call to action, not just for the TRC but also for the twenty-year-old Royal Commission on Aboriginal Peoples, has been for improved education of non-Indigenous Canadians.[10] Education, in a liberal democratic society informed by enlightenment ideals, is seen as the basis for societal change as well as improved quality of life. As educators within a university, we are faced with the question of how to contribute to reconciliation. One of the ways we can do so is through our education efforts as exemplified by our courses. We can also do so through our research, which informs our teaching and our social actions. Should we use the power of our institutions to require students to cultivate the knowledge to participate as informed citizens in the state project of reconciliation? This is the challenge that faces us—and there are many more questions to ask: Can we require students to take a compulsory course in Indigenous history and cultures to make them better citizens? Will we do more harm than good by requiring this? If we do this, then what do we teach? What do we want our students to know? What frame do we use for our course? How should we teach? How do we deal with student resistance?

We asked ourselves these very questions as we moved to have an ICR at Trent. It was important to frame the rationale for the course requirement. As educators, we knew that after an initial heightened period of attention, reconciliation would eventually fade from public view. We knew that the key to student engagement was a proper framing for what we were doing. Instead of reconciliation, we framed the knowledge and skills the ICR provided as foundational to the skills needed to live and work in a twenty-first-century Canada. Our view was that sustaining reconciliation action was going to be challenging over the long term (ten to twenty years) no matter how we framed it, but that students would react more positively to a labour-market frame. Within this frame, however, we did not take a conventional approach. We took what we called an "anticolonial approach" (an approach Gerald Vizenor would frame as "survivance"[11]). By this, we meant that we would ground our course in Indigenous thought, knowledge, and ideas, and that we would use Indigenous cultural foundations (in our case, Anishinaabe and Haudenosaunee foundations, as they are the two nations in our area) to teach the course. Our anticolonial approach required that we present Indigenous peoples not just as cultural beings but as thinking, theorizing, feeling beings acting upon their own ideas and desires, pursuing their own goals and objectives, informed by their own theories and understandings of the social and physical worlds. Our focus was on the actions and thoughts of Indigenous peoples rather than the actions and thoughts of colonizers.

On December 15, 2015, Canadian Prime Minister Justin Trudeau accepted the TRC's final report on behalf of the country and committed to implementing its ninety-four calls to action.[12] In our view, the prime minister's comments indicate that Canada has entered an official period of reconciliation and has started the process of overhauling many of its institutions and processes to accommodate Indigenous peoples and their interests. Reconciliation is a large, complex, national, multiyear project that is proving to be challenging and emotional. This important project requires Canadians to change their attitudes and beliefs about Indigenous peoples and to engage in actions that assist in healing the effects of "The Long Assault."[13] Reconciliation, as we have already stated, is also about reimagining sovereignty in Canada—that is, reconciling the sovereignty of Indigenous peoples with the sovereignty of the British Crown. It is a process that has been underway since the landmark 1972 Calder decision[14] that provided a foundation for this reimagination in law. The TRC extends this reimagination to all aspects of Canadian life.

The TRC—along with other groups including Universities Canada, the organization representing all universities in Canada, and The Association of Deans of Education, representing all Canadian faculties of education—has been clear in its statements that education has a central role in this large national effort. As a result, education systems from kindergarten to postsecondary have started to revise their Indigenous programming. At the postsecondary level, the Association of Canadian Deans of Education (in 2010) and Universities Canada (in 2015) set out principles that were to be followed in this reform.[15] They were designed to ensure that current and upcoming generations were educated in Indigenous cultures, traditions, and history, including in the treatment of Indigenous peoples by the Canadian state. Some universities, such as the University of Manitoba (in 2011) and the University of British Columbia (in 2018) apologized for their role in colonization.[16] Most universities launched Indigenization efforts that were intended to demonstrate the institutions' commitments to reconciliation as well as to improving their educational programs. The Canadian Association of University Teachers adopted a policy for Indigenizing the academy that acknowledges the pioneering work that Indigenous studies faculty members have done in laying the foundations for the work that is now underway in universities across the country.[17] Indigenous studies programs have been at the forefront of Indigenizing efforts since their establishment in the 1970s. They served as academic homes for Indigenous faculty, students, and programs, and provided leadership and advocacy for university reforms, often unsettling the university in their efforts.

Background: Indigenous Studies at Trent University

Since its founding in 1966, Trent University has demonstrated itself to be an institutional agent of change, measurably contributing to foundational initiatives that seek reconciliation. In 1969, Trent implemented an Indigenous studies program. Since that time, it has expanded the program to offer a full undergraduate honours degree (1973); created Indigenous spaces within the university (1972); named one of its largest teaching spaces after Chanie Wenjack, a young Indigenous boy, thus acknowledging the impact of Indian residential schools (1973); and developed the first Indigenous studies PhD program (1999). Further, in 2017 Trent created the

Chanie Wenjack School for Indigenous Studies[18] as a commitment to fostering the world that Chanie Wenjack was running towards: a place of dignity, respect, and love, which were missing from his residential school experience. In the mid-1970s, Trent also made a significant and seminal commitment to Indigenous knowledges through the hiring of Indigenous Elders as tenured faculty, thereby bringing Indigenous Knowledge Holders into the university as full-fledged members of the academy. Indigenous Elders were appointed as professors with all the rights and privileges of faculty members, including sabbaticals, progress through the ranks, eligibility for promotion, and the ability to serve as co-supervisors on graduate committees. In 2011—as stated above—the university revised its vision statement to reflect its continuing commitment to creating an environment in which Indigenous knowledges are understood to be "valid means by which to understand the world."[19]

Two Trent University reports—the 2014 Presidential Task Force on Indigenous Education report and the 2017 Special Committee on Indigenous Education report[20]—defined Indigenous education as the education of Indigenous and non-Indigenous students about Indigenous peoples. Consistent with the latter part of this definition, in May 2017, the university senate approved an ICR for all degrees. As a result, since September 2018, each undergraduate student has been required to include a 0.5-credit [21] ICR course as part of their program of studies. Consistent with other universities' approaches to ICRs, Trent's Senate approved a list of courses that were eligible to meet the Indigenous requirement. The Trent criteria for inclusion state that the course must (a) contain fifty percent Indigenous content, measured in eighteen contact hours, and (b) cover three of seven identified theme areas. [22]

Since the Indigenous Studies program began at Trent in 1969, the university has offered a first-year, twenty-four-week course (INDG1000Y). Prior to 2018, enrolment in the course averaged about 200 students per year. Most of these students (approximately 80%, according to Trent's registrar's office) were non-Indigenous, and most took the course voluntarily. For some students, the course was a degree requirement in disciplines such as nursing, Canadian studies, and anthropology. In 2017–2018, anticipating the implementation of the new, university-wide ICR, we divided the full-year course into two one-term courses— INDG1001H Foundations of Indigenous Studies and INDG1002H Critical Incidents in Modern Indigenous Life—and piloted them. The registrar's office estimated that about 1200 to 1600 students would enrol in these new courses, a six- to eight-fold increase in enrolment over the previous year.

The educational climate within which the ICR is taught has changed considerably over the last half century as has the Indigenous landscape. The course content has subtly evolved to reflect this. In 2018, students wanted their education to be practical and relevant to the labour market and to their careers. As a result of increased costs, students are now more likely to see the university through the lens of a market transaction, seeing themselves as consumers of education. They also tend to expect that, as education consumers, their needs and desires will be satisfied. What they learn at university is expected to result in knowledge and skills that will be immediately applicable to getting a job. As a result, the Senate Committee on Indigenous Education at Trent did not frame the ICR through the lenses of reconciliation or decolonization. The committee believed that doing so, while important, would increase resistance to the course. The Committee instead chose to frame it through the lens of twenty-first-century citizenship and job skills: the ability to work in diverse environments with different knowledge systems; the ability to communicate well across cultures; the ability to analyze the broader context of issues; and an understanding of one's own values, attitudes, and beliefs, as well as the impacts these have on their own actions and those of society more broadly. Knowledge of Indigenous people's cultures, languages, traditions, histories, knowledges, and aspirations is important for life as a citizen and labour-force participant in twenty-first-century Canada.[23] Governments, businesses, and NGOs are more likely to hire someone who has these skills and knowledges.

At Trent, in an anticolonial fashion, we also believe that traditional knowledge is important and ought to be communicated to students for use in their work and personal lives. In our experience, Elders insist that traditional teachings and values be interpreted for the world in which we live. They emphasize the importance of understanding one's history, culture, language, and traditions, as well as the ability to make a living. Like them, our goal is also to demonstrate the continued relevance of traditional teachings—not just to Indigenous peoples but to all our students. Asking students to engage with and consider how traditional teachings are important to their lives and to Canada is unsettling as many have not considered Indigenous peoples as intellectual beings. We ask students to think of the Medicine Circle[24] as a theory of health and the Seven Grandfather/Grandmother Teachings[25] as a system of ethics. We use these as analytic tools. We ask students to use the leadership qualities set out in the *Gayanasogowah* (the Great Law of the Haudenosaunee Confederacy) to evaluate the behaviours of Canadian and American leaders. It is unsettling for many to realize that the world can be seen and evaluated through Indigenous lenses.

Indigenous Studies, Reconciliation, and Decolonization

Within academia, Indigenous studies is a relatively new discipline, with the oldest programs having existed for just over a half century. These programs brought Indigenous scholars, Indigenous knowledge, and students to the academy, and connected the academy to Indigenous leaders and communities. Indigenous studies programs served as important educative efforts for non-Indigenous students, faculty, and administrators, and advocated on behalf of Indigenous communities and students. In many cases, they supported community and political activists seeking to establish sites for dialogue, debate, and discussion. They helped sensitize administrators to the reality of working with Indigenous peoples; taught generations of students about Indigenous history, politics, goals, and aspirations; and helped Indigenous students to explore their own history, cultures, lands, languages, and traditions.

In short, Indigenous studies programs sought to Indigenize parts of the university, support the anticolonial aspirations of Indigenous faculty and communities, respond to the labour-market desires of their students, contribute to the continued development of Indigenous peoples and communities, and build a scholarly community and body of work that was seen as legitimate, both in the eyes of Indigenous communities and the academy.

As instructors in an introductory Indigenous studies course and members of broader academy, we found that the need to be seen as legitimate by the academy, Indigenous communities, and our students, all at the same time, created a set of tensions that had to be continually negotiated. Where is the line between fitting in and selling out? How do we support Indigenous aspirations while building a body of scholarly work? What constitutes scholarship? These became important questions that required constant discussion.

Early Indigenous studies programs were not conceived using decolonizing, reconciliatory, or anticolonial frames. These terms were not part of the academic vocabulary in the 1970s and 1980s. Over time, as Indigenous scholars grew in number and moved beyond appointments in Indigenous studies, they began to critically reflect upon the power and position of the academy. Many began to challenge the academy and its role in colonization, and began to redefine the academy as a possible site for decolonization and, with reconciliation becoming a national priority in 2015, as an important contributor to reconciliation.

Despite this national priority, Indigenization and decolonization continue to be contested social and political actions. There is a general consensus among Indigenous academics that these actions go beyond hiring Indigenous faculty, establishing Indigenous programs and student supports, and recruiting and graduating more Indigenous students. David Newhouse provides an overview of the elements that universities consider to be part of Indigenization efforts.[26] Adam Gaudry and Danielle Lorenz place Indigenization on a spectrum ranging from the relatively easy approach of inclusion, to reconciliation, to the more difficult decolonization.[27] Inclusion doesn't change the academy in any significant fashion, while decolonization posits a radical shift in the university, perhaps requiring the emergence of a dual university with one part based upon Western epistemologies and one part based upon Indigenous epistemologies. Newhouse argues that unless Indigenous Epistemologies and Knowledges are included within the set of knowledges taught in universities, the university itself will become an extension of residential schools and continue their assimilative mission.[28] One of the aspects of colonization is the devaluing and erasure of the knowledge of Indigenous peoples. Teaching Indigenous Knowledge in a university classroom, on university lands, and in an institution that represents the highest educational ideals is one of the strongest anticolonial acts. Still, the structure of the academy may not be changed significantly by the simple addition of Indigenous Knowledge. Indeed, some can see the addition as assimilative. However, asking non-Indigenous peers to grapple with Indigenous Knowledge in, for instance, the tenure process can trouble this assimilative system.

Our teaching in Indigenous studies at Trent has a decidedly social-justice-oriented objective that goes beyond knowledge transmission, development of critical-thinking skills, and development of labour-market skills. Indigenous studies courses are expected to play a key role in helping to undo the colonial work of the last century and a half, create the conditions for Indigenous society development, and contribute to the improvement of the relationship between Indigenous and non-Indigenous peoples. Our vision in redesigning the course is to provide an individualized, transformative educational experience: the target effect of our enterprise is to foster a postcolonial consciousness. We want our students to understand colonization and its impacts, to possess knowledge and skills to mitigate its effects, and to have a desire to ensure that colonization doesn't happen again. These are elements of a decolonizing mission. We see decolonization as a set of ongoing actions rather than a single event that takes place all at once. Decolonization involves an ongoing critical examination not only at the individual level of one's own personal values, attitudes, and beliefs but also at the societal level of the structures and processes that keep these beliefs in place.

The mission statement of the Chanie Wenjack School for Indigenous Studies, where we teach, reflects this dual objective: "to constantly advance the knowledge of and about Indigenous peoples with a view to the overall improvement of quality of life and contribute to the creation of places of respect, dignity and power for Indigenous peoples."[29] The school's teaching goals are "to prepare students for positions of leadership within contemporary society. We endeavour to provide our students with leading knowledge and skills that enable them to foster improved understanding between Indigenous and non-Indigenous peoples, to engage in high quality Indigenous scholarship and to explore emerging identities and cultural expression."[30]

The original first-year Indigenous studies course at the school was designed as an introduction to the study of Indigenous peoples and the discipline of Indigenous studies. It explored issues of Indigenous cultures, languages, histories, and experiences, and attempted to provide a suite of ideas, analytic frames, history, traditional teachings, and worldviews as a foundation for further study. The new courses are designed to provide an understanding of the history of Indigenous-settler relations so that students can engage as more informed and empathetic social and political actors. The course mission has evolved from an introduction to an academic discipline to a decidedly anticolonial process that challenges students to ask: Now that I have all of this new knowledge, what am I to do with it? In this way we ask student to engage with one of the key elements of Indigenous Knowledge: personal responsibility. We also confronts students' desire for content that helps them get jobs. There are, in their opinions, few jobs available for decolonial or anticolonial agents, but employers like employees who can take personal responsibility. In the redesigned class, we shift our language away from decolonization, anticolonialism, and reconciliation as these terms are often perceived as too vague or, in some cases, too strong. We speak instead of being a good citizen, of nation building, and lastly of the knowledge and values that employers are looking for. We also speak to the value set of Generation Z: fairness, equity, and inclusion.

An Anticolonial Approach

Over the last half century, before the redesign, Trent did not frame its first-year Indigenous studies course with the concepts of decolonization or reconciliation. When we began redesigning the course in 2017, we deliberately chose what Marie Battiste, in coversation with David Newhouse, called an "anticolonial approach." An anticolonial approach focuses on the actions of the colonized rather than the colonizers. It asserts that the colonized are aware of their situation and are choosing to resist the actions of the colonizers and advance their own agendas, acting on their own will and desire. In our courses, we present Indigenous peoples as real, live human beings with political and social objectives who pursue these using a combination of ideas and actions from both Indigenous and Western intellectual traditions. We ground our courses in the local—presenting the history, culture, and aspirations of local First Nations, Métis, and urban communities—and then connect the local with the national and international. Using the Anishinaabe Medicine Circle,[31] we developed a Four Directions analytical model for use in the analysis of social phenomena. This model demonstrates the interrelatedness of the parts of a social phenomenon, the context of that phenomenon, and how it moves through time. We use the model to analyze the phenomenon through lenses important to Indigenous people: women, youth, and Elders. We also create opportunities for Indigenous leaders, including Elders, to speak to our classes.

We present Indigenous peoples as having national cultures. Our underlying assumption is that Indigenous peoples are peoples with knowledge and distinct cultures. In this sense, the courses we designed are decidedly anticolonial in their centring of Indigenous agency. They are deliberately designed to challenge non-Indigenous students' understandings of Indigenous peoples and to create cognitive dissonance for them: Indigenous peoples can be traditional and modern at the same time. As we began piloting the course in 2017, we hoped that this dissonance would create the conditions for students to leave the course with an understanding that Indigenous peoples are working to create the best lives they can in much-changed but still colonial circumstances. Our teaching approach was to simply present what Indigenous peoples are doing, what they are creating, and how they are living within North American modernity.

Anticolonialism, Decoloniality, and ICRs: Our Challenges

> I took this course just because it was a requirement, but slowly as I
> moved towards the end of this term I realized the importance of this
> course which actually helps me appreciate and respect the values and
> culture of Indigenous people.
> —INDG1001H/1002H student response

In 2017, the Chanie Wenjack School for Indigenous Studies engaged in a transformational curricular project as it prepared for a new role in educating an entire incoming class of students. Transformation is not a new teaching and learning objective for the community of people who work in the school: it has been the bedrock of the enterprise for fifty years.

When the new ICR was announced in 2017, we had the challenge of designing new courses that would both anticipate the requirements of the ICR and be able to adapt to the new teaching environment—the product of drastically increased enrolment including students who may not have otherwise wanted to take the course. The two courses that we piloted in the 2017–2018 year each consisted of weekly, three-hour, large-group lectures of 200 students and twelve two-hour seminars of fifteen to twenty students. Our assumption was that many of the students enrolling in the redesigned courses starting in September 2018 were taking them solely because of the ICR, and that this would be the only Indigenous content course they would take in their academic career. We also made the assumption that while many of the students had little background knowledge about Indigenous peoples, they had some understanding of the Canadian treatment of Indigenous peoples, especially the residential school experience.

Some students, we assumed, would resent having to take a course that they perceived to be unrelated to their programs of studies. The students in our courses were expected to be overwhelmingly non-Indigenous Canadians. We anticipated that there would also be a significant number of international students. This class demographic has been the experience of Trent's Indigenous studies program over the last half century: the Faculty of Indigenous studies reported that between 75% and 80% of the students who enroll in Indigenous studies courses were non-Indigenous.[32] In our redesigned courses, a minority of international students self-identified as Indigenous at the beginning of the semester, though more began to identify as such over the course of the semester as they found a similarity in experience between themselves and Canadian Indigenous peoples. Local Indigenous students made up a significant minority in the courses. All of these students have lived experiences as Indigenous persons and many come to the courses with significant knowledge of their culture and language.

Bringing all three sets of students together in one course poses a number of specific pedagogical challenges. One of the challenges we encountered was creating a common classroom culture. Common languages and classroom rituals must be created that do not position students of Indigenous descent as "experts" in all things Indigenous. Often, students will look across the classroom and ask students of Indigenous descent to weigh in on a question or a challenge as one might ask the advice of a grandparent. However, these students are, in fact, young men and women who, like everyone else, need the time and space to explore at their own pace and in their own way. Seminar leaders have a responsibility to intervene and reposition the dialogue when this occurs. Being continually positioned within the class as "resident experts" is disrespectful and impedes the development of intellectual curiosity.

For students of non-Indigenous descent and for those who come to this experience with no background in the history that colonization produced, there is a grieving process. This is another challenge. It is not unusual to hear a student comment, "Why is this the first time I am hearing this?" For many students, this grief is expressed as anger, which must be processed before effective listening can occur. Enhanced office-hour availability with faculty members and other targeted and integrated approaches to student services are essential tools to managing this process.

We have also found that it is essential to create classroom environment where students reach out to one another for help. We must get them over the dominant culture's grade-centred embarrassment of not knowing—and this, too, can be very challenging. To address these challenges, it was essential to integrate skills-oriented lessons into the course, focusing on notetaking, reading for results, effective techniques to enhance research and writing, and practical tools for making presentations. Skills-oriented lessons and workshops in Indigenous studies foundations courses are not the exclusive responsibility of academic skills personnel. These lessons and workshops (within redesigned courses) are essential building blocks in the creation of a community of learners. They create relationships among students: they acknowledge who has expertise and build relational bridges between diverse communities of learners. Most significantly, they directly challenge the notion that "basic" skills development is someone else's responsibility. Student success is a shared responsibility that requires our students to confront a natural inclination to isolate themselves when they should, in fact, reach out.

In a larger context, these pedagogical challenges can be organized into two categories: (1) presenting the content in a way that describes and analyzes the colonial brutality and impact without whitewashing or minimizing it, and (2) helping students negotiate challenges to their learned national identity. Learning the details of the history of the treatment of Indigenous peoples by the Canadian state is a particularly emotional exercise for all. Non-Indigenous students tend to become angry and filled with guilt over colonial history. Indigenous students react to the overwhelming white presence and wonder for whom the course is intended. International students react within the national framework that they have learned in their home countries. For example, Peruvian students learn that Indigenous peoples are peasants and occupy the lowest level of Peruvian society. Chinese students learn about "ethnic minorities." Some other Asian students learn of "tribal peoples." Japanese students did not, until recently, learn anything about the Ainu as a distinct Indigenous people in Japan.

Most of our students in our Indigenous studies course (rural, urban, or reserve, Indigenous or non-Indigenous descent) commented, either in class or in year-end reflective papers, that this was their first exposure both to the history of colonialism with respect to Indigenous peoples and to being taught using Indigenous pedagogies. Most had not experienced a curriculum framed through story and containing elements of ritual and ceremony. In the curricular system that they have come from, many—and maybe even most—have concluded the end grade is more important than the learning process. A decolonial experience for them is understood to be a one-time experience rather than a life-long process of engagement with their country. In the context of an anticolonial Indigenous studies learning enterprise, this is often the first time that students have been asked to play an ownership role in connecting a set of Indigenous values—recognition, responsibility, reciprocity, and relationality—to their own learning. We often quote Thomas King's *The Truth about Stories*: "To every action there is a story...take this one...it's yours. Do with it what you will. Tell it to friends...Forget it. But don't say in the years to come you would have lived your life differently if only you had heard this story. You've heard it now."[33]

The anticolonial classroom is not just a site of intellectual learning but also a site of emotional engagement. In presenting the history of what happened, we are challenging students' identities, both as individuals and as Canadians. We are also telling them and demonstrating that the past is not over—that it is still present, and that the students are unknowingly part of the continuing enterprise of settler colonialism. This is unpleasant for students to learn. Our experience in teaching introductory Indigenous studies courses is that students have shifted between anger (Why didn't I learn this before?), guilt (Why did we do this?), and understanding, which comes with new questions: What can I do to ensure this doesn't happen again? How do I help? For Indigenous students, some have indeed been angry and shown that anger to their non-Indigenous classmates. For many, the course material illustrates some difficult experiences within their own lives and the lives of their family and community. Some want a space where they can discuss in relative safety the impact of the last century on their lives. It is an emotional teaching terrain for all.

We accept that decolonization and reconciliation are long-term individual and state processes with stopping places along the way. We also recognize that, as instructors in a university course, all that we can do is point people toward the path of decolonization and reconciliation and provide them with a reason for choosing to follow it. We also want to dispel some students' fear of going down that path. We have to come to terms with the notion that the results of our efforts will not be known for many years, even as other concerns persist. Can we create an anticolonial classroom with 1600 students? Can we find a way to continue our Indigenous

Knowledge pedagogical approach with a set of students who take the course only to satisfy a university requirement? How will the language of decolonization, reconciliation, and resurgence sit with these students? Will students accept the anticolonial presentation of Indigenous peoples as real, live human beings with all of the foibles, goals, and aspirations that human beings have rather than the standard presentation of Indigenous peoples as problems or as people with problems or as Hollywood stereotypes? How will students react to the presentation of a Canada founded on Indian treaties or of a Canada composed of provinces, territories, and First Nations? Can we redefine the idea of the "Indian problem" that is at the centre of mainstream public policies concerning Indigenous peoples?

We do not overtly engage with or present Indigenous cultures within the classroom. We simply do things in a cultural way. We start each class with an opening and end with a closing, as is now standard in Indigenous societies. Occasionally, we'll start with a smudge and take the opportunity to teach about what it means. We use a Medicine Circle to explain Anishinaabe views of the person and social structure and the Seven Grandfather/Grandmother Teachings to discuss ethics. Our Four Directions analytic model for social phenomena is based upon the same iconic view.[34] We use the Haudenosaunee ideal of the Good Mind,[35] the condolence ceremony,[36] and the Thanksgiving Address[37] to explain Indigenous ontologies, education, and political theories. Indigenous culture becomes part and parcel of what we *do* rather than a separate aspect of human existence to be reified and separated from us. We want our students to do more than understand *that* Indigenous peoples do certain things; we want them to understand *why*.

A Vision Statement: Creating a Postcolonial Awareness

Our anticolonial pedagogy is a pedagogy of transformation. In a faculty meeting, one of our colleagues commented that this seemed to be a lofty goal that will be difficult to measure. Our response was to try to put the goal of transformation in strategic planning terms so that we might be able to think of measures that guide our actions and allow us to see whether or not we are making progress toward this objective. In this context, transformation is, itself, our vision statement. It compels us to find organizational strategies and classroom approaches that nurture the development of critical-thinking skills that will enable our students to make decolonizing links in other parts of their lives. This vision moves beyond learning a history and its effects: the aim of transformation extends to creating a capacity to recognize and acknowledge colonizing influences as they emerge and impact our students' families, homes, and workplaces long after they have left the university.

As scholars, we recognize that colonization is an ongoing process and that its impacts continue to be felt by Indigenous peoples throughout the world. Colonization, however, has not been without resistance—a resistance fueled by "postcolonial consciousness."[38] In more measurable terms, then, our mission is to be a catalyst in the development of a postcolonial consciousness: we want students to understand how colonization has affected and impacted Indigenous peoples, how colonization worked and continues to work, and how they have a responsibility in ending it and ensuring that it doesn't happen again.[39] Can we create this new consciousness in twelve weeks, with each week consisting of 150 minutes of lecture and 90 minutes of seminar? Can we move students around a kind of Medicine Circle, teaching from recognition to responsibility to reciprocity, culminating in a type of self-awareness that sees all of us as bound in relationship? Can our anticolonial approach help to create a postcolonial awareness?

What We Have Learned from Our Redesign, Pilot, and Delivery Project

> I'm very glad I got the opportunity to read *The Truth about Stories...*
> Realizing the truth about stories has caused me to reinterpret the
> stories I've been told, and in some instances understand the greater
> importance of those stories. Moving forward with my life and my
> studies, I'll interpret stories differently and be thankful for getting to
> hear them. After all, who knows, maybe I will live my life differently
> after hearing them.
> —INDG1001H/1002H student response

In this section, we present lessons that we learned from piloting our redesigned courses, and from continuing to deliver them in the years that have followed their inaugural semesters.

ANTICOLONIAL, NOT DECOLONIAL

Decolonial approaches place the colonizer at the centre; anticolonial approaches place Indigenous peoples at the centre. The difference is critical. We start from the Indigenous and move outward to the colonial. For example, we use the *Gayanasagowah* (the Great Law) as a way of analyzing the actions of Canadian leaders, the Medicine Circle as model for assessing the health of a community, and the Seven Grandfather/ Grandmother Teachings as an ethical frame for examining childcare policy developed by First Nations communities.

The anticolonial framing of the course is important. It creates an interpretative frame for the students and demonstrates that Indigenous peoples have intellectual histories and well-developed theories about the social and political. It also helps to improve students' receptivity to the material as they become intrigued with new theories and approaches that have applicability beyond the course. When Trent's introductory Indigenous studies course was optional, every student who enrolled in the course wanted to take it and was predisposed to learning the material. Many were aware of some aspects of the historical relationship between Canada and Indigenous peoples but were not aware of its impacts upon Indigenous lives today. Most did not see poverty as an outcome of colonization and its institutions but mostly as a result of the lack of individual Indigenous effort to improve their lives. All of the efforts undertaken by Indigenous leaders and communities to improve their lives over the last century and a half have been largely invisible to the students.

An anticolonial narrative centres Indigenous peoples, their lives, cultures, traditions, and actions, presenting them as peoples who are acting upon their own ideas, values, desires, and cultural traditions to create a society that reflects these. An anticolonial narrative therefore presents Indigenous peoples as peoples who interact with the larger social, economic, political, and cultural forces around them. Our anticolonial pedagogical goal is to interrupt the old narratives—of Indian as problem, Indian as helpless victim, and Indian as frozen cultural being—that have dominated public and academic perception and analysis of Indigenous people over the last century and a half.

Indigenous peoples are not solely presented through the frame of victim (although this is the case when state forces overwhelm), but also through a lens of complexity and multiple perspectives. Using our Four Directions analytic model, we organize, classify, and examine the forces that affect Indigenous people's lives. As the Medicine Circle—which is part of the model—is in constant movement, we are also able to examine the links between past, present, and future, as well as those between individual, clan, community, and nation.

A decolonial approach starts from the state and its structures, policies, and processes. It frames Indians as problems for state sovereignty, stability, and existence. Indigenous reaction to state action is labelled as resistance and insurgence. The state then moves to accommodate Indigenous peoples and their interests in order to assure its legitimacy. The state education system is used to reinforce its absolute sovereignty and frames its accommodative efforts as decolonization, at best. Unlike anticolonial pedagogies, however, decolonial pedagogies are based in anthropology, sociology, or political studies rather than Indigenous studies and Indigenous Knowledge.

BRAVE SPACES, NOT SAFE SPACES

> Looking back, it makes me think of Thomas King's book *The Truth about Stories*, and his overarching message that stories matter...And that's really what this class was, we didn't get told the history we got told stories, and those stories taught us so much.
> —INDG1001H/1002H student response

Students come to the course with expectations as to what they will encounter, how they will be treated, and what they will learn. In effect, they bring their backgrounds, fears, and dreams into the space and project them upon it. Indigenous pedagogical approaches ask us to start where the students are and where we are. And so we do. Students want to have a learning experience free from conflict and emotional entanglement. They want a safe-space experience.

As illustrated in the student response excerpts at the beginning of this chapter, students experienced the classroom differently. The first student felt that the classroom space was an Indigenous space constructed for Indigenous peoples, which caused him, a non-Indigenous person, to feel excluded and disrespected. His view of himself and Canada was challenged in ways he did not appreciate. The third student, who was Indigenous, was tired of learning and relearning history that she already knew. She found that the content depressed and angered her. The first student rejected the overall premise of the course and wanted an experience that reinforced his views. The third student, weary of having to sit through another learning experience for non-Indigenous students, wanted a more intellectually challenging experience. Both expressed intellectual and emotional reactions to the course material.

We acknowledged to all students that they would have emotional reactions to the material, and that it would challenge their ideas of Canada and their own positionality. We detailed for them some of the ways past students had reacted, including their emotions of guilt and anger. We stated that our purpose was not to make anyone feel guilty, as none of those in the room had acted as colonial agents for past state organizations. Further, we expressed that our concern was for the future and noted that learning the past was the best way of ensuring that it didn't happen again. We used a Medicine Circle to explain the process of learning and translating knowledge into action.

As instructors, we shared our own stories, backgrounds, and passions. We used the power of story to try to create a "brave space." We used the idea of brave space as opposed to safe space, since we could not guarantee the intellectual safety of our students. Robert Boost Rom argues that dialogue about social justice—and reconciliation is about social justice—cannot be fostered "by turning the classroom into a 'safe space' a place where teachers rule out conflict...We have to be brave because along the way we are to be 'vulnerable and exposed'; we are going to encounter images that are 'alienating and shocking' We are going to be very unsafe."[40] Bravery is, moreover, one of the Anishinaabe Seven Grandfather/ Grandmother Teachings.

The use of the brave-space paradigm was controversial among our seminar leaders. It required an acknowledgement of risk and conflict as well as emotionality. Brave spaces see differences as an opportunity for learning rather than for suppression. Teaching in brave spaces require a different set of teaching skills than are required in other spaces. To start, one needs personal bravery—a steadiness to handle classroom emotions and a willingness to tackle tough questions. A sense of humour is essential. One needs to be adept at preventing "ganging on," as can too easily happen in emotionally challenging situations.

TRANSFORMATION IS DIFFICULT AND LARGELY UNMEASURABLE

The learning outcomes listed in the INDG1001H course syllabus were:

1. To learn what happened and why. Students will understand the contours of the history of Indigenous-state relations in Canada and around the world.
2. To learn the effects and impacts of what happened. Students will understand the nature of the Long Assault/colonization and its impact upon Indigenous peoples in Canada.
3. To learn Indigenous goals and aspirations. Students will understand the concepts of Indigenous sovereignty, nationhood, self-determination, self-governance, treaty, and Indigenous modernity. Further, they will demonstrate an understanding of how these concepts are being advanced by Indigenous peoples in contemporary Canada.
4. To understand reconciliation and one's role within it. Students will use the findings and calls to action of the Truth and Reconciliation Commission to demonstrate an understanding of reconciliation and their role in achieving its goals.[41]

We can measure whether students achieved these outcomes through the usual assignments, projects, presentations, and exams. These can all be understood to fall under the broader goal of aiding in the transformation of student understanding of and setting the stage for future social-justice actions. This has been the goal of Indigenous Studies at Trent since its inception, with our pedagogies being broadly Freirean and anticolonial in their centring of Indigenous peoples' thinking and action since the Chanie Wenjack School was established.[42] Unlike the stated course outcomes, however, transformation is hard to measure and report on. How do we measure the transformation of students? How do know if we have helped to create a postcolonial consciousness?

The truth of the matter is that we must wait a generation. In time we will begin to see the outcome in our students' life work. Some proposed long-term measurement criteria include:

- Who runs for office and what kinds of legislation they enact
- Who starts a business and how do they root their vision and mission to a multigenerational understanding of our collective responsibility to people, planet, and profit
- The kinds of families that former students raise (e.g., Do they raise children who reject the binary pursuit of redressing inequity for the more substantive responsibility entailed in achieving equality rooted in community?

We can, however, begin to measure whether students are likely to achieve the transformation outcome today through the usual assignments, projects, presentations and exams. To measure transformation, we used reflective learning statements. These statements are a concrete expression of an Indigenous pedagogy; Elders teach us that we have to take the knowledge inside of us and be able to feel it within ourselves if we are to be able to say that we know it.

We asked students to reflect upon the material (readings, lectures, films, Elders, leaders, music) and to prepare a statement that described their learning in a summary fashion, expressing how their learning impacted them. Notwithstanding the issues surrounding a marked assignment, the statements were breathtaking in their honesty. Many students wrote more than the required 500 words, often writing two to three times as much as was required. Taken as a whole, the approximately 1600 statements show a remarkable consistency in changed attitudes towards Indigenous peoples and Canada. Many remarked that they never knew about colonization and its impact or about the efforts of Indigenous peoples to improve their relationship with Canada and to improve their own lives. Most walked away from the course with a newfound respect for Indigenous peoples.

Does it matter that the student assignments were submitted for grades? Yes and no. Some—a minority—knew what would give them an A on the assignment and gave it to us. The vast majority, however, were sincere about the impact of the course upon them. (They were also sincere in their criticism of the course, offering concrete suggestions for future improvements, such as expanding the international aspects of the course, grounding the course more in spirituality, and having fewer assignments). Yet we cannot ignore the power of writing to clarify one's thinking. Writing the words, *even if they are insincere*, has an impact that will be felt.

RESISTANCE MUST BE ANTICIPATED AND ADDRESSED DIRECTLY

We anticipated resistance to the new ICR despite the fact that it was advocated for and supported by the student members of the Trent Senate and was one of the key recommendations of the Special Committee on Indigenous Education. While the measure was unanimously adopted by Senate, the reality is that the ICR reduces student choice and imposes what some may feel is an undue burden on them to take a subject that they have little interest in. Accordingly, we framed the requirement in a variety of ways, trying to address the practical needs of students. Using the lens of twenty-first-century skills, we argued that many workplace organizations would be seeking individuals who had knowledge and skills that mirrored the four learning outcomes listed in the course syllabus. For those students with a more social-justice bent, we spoke of the creation of places of dignity and respect for Indigenous peoples within the Canadian federation. For those with a nationalist desire, we spoke of the need to correct one of the founding errors of Canada. We deliberately did not use a multicultural frame, as this approach to Indigenous inclusion had been rejected by Indigenous peoples themselves since the 1970s. We emphasized the unique constitutional status of Indigenous peoples as requiring a different and unique approach to public education.

OPENING AND CLOSING RITUALS PROVIDE INTRODUCTION TO INDIGENOUS SPIRITUALITY

Each class, we begin with an opening ritual grounded in Indigenous tradition and end with a ritual closing. We explain that this practice has been adopted by many Indigenous organizations, and frame the opening using the Haudenosaunee ideal of the Good Mind. The closing is framed as a covering of the council fire and a return to family and friends. We also use the Haudenosaunee Thanksgiving Address and an Anishinaabe thanksgiving song as well as traditional teachings available on the internet from respected Indigenous Elders. These afford opportunities for discussion of Indigenous spirituality and worldview.

We also create classroom traditions with our students. For example, in Haudenosaunee tradition, a single individual recites the Thanksgiving Address at the start of a meeting. In our class tradition, the students read the various stanzas of the address aloud, moving through individual students until the entire address has been recited. The recitation becomes a form of engagement: students have to speak the words into the classroom. It's a powerful exercise for students, as it demonstrates the power of orality and the spoken word. In our classes, it has helped to create a classroom that is a simultaneously brave, safe, and sacred space.

We also demonstrate a link to Western psychology, situating practice as a transition ritual that helps one to move from a space of busyness to one of attention and readiness to learn. The transition ritual allows the mind to move from attention in the busy world of students and their relationships to the world of listening and participating in a lecture or seminar. In this way we demonstrate an anticolonial approach by starting with the Indigenous and moving to the Western.

The closing of the class has taken many forms, but follows a standard format: a thanking of the students for their time and a wish for safe return to family and friends. In our closing, we always paraphrase and reimagine the words of Thomas King, quoted above: "Don't say in the years to come that you would have lived your life differently if only you had heard this story. You've heard it now."[43]

In order to help students understand the nature of Indigenous spirituality, we developed an exercise called, simply, the thanksgiving exercise. In it, students are asked to draw a circle and to list around the outside all of the people, animals, and objects that helped to get them to where there are today. Upon completion of the exercise, we ask students to report on what they saw in their circles, and how they felt while preparing them. After the report-back, students are asked to thank each of the individuals and items on their circle, in person if possible, and to report on the experience in the next seminar. We use this exercise to demonstrate the core ideas of gratitude and interconnectedness, and the manner in which these can be expressed in everyday action.

We perform a smudging ceremony to open one class in the semester, explaining the nature and purpose of the smudge, discussing Indigenous medicines and their uses, and inviting students to participate. Participation in all Indigenous ceremony is always voluntary. In our experience, about half of the students participate. We ground our pedagogical approach to the issue of tradition and spirituality in traditional Indigenous approaches, providing students with an opportunity to participate and engage, and then to reflect upon the experience. In this manner, their bodies, minds, emotions, and spirits are engaged in a process we call Four Directions learning. Again, we try to practice an anticolonial approach.

During our pilot, we attempted to have students take charge of the class openings after the first three weeks of class. This was less successful. Most expressed discomfort with the notion of participating in what was considered to be an Indigenous spiritual exercise and confused spirituality with religion. The discomfort allowed for a discussion about Indigenous spirituality to occur in seminars and led to an improved understanding of its nature and importance in contemporary Indigenous life.

By engaging in common Indigenous practices (the opening and closing rituals) and using simple class exercises, we bring the issue of Indigenous spirituality to the forefront and try to demonstrate that spirituality is a form of communication and respect, as well as a reminder of our relationships and responsibilities to each other and to all parts of the universe. We demonstrate though our actions the adaptability of Indigenous spiritual traditions to a modern environment.

INDIGENOUS PEDAGOGIES CAN HELP STUDENTS BECOME ENTHUSIASTIC READERS AND LEARNERS

Indigenous pedagogies place the responsibility for learning on the student: the role of the teacher is to create the conditions that enable the students to learn from each other and from the material presented. Accordingly, the presentation of course readings in seminars is the exclusive responsibility of the students. Although there is a stereotype that the contemporary student cohort does not read articles or books, our experience in this redesign and delivery project has been that this is not true. Students in our classes are also required to deliver a presentation during seminar. We frame the seminar presentations through the lens of traditional Indigenous values of responsibility and reciprocity, in which students are part of a community of learners and have responsibilities not just to themselves but to the other members of the community. Students have been given some knowledge by others, and seminar presentations function as acts of reciprocity—that is, opportunities to give back.

For those who do not know how to read critically, the peer dialogue that emerges in the presentation process models the principles and skills of critical thinking in ways that provide gentle instruction for those who needed a "how to" example. A by-product of requiring students to present to their peers is that it improves attendance and participation at the seminar. Students arrive on time and prepared because we emphasize the community-of-learners approach in which everyone has a responsibility to help others learn.

Making the students responsible for the presentation of readings each week also models responsibility and reciprocity. Again, we ground our explanations using Indigenous values, particularly those of the Seven Grandfather/Grandmother Teachings and a version of the Medicine Circle that stresses movement from acknowledgement to responsibility to relationship. In the presentation process, students are positioned as experts in the way that Elders position individuals in community ceremonies. Over time, the experience of being responsible creates cycles of responsibility and reciprocity that are self-perpetuating and decolonizing. In terms of peer connections, students engage because, when it is their turn to present, they understand the importance of having an unqualifiedly engaged audience.

We reinforce these ideas by asking students to prepare a statement of contribution that demonstrates five concrete ways in which they helped their seminar peers learn. Student responses tend to range from seminar presentations, to sharing notes, to establishing study groups, to conducting smudges, to providing peer support in times of stress. We explain that the statement of contribution is meant to demonstrate core Indigenous values of contribution, responsibility, reciprocity, and interrelatedness.

BIOGRAPHY PRESENTATIONS HELP CREATE A COMPLEX UNDERSTANDING AND LEARNING COMMUNITY

Between the 1970s and the 2000s, students at Trent used to call Indigenous Studies— which was formerly called Native Studies—"negative studies." Courses focused on the impact of colonization on Indigenous peoples, presenting an overwhelmingly negative story. Starting in the early 2000s, a cadre of Elders and traditional teachers began to add to the curriculum in important ways. Elders teach that communities and individuals develop through building upon their strengths rather than conducting a detailed analysis of and focusing on their weaknesses. Each individual has a contribution to make, even if that contribution may be contested by some.

In accordance with these teachings, we ask students in our courses to research and present a biography of an Indigenous person or group who made a noteworthy contribution to community. Selecting from an instructor-prepared list, students have an opportunity to investigate the strengths of Indigenous individuals and communities and to learn to see what an Elder might see. We do not tell the students what contribution was made, but leave it to them to undertake the research necessary to identify the contribution. The list includes prominent Indigenous community and political leaders, artists, writers, and educators such as Big Bear, Joseph Brant, Louis Riel, Matthew Coon Come, Thompson Highway, Pauline Johnson, and Buffy Saint Marie, as well as people like Anna Mae Aquash, Tina Fontaine, Colton Boushie, and Leonard Pelletier. In completing this assignment, students must grapple with the questions of who determines whether someone has made a contribution and, more fundamentally, what a contribution is. It is a complex issue. For example, Peter Jones, a local Anishinaabe leader, was also a Methodist minister. Joseph Brant, a Mohawk leader, is both revered and reviled within the Mohawk community. Buffy Saint Marie was adopted out of her community at a young age and reclaimed her culture in her twenties.

We hope that this project helps students begin to understand the complexity of the impact of colonization in the lives of the Indigenous peoples they choose to investigate. In fact, we ask them to identify the aspects of the Long Assault that affected the life of their chosen person, and what actions the person took to address these forces. We want the students to understand that the actions of Indigenous leaders occur in a particular social and political context, which the leader then grapples with. We also want students to grapple with the notion that something that is considered a positive contribution in the eyes of Indigenous peoples may not necessarily be seen as positive in the eyes of Canada and Canadian leaders. For example, the Colton Boushie case can be, at once, a powerful catalyst for Indigenous solidarity and the basis for a strong critique of the Canadian justice system, challenging existing structures of power and domination.

Our anticolonial approach, based in Indigenous Knowledge, focuses not on a search for one truth, but the creation of what we call a "complex understanding"— that is, a view that truths are contextual and based upon perspective. We do not attempt to reconcile differing views of truth, instead allowing a variety of contradictory views to exist simultaneously. This is somewhat unsettling for some students accustomed to the idea of a single truth that dominates all others.

In the inaugural year of the redesigned program, we asked students to work in groups on the biography assignment. They enjoyed the research and presentation parts of the assignment experience in ways that built community beyond the classroom. Those students whose presentation skills lacked sophistication were often stronger researchers than those who were comfortable making a presentation. The end result of the exchange was groups of students sharing skills with one another in line with the relationality quadrant of the Medicine Circle. When something unexpected occurred or the technology was uncooperative, an ethic of cooperation emerged among the students, who rallied to support one another.

MAKING INDIGENOUS CREATIVITY VISIBLE IS IMPORTANT

Each class in the redesigned courses follows a similar structure: opening, creativity, news, lecture, closing. The creativity section was developed and included as part of the course based on feedback given in the late 2000s to one of this chapter's authors who asked his third-year class to list the adjectives used to describe Indigenous peoples. *Creative, innovative,* and *resilient* were not among the list of mostly negative terms that emerged from this exercise. The creativity section of the redesigned program consists mostly of videos demonstrating the artistic creativity of Indigenous peoples. The videos range from professionally produced contemporary music and dance videos, to amateur videos of Indigenous youth performers, to videos explaining traditional teachings using animation and other nonconventional forms, to traditional teachers explaining aspects of Indigenous world view, to short videos produced by Indigenous youth.

The themes and issues of creativity and innovation are interwoven throughout the course, initially arising in discussions of the Long Assault. In this way, we demonstrate that Indigenous peoples have always been acting to create good lives for themselves, often in the face of horrendous assaults. We also use the creativity section to demonstrate Indigenous peoples' use of new forms of media and communication to resist colonization, to advance their own political agendas, to create and enhance community, and to both support and challenge identities.

We present creativity as an important foundational aspect of what we call "the Great Healing"—a period beginning in the 1970s and continuing into the present, which consists of an impressive array of activities that are intended to advance Indigenous self-determination and self-governance. Weaving the story of the Long Assault with the story of the Great Healing illustrates an Indigenous view of history as something that is not disconnected from but intertwined with the present, and influencing the future.

We ask students to send us examples of Indigenous creativity that we might use in this section of the course. In the first year of the redesigned course, it took almost half a term before students became comfortable seeking out and bringing forward examples that could be shared. Many had simply not previously seen creativity as an important aspect of Indigenous cultures and societies.

Our anticolonial approach again foregrounds Indigenous perspectives, theories, and actions, and is intended to demonstrate that Indigenous peoples are working to create new societies and communities based upon their own desires, goals, and ideas, rather than only reacting to their environment.

THE QUESTION OF TESTS AND EXAMINATIONS

In our pilot year, we ran one semester with sit-down tests and exams and one semester with no sit-down tests or examinations. The feedback was consistent and surprising. First-semester students felt the large-group sessions were better connected to the seminars. Attendance in the first-semester large-group lecture sessions was remarkably better with tests and exams as a fixture in the schedule.

In both semesters, every written submission was paired with a group or individual presentation, but students reported greater "rigour" in the semester with tests than the semester without. Ironically, the overwhelming majority of students reported that they disliked taking tests and believed that test results did not reflect what they had actually learned. We did not overtly link tests and exams to Indigenous teachings or values in either of the two classes.

Each test was a product of consensus among instructors and seminar/ workshop leaders. In the week before a test, faculty and seminar leaders developed the questions and then worked to arrive at a model answer for each question posed. When tests were graded, the model answers were divided up among the instructors and test scoring became a collaborative process. The outcome effect was two-fold: student and curriculum assessment were understood to be an ongoing responsibility in the day-to-day work of seminar leaders, and test reliability was improved. Using model answers that were the product of staff consensus enhanced the capacity of seminar leaders to compare and contrast student performance in essay writing and seminar presentations. More particularly, seminar leaders who had no previous training or experience as classroom teachers were themselves engaged in a professional dialogue regarding how their students internalize knowledge.

After examining our experience, we decided to frame testing in future iterations of our courses through an Indigenous lens: Young people are continually tested by Elders to determine if they have understood the teachings and can explain and act upon them in their daily lives. Becoming a self-aware and empowered learner is an extremely rigorous and challenging process that is undertaken with the guidance of others. The ability to demonstrate what one has learned to others is an important skill.

Going forward, tests will therefore be used to punctuate the learning process in ways that recognize the need for students to demonstrate their knowledge. We decided to have weekly quizzes, which help us to gauge student understandings, and a final exam. We ask students to demonstrate what they learned in the course and, in accordance with the final learning objective, to write what they will do with their new knowledge.

DECLARATIONS, TRIGGER WARNINGS, AND COLONIAL VIOLENCE

> Learning about my ancestors and trauma of my people is hard emotionally.
> —INDG1001H/1002H student response

During our pilot year, the First Peoples House of Learning experienced a surge in the number of students who requested support to address anxiety-related challenges arising from their participation in the course.[44] While this surge paralleled a rise in the number of students in the larger university community who requested support from other student services (as reported by Trent Student Affairs), its origins were different. In many cases, in their dialogues with the First Peoples House staff, it emerged that the chronology and facts of the history of colonization (and of its impact on Indigenous peoples) was either traumatizing or retraumatizing to students in the courses. In a series of dialogues among teaching staff about how to address these issues—informed by the concepts of safe spaces, brave spaces, and trigger warnings—we agreed that is was fair to provide a notice to students about the content that was to be covered. We considered adding a note to our future course syllabi: "This course contains depictions of colonial violence against Indigenous peoples. Some of the students in this course will have family and friends who may have been affected by this violence. First Peoples House staff are available to talk if you need assistance."

After the ritual opening and land acknowledgements at the beginning of each session, we shared a summary of the content for the day. This summary acknowledged that for some students the content would be upsetting. To this end, the declaration is as an act of respect and transparency. It also confirms that the business of the university is to be an oasis of free and open discourse that asks challenging questions and engages in discomforting dialogue. Decolonization starts with an acknowledgement and sharing of often uncomfortable truths that have in the past remained invisible or unsaid. The resulting seminar dialogue is often punctuated by comments such as "Wow, I didn't know that" and "How can this be true?" Time is needed to allow students to intellectually and emotionally process the knowledge.

OFFICE HOURS AND STUDENT ENGAGEMENT

The relationship between student and professor is often fraught with power and distance, which can inhibit learning. At the same time, we are not our students' friends and we suspect that they don't want us to be. However, we feel that it is important to foster a different learning environment for students who sees us as teachers in the traditional Indigenous sense: as guides and mentors who are willing to help and assist in the learning journey rather than just as sages on the stage, so to speak.

In 2018, the staff of INDG1001H and INDG1002H engaged in an office hours experiment. Seminar leaders offered office hours to students in traditional academic fashion: in their office on the third floor of the Enwayaang Building, which hosts the Chanie Wenjack School for Indigenous Studies. With rare exceptions, students asked questions at the end of seminars and did not avail themselves of the personal contact that comes with office hours.

At the same time, one of the faculty members conducted office hours next to the lecture hall three times a week, in the coffee shop and dining halls where students tended to congregate. Appointments were not required, and it didn't matter to whose seminar the student was assigned. Over the course of the semester, a steady and growing number of students used the common-area approach to office hours. In preparation for the end-of-term examination, a seminar/workshop exam-preparation session was offered, and thirty-eight students made the time on a Wednesday evening to attend. The students who attended came from two groups: students who regularly used common-area office hours and the friends of students who regularly used common-area office hours. In our experience, when the office-hour process was presented in an accessible public setting, students attended and encouraged others to do so, as well. It should come as no surprise that the students who used either office-hour process were more successful than those who did not. Ultimately, based upon our conversations with students, participating in office hours reduces student anxiety and raises student achievement in measurable ways.

We are making efforts to incorporate office hours at the end of the large-group lecture in the lecture hall or the public spaces connected to it. We hope this will more effectively communicate to students that, in our learning process, we put a high priority on the individual relationship of teachers and students. We hope, too, that this will reduce some of the stress and anxiety expressed by students about the course material. Holding office hours in public spaces and at times when the students are likely to be in the space models processes taught by Elders in the community.

GRADUATE TEACHING ASSISTANTS FUNCTION AS TEACHERS WORKING IN CLASSROOMS WITH STUDENTS

Each year, graduate teaching assistants (GTAs) are assigned to various courses in every school and department across the university. These individuals participate in every phase of the delivery of curriculum. They are the frontline workers in the university enterprise. They assist students in understanding what the professor is saying; answer questions about the syllabus and course material; clarify expectations about assignments; grade student presentations, assignments, and exams; lead small-group discussions; and support students who experience difficulty, intellectually and emotionally, with the class and its material. In most cases, graduate students bring little formal training or experience to the appointment. Even if they do have some kind of teaching experience, it is very rare for any to have had formal training that would prepare them for leading and teaching seminars in a multicultural classroom at the university level.

The situation is no different for GTAs who teach in our courses, except for the fact that, in the context of a foundation-year course that aspires to be a transformational decolonizing experience (such as our Indigenous studies courses), the challenges are particularly stark. GTAs assigned to the introductory Indigenous studies courses are students in the Indigenous studies PhD program or the MA program in Canadian studies and Indigenous studies. They often have excellent content knowledge, even though they have little teaching experience.

GTAs play a key role in the student experience of our courses. Experienced faculty have a responsibility to nurture and mentor them. In the last decade or so, university teaching and learning centres have also been created to fill the gap in teaching experience. Teacher training is provided on a voluntary basis. While some GTAs are enthusiastic participants, the service is challenged by the fact that GTAs are also students who are themselves expected to be high achievers in their course work and therefore have difficulty setting aside the time to complete this program.

The university teaching and learning centres play critical roles in training GTAs for Indigenous studies courses. Teaching Indigenous studies is challenging and requires more than an orientation to the course material. Graduate students need to receive training that ensures they understand the challenges of the classroom and how to navigate them. Training should cover topics such as how to deal with the emotional challenges of the course material as well as Indigenous-non-Indigenous relationships.

The delivery of large-volume foundations courses, such as our redesigned program, also brings with it the challenge of consistent course delivery. Such courses require lesson planning for both the large-group sessions and the seminars. To address this challenge, GTAs are fully briefed and have input into final lesson plans several weeks before the topics are delivered in class. A weekly briefing and debriefing session is held with GTAs and faculty to try to ensure a high degree of consistency in delivery and course messaging. As well, many GTAs for our course are initially unfamiliar with anticolonial pedagogy, the Medicine Circle, or the Four Directions analytical model. We therefore deliver training meant to allow them to feel comfortable in using these frameworks in the classroom.

The faculty need the time to build a GTA relationship that does not overwhelm the graduate students. Nurturing takes time, and high-volume, first-year foundations programs can be an impediment to meeting the responsibility that faculty has to take care of the GTAs. These graduate students are essential to the process and must be treated with the same consideration, deference, and respect as the students assigned to their classroom seminars.

THE QUESTION OF THE INDIGENEITY OF THE INSTRUCTOR AND GRADUATE TEACHING ASSISTANTS

> White folks should not be lecturing in this course. [The lecturer] said extremely offensive and factually incorrect things on several occasions in lecture. The overall whiteness of his perspective was in no way constructive. He centred whiteness always, which is entirely unnecessary in a course like this. His personal anecdotes were steeped in settler mentality, which only further marginalized Indigenous and racialized students. He is a complete disservice to them and they should be the ones centred in a space like this. Speaking about Indigenous people as if they aren't in the room is a painfully white thing to do.
> —INDG1001H/1002H student response

Students enter Indigenous Studies with expectations about the teaching staff. Some expect that they will be taught by Indigenous instructors; others expect that the space will be similar to the teaching spaces they have encountered in the past. We use an Anishinaabe term *Enwayaang*[45] to characterize our teaching space as one of consensual dialogue and discussion. We also use the term *Guswentah space*[46] and the Seven Grandfather/Grandmother Teachings to describe the ethics that govern dialogue.

At Trent over the last half century, the Chanie Wenjack School teaching staff has consisted of a majority of Indigenous faculty. The non-Indigenous faculty have significant experience within Indigenous communities and have developed considerable understanding of Indigenous Knowledge in addition to their academic credentials. The school is positioned as a site where Indigenous and non-Indigenous faculty and students can work and learn together. For more than a decade, we have used a co-instructor model for our first-year course—both before and after the redesign—in which one instructor is Indigenous, the other non-Indigenous. In the context of Guswentah space (which defines the relationship between Europeans and Indigenous peoples as one based on peace, friendship, and respect), these collaborative partnerships are essential to the process by which we work to create a consensual, transformational learning environment.

Our classrooms and our partnerships reflect our commitment to address the individualized needs of each student who enrolls in an Indigenous Studies foundations course. This is reflected in the comments of the students at the beginning of the chapter. Two of these students struggle with the challenges of internalizing a Medicine Circle curriculum model. Each has moved from recognition to responsibility; each is struggling with the daunting task of moving from internalized responsibility to becoming actively reciprocal. In the end they will have to navigate a path from reciprocity to relationality.[47] For this they will need other teachers and time in the company of Elders. In this space, our mission is to become catalysts for transformation. Self-awareness and relationality are achievements that will very likely take longer than a semester.

For decades, the Chanie Wenjack School faculty have taken great care in the presentation of our changing curriculum to ensure that Indigenous culture and knowledge are taught and/or presented by Indigenous peoples with the appropriate traditional Indigenous qualifications. We've learned to treat Indigenous Knowledge as a discipline within Indigenous Studies, with its own set of educated knowledge holders qualified to teach in the area.

We've learned that the Indigeneity of the instructor is critical for courses that deal explicitly with Indigenous culture and Indigenous Knowledge. Over time, we also pursued and nurtured professional partnerships between scholars. These collaborations match skill sets and life experiences in ways that complement each other as they serve to anticipate the individual needs of our students. As faculty in the Chanie Wenjack School, we recognize the limits of our knowledge, be it academic, traditional, or experiential knowledge. We work hard to ensure that the appropriate knowledge is present in our classrooms when required. On a very good day, our students are left with an unsettling, inconvenient, troubling, and potentially transformational question: Now that I know, what am I to do?

Changing the Stories We Live By

Transformational teaching is unsettling to the student, teacher, and institution. It requires careful attention to context, pedagogies, and instructional material. Based upon our years of teaching, we learned that transformational teaching challenges our very sense of self and other, and that this unsettles our world. As educators teaching about reconciliation, we need to stand with our students on this journey as they negotiate their own unsettledness.

At the end of the first year with a new curriculum, we began another new process: we moved from pilot to delivery of the ICR. We anticipate that most of our incoming students will not have closely examined the available range of courses and will not independently choose an elective credit that meets the requirement outside of INDG1001H or INDG1002H. As we have shown, this environment will create challenges for the Medicine Circle approach of fostering a transformational experience. The good news in this process is that our instinct is to continue with a decades-old commitment to small-group seminars of less than twenty students in partnership with lectures of less than 200. The deans and Provost/Vice President Academic have accepted this approach. While we will be sorting through the challenges of several sections of students and thirty-six separate seminar sections, we know our students have the support of a university community that understands the rationale for this large effort.

Our foundational approach is anticolonial in nature: it starts with Indigenous perspectives, ideas, theories, actions, and experiences, and proceeds from there. It also uses a story-telling approach, framing the course material through two intertwined stories: the Long Assault and the Great Healing. Students are asked to perform analyses based upon methods derived from the Medicine Circle, bringing Western theories to the Indigenous site rather than the other way around. Developing a postcolonial consciousness means learning to read the world through an Indigenous lens,[48] which is the fundamental anticolonial act.

Reconciliation and decolonization require bravery of the instructor and of the learner. If both are to be achieved, we have to learn to be uncomfortable together, to confront and discuss old truths while creating new ones. However, the ultimate act of bravery is to adopt an anticolonial intellectual stance and to trust that Indigenous teachings and knowledge will provide a solid foundation for being brave together. Creating a simply *safe* space only perpetuates the status quo.

We return to Thomas King, who quotes from Nigerian storyteller Ben Okri's 1997 book *A Way of Being Free*: "In a fractured age, when cynicism is god, here is a possible heresy; we live by stories, we also live in them. One way or another we are living the stories we planted—knowingly or unknowingly—in ourselves. We live stories that either give our lives meaning or negate it with meaninglessness. If we change the stories we live by, quite possibly we change our lives."[49] In the spirit of the Elders who provide us with the Medicine Circle teachings—the strategic directions, strategic objectives, and work plans that flow from the transformational vision of our Indigenous studies foundation programs—we are engaged in a process of shared responsibility that has the potential to change lives, one person at a time, from the inside out. This can be unpredictable; it is often messy, but never dull.

The measure of our work is best understood in the words of our students, which serve to remind us that this work matters. As one student said, "Prior to this course, my judgments regarding Indigenous peoples paralleled the results of Canadian polls. I felt as if it was enough to be a bystander. I thought my actions, or lack thereof was an illustration of support. Through this course I have learned that it is never enough to be passive, we need to actively participate in the process in order to aid in the reimagination of Aboriginal peoples."

NOTES

1. Regan, *Unsettling the Settler*.
2. Manuel and Derrickson, *Unsettling Canada*.
3. Unless otherwise indicated, all student response excerpts in this chapter were collected in writing at the end of the 2017–2018 winter term. The excerpts are responses to a pilot of redesigned Indigenous studies introductory courses INDG1001H and INDG1002H taught by the authors at Trent University.
4. Sinclair, interview by Peter Mansbridge, *The National*.
5. *Truth and Reconciliation Commission of Canada: Calls to Action*, hereafter cited as TRC calls. See also Truth and Reconciliation Commission of Canada, *Final Report*.
6. Samson, "Indigenization."
7. Gaudry and Lorenz, "Indigenization as Inclusion," 218.
8. Trent University, *Vision and Mission*, Vision sec., pt. 4.
9. Newhouse, "Indigenous Peoples, Canada," 3–4.
10. See TRC calls 6–12, 62–65. See also Royal Commission on Aboriginal Peoples, *Restructuring the Relationship*.
11. Vizenor, *Survivance*.
12. Trudeau, *Statement by the Prime Minister*.
13. Newhouse, "Indigenous People, Canada." The Long Assault is the period in Canadian history stretching from the 1857 passage of the Gradual Civilization Act to the 1971 withdrawal of the Statement of Indian Policy of the Government of Canada (also known as the White Paper). This period is characterized by a series of outright attempts to eradicate and assimilate Indigenous people into Canada. It's a way of describing colonization and its impact to Canadian audiences without stopping the conversation, which the use of the word *colonization* does.
14. Calder et al. v. Attorney-General of British Columbia, [1973] S.C.R. 313.
15. Archibald et al., *Accord on Indigenous Education*; Universities Canada, *Principles*.
16. Barnard, *University of Manitoba Statement of Apology*; Ono, *Statement of Apology*.
17. Canadian Association of University Teachers, "Indigenizing the Academy."
18. In May 2017, the Department of Indigenous Studies was dissolved and the Chanie Wenjack School for Indigenous Studies was created. It houses Trent's Indigenous studies programs, the First Peoples House of Learning, the Boodweh Centre for Indigenous Knowledge and Languages,

the Centre for Indigenous Environmental Studies and Science, and the Enweying Institute for Professional and Community Learning.

19. Trent University, "Vision and Mission," Vision sec., pt. 4.

20. Trent University, *Preparing Students.* For information on the 2014 presidential task force report, see pp. 22–23, 29–31.

21. At Trent, term courses (12 weeks) are identified as 0.5 credit, full year courses (24 weeks) are identified as 1.0 credit.

22. Trent University, "Indigenous Course Requirement."

23. Trent University, *Preparing Students.*

24. The Medicine Circle can be used to describe human existence as being comprised of four elements: physical, mental, emotional, and spiritual. These are in constant motion, moving from past to present to future. Each element is arranged in the Circle in one of the four cardinal directions.

25. The Seven Grandfather/Grandmother Teachings are the foundational ethical values as taught by Anishinaabe Elders. They are love, respect, wisdom, honesty, truth, humility, and bravery.

26. Newhouse, "The Meaning of Indigenization."

27. Gaudry and Lorenz, "Indigenization as Inclusion."

28. Newhouse, "The Meaning of Indigenization."

29. Trent Indigenous Studies, "Vision Statement" (unpublished document, 2011), Trent Indigenous Studies archives.

30. Trent Indigenous Studies, "Vision Statement."

31. We use the term *Medicine Circle* instead of *Medicine Wheel* as the Elders who advise us argue that there were no wheels on this continent prior to the arrival of Columbus, and hence the the term *wheel* would be a misnomer and inaccurate. They report that the Medicine Circle is a pre-Columbian phenomenon. Some prefer the term *teaching circle.*

32. Figures are based on class discussions and student self-reporting.

33. King, *Truth about Stories,* 29.

34. The Four Directions Analytic model is based on the Medicine Circle's four cardinal directions. We ask students to use our Four Directions model to analyze and structure social phenomenon. Western theories can be used to analyze aspects of the phenomenon within an Indigenous frame.

35. The Good Mind is a Haudenosaunee theory of mind. It postulates that the human mind consists of both reason and passion, that both are essential to human existence, and that a person with a good mind desires and constantly engages in action designed to improve peace among all forms of life. The qualities of a Good Mind are fostered by a sense of interconnected, as described in the Thanksgiving Address.

36. The condolence ceremony is a ritual developed by the Peacemaker, the founder of the Haudenosaunee Confederacy, and designed to restore the Good Mind. It wipes tears from the eyes and opens the ears and throat so that one may again think and feel clearly and act for the benefit of all.

37. The Thanksgiving Address, commonly known as the Opening address, is a recitation spoken at the beginning of important events in Haudenosaunee communities. The address reminds those gathering of the interconnectedness and interdependence of all living things and gives thanks for all that is part of the world that we live in. It reminds human beings of the web of relationships that are part of our lives. The address binds us together as a community and helps us to act with kindness and respect. The Peacemaker, the founder of the Confederacy, asked the Chiefs to recite it at the start of council meetings.

38. Newhouse, "Indigenous Peoples, Canada," 12–13.

39. Newhouse, "From the Tribal."

40. Boom Rom, "Safe Spaces," 407.
41. Newhouse and Quantick, INDG1001H course syllabus, 2018.
42. Newhouse, McCaskill, and Milloy, "Native Studies at Trent."
43. King, *Truth about Stories*, 29.
44. The First Peoples House of Learning in the Chanie Wenjack School for Indigenous Studies provides academic and personal support for Indigenous students enrolled at Trent University. In addition, it provides support for all students enrolled in Indigenous Studies courses. Over the course of the pilot year, we met regularly with the counselling staff of the First Peoples House to receive feedback from them on student reaction to the course.
45. Enwayaang is translated to English from Nishinaabemowin as "how we speak together." It is also the name of the building that houses the Wenjack School and Peter Gzowski College.
46. Guswentah, commonly referred to as the Two-Row Wampum, sets out the principles that define the historic relationship between Haudenosaunee and Europeans. Made of wampum beads, it consists of two parallel purple rows separated by three rows of white beads. The term *Guswentah space* refers to the three-row-wide white space between the two purple rows of the Guswentah. The white rows have varying meanings. We interpret them as peace, friendship, and respect.
47. Wilson, *Research Is Ceremony*, 99.
48. Newhouse, "On Reading Basso."
49. Ben Okri, quoted in King, *Truth about Stories*, 153.

BIBLIOGRAPHY

Archibald, Jo-ann, John Lundy, Cecilia Reynolds, and Lorna Williams. *Accord on Indigenous Education*. Delta: Association of Canadian Deans of Education, 2010. https://csse-scee.ca/acde/wp-content/uploads/sites/7/2017/08/Accord-on-Indigenous-Education.pdf.

Barnard, David T. *University of Manitoba Statement of Apology and Reconciliation to Indian Residential School Survivors*. University of Manitoba, October 27, 2011. https://umanitoba.ca/about/media/StatementOfApology.pdf.

Boost Rom, Robert. "'Safe Spaces': Reflections on an Educational Metaphor." *Journal of Curriculum Studies* 30, no. 4 (1998): 397–408.

Canadian Association of University Teachers. "Indigenizing the Academy." CAUT Policy Statement, approved November 2016. https://www.caut.ca/about-us/caut-policy/lists/caut-policy-statements/indigenizing-the-academy.

Gaudry, Adam, and Danielle Lorenz. "Indigenization as Inclusion, Reconciliation, and Decolonization: Navigating the Different Visions for Indigenizing the Canadian Academy." *Alternative* 14, no. 3 (2018): 218–27.

King, Thomas. *The Truth about Stories: A Native Narrative*. Toronto: House of Anansi Press, 2003.

Manuel, Arthur, and Ronald M. Derrickson. *Unsettling Canada. A National Wake-Up Call*. Toronto: Between the Lines, 2015.

Newhouse, David. "From the Tribal to the Modern: The Development of Modern Aboriginal Society." In *Expressions in Canadian Native Studies*, edited by Ron F. Laliberte, Priscilla Settee, James B. Waldram, Rob Inness, Brenda Macdougall, Lesley McBain, and F. Laurie Barron, 395–405. Saskatoon: University of Saskatchewan Extension Press, 2000.

———. "Indigenous Peoples, Canada and the Possibility of Reconciliation." *Institute for Research on Public Policy Insight* 11 (2016). https://on-irpp.org/3uvuyNJ.

———. "The Meaning of Indigenization in Our Universities." *CAUT Bulletin* 63, no.6 (June 2016). https://bulletin-archives.caut.ca/bulletin/articles/2016/06/the-meaning-of-indigenization-in-our-universities.

———. "On Reading Basso: Towards an Indigenous Theory of Reading." In *Indigenous Poetics*, edited by Neal McLeod, 73–81. Waterloo: Wilfrid Laurier University Press, 2014.

Newhouse, David, Don McCaskill, and John Milloy. "Native Studies at Trent." In *Native American Studies in Higher Education Models for Collaboration between Universities and Indigenous Nations*, edited by Dwayne Champagne and Jay Stauss, 61–81. Lanham: Altamira Press, 2002.

Ono, Santa J. *Statement of Apology.* University of British Columbia, Office of the President. Delivered April 9, 2018. https://president.ubc.ca/homepage-feature/2018/04/09/statement-of-apology/.

Regan, Paulette. *Unsettling the Settler Within: Indian Residential Schools, Truth Telling and Reconciliation in Canada.* Toronto: University of Toronto Press, 2010.

Royal Commission on Aboriginal Peoples. *Restructuring the Realtionship.* Vol. 2 of *Report of the Royal Commission on Aboriginal Peoples.* Ottawa: The Commission, 1996.

Samson, Natalie. 2019. "Indigenization Efforts Vary Widely on Canadian Campuses, Study Finds." *University Affairs*, April 16, 2019. https://www.universityaffairs.ca/news/news-article/indigenization-efforts-vary-widely-on-canadian-campuses-study-finds/.

Sinclair, Murray. Interview by Peter Mansbridge. *The National*, CBC, May 31, 2015. https://www.cbc.ca/news/politics/truth-and-reconciliation-chair-urges-canada-to-adopt-un-declaration-on-indigenous-peoples-1.3096225.

Trent University. "Indigenous Course Requirement." https://www.trentu.ca/vpacademic/committees-policies/undergraduate-studies-committee/indigenous-course-requirement.

———. *Preparing Students for a 21st Century Canada: Report of the Special Senate Committee on Indigenous Education.* Trent University Senate, March 7, 2017. https://www.trentu.ca/vpacademic/initiatives/special-committee-indigenous-education-report.

———. "Vision and Mission." Trent University, 2011. www.trentu.ca/about/vision-mission.

Trudeau, Justin. *Statement by the Prime Minister of Canada on Release of the Final Report of the Truth and Reconciliation Commission.* PMO office. Delivered December 15, 2015. https://pm.gc.ca/eng/news/2015/12/15/statement-prime-minister-release-final-report-truth-and-reconciliation-commission.

Truth and Reconciliation Commission of Canada. *The Final Report of the Truth and Reconciliation Commission of Canada.* 6 vols. Montreal: McGill-Queen's University Press, 2015.

———. *Truth and Reconciliation Commission of Canada: Calls to Action.* Winnipeg: National Centre for Truth and Reconciliation, 2015. https://ehprnh2mwo3.exactdn.com/wp-content/uploads/2021/01/Calls_to_Action_English2.pdf.

Universities Canada. *Universities Canada Principles on Indigenous Education.* Posted June 29, 2015. https://www.univcan.ca/media-room/media-releases/universities-canada-principles-on-indigenous-education/.

Vizenor, Gerald. *Survivance: Narratives of Native Presence.* Lincoln: University of Nebraska Press, 2008.

Wilson, Shawn. *Research Is Ceremony: Indigenous Research Methods.* Halifax: Fernwood Publishing, 2009.

14

**JEANNIE KERR AND
AMY PARENT**

Contemporary Colonialism and Reconciliation in Higher Education

A Decolonial Response Through Relationality

IN THIS CHAPTER, WE TROUBLE THE notion that postsecondary institutions are currently able to address the 2015 Truth and Reconciliation Commission of Canada's (TRC) calls to action for reconciliation in education,[1] and offer what we see as pedagogical opportunities for instructors in higher education to gesture towards decolonial possibilities. This co-authored chapter emerges from our time collaboratively teaching mandatory Indigenous education courses in a postsecondary institution in British Columbia, and our ongoing work engaging the complexity of addressing this context in our teaching and theorizing.

Drawing on Indigenous, decolonial, and settler-colonial scholarship, we illustrate particular ways that the contemporary colonial context is obscured in Canadian society and higher education, and outline how we trouble this in our work as instructors. Considering colonialism as a fundamentally relational problem that is laden with inequalities, we foreground relational priorities in our work as instructors to trouble the colonial logics that continue to structure higher education. We also centre relational priorities in recognition of Indigenous sovereignty and teachings in the places we live and teach. We understand that our collaborative practices involve

281

providing pedagogical opportunities wherein we strategically engage with our positionalities as Indigenous and Settler instructors. In doing so, we draw attention to relational priorities across difference and provide opportunities to unlearn colonial logics of relation for our students and ourselves.[2] In this chapter, we share four relational commitments in our educational work: embodied decolonial relations, relation as a storying of land and Indigenous territory, ethical relationality as an educational practice, and interrelatedness as the foundation of whole human being. As we do this work with humility, we are not seeking to find and argue for the answer to the decolonization of higher education. We are mindful of our complicities in a neoliberal university, and instead aim to share our pedagogical practices based in relationality in order to strategically gesture towards decolonial futures and Indigenous sovereignty in the midst of the complexity of a colonial present.

Introductions

NOX̱S TS'AAWIT, AMY PARENT

My name is Amy Parent, and I begin by raising my hands high to show my deep appreciation to the Musqueam, Squamish, and Tsleil-Waututh Nations for providing me with a place to live, study, and teach. Following an insightful conversation with scholar Kaui Kellipio, I acknowledge that I am an "uninvited guest" on their traditional, ancestral, unceded, and overlapping territories. My Nisga'a name is Nox̱s Ts'aawit (Mother of the Raven Warrior Chief). This name connects me to my mother and signifies the importance of the matrilineal culture that flows through my bloodlines. My mother's side of the family is Nisga'a from the House of Ni'isjoohl and we belong to the Ganada (frog) Clan. Two of my grandparents were residential school survivors. My grandmother also spent a significant portion of her childhood with her mother, my great-grandmother, in the Miller Bay Indian Hospital due to tuberculosis. My great-grandmother ultimately passed away from the disease when my grandmother was fourteen years old. On my father's side, I am French Canadian and German. I recognize that my European ancestors were implicated in two distinct genocides in recent memory: the Holocaust and the Indian residential school (IRS) system. I am a mother, a researcher, and an educator. I am an associate professor of education at Simon Fraser University, and an assistant professor of education in the Department of Educational Studies at the University of British Columbia.

JEANNIE KERR

My name is Jeannie Kerr and I am a Settler-scholar-teacher who is grateful to be thinking, writing, and teaching on the traditional territories of the Anishinaabeg, Nêhiyawak, Dakota, Oji-Cree, and Dene peoples, and on the homeland of the Métis nation. I greatly appreciate the welcoming I have received in Treaty I territory through my role as an associate professor at the University of Winnipeg. On my mother's side, I am from the Couch family of Cork County, Ireland. On my father's side, I am from the Kerr Clan from the Scottish borderlands, and more recently Glasgow. I am the first of my family to be born in what is now known as Canada. My parents immigrated here with my older sister with no understanding of Indigenous perspectives and governance. Following Paulette Reagan, I identify as a Settler in Canada,[3] not as a way to stake a claim to land, but as a way to acknowledge my and my ancestors' participation in problematic and ongoing colonial ways of relating and my ongoing complicity in settler colonialism. I am currently learning about the spirit and intent of the treaties and my responsibilities in Treaty 1 territory.

Troubling Reconciliation Work in Higher Education in Canada

In September of 2009, Stephen Harper, then Prime Minister of Canada, addressed a news conference at the end of a G20 Summit in Pittsburgh. He touted Canada's 150 years of trouble-free parliamentary democracy and added, "We also have no history of colonialism. So we have all of the things that many people admire about the great powers but none of the things that threaten or bother them."[4] That a prime minister of Canada could confidently share these words in the media less than a year after providing a formal apology in Parliament to the survivors of Canada's IRS system is stupefying. On the one hand, it's difficult, if not impossible, to even make sense of a ceremonial, public apology regarding a paradigmatic example of Canada's colonial violence that is followed in short order by a proud claim, to an international audience, that Canada has no history of colonialism at all. It is difficult, too, to understand why the "great powers" would be, ironically, *threatened* by histories of colonialism. On the other hand, Harper's comments are less shocking and less nonsensical when seen as part of the ongoing work to obscure the reality of Canada as a settler-colonial nation-state that is historically bothered and threatened by the presence of Indigenous Peoples—a narrative used to justify colonial violences. Following the important work of scholars Taiaiake Alfred, Glen Coulthard, Eva Mackey, Pam Palmater, and Leanne Betasamosake Simpson, we recognize the ongoing settler-colonial project in Canada and the Indigenous resurgence that has been a prominent response.[5] We have also learned from Michael Marker and Leanne Betasamosake Simpson that educational institutions are powerful actors in erasing and obscuring colonial realities in support of settler-colonial futurity.[6]

In our experience, since the publication of the TRC's formidable work and calls to action,[7] there has been widespread interest in and commitment to the difficult work of reconciliation. We hold our hands high to the work of the TRC and the survivors of the IRS system, as well as to all Indigenous Peoples who are subjected to colonial violences. Within our current, respective university contexts, we have seen institutional efforts to begin addressing the TRC's calls to action. While these directions can be seen as promising, we see little if any recognition of the contemporary colonial encounters that continue to obstruct the work of reconciliation. Settler-Indigenous encounters—whether in the courts, in child and family services, in hospitals, in educational institutions, or any other context authorized by colonial structures—are still marked by both subtle and overt violences. These colonial violences are directly related to colonial practices such as erroneous legislation that provides settler-colonial governments with self-appointed authority to act on Indigenous territory.[8] They are also related to assumptions about the nature of land ownership,[9] the superiority and benevolence of settler systems and Settler actors,[10] and the universalizability of Euro-Western knowledge.[11] These collective understandings of the colonial present in Canadian society provide a troubling context for the work of reconciliation. How is reconciliation possible when institutions fail to recognize that we are in a colonial society and, in some cases, deny that we ever have been so? The idea of reconciliation has also been aptly critiqued by numerous Indigenous scholars, activists, and allies, in particular Arthur Manuel and Grand Chief Ronald Derrickson, for being steeped in liberal values that uphold the legitimacy of the Canadian nation-state.[12] We raise our hands high in appreciation for Stó:lō scholar, writer, and activist Lee Maracle, whose response to the question "What is reconciliation?" was: "Well, stop killing us would be a good place to begin… Then maybe stop plundering our resources, stop robbing us of our children, end colonial domination—return our lands, and then we can talk about being friends."[13] Maracle's poignant response reminds us of the depth of the colonial logics obscuring the violence of the colonial present in Canadian society, and of the requirement to trouble these logics through truth-telling about ongoing colonial violence. This is a first step toward decolonial possibilities in and beyond higher education.

Bringing to Light Settler Colonialism and Coloniality/Modernity

The conceptions of contemporary colonialism in both settler-colonial nation-states and world politics are growing areas of scholarship that are troubling the notion that we could possibly be in postcolonial times or that settler-colonial societies have ever been free of colonialism. In our own work in higher education, we engage with two areas of scholarship that help us trouble colonial logics: decolonial scholarship and settler-colonial studies. Each are grounded in the premise that fifteenth-century European colonialism not only is a historical event, but also has served to create a pervasive contemporary structural phenomenon, which decolonial scholars refer to as coloniality/modernity.[14] In other words, fifteenth-century European colonialism is more than a violent system of labour and capital that has ended. As Ramón Grosfoguel argues, it is a historical event of the late 1400s that created *coloniality*.[15] In Grosfoguel's scholarship, coloniality is revealed to be a complex world system that was established through the embodied arrival of "European, capitalist, military, Christian, patriarchal, white, heterosexual, male" human beings who self-proclaimed the land as the *Americas*, and thus "established in time and space several entangled global hierarchies."[16] Decolonial scholars such as Walter Mignolo and Aníbal Quijano—originators of the coloniality/modernity concept—point out that self-constructed notions of Western exceptionalism and Western civilization as the "arrival point of human history" are key features of modernity, and are made possible by and through the structural violence of coloniality.[17] Coloniality is thus the darker, hidden structure that is entangled in the promises of modernity, constituted by material, spatial, and epistemic inequality and violence for Indigenous and non-Western Others (human and more-than-human). In this theorization, modernity is only possible through the structural violence of coloniality.

As we look to higher education and the context of our own work, we are cognizant of the Canadian settler-colonial context. The constructed narratives of modernity continue to be upheld and formed within institutions of higher education in Canada. Simpson acknowledges that there have been some decolonizing in-roads in the academy, but there has been far less success in dismantling oppressive systems. She argues, "While there are sites of decolonization within academic institutions, they still remain a colonizing force upholding the values of heteropatriarchy, settler colonialism and capitalism."[18] We are also informed by a project by Vanessa de Oliveira Andreotti and colleagues that maps orientations to decolonization in higher education as a pedagogical exercise to reveal the ways responses in higher education to the violences of coloniality/modernity are filled with tensions and contradictions.[19] In particular, the authors of this study recognize the dominance of Euro-Western knowledge and the contradictory ways it is naturalized and challenged within different decolonizing approaches. They conclude that anything we do within the university takes place through the structures and grammars of modernity, placing us within the systems we critique. As we look at lessons of the past and imagine something different, they advise us also to avoid the colonial ontology that seeks a single story based in linear "notions of progress and betterment."[20] In our work, we inhabit our places within our universities with great humility, understanding that we are complicit in the systems we seek to change. We see the university as an institution immersed in capitalism and colonial structures. Still, when we engage this institution strategically and with awareness and humility for the ways we can be co-opted into its projects, it has the potential to be useful. As such, we are not seeking to find the best way to approach reconciliation. Instead, we wish to be responsive, collaborative, and aware of the contradictions and complicities, and to attend to the ways our institutions are obscuring the colonial present through colonial logics. We seek to engage in truth-telling to trouble colonial logics within our roles as instructors by openly acknowledging the colonial framing that surrounds contemporary encounters between Indigenous and Settler peoples. We seek to gesture towards something different. We recognize that within our future there are many uncertainties and possibilities in our work, but we remain committed to upholding self-determination and sovereignty for Indigenous Peoples in any of our efforts.

In our view, following Dolores Calderon, the work begins in our classrooms: we must reveal settler-colonial grammars that naturalize colonialism by obscuring the colonial present and its violences.[21] In the Canadian context, we are guided by the work of Indigenous scholars that draw out the Canadian narratives that form located settler-colonial grammars. Dwayne Donald argues that there are deeply learned habits arising from the colonial experience in Canada, which reinforce a notion that Indigenous Peoples and Settler Canadians inhabit separate realities. Donald analyzes the fort as a mythic symbol in the Canadian frontier imaginary that signifies the teleological dream of *civilization* and positions Indigenous Peoples as "outside accepted versions of nation and nationality."[22] The narratives of civilization, progress, and separate realities continue to configure relations through colonial logics.

We also appreciate the work of Verna St. Denis, who draws out the colonial nature of the narratives of multiculturalism in Canada. These narratives, she argues, work to distract us from recognizing and redressing Indigenous rights, which are constituted by the sovereign status of Indigenous Peoples.[23] St. Denis argues that, by centring dominant narratives that situate Indigenous Peoples as one more cultural group in the multicultural Canadian mix, Indigenous demands for Nation-to-Nation sovereignty are completely misunderstood and seem to offer undeserved benefits to Indigenous Peoples. St. Denis points out that multicultural policy erroneously equates Indigenous Peoples with cultural minority groups, ignores their sovereign status, and thus assumes "the legitimacy of the current colonial government."[24] Further, this policy serves to reaffirm the benevolent and innocent Settler-controlled nation-state as purveyor of human rights, thus ignoring the violence of land dispossession within settler colonialism. In sum, multicultural policy and narratives reproduce the colonial relationship through denying Indigenous sovereignty and rights, and by naturalizing the violence of colonialism.

Collaborative Pedagogies Focused on Relationality

We are grateful for our collaborative work together. This work first emerged when we were fortunate enough to be taught by, and work as teaching assistants for, Dr. Jo-ann Archibald (Q'um Q'um Xiiem). One of the significant teachings that Dr. Archibald gave us in our time with her was the centrality of relationality within Indigenous ontologies. We have continued to appreciate the diverse work of Indigenous scholars such as Vine Deloria Jr., Leanne Betasamosake Simpson, and Richard Atleo, whose works engage in the complexity of articulating the ways Indigenous ontologies are specific to place, yet who all commonly understand Mother Earth to be a dynamic, sacred being constituted by ethics and relationality.[25] In our view, efforts in post-secondary that seek to unlearn colonial logics need to meaningfully engage with Indigenous perspectives, knowledges, and ontologies if they are to disrupt the Eurocentrism that is dominant in postsecondary education.

A relational focus is key to troubling colonial dominance. As we discuss elsewhere, our courses engage with knowledge that is often difficult for our students to apprehend.[26] We feel that a relational focus supports our students' engagement while lessening some of the common resistances that emerge. We also believe that a relational focus challenges the erroneous teaching within settler-colonial society that Indigenous and Settler peoples are inherently separate and unrelated, and puts this belief into practice. Since our time as teaching assistants in Dr. Archibald's class, we have taught postsecondary courses together in British Columbia and continue to work together in research and publishing endeavours with a focus on relations. In line with that priority, in all of our co-authored texts, we place our names in alphabetical order without designating a first or second author. We often learn and explore ideas with a familiar friend, Txeemsim (the trickster character in Nisga'a culture). Through collaborative co-teaching and designing Indigenous course requirements in teacher education (based in relationality), our work engages the following commitments: embodied decolonial relations, relation as a storying of land and Indigenous territory, ethical relationality as an educational practice, and interrelatedness as the foundation of whole human being.

COMMITMENT TO EMBODIED DECOLONIAL RELATIONS

Settler-colonial and decolonial scholarship highlights that the experiences of Indigenous and Settler peoples have been drastically different and marked by violence to Indigenous Peoples. As Donald argues, however, these experiences are related and interreferential.[27] We recognize that the work of reconciliation requires unlearning colonial logics that deny relations, and then learning how to engage in respectful dialogue and approaches that will not exacerbate the problematic ways of engaging that have been forming for hundreds of years. We appreciate the pedagogical possibilities that emerge from embodying our differing subjectivities related to Settler and Indigenous positionalities—for instance, implementing different speaking patterns in class and engaging in questions about who designs and responds to which specific topics.

In terms of speaking patterns, we do not interrupt or interject when the other is speaking. We ask thoughtful questions when the other is finished speaking to obtain more clarity on points that we know students tend to struggle with. We invite each other to share ideas. For example, when Amy engages students with Indigenous ontologies that disrupt assumptions based in Western scientific materialism, we anticipate that some students will question the legitimacy of these Indigenous approaches. In anticipation, Amy invites Jeannie to share her thoughts. Jeannie will ask questions that acknowledge the difference, but engage with Amy, asking what she has understood from approaching learning in that way. We hope to demonstrate respectful ways that non-Indigenous peoples can engage Indigenous perspectives to learn and expand instead of reentrenching dominant perspectives. We try to demonstrate that we are not debating which perspective is right; rather, we are exploring how different perspectives, experiences, and affiliations lead to different ways of seeing and understanding ourselves and phenomena. We try to show that we need to take time to understand each other through asking questions of each other rather than responding with a counter-perspective.

By living respectful relations in the classroom, we can draw out topics that reveal the current nature and problematics of settler colonialism and strategically take the lead in different areas. Jeannie, for example, leads experiences in which Settler narratives around multiculturalism, whiteness, and racism are deconstructed. She draws on Verna St. Denis's critique of multicultural narratives and on the analysis, by R. Patrick Solomon and colleagues, of white teacher candidates' discourses of denial around racism and white privilege.[28] Jeannie understands that engaging with student resistance in these experiences is a form of allied work. Elsewhere, we have written in detail about our understanding, influenced by Richard Atleo, of this type of resistance as a condition of being out of balance or harmony.[29]

Amy, speaking from her own community experience, research, and encounters with Txeemsim, leads experiences in which Indigenous perspectives and knowledges are engaged. Influenced by Donald's articulation of colonial frontier logics,[30] we disrupt the notion that Indigenous and Settler peoples have separate realities by detailing our unique positionalities and highlighting how we embody a shared reality. Through this pedagogical relationship, we have the opportunity to demonstrate ways that respectful Indigenous-Settler relations can be enacted—especially when having difficult conversations concerning settler-colonial violence. We also attempt to reflect Indigenous priorities in the oral tradition through sharing carefully chosen personal experience stories that draw attention to our own mistakes and vulnerabilities, and that show reverence to our human and more-than-human teachers. We have found that showing our own fallibilities—those that emerge from our complex Indigenous and Settler positionalities as well as from our limitations as humans—can support prospective educators in overcoming the common fears of engaging Indigeneity in the classroom. We are thankful for the humorous, challenging, and complex moments in which Txeemsim, Moose, Mouse, Deer, Gaahl (shrew), and friends help us to learn from our students and colleagues as we endeavour to create balanced, ethical relationships in our practice.

COMMITMENT TO STORYING A RELATION TO LAND / INDIGENOUS TERRITORY

The dominant multicultural narratives that centre a white, Western, liberal imaginary of Canada and obscure the significance of Indigenous territory and sovereignty are powerful stories that many of our students bring to class. Multicultural narratives, as St. Denis clarifies, cause Settler Canadians (as well as those who have more recently immigrated to Canada) to question why a special focus is put on Indigenous Peoples, and why they are deserving of specific territorial recognition.[31] While territory and treaty acknowledgements are important in this work, we find this to be only an introductory step. More needs to be done, for instance, to interrogate the diversity of Settler identities and how they can build relations with and within Indigenous territories.

Our initial teaching assistant work together took place in a diverse urban location in which a significant number of our students did not neatly fit into either Euro-Western / white Settler or Indigenous positionalities. Many of our students had themselves been displaced from their ancestral places by colonial forces and subjected to racialization tied to their migration experience. As settler-colonial theorist Lorenzo Veracini argues, we should consider deeply the ways in which racialized Settlers do not always carry a sovereign capacity in their experience of migration.[32] We find that some of the resistance we experience with students around territory can emerge from our assumptions that our students have homogenous experiences and static identities. We realize that we need to provide space for students to share their unique lives, stories, and experiences, but also to come into relation with the territory, with Indigenous Peoples, and with Indigenous perspectives in the places in which they live and study. We also work to disrupt Eurocentric assumptions of teaching and learning by centring the Indigenous knowledges, cultures, and perspectives of these places.

Drawing on and extending the work of Celia Haig-Brown on decolonizing autobiographies,[33] we have our students write their place-based relational autobiographies in relation to both Indigenous territory and the Canadian political governance structure. The students then trace the journeys that led them to the Indigenous territory where they currently reside. We also have our students, as prospective teachers, detail their ideas of teaching and learning in relation to their own history and current place. Importantly, students return to and extend their biographies as they engage with the course's central themes and learn from local Indigenous teachers and pedagogies. We provide recursive opportunities for our students to articulate and receive feedback about their work as prospective teachers and about their evolving perspectives on their own relations to land, territory, and Indigenous peoples. All of these encounters are designed to open up their perspectives and challenge dominant Canadian narratives and Eurocentrism. In general, we have found that these supported opportunities produce deeper and more respectful engagements on the part of our students and lessen some of the Eurocentric practices within curriculum.

A good number of our students today come from white Settler histories, but we have many students of other backgrounds, too. We tend to have a number of non-Indigenous students who trace their histories and experiences to colonial displacement and racialization, but who have now settled on Indigenous territory. We also regularly have a very small number of Indigenous students in our classes. Within this context of mixed experiences, identities, and affiliations, we find that these practices allow us to respond to our students in ways that help them explore their own identities and memories in relation to course themes without being boxed into a static identity created for them by an external figure of presumed authority.

COMMITMENT TO ETHICAL RELATIONALITY AS AN EDUCATIONAL PRACTICE

Donald foregrounds ethical relationality as an educational priority in unlearning colonial logics,[34] and we have found his ideas incredibly generative in our practice of troubling relations based in colonial logics. Donald notes the divisiveness taught in Canadian narratives of naturalized separation of Indigenous and Settler peoples, and the ways in which these divisions are replicated in the current market logics of Canadian society. He argues that these logics deny ethical Settler relationality to Indigenous land and people and thus promote violence and exploitation. He argues that the key to ethical relationality in education is not valorizing sameness, but rather deepening our understanding of the need for difference. Methodologically, Donald suggests that this be approached through attention to the "historical, cultural and social contexts from which a person or community understands and interprets the world," and by seeking greater understanding through an ethics of balance and reciprocity within relations.[35] In our course, we set up the readings and activities in a way that allows students the time required to acknowledge and learn from different perspectives. Our purpose is to provide our students with an opportunity to enlarge their personal perspectives by having them learn from Indigenous perspectives, histories, and memories. We further aim to support them in developing an increased awareness of their own ways of knowing the world. In this way, we attempt to uphold the productive tension of difference rather than suppress it.

We also challenge the norms of the university within the neoliberal strategies of individualism and separation by doing this work in relation with each other instead of individually. We initially acted upon our idea to co-teach when we were scheduled to teach different sections of the same course at the same time. We decided to teach these courses together rather than teaching them separately. After this experience, we asked for an institutional reconfiguration that would allow us to officially work together. This move was meant to trouble the academy's assumptions of hierarchy among and separation between course instructors. Following the commitments of Linda Tuhiwai Smith to decolonize research methodologies,[36] we chose to share our resources, time, and opportunities (through relationships, access to space, and institutional knowledge) as a way of challenging the hegemonic norms of the university. This configuration also supports an embodied way of upholding the productive tension that emerges from our own experiences within settler-colonial society. In doing so, we are able to draw upon each other's gifts and strengths, provide more opportunities for our students to engage with our different subjectivities, emotionally support each other, and enact a collectivist orientation that reflects Indigenous pedagogical values. The emotional support we create for each other is also a valuable strategy for dealing with resistances to our approaches within the academy and helps to lessen the emotional labour and deleterious impacts of teaching what Alice Pitt and Deborah Britzman refer to as "difficult knowledges."[37] We also feel that this shared model challenges the reimposition of colonial violence on Indigenous instructors who work alone in what are sometimes unsafe classrooms. Co-teaching can provide an opportunity to balance the emotional toll of these encounters in the classroom. Collaborations may be a way for Indigenous instructors to lead on the priorities and tone of the course while their Settler colleagues absorb more of the resistance and violence that take place within these courses.

COMMITMENT TO LEARNING TO BECOME WHOLE HUMAN BEINGS: INTERRELATEDNESS

It is impossible to reconcile anything until we can learn how to become whole human beings. We feel that structuring our course to reflect Indigenous philosophical conceptions of *wholism*, a concept we have learned from Indigenous Elders and knowledge holders, is important to illustrate the interrelatedness between the intellectual, spiritual, emotional, and physical realms that form a whole, healthy person. This perspective in education works against the practice of a sole focus on our students' and colleagues' intellect. We feel it is important to begin providing a learning environment that fosters understandings of wholism that are expressed by local Indigenous communities. We attempt to teach in a way that offers our students the opportunity to begin reconciling the spiritual, emotional, physical, and intellectual realms within themselves (as they see fit) so that they can begin to engage Indigenous knowledges and perspectives in their own teaching practices. We share the ways in which a wholistic conception clashes with the views of secularism, segmentation, polarization, fragmentation, and abstraction that are found in most Euro-Western educational contexts. This also includes framing our class code of conduct to reflect Verna Kirkness's and Ray Barnhardt's four *R*'s—respect, relevance, reciprocity, responsibility—which we see as intimately connected to ethical relationality and supporting interrelatedness as wholeness.[38] We see this as a way of supporting ourselves and our students in our life-long and life-wide journeys to become whole human beings from an ethical orientation.

We have attempted to trouble the context of higher education in Canada as a colonial structure that takes up the words of reconciliation in the lineage of the TRC while simultaneously maintaining colonial logics and violences. We considered the possibilities for instructors to engage in decolonial practices in this complex context. In particular, we theorized and detailed colonialism from a political and theoretical orientation in Canadian society and higher education, troubling the notion that postsecondary institutions are actually undertaking the work of reconciliation in the TRC's sense. We shared in some detail our collaborative pedagogies to illustrate our commitment to relationality in our work in higher education, which helps us engage our students in unlearning colonial logics. We believe that our work remains within the complicities of a capitalist system that configures possibilities, but know that we also seek to strategically disrupt the alienation and fragmentation embedded in colonial institutions.

As of the time of this writing, we note that it has been thirty years since Verna Kirkness and Ray Barnhardt—another example of Indigenous and Settler collaboration—published their seminal article "First Nations and Higher Education: The Four *R*'s—Respect, Relevance, Reciprocity, Responsibility." Their ethically focused article argued that universities should meaningfully enact the four *R*'s to better reflect Indigenous educational priorities in support of Indigenous students. We continue to appreciate their thoughtful work as we consider the current obstructions to reconciliation. We recognize that there continue to be many (im)possibilities and complicities in higher education due to the current context of colonial violence, but we do believe that an overt and critical focus on settler colonialism that centres ethical relationality, truth-telling, and Indigenous sovereignty provides pedagogical opportunities for instructors in higher education to gesture toward decolonial futures.

Authors' Note
The authors contributed equally to this chapter—neither is the lead author.

NOTES

1. *Truth and Reconciliation Commission of Canada: Calls to Action*, calls 62–65.
2. The idea of "unlearning" colonial relations that we use in this chapter emerged from many years of personal conversations with Dwayne Donald regarding his concept of "ethical relationality." See also Donald, "Forts, Colonial Frontier Logics"; Donald, "From What." (2012; 2016).
3. Regan, *Unsettling the Settler*, 11–12.
4. Stephen Harper, quoted in Ljunggren, "Every G20 Nation," para. 11.
5. Alfred, *Peace, Power, Righteousness*; Coulthard, *Red Skin, White Masks*; Mackey, *Unsettled Expectations*; Palmater, *Indigenous Nationhood*; Simpson, *Dancing*.
6. Marker, "After the Makah Whale Hunt"; Simpson, "Land as Pedagogy."
7. Truth and Reconciliation Commission of Canada, *Final Report*.
8. Palmater, *Indigenous Nationhood*.
9. Mackey, *Unsettled Expectations*, 3; Marker, "After the Makah Whale Hunt," 4–5.
10. Battiste, "You Can't Be the Global Doctor," 133; Thobani, *Exalted Subjects*.
11. Battiste and Henderson, "Naturalizing Indigenous Knowledge," 6; Kuokkanen, "Toward a New Relation," 267.
12. Manuel and Derrickson, *The Reconciliation Manifesto*.
13. Maracle, *My Conversations with Canadians*, 137.
14. Wolfe, "Settler Colonialism," 388; Mignolo, *Darker Side*, xxi.
15. Grosfoguel, "Transmodernity."
16. Grosfoguel, "Transmodernity," Coloniality of Power sec., para. 3.
17. Mignolo, *Darker Side*, xiv; see also Quijano, "Coloniality and Modernity/Rationality."
18. Simpson, "Land as Pedagogy," 13.
19. Andreotti et al., "Mapping Interpretations of Decolonization."
20. Andreotti et al., "Mapping Interpretations of Decolonization," 6.

21. Calderon, "Uncovering Settler Grammars."
22. Donald, "Forts, Colonial Frontier Logics," 100.
23. St. Denis, "Silencing Aboriginal Curricular Content."
24. St. Denis, "Silencing Aboriginal Curricular Content," 311.
25. Deloria, *God Is Red*; Simpson, *Dancing*; Atleo, *Tsawalk*; Atleo, *Principles of Tsawalk*.
26. Kerr and Parent, "Being Taught by Raven."
27. Donald, "Forts, Colonial Frontier Logics."
28. St. Denis, "Silencing Aboriginal Curricular Content"; Solomon et al., "Discourse of Denial."
29. Kerr and Parent, "Being Taught by Raven." See also Atleo, *Tsawalk*; Atleo, *Principles of Tsawalk*.
30. Donald, "Forts, Colonial Frontier Logics."
31. St. Denis, "Silencing Aboriginal Curricular Content."
32. Veracini, *Settler Colonialism*.
33. Haig-Brown, "De/colonizing Diaspora."
34. Donald, "Forts, Colonial Frontier Logics."
35. Donald, "Forts, Colonial Frontier Logics," 103–04.
36. Smith, *Decolonizing Methodologies*.
37. Pitt and Britzman, "Speculations on Qualities of Difficult Knowledges, 756.
38. Kirkness and Barnhardt, "First Nations Higher Education."

BIBLIOGRAPHY

Alfred, Taiaiake. *Peace, Power, Righteousness: An Indigenous Manifesto*. 2nd ed. Don Mills: Oxford University Press, 2008.

Andreotti, Vanessa de Oliveira, Sharon Stein, Cash Ahenakew, and Dallas Hunt. "Mapping Interpretations of Decolonization in the Context of Higher Education." *Decolonization: Indigeneity, Education & Society* 4, no. 1 (2015): 21–40.

Archibald, Jo-ann [Q'um Q'um Xiiem]. *Indigenous Storywork: Educating the Heart, Mind, Body, and Spirit*. Vancouver: University of British Columbia Press, 2008.

Atleo, E. Richard. *Principles of Tsawalk: An Indigenous Approach to Global Crisis*. Vancouver: UBC Press, 2011.

———. *Tsawalk: A Nuu-chah-nulth Worldview*. Vancouver: UBC Press, 2004.

Battiste, Marie. "You Can't Be the Global Doctor If You're the Colonial Disease." In *Teaching as Activism: Equity Meets Environmentalism*, edited by Peggy Tripp, 121–33. Montreal: McGill-Queen's University Press, 2005.

Battiste, Marie, and James Sa'ke'j Henderson. "Naturalizing Indigenous Knowledge in Eurocentric Education." *Canadian Journal of Native Education* 32, no. 1 (2009): 5–18.

Calderon, Dolores. "Uncovering Settler Grammars in Curriculum." *Educational Studies* 50, no. 4 (2014): 313–38. https://doi.org/1010/00131946.2014.926904.

Coulthard, Glen Sean. *Red Skin White Masks: Rejecting the Colonial Politics of Recognition*. Minneapolis: University of Minnesota Press, 2014.

Deloria, Vine, Jr. *God Is Red*. 30th anniversary ed. Golden: Fulcrum Publishing, 2003.

Donald, Dwayne. "Forts, Colonial Frontier Logics, and Aboriginal-Canadian Relations: Imagining Decolonizing Educational Philosophies in Canadian Contexts." In *Decolonizing Philosophies of Education*, edited by Ali A. Abdi, 91–111. Rotterdam: Sense Publishers, 2012.

———. "From What Does Ethical Relationality Flow: An 'Indian' Act in Three Artifacts." *Counterpoint*, no. 478. (2016): 10-16,

Grosfoguel, Ramón. "Transmodernity, Border Thinking and Global Coloniality: Decolonizing Political Economy and Postcolonial Studies." *Eurozine*, July 4, 2008. https://www.eurozine.com/transmodernity-border-thinking-and-global-coloniality/.

Haig-Brown, Celia. "De/colonizing Diaspora: Whose Traditional Lands Are We On?" *Cultural and Pedagogical Inquiry* 1, no. 1 (2009): 4–21.

Kerr, Jeannie, and Amy Parent. "Being Taught by Raven: A Story of Knowledges in Teacher Education." *Canadian Journal of Native Education* 38, no. 1 (2015): 62–79.

Kirkness, Verna J., and Ray Barnhardt. "First Nations and Higher Education: The Four R's—Respect, Relevance, Reciprocity, Responsibility." *Journal of American Indian Education* 30, no. 3 (1991): 1–15. http://www.jstor.org/stable/24397980.

Kuokkanen, Rauna. "Toward a New Relation of Hospitality in the Academy." *American Indian Quarterly* 27, no. 1/2 (2003): 267–95.

Ljunggren, David. "Every G20 Nation Wants to Be Canada, Insists PM." *Reuters*, September 25, 2009. https://www.reuters.com/article/columns-us-g20-canada-advantages-idUSTRE58P05Z20090926.

Mackey, Eva. *Unsettled Expectations: Uncertainty, Land, and Settler Decolonization.* Halifax: Fernwood Publishing, 2016.

Manuel, Arthur, and Chief Ronald Derrickson. *The Reconciliation Manifesto: Recovering the Land, Rebuilding the Economy.* Toronto: Lorimer Press, 2017.

Maracle, Lee. *My Conversations with Canadians.* Toronto: Book*hug Press, 2017.

Marker, Michael. "After the Makah Whale Hunt: Indigenous Knowledge and Limits to Multicultural Discourse." *Urban Education* 41, no. 5 (2006): 1–24.

Mignolo, Walter D. *The Darker Side of Western Modernity: Global Futures, Decolonial Options.* Durham: Duke University Press, 2011.

Palmater, Pamela. *Indigenous Nationhood: Empowering Grassroots Citizens.* Winnipeg: Fernwood Publishing, 2015.

Pitt, Alice, and Britzman, Deborah. "Speculations on Qualities of Difficult Knowledge in Teaching and Learning: An Experiment in Psychoanalytic Research." *International Journal of Qualitative Studies in Education* 16, (2003): 755–76.

Quijano, Anibal. "Coloniality and Modernity/Rationality." *Cultural Studies* 21, no. 2–3 (2007): 168–78.

Regan, Paulette. *Unsettling the Settler Within: Indian Residential Schools, Truth Telling, and Reconciliation in Canada.* Vancouver: UBC Press, 2010.

Simpson, Leanne. *Dancing on Our Turtle's Back: Stories of Nishnaabeg Re-Creation, Resurgence and a New Emergence.* Winnipeg: ARP Books, 2011.

Simpson, Leanne Betasamosake. "Land as Pedagogy: Nishnaabeg Intelligence and Rebellious Transformation." *Decolonization: Indigeneity, Education & Society*, no. 3 (2014): 1–25.

Smith, Linda Tuhiwai. *Decolonizing Methodologies: Research and Indigenous Peoples.* London: Zed Books, 1999.

Solomon, R. Patrick, John P. Portelli, Beverly-Jean Daniel, and Arlene Campbell. "The Discourse of Denial: How White Teacher Candidates Construct Race, Racism and 'White Privilege'." *Race Ethnicity and Education* 8, no. 2 (2005): 147–69.

St. Denis, Verna. "Silencing Aboriginal Curricular Content and Perspectives through Multiculturalism: 'There are Other Children Here'." *Review of Education, Pedagogy, and Cultural Studies* 33, no. 4 (2011): 306–17.

Thobani, Sunera. *Exalted Subjects: Studies in the Making of Race and Nation in Canada.* Toronto: University of Toronto Press, 2007.

Truth and Reconciliation Commission of Canada. *The Final Report of the Truth and Reconciliation Commission of Canada.* 6 vols. Montreal: McGill-Queen's University Press, 2015.

———. *Truth and Reconciliation Commission of Canada: Calls to Action.* Winnipeg: National Centre for Truth and Reconciliation, 2015. https://ehprnh2mwo3.exactdn.com/wp-content/uploads/2021/01/Calls_to_Action_English2.pdf.

Veracini, Lorenzo. *Settler Colonialism: A Theoretical Overview.* London: Palgrave Macmillan, 2010.

Wolfe, Patrick. "Settler Colonialism and the Elimination of the Native." *Journal of Genocide Research* 8, no. 4 (2006): 387–409.

Contributors

DANIELA BASCUÑÁN was exiled from Chile as a child due to the dictatorship there and has lived in Tkaronto since then. Questions of uprootedness, belonging, resistance, erasure, and revitalization have shaped her research and teaching trajectory. She is currently a doctoral candidate in the Department of Curriculum, Teaching, and Learning at the Ontario Institute for Studies in Education, University of Toronto, and a full-time elementary teacher at the Toronto District School Board. Bascuñán engages a practitioner inquiry stance with elementary students to gain understandings of storied approaches to ethical relationality. Her doctoral research focuses on the possibilities of weaving Indigenous treaty teachings in students' lives and tracing how students spatially construct concepts about Land, explore historical narratives of encounter, contest current issues, and mobilize their own subjectivities. Her co-authored work includes "Teaching as Trespass: Avoiding Places of Innocence" (*Equity & Excellence in Education*, 2021) and "How Discomfort Reproduces Settler Structures: Moving Beyond Fear and Becoming Imperfect Accomplices" (*Journal of Curriculum and Teaching*, 2020).

Contributors

DR. JENNIFER BRANT of the Kanien'keh:ka (Mohawk Nation) is a mother-scholar with family ties to Six Nations of the Grand River Territory and Tyendinaga Mohawk Territory. Dr. Brant is currently an Assistant Professor at the Ontario Institute for Studies in Education. Her dissertation "Journeying toward a Praxis of Indigenous Maternal Pedagogy: Lessons from Our Sweetgrass Baskets" (Brock University, 2017) provides insight into the value of a unique pedagogical approach as it relates to cultural identity development and academic success. Dr. Brant's work positions Indigenous literatures as educational tools to move students beyond passive empathy and compassion, inspire healing and wellness, and foster sociopolitical action. She is the co-editor of *Forever Loved: Exposing the Hidden Crisis of Missing and Murdered Indigenous Women and Girls in Canada* (Demeter Press, 2016), and calls for immediate responses to racialized and sexualized violence. Through her community work, teaching, research, and writing, Dr. Brant is dedicated to encouraging all to engage in effective responses to the Truth and Reconciliation Commission of Canada's 94 calls to action and the 231 calls for justice released in the final report of the National Inquiry into Missing and Murdered Indigenous Women and Girls.

LIZA BRECHBILL currently works as an online educator within the healthcare and public service sectors across what is colonially known as Canada. They graduated from Ontario Institute for Studies in Education, University of Toronto, with a master's degree in social justice education. They also have a bachelor's degree in psychology with a focus on narrative therapy and working-class experiences of postsecondary education. With a community-education background in gender-based violence, their graduate thesis "Unsettling White Settler Subjectivity in Social Justice Education: Towards a Pedagogy of Risk" (ProQuest, 2020) focused on the relationships between white settler subjectivity and colonial violence, as well as the risks and roles of emotion and psychic life in addressing white settler investment in Canada's ongoing colonial legacy.

DR. SHAWNA M. CARROLL is a senior assistant professor at Okayama University in the Graduate School of Education. Their research expertise focuses on antioppressive and anticolonial English teaching and research methods. Most recently, Dr. Carroll is the author of "Anti-Colonial Book Clubs: Creating a Different Kind of Language for a New Consciousness" (*Art/Research International*, 2021) and co-author of "How Discomfort Reproduces Settler Structures: Moving Beyond Fear and Becoming Imperfect Accomplices" (*Journal of Curriculum and Teaching*, 2020).

DR. FRANK DEER is a Canada Research Chair and member of the Royal Society of Canada. He is Associate Professor of Education in the Faculty of Education at the University of Manitoba in Winnipeg, Canada. Dr. Deer is Kanienkeha'ka from Kahnawake, a community that lies just south of Tiotia'ke in the eastern region of the Rotinonshonni Confederacy. Frank earned his PhD in educational administration from the University of Saskatchewan and is published in the area of indigenous education. Dr. Deer conducts research on indigenous language education and indigenous religious and spiritual orientations. He has previously served as a classroom teacher in northern Manitoba and in the inner city of Winnipeg.

DR. GEORGE J. SEFA DEI (NANA ADUSEI SEFA TWENEBOAH) is a professor of social justice education and the director of the Centre for Integrative Anti-Racism Studies at the Ontario Institute for Studies in Education, University of Toronto. Dr. Dei is a 2015, 2016, and 2018–2019 Carnegie African Diaspora Fellow. In June of 2007, Dr. Dei was installed as a traditional chief in Ghana—specifically, as the Gyaasehene of the town of Asokore, Koforidua, in the New Juaben Traditional Area. His stool name is Nana Adusei Sefa Tweneboah. Dr. Dei is the author of *Fanon Revisited* (DIO Press, 2020) and co-author of *Cartographies of Blackness and Black Indigeneities* (Institute of Education, 2020). Most recently, he is the co-editor of *Africanizing the School Curriculum: Promoting an Inclusive, Decolonial Education in African Contexts* (Myers Education Press, 2021).

LUCY EL-SHERIF is an Arab Muslim mother and immigrant to Turtle Island. She is a doctoral candidate in education at the Ontario Institute for Studies in Education, University of Toronto, specializing in curriculum and pedagogy. Her doctoral research on Palestinian folk dancing and its engagement by youth on Turtle Island examines how race unevenly fashions the structural subject positions available to settlers and the pedagogical processes of social citizenship that shape their subjectivities. By tracing what it means for racialized people to belong to a settler state, El-Sherif's work examines how citizenship functions at the intersection of orientalism and settler colonialism. Her most recent publication is "Webs of Relationships: Pedagogies of Citizenship and Modalities of Settlement for 'Muslims' in Canada" (*Lateral*, 2019). She is the 2020–2021 New College Senior Doctoral Fellow in Critical Studies in Equity and Solidarity at the University of Toronto.

DR. RACHEL YACAA?AŁ GEORGE is an assistant professor in the Department of Political Science at the University of Alberta, specializing in Indigenous politics. She is nuučaańuł of Ahousaht and Ehattesaht First Nations and grew up in the Metro Vancouver area of British Columbia on the territories of the Qayqayt, Musqueam, Skwxwú7mesh, and Tsleil-Waututh peoples. Her research has focused on reconciliation, justice, and pathways of decolonization through storied practice. Most recently, she is the lead author of "Fluid Decolonial Futures: Water as a Life, Ocean Citizenship and Seascape Relationality" (*New Political Science*, 2020), and author of "A Move to Distract: Mobilizing Truth and Reconciliation in Settler Colonial States" (in *Pathways of Reconciliation*, University of Manitoba Press, 2020).

DR. RUTH GREEN (Kanien'kehá:ka) is an activist-turned-accidental-academic and associate professor in the School of Social Work at York University. She has served as the co-chair of the Indigenous Council at York University and as the special advisor to the president on Indigenous Initiatives. Dr. Green identifies as an urban Indigenous person and is a citizen of the Haudenosaunee Confederacy. She is from the Kanien'keha:ka Nation and is a member of the Turtle Clan. She was born a Canadian but was half-disenfranchised when she was 10 years old. By the time she was 34.5 years old, she was completely disenfranchised. She acknowledges the privileges she has in a world of identity politics where she is governed by legislation that is 100 years older than she is! She also acknowledges her paternal Celtic heritage. She holds a PhD in adult education and community development from the Ontario Institute for Studies in Education, University of Toronto. Her work focuses on the institutional and interpersonal relationships between Host (Indigenous) and Guest (non-Indigenous) peoples. Dr. Green likes to think about Indigenous education and social issues that impact Indigenous communities. And her favourite two people are Elijah and Ani!

DR. CELIA HAIG-BROWN is a full professor at York University in Toronto, Canada. A Euro-Canadian ethnographer committed to decolonizing approaches to research, her major interests are based in work with Indigenous communities, nationally and internationally. Her book, *Resistance and Renewal: Surviving the Indian Residential School* (Arsenal Pulp Press, 1988), is a retrospective ethnography of the Kamloops Indian Residential School based on interviews with former students as well as church and government documents. She has published three other books, authored numerous articles and reports, and co-directed three films including *Pelǫ́ilc (Coming Home)* (2009), made in collaboration with the children and grandchildren of former Kamloops Indian Residential School students. Her latest SSHRC-funded film, *Listen to the Land* (2018), is a lyrical look at the complexities of the Naskapi Nation's commitment to the land and their culture in the contemporary economic reality of their involvement with open-pit mining.

DR. ARLO KEMPF is a settler Canadian living and working in Tkaronto, on the Treaty 3 land of the Toronto Purchase. He is an assistant professor in the Department of Curriculum, Teaching and Learning at the Ontario Institute for Studies in Education, University of Toronto. His research and teaching areas include antiracism and anti-colonialism in education, neoliberalism in education, and whiteness. He is the author of "Of Word, World, and Being (Online): A Brief Response to Paulo Freire's 'The importance of the Act of Reading'" (in *The SAGE handbook of critical pedagogies*; SAGE, 2020); and "If We Are Going to Talk About Implicit Race Bias, We Need to Talk About Structural Racism: Moving Beyond Passivity and Ubiquity in Teaching and Learning About Race" (*Taboo*, 2020). He has also recently co-authored "Primary and Secondary Education: Afrocentric Schooling" (in *International Encyclopedia of Education*, 4th ed., Elsevier, 2022).

DR. JEANNIE KERR is an associate professor in the Faculty of Education at The University of Winnipeg. Her research examines the reproduction of societal inequalities in K to 12 education, teacher education, and higher education. Dr. Kerr's scholarship is committed to an explicit analysis of contemporary colonialism, addressing inequalities in processes of schooling and public knowledge production, and collaboratively repairing and renewing relations in urban landscapes and Canadian society. Her publications engage the complications and complicities of her Settler positionality on Indigenous territory. Dr. Kerr is the author of "Ethics, Relationality and Global Citizenship Education: Decolonial Gestures within Complicity" (in *Global Citizenship*, Canadian Scholars Press, 2020) and lead author on the article "Engaging Ethical Relationality and Indigenous Storywork Principles in Research Methodology: Addressing Settler-Colonial Divides in Inner-City Educational Research" (*Qualitative Inquiry*, 2020). Her article "Western Epistemic Dominance and Colonial Structures: Consideration for Thought and Practice in Programs of Teacher Education" (*Decolonization: Indigeneity, Education & Society*, 2014) received the publication award from the Canadian Association of Foundations of Education.

PROF. DAVID NEWHOUSE is Onondaga from the Six Nations of the Grand River near Brantford, Ontario. He is a professor in the Indigenous studies program at Trent University and director of the Chanie Wenjack School for Indigenous Studies. His research interests focus on the emergence of modern Indigenous society through the ideas that animate the individuals and collectivities within it, and the shape and nature of Indigenous governance as a key institutional idea that gives expression to Indigenous modernity. Prof. Newhouse is particularly interested in the manner in which Indigenous traditional knowledges and thought are incorporated into contemporary social action.

Contributors

DR. AMY PARENT, NOX̱S TS'AAWIT (Mother of the Raven Warrior Chief), is an associate professor of education at Simon Fraser University, and an assistant professor in the Department of Educational Studies in the Faculty of Education at the University of British Columbia. On her mother's side, she is Nisga'a from the House of Ni'isjoohl and is a member of the Ganada (frog) clan in the village of Laxgalts'ap. On her father's side, she is of Settler ancestry (French and German). Her research expertise is focused on two areas: (1) teaching and mentoring practices aimed at capacity-building in Indigenous communities, K to 12 contexts, teacher education, and higher education in British Columbia; and (2) Nisga'a language revitalization, educational governance, and policy. Most recently, Dr. Parent is the author of "Txeemsim Bends the Box to Bring New Light to Working with Indigenous Methodologies" (in *Critical Theorizations of Education*, ed. Abdi; Brill, 2021). She is also producer and writer for the film series *Critical Understandings of Land & Water: Unsettling Place at SFU*.

DR. MICHELLE PIDGEON is an associate professor in the Faculty of Education at Simon Fraser University. Her research agenda is located within the areas of higher education and Indigeneity. In particular, her scholarship focuses on intersections between student affairs and services, recruitment and retention, and Indigenous peoples' experiences in postsecondary education. Dr. Pidgeon's most recent research aims to understand Indigenous research processes and ethical protocols. She has authored "Moving Between Theory and Practice within an Indigenous Research Paradigm" (*Qualitative Research*, 2019) and co-authored "Indigenous University Student Persistence: Supports, Obstacles, and Recommendations" (*Canadian Journal of Education*, 2020).

DR. ROBIN QUANTICK is an assistant professor at the Chanie Wenjack School for Indigenous Studies at Trent University. He has spent his entire professional life in education. Dr. Quantick began his career as an elementary school teacher, then as a high school teacher. He worked in correctional education for twenty-eight years, supporting federally incarcerated men and women in various prison settings. This work was largely centred on the community of Indigenous men and women who are disproportionately incarcerated in Canada. It led to a PhD in Indigenous studies and, most recently, to working with first-year students around the challenges of decolonization. In all of this work, there has been a key decolonizing question that has served him in navigating the student experience: Now that you know this, what will you do?

DR. JEAN-PAUL RESTOULE is a professor and chair of the Department of Indigenous Education at the University of Victoria. He is Anishinaabe from Dokis First Nation in Ontario, and his research focuses on bringing Indigenous worldviews to a wide audience. His interests include Indigenizing and decolonizing teacher education and investigating the use of Indigenous knowledge in online learning environments. He is also co-editor of *Indigenous Research: Theories, Practices, and Relationships* (Canadian Scholars Press, 2018), a ground-breaking collection for students and scholars interested in learning how Indigenous research is carried out in practice.

DR. TOBY ROLLO is an assistant professor at Lakehead University. Their research expertise is in democratic theory, Canadian law and politics, and feminism and childhood. They are the author of numerous articles and book chapters on the figure of the child, democracy, and colonialism in the Canadian context.

DR. MARK SINKE is an elementary school teacher who lives on the territory of the Anishinaabe and Haudenosaunee Nations in Hamilton, Ontario. He received his PhD in curriculum studies from the Ontario Institute for Studies in Education, University of Toronto, in 2020. Dr. Sinke is a settler whose family migrated from the Netherlands onto Indigenous lands following World War II. His research focuses on pulling apart pedagogies of nationhood and settler colonialism to understand how children receive education about particular settler-Indigenous relationships, and how children understand and enact their own positionalities within these educational contexts. His doctoral work focused on the figured worlds of fifth-grade students in public schools as they learned about settler-Indigenous relationships through the formal curriculum of the Ontario Ministry of Education's social studies program. Other topics of published academic writing include the public pedagogy of settler-colonialism in Canada, teacher understandings and practices of Indigenous pedagogies in schools, and student experiences of formal education after arriving in Canada as refugees. He has taught social studies, history, and geography at Brock University's Faculty of Education for four years and continues to work as a full-time educator of young students in K to 8 schools.

Contributors

DR. SANDRA D. STYRES is of Kanien'kehá:ka (Mohawk), English, and French descent, and is a member of the Six Nations of the Grand River community. Dr. Styres is a Canada Research Chair and an associate professor with the Department of Curriculum, Teaching, and Learning at the Ontario Institute for Studies in Education, University of Toronto. She is co-chair of the Deepening Knowledge Project and director of the Indigenous Educational Research Centre. Her research interests are Land-centred education, Indigenous resurgence, the politics of decolonizing reconciliation in education broadly, the appropriate inclusion of Indigenous perspectives into teacher education programming and K to 12 classrooms, Indigenous philosophies and perspectives, culturally aligned methodologies and theoretical approaches to Indigenous research, and the ethics and protocols that guide the work in Indigenous and non-Indigenous research collaborations and community engagement.

DR. LYNNE WILTSE is a professor in the Department of Elementary Education at the University of Alberta where she teaches courses in children's literature and in language and literacy. Dr. Wiltse's research interests include minority language education, literacy pedagogy, postcolonial children's literature, teaching for social justice, sociocultural theory, and teacher education. Recent publications include "After They Gave the Order: Students Respond to Canadian Indian Residential School Literature for Social Justice" (*Bookbird*, 2021); "Seeing Self and Students Through Richard Wagamese's *Medicine Walk*" (*English Practice*, 2020); "Can Diversity Really Be Used in Teaching Minority Language Students?" (in *Perspectives on Educational Practice Around the World*; Bloomsbury Publishing, 2019); "Following the Headlines through Reading and Responding to Children's Refugee Literature" (*Alberta Voices*, 2018); and "Filling in the Gaps: Lessons Learned From Preservice Teachers' Partnerships with First Nations Students" (*In Education*, 2016). She is co-author of "Opening Doors, Opening Minds: The Role of the Inquiry Group in Teaching for Social Justice" (in *Challenging Stories*; Canadian Scholars Press, 2017).

DR. DAWN ZINGA is a Canadian of several-generations-removed European descent. She is a professor in the Department of Child and Youth Studies at Brock University. Dr. Zinga has had the privilege of working with a number of Indigenous scholars, communities, and youth. Her research interests include Indigenous pedagogies and practices, integration of Indigenous approaches to teaching and learning in higher education, and responses to the TRC calls to action in postsecondary contexts. Most recently, she is one of four co-editors of *Indigenous Education: New Directions in Theory and Practice* (University of Alberta Press, 2019).

Printed in the USA
CPSIA information can be obtained
at www.ICGtesting.com
LVHW040854201223
766647LV00008B/163